OXFORD CLASSICAL MONOGRAPHS

Published under the supervision of a Committee of the
Faculty of Classics in the University of Oxford

The aim of the Oxford Classical Monographs series (which replaces the Oxford Classical and Philosophical Monographs) is to publish books based on the best theses on Greek and Latin literature, ancient history, and ancient philosophy examined by the Faculty Board of Classics.

Pindar's Library

Performance Poetry and Material Texts

TOM PHILLIPS

OXFORD
UNIVERSITY PRESS

Great Clarendon Street, Oxford, OX2 6DP,
United Kingdom

Oxford University Press is a department of the University of Oxford.
It furthers the University's objective of excellence in research, scholarship,
and education by publishing worldwide. Oxford is a registered trade mark of
Oxford University Press in the UK and in certain other countries

© Tom Phillips 2016

The moral rights of the author have been asserted

First Edition published in 2016

Impression: 1

Published in the United States of America by Oxford University Press
198 Madison Avenue, New York, NY 10016, United States of America

British Library Cataloguing in Publication Data

Data available

Library of Congress Control Number: 2015944996

ISBN 978-0-19-874573-0

Printed in Great Britain by
Clays Ltd, St Ives plc

Preface

This book is a revised version of a DPhil thesis completed in July 2012. It is a great pleasure to acknowledge the many debts I have incurred before and during its composition. The oldest and perhaps the deepest is to my Classics teachers at Monmouth School, Peter Dennis-Jones and David Jenkins, and later Ben Giles and David Hope, who first fostered my interest in the classical languages. During my time at Oxford I have been fortunate to share the company of numerous scholars who have informed and changed the way I approach literature; particular thanks are due to Rhiannon Ash, Bruno Currie, Aneurin Ellis-Evans, Peta Fowler, Gregory Hutchinson, Adrian Kelly, Francesca Martelli, Dirk Obbink, Jonathan Prag, Scott Scullion, Barnaby Taylor, and Rosalind Thomas. It would be impossible to list all the other friends and colleagues from whom I have learnt so much over the years, but I must mention Emily Dreyfus, who has frequently caused me to rethink my views about a whole host of issues, and Guy Westwood, who has been a constantly stimulating companion and scholarly exemplum. I also owe a great deal to Oliver Thomas, who has read much of what I have written over the last few years, and given much exacting advice.

Without the support of funding from the AHRC I would not have been able to undertake graduate study, and I am very grateful for their assistance. During the academic year 2012–13, I held a lectureship at Corpus Christi College: there can be few more inspiring places to study the ancient world, and I would like to thank my students, and Ursula Coope, Jaś Elsner, Peter Haarer, Stephen Harrison, John Ma, Neil McLynn, and numerous other colleagues for making my time there so enjoyable. More recently, the task of converting the thesis into a monograph was undertaken during the first year of a Junior Research Fellowship at Merton College, and I am deeply indebted to the Warden and Fellows of the college for electing me to this post.

My doctoral examiners, Giambattista D'Alessio and Tim Whitmarsh, greatly improved the final product and saved me from numerous errors, as did Patrick Finglass, my reader for the press, before Felix Budelmann shepherded the book through its final stages with a keen eye and critical pen. Any failings and errors that remain are of course my own responsibility. My most longstanding academic obligations are to Tim Rood, my undergraduate tutor, and my doctoral supervisor, Armand D'Angour, who have both provided advice, criticism, and encouragement well beyond the call of duty. It is more than convention, however, that prompts me to thank my parents Paul and Claire last of all: for their unfailing kindness, patience, and support the present work seems a most inadequate return.

T.R.P.

Merton College, Oxford
January 2015

Contents

Abbreviations

AB	C. Austin and G. Bastianini, *Posidippi Pellaei Quae Supersunt Omnia* (Milan, 2002)
AP	*Anthologia Palatina*
BNJ	*Brill's New Jacoby*, Brill Online Reference Works
Broggiato	M. Broggiato, ed., *Cratete di Mallo. I Frammenti* (Rome, 2001)
Chantraine	P. Chantraine, *Dictionnaire étymologique de la langue grecque: histoire des mots* (Paris, 1968)
Cults	R. Farnell, *The Cults of the Greek States*, I–V (Oxford, 1896–1909).
DFA	A. Pickard-Cambridge, *The Dramatic Festivals of Athens*, 2nd edition revised by J. Gould and D. Lewis (Oxford, 1988)
D–K	H. Diels and W. Kranz, eds., *Die Fragmente der Vorsokratiker*, I–III (Berlin, 1974)
Dr	A. B. Drachmann, ed., *Scholia Vetera in Pindari Carmina*, I–III (Leipzig, 1903–27 [reprinted Stuttgart, 1997])
EG	D. L. Page, ed., *Epigrammata Graeca* (Oxford, 1975)
FGrH	F. Jacoby et al., eds., *Fragmente der Griechischen Historiker* (Leiden, 1923–)
FHG	C. Müller, ed., *Fragmenta Historicorum Graecorum* (Paris, 1849)
Fowler	R. L. Fowler, ed., *Early Greek Mythography I: Texts* (Oxford, 2000)
GP	A. S. F. Gow and D. L. Page, eds., *The Greek Anthology: Hellenistic Epigrams* (Cambridge, 1965)
Harder	M. A. Harder, *Callimachus* Aetia Vol. I (Oxford, 2012)
Hummel	P. Hummel, *L'épithète pindarique: étude historique et philologique* (Bern, 1999)
LIMC	*Lexicon Iconographicum Mythologiae Classicae*, I–VIII (Zurich/Munich, 1981–99)
K–A	R. Kassel and C. Austin, eds., *Poetae Comici Graeci* (Berlin, 1983–)
LfgrE	*Lexikon des frühgriechischen Epos* (Göttingen, 1979–)
LSJ	H. G. Liddell, R. Scott, H. S. Jones, and R. Mackenzie, eds., *A Greek–English Lexicon* (9th edition, Oxford, 1940)
Müller	C. Müller, *Geographi Graeci Minores* (Paris, 1855–82 [reprinted Hildesheim, 1965])
M–W	R. Merkelbach and M. L. West, eds., *Fragmenta Hesiodea* (Oxford, 1967)

Olimpiche   *Pindaro Le* Olimpiche: *introduzione, testo critico e traduzione*
                di Bruno Gentili, *commento a cura di* C. Catennaci,
                P. Giannini, and L. Lomiento (Milan, 2013)
P.Ant.   *The Antinoopolis Papyri* I, ed. C. H. Roberts (Egypt
                Exploration Society, Graeco-Roman Memoirs 28, 1950)
PEG   A. Bernabé, ed., *Poetarum epicorum Graecorum testimonia et
                fragmenta* I (Leipzig, 1987)
Pf.   R. Pfeiffer, ed., *Callimachus*, I–II (Oxford, 1949, 1953).
Pitiche   *Pindaro Le* Pitiche: *introduzione, testo critico e traduzione di*
                Bruno Gentili, *commento a cura di* P. Bernardini, E. Cingano,
                and P. Giannini (Milan, 1995)
P.Lond.Lit.   *Catalogue of the Literary Papyri in the British Museum*, ed.
                H. J. M. Milne (London, 1927)
PMG   D. L. Page, ed., *Poetae Melici Graeci* (Oxford, 1962)
POxy   *The Oxyrhynchus Papyri* (London 1898–)
Race   W. H. Race, ed., *Pindar, Olympian, Pythian, Nemean,
                Isthmian Odes*, I–II (Cambridge, Mass., 1997)
Scholies   C. Daude, S. David, M. Fartzoff, C. Muckensturm-Poulle, eds.,
                Scholies à Pindare: Volume I Vies *de Pindare et scholies à la
                première Olympique. 'Un chemin de paroles' (O.1.110)*
                (Besançon, 2013)
SH   *Supplementum Hellenisticum*, ed. H. Lloyd-Jones and
                P. Parsons (Berlin/New York, 1983)
SIG   *Sylloge Inscriptionum Graecarum*, I–IV ed. W. Dittenberger
                (3rd edn., Leipzig, 1915–24)
Slater   W. J. Slater, *Lexicon to Pindar* (Berlin, 1969)
SLG   D. L. Page, ed., *Supplementum Lyricis Graecis* (Oxford, 1974)
S–M   B. Snell and H. Maehler, eds., *Pindari Carmina cum
                Fragmentis* (Leipzig, 1984, 1989)
TGrF   R. Kannicht, S. Radt, and B. Snell, eds., *Tragicorum Graecorum
                Fragmenta*, I– (Göttingen, 1971–2004)
W   M. L. West, ed., *Iambi et Elegi Graeci* (Oxford, 1971)
Wehrli   F. von Wehrli, *Die Schule des Aristoteles: Texte und
                Kommentar*, I–X (Basel and Stuttgart, 1969)
Wendel   C. Wendel, ed., *Scholia in Apollonium Rhodium Vetera*
                (Berlin, 1935)

Introduction

τὸν Ὀλυμπιονίκαν ἀνάγνωτέ μοι
Ἀρχεστράτου παῖδα, πόθι φρενός
ἐμᾶς γέγραπται· γλυκὺ γὰρ αὐτῷ μέλος ὀφείλων
    ἐπιλέλαθ᾽· ὦ Μοῖς᾽, ἀλλὰ σὺ καὶ θυγάτηρ
Ἀλάθεια Διός, ὀρθᾷ χερί
ἐρύκετον ψευδέων
ἐνιπὰν ἀλιτόξενον.

Read out to me the name of the son of Archestratus, the Olympian victor, where it has been inscribed in my mind, for I have forgotten the sweet song owed to him. O Muse, and you, Truth, daughter of Zeus, with upright hand ward off the reproach of harming a friend with falsehoods.[1]

So begins Pindar's ode for Hagesidamus of Western Locri, celebrating his victory in the Olympian boys' boxing competition of 476 BC. Writing as a means of recording information is here contrasted with the contingencies of human mental activity, although with the irony that the organ on which the writing has been inscribed is also responsible for the name being 'forgotten'. A somewhat different and more diffuse focus on writing emerges at O.6.90–1, where the *persona loquens* addresses Aeneas, the chorus-trainer, as a 'true messenger, a message-stick of the fair-haired Muses' (ἐσσὶ γὰρ ἄγγελος ὀρθός, / ἠϋκόμων σκυτάλα Μοισᾶν); Aeneas' responsibilities presumably involved taking a physical copy of the poem to the place of performance and instructing the chorus.[2]

---

[1] Translations are my own unless otherwise noted.
[2] Cf. Hutchinson (2001) 417; *Olimpiche* pp. 469–70; Uhlig (2011) 74–5. On the *choregos* in general see Calame (2001) 43–72.

The phrase evokes the Spartan method of sending written messages.[3] The cκυτάλη was a staff around which a strip of leather or parchment would be wound; one was kept in Sparta and the other, of exactly the same size, was given to, for example, the commander of an army. The writing material would be wound slantwise around the staff and the message written vertically, so that it could only be read correctly when wrapped around its counterpart.[4] Pindar's metaphor draws on this custom, casting poetic performance as a participation in a shared body of specialist knowledge; like the Spartan users of the cκυτάλη, Aeneas, and by extension the performing chorus, have sufficient skill to be able to understand the poem and translate it into a performance.[5] The metaphor uses the separation of a poetic utterance from its author as an opportunity of celebrating the communality of performance culture and, by implication, writing's power to fix and disseminate texts.[6] Both *O*.6.90–1 and *O*.10.1–3 are part of a more general pattern in Pindar's self-referential rhetoric, in which songs are characterized as objects, particularly those which commemorate athletic success such as crowns, fillets, and statues.[7] These characterizations often have an agonistic dimension, as at *P*.6.10–14 where the poem *qua* ὕμνων θηcαυρόc is not vulnerable to the elements in the same way as a real building, or *N*.5.1–5 where song's mobility is contrasted with the fixity of statues. These and other similar passages can be read as insisting on the pragmatic

---

[3] The word occurs first in Archilochus, at the beginning of the fable of the Fox and the Monkey (fr. 185 W): ἐρέω τιν' ὑμιν αἶνον, ὦ Κηρυκίδη, / ἀχνυμένηι cκυτάληι ('I shall tell you a fable, Cerycides, with a grieving message stick'). Pindar's usage may therefore be playing on an established literary topos. For further comments see Jeffery and Johnston (1990) 57–8. The scepticism of Bing (1988) 28 n. 39 about the cκυτάλη as a reference to written text is unnecessary.

[4] This is the explanation of its function given by *Σ O*.6.154b and f (i 189, 190 Dr), although a slightly different account is given by d (i 190 Dr). Cf. also Thuc. 1.131; Xen. *Hist*. 3.3.8; Ar. *Lys*. 991; Plut. *Lys*. 19.

[5] For the musical education and understanding which composers and performers brought to bear on the melodization of poems during this period cf. D'Angour (2007).

[6] Cf. Hutchinson (2001) 415. Herington (1985) 45 argues that in the archaic and classical periods 'texts were no part of the performed poem as such, but merely a mechanical means of preserving its wording between performances'. This, however, mistakenly discounts the possibility of readerly engagement with texts. Hubbard (1985) 67 n. 166 thinks that Pindar would have held written dissemination to be even more important than performance: this inference is unjustified, and oversimplifies the relationship between the two modes.

[7] Cf. Steiner (1994) 92 nn. 107–9.

superiority of song to other artforms,[8] but they also contribute to a metaphorization of the text itself as an object involved in a nexus of social relationships.[9]

In addition to their particular contextual functions, such comparisons can be seen as responses to and manipulations of the technological changes taking place in Pindar's lifetime. By the time of Pindar's poetic career writing was an important part of Greek culture; vase paintings testify to the increasing use of various types of writing materials in teaching,[10] and the Muses are shown carrying papyrus rolls, signalling the connection between writing and poetic composition. Metaphors involving writing become increasingly common from the early fifth century,[11] and although this period cannot be described as fully 'literate' in the manner of, say, the Hellenistic age,[12] writing had for a long time been playing a role in the creative process. Equally, writing influenced other aspects of performance culture; reperformance of epinician odes, for example, probably depended on written texts, and there is some evidence for their preservative function. One such datum is the citation of the Rhodian historian Gorgon about Pindar's epinician for Diagoras of Rhodes, *O*.7, being inscribed in the temple of Lindian Athena (ταύτην τὴν ᾠδὴν ἀνακεῖσθαί φησι Γόργων ἐν τῷ τῆς Λινδίας Ἀθηναίας ἱερῷ χρυσοῖς γράμμασιν, 'Gorgon says that this ode is dedicated in the temple of Lindian Athena in golden letters', Σ *O*.7 inscr., i 195 Dr = *BNJ* 515 F 18). This may well represent a more general practice; while the 'golden letters' are

---

[8] Cf. Svenbro (1976) 172–93; Steiner (1994) 95–6; Ford (2002) 113–30; Thomas (2007); Kowalzig (2011); Fearn (2013).

[9] Thus Steiner (1994) 96–9. See particularly her comments p. 96: 'Through the presence of the monuments, the poet suggests a resolution to two issues central to his craft: first, his own relation to his patron, second the question of the afterlife of his compositions, their ability to go on sounding the athletes' praise.' See also Uhlig (2011) 23–7.

[10] Immerwahr (1964) and (1973) provide an inventory of depictions of books on vases.

[11] Cf. e.g. Aesch. *Supp*. 179; [Aesch.] *PV* 459–62; *TGrF* F 3597. For the connection between these passages and the appearance during this period of school scenes on vases see Ford (2003) 24. Hdt. 6.27 tells a story about children in Chios being taught writing, an episode which occurs in 496. The evidence for written texts pre-431 is collected by Herington (1985) 201–6.

[12] Although the opposition between 'oral' and 'literate' is itself problematic, as numerous studies have shown: see e.g. Thomas (1992); Duguid (1996) 66–73. See Scodel (2001) 125 on the intersection of orality and literacy in Pindar. On the background that informed Pindar's (and Aeschylus') use of writing, both as textual figure and textual practice, see Uhlig (2011) 81–95.

probably apocryphal, the inscription of such poems, or the dedication of written texts in temples and private archives, could well have been widespread.[13]

Despite these hints, however, our understanding of how written texts of Pindar operated in the fifth and fourth centuries is severely limited by lack of evidence. Few papyri from the period, and none of Pindar, survive,[14] and we are in the dark about many of the precise details of textual production. How exactly Pindar made use of writing in the process of composition (or if he did at all—although this seems very probable),[15] what the texts of his poems looked like, how and how widely they circulated, who read them,[16] and the precise details of how they served as bases for reperformance are all largely matters of guesswork. What Pindaric books were like before the Hellenistic period, whether they consisted of single poems or small groups, or of larger collections similar to those of later scholarly editions, is equally obscure.[17] My chief

[13] On the possible dedication of a copy of *O.7.* by Diagoras cf. Carey (2007) 201 n. 13. Writing is also used to describe an act of dedication at *O.3.30*; for the vocabulary of dedication in general cf. Herington (1985) 46; Rutherford (2001) 175–8. Carey (2011) 454–6 argues plausibly that local Spartan archives were the main source for Hellenistic and late classical texts of Alcman. For books as dedicatory objects in the Hellenistic period cf. Johnstone (2014) 371–2.

[14] The exceptions being the Derveni Papyrus and the papyrus of Timotheus *Persae*.

[15] Cf. Herington (1985) 46. The word δέλτου occurs at *Pa.* 7b.24 and may form part of a discussion of poetics, but the fragmentariness of the context precludes certainty: see Rutherford (2001) 250.

[16] The evidence for the book trade in the classical era comes mainly from the late fifth and fourth centuries: cf. Ar. *Ran.* 52–4; Xen. *Anab.* 7.5.14 and Harris (1989) 85 n. 92. Currie (2004) 52 sites the development of the book trade in the late fifth century, but there is no reason to suppose that books were not circulating earlier than this, albeit perhaps on a smaller scale. Hubbard (2004) argues for the importance of written texts in the dissemination of epinician in the fifth century; Carey (2007) 200 n. 5 is more cautious. Cf. also Hubbard (2011) for the importance of family-based networks for the circulation of texts in the fifth century. Pöhlmann (1994) 16 argues that Pindar's poems may have been collected and preserved in Thebes by the Aegeidae, and that this collection could have formed the basis of the Alexandrian edition(s); cf. West (2011) 66. For the early transmission of other lyric authors see e.g. Carey (2011) (on Alcman); Davies and Finglass (2014) 60–5 (on Stesichorus).

[17] Cf. Irigoin (1952) 5–28 for an assessment of the evidence. He argues that the allusions to Pindar in Aristophanes are based on an Athenian edition of a selection of the poems (p. 16), and that regional editions were assembled and edited into larger editions at intellectual centres such as Athens and Rhodes during the late 5th and 4th centuries, editions which served as a basis for Hellenistic scholarship (p. 21). It could, however, be argued that the allusions in comedy (e.g. Ar. *Ach.* 637–9, *Birds* 926–45, *Clouds* 1355–62, *Knights* 1323, 1329) need not reflect the contents of a particular edition, but rather the poems that were, for reasons of perceived aesthetic quality or relevance to Athenian affairs, best known to the audience.

goal in this study, however, is to explore the function of written texts of Pindar in later antiquity. In part this approach aims to correct a disparity between scholarly focus and textual history. Pindaric scholarship has in the main been concerned to analyse the social and historical conditions which shaped the poems' production and initial reception, and to interpret how the poems operated in their fifth-century contexts of performance. While such approaches are obviously important, we should not forget that the vast majority of readers in antiquity encountered Pindaric texts in book form, or in various reperformance scenarios remote from Pindar's own time.

Attempting to understand what was involved in such encounters entails questions about the form of books, the nature of reading practices, and the effects of changing literary and scholarly contexts on readers' approaches to the Pindaric corpus. Yet we should be wary of schematic oppositions between 'performance' and 'books' or 'reading', and between the contexts of Pindar's time and those of later periods. As we have seen, Pindar was acutely aware of the material forms his poems could take, and 'performance' continues to be important, both as a concept with which later authors and scholars reimagined the circumstances of the fifth-century poetic economy, and as a mode of realizing texts in later periods. Similarly, although Pindar's poems are rooted in specific situations and respond in particular ways to the demands of individual social and political contexts, they also make generalizing claims which are easily assimilable to a variety of reading contexts. Indeed, the very specificity of features such as deixis, addresses to historical individuals, and references to particular cultic or political situations allows in later contexts for an imaginative recreation of the poem as a performance piece, permitting the poem to impose its own mode of contextualization upon the context(s) in which it is being read.[18] Pindar's poetry both transcends and embodies historical contingency.

Moreover, the textual dissemination of epinicians can also be seen as making concrete the texts' own rhetorical strategies.[19] One of

---

[18] The poems have little to say about their performance locations, a fact which eases the transition into reperformance and written dissemination: cf. Carey (2007) 199. Deixis in Pindar has received considerable attention: cf. Felson (1999); Athanassaki (2004); D'Alessio (2004a); Felson (2004); Martin (2004).

[19] In addition to this generically specific connection between form and dissemination, my decision to focus on the epinicians is motivated by evidential considerations: for example, we know more about editions of Pindar's epinicians in the

epinician's primary concerns is the construction and perpetuation of the victor's fame, and scholars have become increasingly sensitive to the Panhellenic nature of these claims; as well as composing for particular contexts, Pindar is also writing for the whole Greek world.[20] This study aims to think about this fame as an historical actuality as well as a textual projection, and about how Pindar's immortalization of a figure such as Hiero of Syracuse operates in relation to changing historical circumstances. I shall therefore present readings of various poems through the lens of fifth-century perform- ance in addition to considering their operations in later contexts; the latter cannot be understood without the former, but I shall also try to show how consideration of interpretative issues central to assessment of Pindaric texts in later periods can enhance our understanding of how the poems worked in Pindar's own time.

The opening of *O.*10 quoted at the beginning of this chapter provides a useful starting point for sketching out what is at stake in such dialogues. The relationship between *persona loquens* and victor is presented through the lens of aristocratic guest friendship;[21] the narrator is in danger of 'wronging his friend' (ἀλιτόξενον) by his tardiness in delivering the poem,[22] and the poem is presented as 'owed' (ὀφείλων) to the victor.[23] The metaphor continues in the antistrophe, where the narrator describes his 'deep debt' which 'shames' him (ἐμὸν καταίσχυνε βαθὺ χρέος, 8) and hopes that the 'interest' (τόκος, 9) accrued by the debt will 'loosen the sharp reproach' (λῦσαι ... ὀξεῖαν ἐπιμομφάν, 9) attendant on it. The

---

Hellenistic period than we do even about a relatively well-preserved corpus such as the *Paeans*. Moreover, the scholia offer a wealth of information that allows us to interro- gate the critical climate that related to these poems in much greater depth than we can for the rest of Pindar's corpus. My focus, however, should not be taken as a reflection of an imagined tendency on the part of Hellenistic scholars and readers, for whom Pindar would have been as much a poet of dithyrambs, paeans, partheneia, and the rest as of victory odes.

[20] Cf. e.g. Athanassaki (2011a).   [21] Cf. Verdenius (1988) 57.

[22] For the possible historical circumstances of this situation cf. Verdenius (1988) 56 who suggests that the delay was due to Pindar being occupied with 'the more important odes' *O.*1, *O.*2, and *O.*3. Cf. Erbse (1970) 28 for the reading that Pindar is light-hearted teasing Hagesidamus over his eagerness to have his praises sung. Nassen (1975) 223–4 sees the description of lateness as balancing historical circum- stances and poetic exaggeration.

[23] For the topos of the debt owed to victory cf. e.g. *O.*1.103, *O.*3.7. Cf. Hubbard (1985) 65–8 for some remarks on the role of writing in this passage.

metaphorical structure sites the acts of composition and performance in a network of ethical concepts, and in the context of performance hints at the debt owed by the wider community to the victor's achievements. This is balanced by the figuration of the narrator's mind as a substrate, an imagined material surface upon which the inscription is projected, that is simultaneously preservative and open to the contingencies of human understanding (ἐπιλέλαθ'), in need of assistance from the Muse and Aletheia in order to fulfil its duty. The use of γέγραπται in the context of the debt metaphor is usually interpreted as suggesting a ledger; the victor's name has been written in the narrator's mind in the same way as a debtor records the amounts he owes.[24] But when sung by a chorus, γέγραπται also hints at the distinction between composition and performance, and between the poet and the chorus.[25]

Read in this way, the name having been 'inscribed on my mind' works as a reference to the processes of composition and training the chorus, which doubtless involved (a) written text(s).[26] This connotation playfully, and perhaps humorously, undermines the rhetoric of debt and tardiness by implying that the poem was composed some time before the performance, and hence that the χρέος is not quite as serious as the second stanza makes out. Hagesidamus has (literally) been on the poet's mind, and the choral enunciation of a victor's name previously written down replays in miniature the dynamic of composition and performance.[27] This implication is reinforced by the mention of Hagesidamus (Ἀρχεστράτου παῖδα) preceding the rhetoric of debt; the debt has, in the sequential movement of the text, been repaid before it has been constructed. The implied distinction between poet and

---

[24] Thus Verdenius (1988) 54.

[25] For the debate over monodic versus choral performance of epinicians see Heath (1988) and Lefkowitz (1988), both arguing that monodic performance was the norm, with the counter argument of Carey (1989). Currie (2005) 16–18 is a useful overview. A consensus has grown in recent years that choral performance was common, but that performance is a category which subsumes considerable variations in venue and size: cf. e.g. Carey (2001); Hornblower (2004) 33–6, and D'Alessio (1994) on the difficulties of distinguishing authorial and choral first persons. There is no good reason to think that O.10 was not performed at its 'première' by a chorus.

[26] Cf. Pelliccia (2003) 99–102 on the importance of fixed texts to the process of rehearsal.

[27] D'Alessio (2004a) 291 n. 89 argues that 'what the addressees should read aloud . . . is not the song but the patron's name', but the phrasing of the opening lines allows the victor's name to be understood as a synecdoche of the song as a whole. For discussion of the passage in relation to voice and textuality see also Uhlig (2011) 26–7.

chorus also opens up another way of understanding πόθι φρενός / ἐμᾶς γέγραπται, namely as a reference to the fact that Hagesidamus' name has been more generally 'inscribed' on people's minds by the act of victory, the subsequent announcement of his name at Olympia, and the word-of-mouth spread of the news that doubtless followed his success.[28]

All these lines of interpretation would also have been available to a later reader engaging with a written copy of the poem, even though the distinction between poet and chorus would have taken place at the level of imaginative recreation rather than through the actualities of performance. But the situation of the poem in a book also opens up other meanings, particularly in view of the interaction between the language of writing and the book itself. The act of writing in the poet's mind (γέγραπται) is not identical with any individual act of inscription: each physical copying of the text would have replayed this division and reinforced the phrase's metaphorical force. Together with the description of the poem as a γλυκύ . . . μέλος, the reference to (a metaphorical) writing invokes the difference between performance and reading. Yet the use of γέγραπται also interacts with its material aspect; the metaphor of writing on the mind is converted by the act of inscription into an (almost) literal description of the book itself, or, from another angle, might be read as doubly metaphorical, metaphorizing the book as the poet's mental substrate. Similarly, there is a difference between the enunciative situation of ἀνάγνωτέ μοι in performance and reading. In reading the phrase, the reader describes his own activity, but also addresses the text, whereas the narrator, realized by the chorus in performance, uses the imperative in a way that projects a number of possible addressees.[29] The re-enunciation of ἀνάγνωτέ μοι by the reader as an address to the text highlights another aspect of the book, namely its function in preserving a temporally prior performance and, more generally, as offering a

---

[28] The poem's opening also references epigraphic practice: see Fearn (2013) 248–9 for discussion.

[29] The imperative has caused controversy. Verdenius (1988) 55 sees it as used 'absolutely'. For criticism of this position see D'Alessio (2004a) 291 n. 81, who reads it as addressed to the Muse and Aletheia; this in turn is complicated by the gap between γέγραπται and the address to the Muse. Hubbard (1985) 67 sees it as addressed to the audience, which is then put in the position of 'reading the present ode externalized and objectified into a written text'. I take it as capable of being understood both as an address to the Muse, and as an address from poet to chorus, in line with the remarks about rehearsal above.

means of access to the past. Unlike the narrator, who dramatizes his mind (albeit ironically) as a somewhat unstable substrate, the reader interacts with the secure material frame of the book. Whereas in performance, φρενός / ἐμᾶς γέγραπται gestured to the process of written composition preceding performance, in the situation of the book the phrase points up the book's status as a record of performance which 'has been written'.[30]

These lines illustrate Pindar's dramatic use of the notion of writing. When considered in the light of their place in a book, they also alert us to the additional meanings and resonances that his poems can take on as a result of interactions between the text and its medium. The self-referential characteristics of the passage make it particularly significant in this respect, but in the course of this study I shall demonstrate that similar kinds of arguments can be made about numerous other aspects of Pindar's corpus.

MATERIAL ISSUES

The notion of writing is central to how Pindar is conceived by ancient commentators. Although authorial utterance is frequently referred to by λέγει or φησί, the process of composition is frequently referred to in terms of writing,[31] and his poems are habitually described as written constructs. The scholia frequently comment on what they consider to be his compositional practices. They refer to his location

[30] Cf. Edmunds (2001) 79 'these techniques of orally performed poetry, Pindaric and archaic, are already "grammatological", a potential deferral of the voice of the poet or performer(s) to other, later, voice(s)'. Relevant also is Payne (2006), who argues that Pindar's gnomic maxims have a transhistorical as well as a (temporally and spatially) local force: 'gnomic lyric . . . presupposes its own transhistorical reception by addressing abstract formulations to a universal subject created by its own pronominal structures' (p. 182).

[31] Cf. *Scholies* pp. 216–20, although their remarks on p. 220 do not adequately distinguish between utterance *per se* and composition. Where composition is concerned, ποιεῖν is used occasionally (e.g. Σ O.1.5g = i 20–1 Dr) but γράφειν is common: on the vocabulary of writing used to describe poetic composition in inscriptions and other texts see Prauscello (2006) 48–51. Perhaps more importantly, descriptions of compositions often manifest an awareness of writing as a compositional practice as distinct from the transcontextual utterance it produces: see e.g. Σ O.1.184b (i 56 Dr): εἴη . . . ἐμέ τε ἐπινίκους γράφειν καὶ ὑμνεῖν τοὺς νικῶντας, and the passages cited in the next two notes.

when writing,[32] and glosses on *O*.10, *P*.4, and *N*.4, taking their lead from Pindar's self-referential rhetoric, go into detail about the difference between the time at which the poem was composed and the time of its performance.[33] Pindar's writing practices are occasionally connected to images in the poems. At *N*.3.80–1, Pindar refers to the lateness of the poem, and then employs the image of an eagle catching its prey to indicate the force of his composition ('the eagle is swift among birds, which suddenly seizes, searching from afar, the bloodied prey with its claws'). One of the scholia on the passage comments as follows (Σ *N*.3.138b = iii 61–2 Dr): ἢ οὕτως· εἰ καὶ ὅλως ὀψέ [φησί,] γέγραπταί μοι τὸ ποίημα, ὅμως ὡς ἀετὸς πόρρωθεν ἐλθὼν ταχέως ἤγρευσέ τι καὶ cυνήρπαcεν, οὕτως ἐγὼ τὰ πράγματα ταχέως cυνήρπακα καὶ γέγραφα ('Or thus: even if I wrote the poem very late, just like an eagle coming from far away swiftly hunted something down and seized it, thus have I swiftly hunted down my subject and written it'). Here, poetological imagery is used as a basis for constructing an image of the writer at work, and the text, in turn, is seen as reflecting these working practices. The scholia's comments about writing are not restricted to imagining Pindar's use of the medium; there are also occasions where the scholia manifest a strong sense of being part of a scholarly tradition to which writing is fundamental. This sense emerges in the frequent references to textual readings preferred by various scholars,[34] but it is also made explicit at Σ *O*.7.5b (i 200 Dr), which references the textual critical history of the phrase under discussion: 'some say [the text should read] "sending", and they say that [the reading] "drinking" is an old error of the scribes' (παλαιὸν cφάλμα φαcὶ τῶν γραψάντων). The reader is here made aware of the textual and historical contingencies that affect the texts they read.

---

[32] For Thebes as a site of composition cf. Σ *P*.2.inscr. (ii 32 Dr): ὥcτε ἀπὸ Θηβᾶν δεῖ γράφειν, ὅθεν ἦν ὁ τὸ ποίημα cυνθείc. This scholium is connected to the argument made in Σ *P*.2.6b (iii 33 Dr) that Pindar did not bring the poem to Hiero himself, but sent it in the form of a document: the statement φέρων / μέλος ἔρχομαι (*P*.2.3–4) should therefore be understood as the utterance 'either of the person who carried the poem or of the chorus' (ἤτοι οὖν ἐκ τοῦ διακομίcαντος τὴν ᾠδὴν πρὸς τὸν τύραννόν ἐcτιν ὁ λόγος ἢ ἐκ τοῦ χοροῦ, Σ *P*.2.6b) On the historical scenarios that may underlie this statement see Prauscello (2006) 40–5 with further bibliography.

[33] Cf. Σ *O*.10.101d (i 337 Dr), Σ *P*.4.inscr.a (ii 92 Dr), Σ *N*.4.14a (iii 65–6 Dr). Cf. D'Alessio (2004a) 278–80 for remarks on this gap from a pragmatic perspective.

[34] For the phrase ἐὰν δὲ γράφηται used of disputed readings cf. e.g. Σ *O*.2.42e (i 72 Dr), Σ *O*.7.24c (i 203 Dr), Σ *O*.10.83b (i 332 Dr), Σ *P*.3.75 (ii 73–4 Dr), and see the comments of *Scholies* p. 220.

Writing has a preservative function, but as *Σ N.3*.138b demonstrates, it is also a means of imagining the past and connecting the past with the present. This process is also at work in the scholia's paraphrases of Pindar's metaphorical language. At *Σ N.7*.16a (iii 119 Dr), Pindar's lines εἰ δὲ τύχῃ τις ἔρδων, μελίφρον᾽ αἰτίαν / ῥοαῖσι Μοισᾶν ἐνέβαλε ('if someone succeeds, he throws a sweet-minded cause into the Muses' streams', *N.7*.11–12) are glossed as follows: 'if someone has won success, he has flung a pleasurable cause for encountering [i.e. reading about] him 'in the streams of the Muses', *that is, in the hymns written for him*' (τουτέστι τοῖς ὕμνοις τοῖς εἰς αὐτὸν γραφομένοις). The gloss explains the rhetoric, but it also translates Pindar's imagery into the terms of written composition and stresses the book as the site in which the poem functions.[35] More extended reflections on writing are found at *Σ N.4*.10a (iii 65 Dr), which glosses a reflection on poetry's immortalizing power being dependent on the Graces (ῥῆμα δ᾽ ἐργμάτων χρονιώτερον βιοτεύει, / ὅ τι κε σὺν Χαρίτων τύχᾳ / γλῶσσα φρενὸς ἐξέλοι βαθείας ('a discourse lives for a longer time than deeds, which a tongue seizes from the mind's depths with the Graces' favour', *N.4*.6–8):

παντὸς ἔργου χρονιώτερόν ἐστι τὸ ῥῆμα, τουτέστιν ὁ ὕμνος· οἷον τὰ λεγόμενα πάντα ἢ γραφόμενα χρονιώτερά ἐστι τῶν ἔργων. τὰ μὲν γὰρ ἔργα τῷ γεγονέναι παρήκει, τὰ δὲ γραφόμενα αἰώνια παραδίδοται. ποῖα δέ; ἃ ἂν μετὰ τῆς ἐκ Χαρίτων τύχης τεχθῇ καὶ προαιρεθῇ ἐκ τῆς γλώττης ἑκάστῳ· ὡς ἐάνγε χωρὶς Χαρίτων γράφηται ὁ ὕμνος, ἀπόλωλε καὶ ἔσβεσται, ἐὰν δὲ μετὰ Χαρίτων, μένει πρὸς αἰῶνα εὔδια. καὶ Καλλίμαχος (= fr. 7.13–14 Harder)·

ἔλλατε νῦν, ἐλέγοισι δ᾽ ἐνιψήσασθε λιπώσας
χεῖρας ἐμοῖς, ἵνα μοι πολὺ μένουσιν ἔτος.

The utterance, that is the hymn, lasts for longer than any deed, for all spoken or written things last longer than deeds. For deeds are in the past by virtue of having happened, but writings are handed down so as to be eternal. Which sort? Those that are created with the Graces' favour and selected by each man's tongue. For if a hymn is written without the Graces, the writings perish and are extinguished, but if written with them, it abides in fair weather for all time. And Callimachus says: 'Come now, wipe your shining hands on my elegies, so that they may abide for many a year.'[36]

---

[35] Cf. also *Σ I.5*.67c (iii 248 Dr): ἢ οὕτω· καὶ αἱ τοιαίδε τιμαί, καίπερ ἐν μέλιτι οὖσαι, τουτέστιν ἡδύσαι, ὅμως ἀγαπῶσι τὸ καλλίνικον χάρμα, τουτέστι τὴν ἐκ τῶν γεγραμμένων ἐπινίκων χαρὰν ἀγαπῶσι.

[36] For the place of this fragment in the *Aetia* cf. Massimilla (1996) 246–55, Harder (2012) 133–4. For an analysis of the scholium cf. Phillips (2013c) 167–9.

A tension emerges here between the Graces bestowing value on a text and the necessity of writing to its preservation. While the poetic inspiration and social approbation symbolized by the goddesses is crucial to a text's success, it is the material durability of books that ensures their survival, an implication registered (perhaps unconsciously) by the scholium's shift from referring to the role of 'spoken' and 'written' discourses in a poem's dissemination (τὰ λεγόμενα πάντα ἢ γραφόμενα χρονιώτερά ἐcτι τῶν ἔργων) to emphasizing writing alone (τὰ δὲ γραφόμενα αἰώνια παραδίδοται).[37]

The citation of Callimachus adds an additional level of complexity to the gloss. The citation has explanatory force, but it also implies a literary relationship in which Callimachus has reworked Pindar's conception of the Graces with a greater degree of emphasis on the role played by the book, as well as by individual poetic agency, in literary production.[38] As well as functioning as symbols of poetic agency, then, Pindar's Graces are positioned as figures open to rewriting. Crucially, this openness emerges as part of their immortalizing function; just as the rhetoric of ῥῆμα δ' ἐργμάτων χρονιώτερον βιοτεύει comes to act (at least in part) as a reference to the preservative medium of the book, so the juxtaposition with Callimachus highlights how Pindar's lines have taken on a new significance as a literary model in their contextual and temporal transplantation. This scholium is a particularly explicit instance of writing functioning as both a conduit that links different historical periods and a mode of distantiation. As an imaginary construct, writing allows readers to connect their own activity with Pindar's practices, the image of Pindar the writer also affects later readers' view of the performance economy. For Hellenistic readers, the *origo* of Pindaric discourse is doubled across (written) composition and performance; one effect of the scholia's persistent references to Pindar as writer is that for later readers this notion always lies just behind the self-referential rhetoric of the poems themselves. But the emphasis on writing also shifts the terms within which Pindaric textuality is considered: the performance utterance can be read as an event which unfolds from a prior textual substrate, rather than as itself a privileged locus of meaning.[39] Moreover, the image of Pindar's writing also intimates that

[37] Cf. Barchiesi (2000) 170 n. 7.

[38] This should not be taken as implying that Callimachus did not have other models: cf. Phillips (2013a).

[39] This reading expands on the poems' self-representations, in which a prior instantiation of textuality is often at issue: see e.g. O.6.90–1 and pp. 1–2 above.

the poetry is given over to textual dissemination in the very act of composition; in this sense, performances are part of the poems' afterlife no less than books.

Implicit in this double status of writing is another question, decisive for this study as a whole, that concerns the relationship between books and the performance economy. Thinking about how Pindar's epinicians operate in book form entails asking how different the experience of reading is from attending a performance, or, to put it in different terms, asking how many of the claims we could make about the meanings generated by the poems in book form could also be made about reperformance scenarios. As I mentioned above,[40] drawing a sharp distinction between the two is problematic for various reasons. There are clearly ways in which reading differs from attending a performance. Perhaps most obviously, the action of sitting alone in a colonnade reading a papyrus of the *Olympians* differs markedly from the experience of attending a large-scale choral performance as part of an audience.[41] There are also numerous other, more subtle differences between the two modes. The temporally unique, impermanent performance contrasts with the (at least notional) durability of the material frame. The gathering and order-ing of poems in editions imposes on them a form of collectedness at variance with the temporally discrete status of individually performed songs. Editing poems can affect their functions: perhaps the most obvious instance of this is the placing of poems first or last in a book, which gives them a force that they could not have when performed.[42] The addition of critical signs, the process of colometrization, and the use of scholarly marginalia all likewise shift the grounds of textual engagement. I shall argue below that these forms of reception, together with literary responses to Pindar's texts, add new dimensions to the experience of engaging with epinician poetry. Especially marked in this respect are the intertextual connections developed in commentaries between Pindar and his Hellenistic successors, although I shall also argue that reading commentaries opens up the possibility of more extended reflection on the intertextual relationships between Pindar and, for instance, Homer and Hesiod.

---

[40] See p. 5.

[41] Although the former is not the only reading scenario that we should imagine: see Ch. 4, pp. 170–1.

[42] See esp. Chs. 3 and 5.

Nor is the shift from performance to text only a matter of external relations; the texts' own rhetoric also takes on new resonances in the light of its material resituation, as in the case of *N*.4.6–8 above. References to musical accompaniment, choral singing, and other specific aspects of the performance economy impose on the reader a vivid sense of the difference of the poem's self-projection from the situation in which he himself engages with it, while at the same time influencing the reader's conception of his own activity. When, for example, at the beginning of *P*.4 the narrator says that the Muse 'must stand today by a man who is a friend [Arcesilas]' (σάμερον μὲν χρή σε παρ' ἀνδρὶ φίλῳ / στᾶμεν, 1–2) in order for the activity of praise to take place, the reader is made aware of the temporal specificity of the performance utterance, but also of his own role in continuing the text's project (αὔξῃς [sc. the Muse] οὖρον ὕμνων, *P*.4.3). But this example also makes clear how difficult it is to separate the realms of performance and reading. The most obvious reason for this is that the rhetoric of performance imprints itself on the reading scenario and invites readers' imaginative recreation. Moreover, effects that come about as a result of the spatial and temporal differentiation of the scene of reading from the deictic *origo* constructed in performance could also function in reperformance scenarios remote from the location of the 'original' performance.[43] As discussed above, the materiality of the book is to a certain extent prefigured by Pindar's characterization of his poems as objects, and various poems advertise their connections to others in the corpus even as performance pieces.[44] Likewise, intertextual relationships would have been available for scrutiny for Pindar's first audiences and performers.

In the light of these considerations, my analyses will have a double focus. Some of my readings will be directed at textual phenomena that emerge from the multiple redefinitions of a given poem in a variety of cultural contexts, while others will examine phenomena that emerge specifically from the interaction between poem and book. In some cases, however, my readings will dwell on dialogues between the two types of phenomena. Some of the readings I elaborate in the context

---

[43] Cf. D'Alessio (2004a) 269, 278–80 on deixis as fictionalizing its setting in advance of its realization in performance.

[44] See my remarks on Ch. 6, pp. 238–4 on relations between poems within an edition. On 'performance intertextuality' cf. Pavlou (2008); Morrison (2011).

of the book could also be made in slightly different terms about reperformance scenarios. Numerous differences between listening to a monodic reperformance of, for instance, *O*.14 in Athens in the 440s and reading it in a book in the 180s would have been differences of scale rather than kind; a sense of temporal dislocation from the implied space of performance would have been common to both, as would the metaliterary resonance of the poem's ending. But as I shall argue, there are various phenomena that are either unique to books, or more marked when they take place as part of a reading process. So while there are some distinct differences, the relation between the textual and performance economies is also a matter of dialogue, overlap, and interaction.[45] These tensions are captured by the iconography of a bronze statue dedicated to Pindar in Athens, and described by ps-Aeschines: καὶ ἦν αὕτη καὶ εἰς ἡμᾶς ἔτι, πρὸ τῆς βασιλείου στοᾶς καθήμενος ἐνδύματι καὶ λύρᾳ ὁ Πίνδαρος, διάδημα ἔχων καὶ ἐπὶ τῶν γονάτων ἀνειλιγμένον βιβλίον ('and you can still see it, the statue of Pindar before the Royal Stoa, seated with this cloak and lyre, with his diadem and an unrolled book on his knees', *Ep.* 3.1–3).[46] The statue fuses the image of Pindar the musician, probably directing a chorus, with the paraphernalia of reading. Like the scholia, the image seems to imply the book as a medium that precedes and enables performance, and encourages readers to dwell on the relation between the two modes of textuality, but as a mimesis of the poet's role in performance, the statue also functions as a monument to song culture. In combining these elements, the statue neatly expresses the concerns of this study.

Before considering the methodological issues involved in charting these interactions, I want to analyse the status of books and readers in antiquity, in order to explore further the material realities and imaginative frameworks that underlay ancient reading practices. Recent studies have focused on books as aesthetically significant objects expressive of their owners' status, on their influence on

---

[45] It should also be noted that my remarks are not unique to Pindar; many of the phenomena I comment on would also have been the case in more or less similar terms for other poets.

[46] Cf. also the description at Paus. 1.8.4. On the iconography, dating, and political background of the statue cf. Picard (1952) 16; Kimmel-Clauzet (2013) 235–7. According to Isoc. *Ant.* 166 Pindar was appointed as Athens' *proxenos* on account of his glorification of the city in his dithyrambs: on his relations with Athens see Hubbard (2001).

modes of literary composition, and on how they were produced,
sold, and read.[47] Somewhat less attention, however, has been given
to how the forms of books interact with the texts they contain,[48] and
it is this interaction with which this study is mainly concerned.
Central to my analysis is a conception of the book as an aesthetically
marked object in its own right, not simply as a neutral purveyor of
meanings. Following the lead of contemporary book theorists, I want
to re-examine the division between semantic meaning and material
form by means of which the latter is conceived as an incidental
adjunct to the former, and emphasize instead the book's status as a
part of the processes by which meaning is created and maintained.

This approach runs counter to one of the primary features of
Western aesthetic thinking, in which the marginalization of the
book as a part of aesthetic processes has been symptomatic of a
wider view, derived chiefly from Plato and Aristotle, that privileges
the noetic aspects of aesthetic experience over the material.[49] The
book theorists' emphasis on the material particularity of the book and
its cultural significance problematizes this distinction, and also highlights the importance of the wider intellectual and social contexts in
which books are produced, disseminated, and read. In tracing the
distinction between formalist and materialist tendencies in modern
criticism, Peter McDonald highlights the role of scholars such as
Jerome McGann and Donald McKenzie in questioning New Critical
and poststructuralist reading protocols which abstracted the text
from its material context:

> They insisted on seeing the text, not as an abstract linguistic form, but as
> a mediated material artifact, a redescription which, they urged, entailed
> a significant shift in our understanding of the scene of reading. If this
> scene was defined for close readers by their critical engagement with
> what we could call the transcendent 'text-type'—the free-floating, ideal-
> ized verbal text—*written* by the author, it was structured more imme-
> diately for materialist readers by their physical encounter with an
> immanent 'text-token'—a particular material document—*produced* by

---

[47] Cf. e.g. Houston (2009); White (2009). Lowrie (2009) focuses on how writing is
represented in Latin poetry; cf. also Dupont (2009); Farrell (2009). See Johnson (2010)
17–22 on the importance of books as 'display pieces'.

[48] Cf., however, Eidinow (2009).

[49] On the role of written texts in fostering more abstract ways of thinking about
texts during the fourth century BC see Ford (2003).

various cultural mediators (editors, publishers, printers, etc.) for specific markets.[50]

McDonald's analysis highlights that the act of material inscription is itself meaningful, not only because the material document reflects a variety of social and institutional factors attendant on its production which are themselves part of the ongoing shaping of meaning,[51] but also because it generates the potential for interplay between meaning and medium. On this reading, the space of the document itself becomes a part of literary form. This position also points towards the tension between the book as a (provisionally) fixed structure and the instability of textual meaning, informed by its multiple intertextualities, its potential for indeterminacies and its capacity for dislocating generic and ideological frames. This tension has been central to book theory and responses to it. The 'documentalist' approach to the material particularity of the book was sometimes mobilized to oppose the poststructuralist notion of textuality decoupled from authorial control, even as its insistence on the roles played by extra-authorial and extratextual forces paralleled the anti-Platonizing positions of textualists such as Derrida, Barthes, and Foucault.[52]

And yet the apparent opposition between the documentalist insistence on the centrality of the material document and the poststructuralist commitment to a thinking of textuality which 'dislocates the borders, the framing of texts, everything which should preserve their immanence and make possible an internal reading'[53] is far from absolute. Poststructuralist thinking has often focused on the

---

[50] McDonald (2003) 231. His analysis builds on that of Chartier (1995) 134, who insists that '[r]eaders never confront abstract, idealized texts detached from any materiality', and opposes a mode of reading which attempts to take account of the material conditions of textuality to the phenomenologies of reading promulgated by e.g. Iser (1978) 'which eras[e] the concrete modality of the act of reading and characteriz[e] it by its effects, postulated as universals'.

[51] See e.g. Chartier (1995); McKenzie (1999); (2002).

[52] See Derrida (1978) 20 on 'the theological simultaneity of the book', which he treats in that discussion as an illusory totality linked to a metaphysical conception of the connection between meaning and presence. Cf. also Derrida (1976) 18–26 on the links between the book as traditionally conceived and metaphysics: '[t]he idea of the book is profoundly alien to the sense of writing. It is the encyclopaedic protection . . . of logocentrism against the disruption of writing [and] against difference in general' (p. 18).

[53] Derrida (1990) 92.

potentially infinite variety of contexts and their consequences for textuality; as it is only possible for meaning to emerge in contexts, meaning can never said to be securely finalized. McDonald argues that the poststructuralist approach complements documentalist emphasis on the material text in giving a theoretical framework to deal with the contextual and material variety attendant on the processes of dissemination:

> [I]mmanence [does] not entail stability, since, even in material terms, there is no end to the process of dissemination. Proliferation, not fixity, is the norm as texts are successively put to new uses in new forms. This is not, it should be stressed, simply a reassertion of the scholarly editor's traditional insistence on *textual* variation. It is a matter of recognizing the volatility of material *contexts* and the unpredictability of *readings*. Produced and reproduced by new cultural mediators, in new contexts, and for new readers, the successive versions of texts represent unique episodes in the constitution of meaning.[54]

Using this model to think about books in the ancient world requires some methodological adjustment. Contemporary book theorists pay considerable attention to bibliographical issues and social analysis of book production in a way precluded for classicists by lack of detailed evidence.[55] However, McDonald's emphasis on contextual variation is a useful starting point for thinking about the cultural issues which affected the Pindaric corpus in different periods of antiquity, as the texts became sites for scholarly contestation and mediation by individual readers, and were opened up to the influences of literary receptions. Equally, 'the volatility of material contexts' is an apt formulation of the physical variety of ancient books. In antiquity, each book was a physically unique object, written out by a reader or a professional scribe.[56] These inscriptional processes were shaped by economic considerations, by the professionalism of individual scribes, and by changing fashions in the style of book hands, which were themselves of aesthetic significance.[57] Books were consequently idiosyncratic, often produced for

---

[54] McDonald (2003) 232.

[55] e.g. McGann (1991); McKenzie (1999). Fundamental also is Genette (1997) on the role of paratexts (titles, prefaces, etc.) in presenting literary works and affecting their consumption.

[56] See the remarks of Johnson (2010) 179.

[57] On the concept of 'deluxe editions' cf. Johnson (2004) 155–60; for a typology of Pindaric book-rolls in later antiquity cf. Ucciardello (2012) 113–18.

and tailored to the needs of specific consumers, as well as modified by individual readers' additions of marginalia. One of the concerns of this study will be to establish a dialogue between these material features (actual or deduced) and the texts themselves.

While the distinction between text-type and text-token is helpful in focusing attention on the materiality of the book, we should resist an overly schematic application of this opposition. Every act of reading involves a certain abstraction of the text from its material instantiation, and in the case of Pindar's epinicians, as I noted above, deixis, self-referential discourse, and contextual references encourage an imaginative engagement with the situations the poems project.[58] This mode of reading is also encouraged by the ancient literary critical discourses and literary receptions which emphasize the connection between poetic utterance and the historical figure of the author. Yet this mode of reading, while important, is not a 'natural' approach which should be privileged, but rather one means of reading among others, subject to influence by contextual factors. The distinction between text-type and text-token provides a useful starting point for considering the various kinds of interactions that occur between signified structures and their material frames.

Any account of the reception of a textual corpus in antiquity must take account of ancient reading practices and the various ways in which these were conceptualized by literary critics. It was long a commonplace that reading in antiquity meant reading aloud, even when the reader was alone.[59] This position has been challenged by numerous scholars who have pointed out that, although voiced reading was clearly common, there is also much evidence for silent reading, and we should not think that voiced reading was the norm.[60] Debates about which form of reading predominated are less important for this study than the variety of reading situations in which texts would have been realized; reading aloud to oneself, to a small group of friends, reading silently on one's own, and engaging in

---

[58] On deixis and the relation between historical and projected context cf. pp. 5, 14.

[59] Cf. e.g. Balogh (1927); Hendrickson (1929); Rohde (1963); Kenney (1982) 12; Porter (2010) 314–15, 353–4; for further references cf. Gavrilov (1997) 56–8. On Roman reading practices cf. e.g. Quinn (1982); Cavallo (1999); Johnson (2000). Cf. Johnson (2010) 4–9 for a helpful overview of the voiced versus silent reading debate.

[60] Knox (1968) argues against the view that silent reading was not viewed as 'abnormal' even if it was less common than voiced reading: cf. also Burnyeat (1997). Parker (2009) offers an overview of the Roman evidence and argues for the prevalence of silent reading.

a more dramatic performance before a larger group of a previously
memorized poem (or part of a poem) were all possible scenarios, and
having slaves read aloud was also a common practice.[61] Therefore,
while we should be cautious about thinking that reading was usually
or predominantly voiced, we need to think about the interpretative
consequences of voiced reading and how this practice may have
affected how readers orientated themselves towards texts. We also
need to bear in mind the effects of literary theoretical discourses
about the voice, and the role of poets' voices in literary receptions.[62]
Given the prominence of the emphasis on the voice in these texts, it is
reasonable to assume that even when reading silently, ancient readers
would sometimes have conceived of the texts they were engaging with
as the 'written voice' of an author, or at least entertained the possibility, as we still do today, of so conceptualizing the text.

The notion of writing as inscribed/written voice (ἐγγράμματος
φωνή) is common in ancient theoretical literature.[63] Speech as an
emitting of 'breath' (πνεῦμα) was transcribed into the written document, which then became a trace not only of meanings but of the
physicality of enunciation: 'voice inscribed in letters is the culmin-
ation of the breath that is stored within us' (ἐγγράμματος δὲ φωνή
ἐστιν ἀποτέλεσμα τοῦ ἐν ἡμῖν ἐντεθησαυρισμένου πνεύματος, Σ Dion.
Thrax 212.23–4 Hilgard). This physicality could be foregrounded as a
central part of the reading experience: Arcesilaus, head of the Middle
Academy in the mid-third century BC, is quoted by Diogenes Laertius
as describing Pindar as 'terrific at filling [the reader] with voice', a
power he associates with the poet's ability to furnish readers with rich
verbal resources (τόν τε Πίνδαρον ἔφασκε <u>δεινὸν εἶναι φωνῆς ἐμπλῆσαι</u>
καὶ ὀνομάτων καὶ ῥημάτων εὐπορίαν παρασχεῖν, Diog. Laert. 4.31).
Reading (aloud) is, on these terms, an excavation of the authorial
voice which inheres in the text: '[t]he discourse produced by the
reader's voice is a re-enactment of the writer's voice that was transcribed in the act of writing'.[64] The propositions that the sound of

---

[61] Cf. Johnson (2000).   [62] See pp. Ch. 1, pp. 72–3.

[63] For further examples cf. Porter (2010) 350 n. 212.

[64] Bakker (2005) 41. Cf. Porter (2010) 310–11 for a characterization of this critical
standpoint: 'render[s] the voice audible no matter how many layers of writing,
transmission, quotation, or time have intervened . . . "the view that within all linguistic
expressions, oral or written, lies buried a voice that animates them"'. Cf. further ibid.
351–3. See Prauscello (2006) 51–8 for the conceptualization of voiced reading in
Dionysius Thrax and the accompanying scholia.

words has a function distinct from their meaning, that sound could be pleasing to the hearer, and that sound could reinforce meaning, were widely accepted by Hellenistic literary theorists, and form the background to the stylistic analyses of Cicero and Dionysius of Halicarnassus. The precise nature of linguistic sound and its relations to semantic meaning, however, were contested issues.[65]

The materiality of language is also a problematic figure in these debates; not only is there the primary argument about whether poetry is to be valued according to sound or meaning, but the status of the sound of language itself is in question. Whereas φωνή is often conceptualized as the voice of the author, it can also be employed to mean 'sound', and the euphonist thinkers cited by Philodemus often refer to a materiality inherent in language itself rather than a personalized voice.[66] This distinction will be significant when considering, for instance, the ways in which literary receptions of Pindar depersonalize the poetic utterance by comparing it to other types of sounds which exceed normative human capacities.[67] Furthermore, the thinking of the text as 'inscribed voice' need not be privileged as a dominant way of conceiving readerly activity; rather, we need to recognize its theoretical shortcomings, as well its limitations as an 'historical' description of what reading entailed. First, the conception of authorial φωνή is distinctly problematic as a means of thinking about performance, involving as it does a deformative construction which reduces the complex vocal and musical aspects of performance to an essentialized notion of authorial utterance. Moreover, thinking about the text as a transcription of authorial φωνή glosses over important distinctions between author and narrator, and hence limits the possibility for attention to the specific ways in which narratorial voice is constructed.[68] Authorial voice should not be conceptualized

---

[65] Crates of Mallos, for instance, held that the quality of verbal sound was the most important factor is judging the value of a poem: cf. Asmis (1992); (1995b) 152. Cf. further Philod. *On Poems* 5 (Mangoni) col. xxv 2–xxix 18 for Crates' argument that sound quality is not determined by rules but inheres naturally in an arrangement of words. This view is contested by Philodemus *On Poems* 1 fr. 184 when he asserts that 'everyone's hearing or mind is pleased not without reason'. Cf. also *On Poems* 5 col. xxxii 6–10, where Philodemus says that an unnamed opponent 'speaks only about lexis, while leaving aside thoughts, which have the far greater importance'.

[66] Cf. *On Poems* 1 fr. 117.17 for φωνή as explicitly non-authorial sound.

[67] See Ch. 2, pp. 92–6.

[68] For an overview of the controversial issue of first persons in Pindar cf. Currie (2005) 19–21, and Fearn (2007) 7–9. The fullest treatment is Lefkowitz (1991), and

only as a productive ground which generates the text, but as a figure produced by the processes of textuality.

Too essentializing a conception of the authorial 'voice' also risks neglecting how it is constructed according to generic and contingent influences; no author writes with a 'voice' that is entirely 'his own'. These issues also affect the historical resitings of texts. Even thinking in materialist terms, a later reading is a *re*-enactment, a confluence of the reader's voice with that of the text which presupposes the absence of the 'actual' voice of the historical author.[69] This absence raises the question, connected to the constructedness of authorial voice just discussed, of whose 'voice' is being re-enacted—the voice of Pindar the historical individual, Pindar *qua* constructed narrator, or the voice of the performing chorus. As my readings will demonstrate, reading Pindaric texts often brings to the fore the impossibility of a complete 're-enactment' of the text, not least because of the texts' dramatizations of the limitations of their own enunciative strategies.[70] A voiced reading is a transformative encounter which entails the reader's physical disposition being given over to the text's voice(s) while simultaneously affirming the uniquely contingent status of each recreation of the text.

The transcription-and-revivification model also ignores the considerable distantiations involved in the processes of textual dissemination and their potential to generate new meanings. The differences mentioned above between the sites of performance and reading would have been strengthened in later antiquity by other factors such as the oddities of Pindar's dialect, as well as the growing body of literary and scholarly receptions. Moreover, books are not simply transcriptions of a prior body of language but visual and tangible objects. The materialists' stress on the embodied particularity of text-as-voice discounts the role of material factors such as the use of critical signs and the more general visual appearances of and physical forms of books in shaping readers' access to texts.[71] An examination of Pindar's texts in later antiquity also needs to take account of interpretative and

note her supplementary comments in Lefkowitz (1995). A particularly interesting aspect of this problem is whether certain utterances are felt to be spoken/sung in the persona of the *laudandus*: cf. *Σ P*.8.78a (ii 214 Dr), *Σ P*.9.161 (ii 235–6 Dr), *Σ N*.10.73b (iii 175–6 Dr), *Σ I*.7.55b (iii 267 Dr).

[69] My reading of enactment differs from that of Nagy (1990) 42–5: for further details see Ch. 6, pp. 256–63 and p. 257 n. 52.

[70] See Ch. 5, p. 226 and Ch. 6, pp. 262–3.

[71] I examine this aspect of critical signs on Ch. 2, pp. 114–17.

literary receptions, and in this respect the corpus of ancient scholarship represented by the Pindaric scholia is particularly important. Not only are the exegetical and historical questions foregrounded by the scholia remote from the materialist emphasis on the here-and-now of the physicality of language,[72] but they also implicate the texts they comment on in a series of intertextual, cultural, and historical networks which demand readerly attention to the contexts, both those of Pindar's own time and later, in which meaning arises and is remade, debated, and contested. In short, ancient reading, voiced or silent, was a dynamic process wherein the text both imposes its particular economies of meaning on its readers and is reshaped by the contexts in which it is encountered. Reading is an encounter with the other, and this otherness is reinforced by cultural and historical distantiations, as well as being reconfigured by the receptions to which it is subject.

The literary theoretical validation of the voice in antiquity is an episode in what Derrida terms the 'logocentric' or 'phonocentric' metaphysics of Western thought, in which live utterance is seen as a privileged space where meaning is informed by its co-presence with the intentions of the speaker, and writing is seen as a parasitic copy of speech. Derrida attempted to show that speech no less than writing partook of the deferrals and indeterminacies of meaning operative in language; the broader correlative of this position is that performances should no more be thought as sites of unified self-present meaning than written texts.[73] In classical scholarship, and particularly in analysis of classical and archaic Greek literature, this dichotomy has often been expressed in the tendency to privilege performance as a dominant site of meaning and significance, and in the concomitant view of books as a secondary medium mechanically reproducing texts which find their fullest meaning in performance. Classical scholarship has often sought to organize oral and written literature around a series of such oppositions, sometimes with a strongly fetishizing stress on the alterity of ancient cultural practices: reading is an individual, playful activity which takes place at a remove from society, whereas performance, as the ultimate expression of oral culture, dramatizes considerations of communal importance.[74]

---

[72] Cf. Porter (2010) 308–64.
[73] Foundational are Derrida (1976) 3–93 and (1981) 17–33.
[74] Cf. Fowler (forthcoming) 1–16. I am grateful to Peta Fowler for allowing me to consult this work. Uhlig (2011) 4–8 and *passim* provides a useful complication of this opposition by examining Pindar's construction of a 'scriptory poetics'.

While few scholars nowadays would accept this division and its conceptual apparatus as an historical account of how readers encountered texts, debates over the interrelation of oral and written cultures are still largely structured around these underlying oppositions.[75] One manifestation of this tendency is the construction of idealized modes of performance reception, which either explicitly posit or implicitly assume a privileged mode of comprehension attendant on the 'original' performance or reception of a literary work.[76] In a similar way to the construction of authorial/textual voice by the ancient literary theorists, this conceptualization of 'original' receptions denies the temporally extended and multiple nature of any (set of) receptive event(s). Don Fowler's discussion clarifies the issues:

> [T]he reception of a work even in its most primary context cannot be identified with a single aesthetic experience but is constituted by an extended set of acts and events ... in archaic and classical Greece, the meaning of a lyric or dramatic text was not used up on its first performance but is crucially constituted precisely through its reperformance and reuse. This is true whether or not we are looking to empirical data about actual reception or to the various constructs of 'implied' or 'model' audiences, to the figurations, that is, of an audience that a reading of a text constructs as necessary for its interpretation. Even those who are prepared to admit that the reception of a literary work is in fact always extended in time and composed of an indefinite number of different events will often wish to construct a more ideal encounter as the implied moment of reception, and to track the implied audience's interpretation of the text *as if* it took place ... during a first reading.

This analysis is particularly relevant to the fifth-century reception of Pindar, informed as it was by a variety of events separate from the first or official performance of a poem. Rehearsals, in which the performers would, in learning the song, have participated in a lengthy contact with the text which would have operated as a powerful conduit for the text's ethical demands; reperformances, whether choral or monodic,[77] interactions between epinician performances, and other modes of dissemination such as commemorative epigrams,

---

[75] e.g. Habinek (2005).

[76] Cf. Hirsch (1967); Bundy (1962) 4–5. For a counter-argument about the temporally extended nature of receptions cf. Fowler (1996).

[77] On reperformance scenarios cf. Currie (2004); Hubbard (2004); Morrison (2007); (2011); Hornblower (2012) 102–3.

announcements at the games, and general rumour and conversation, are all part of the extended receptive dynamics Fowler outlines.

The recent focus on reperformances in the classical period has somewhat diminished the idealizing tendency Fowler describes, even if the 're-' has inscribed a concept of secondariness that is in some respects unhelpful. The lexis is symptomatic of an essentializing focus on the original performance still common in Pindaric scholarship, as in Ilja Pfeijffer's argument that '[a]n [epinician] ode had the deepest significance for its first audience attending the official celebration for which it was written'.[78] Aside from its reductive implications for reperformance scenarios, this position neglects the richness and multiplicity of the *Nachleben* of the Pindaric corpus. This type of thinking is in part a response to the localizing rhetoric of Pindaric poems; in the light of the poems' emphasis on the circumstances of their performance and their local ethical and encomiastic aims, it is easy to see why critics have tended to see them as sites for the circulation of sociopolitical energies and for the creation and maintenance of forms of symbolic capital with an occasional function, but, as I suggested above, we should be wary of equating these functions with a unifying dynamic.

While acknowledging the importance of performance culture, this study will make an argument almost diametrically opposed to Pfeijffer's essentializing construction. Epinicians, and other types of performance poems, take on additional meanings and significances in their transhistorical journeys, and can in some respects be seen as more richly meaningful and suggestive as a result of their interaction with later literature, scholarship, and sociocultural developments. As such, my arguments seek to extend Fowler's stress on the multiplicities of the receptive process to the functions of the Pindaric corpus in later antiquity. The study of performance poems as written texts is also an underexplored means of addressing the ongoing interaction of performance and writing, wherein 'performance' is not simply an idealized prior event but a cultural construct open to continual reimagining, subject to the dynamics of the receptive tradition, and frequently put to interpretative and other ends. We shall also see that, in parallel to these developments, the book itself is subject to

---

[78] Pfeijffer (1999a) 10. This view is endorsed by Currie (2004) 53–4 in his examination of reperformance scenarios for Pindar's epinicians. Cf. Steiner (1994) 98–9 on performance as a unifying modality.

particular kinds of transformation when it interacts with the Pindaric corpus, a relationship that differs significantly from that which obtains between book and text in later, more 'bookish' literatures. As a prelude to detailed examination of these issues, I shall now analyse further the role of contexts in shaping literary encounters.

DIACHRONIC TEXTS

Our evidence for these encounters is problematic. The mental events which constitute the reading process are irrecoverable, and the traces left by individual readings are mediated to the extent that they can only give partial access to the thoughts that preceded them.[79] When we read passages in Callimachus which interact with Pindar's poems, there are various literary critical tools at our disposal for formulating how one author might be responding to the other, and how the texts might be interacting, but most modern scholars would be sceptical of using these formulations to reconstruct Callimachus' experiences when reading Pindar. Even ancient scholarship on the Pindaric corpus, which might seem more promising evidence for reading practices, is not straightforward; quite aside from the difficulties of reconstructing ancient scholarship on the basis of the scholia preserved in the mediaeval manuscripts, we cannot be sure how individual readers responded to scholarly comments. While the scholia can give us an outline of the kind of interpretative and exegetical questions with which their readers would have been confronted, they also give rise to effects which go beyond their own interpretative frameworks, and raise questions which they themselves do not answer. I shall explore these issues in Chapter 1;[80] for the moment, I simply note that the reading protocols formed by such metatextual bodies should not be seen as determinative for individual readings. Readers always have a certain licence to form their own judgements and contest those of others, practices encouraged by the openness of

---

[79] Cf. Chartier (1995) 147: 'reading...cannot be recursively deducted from the texts to which it is applied...the tactics of readers, infiltrating the "special space" produced by the strategies of writing obey certain rules...Thus...any history of reading...must postulate the freedom of a practice of which, broadly, it can only grasp the determinations.'

[80] Ch. 1, pp. 60–9.

ancient scholarly texts, and their juxtaposition of the views of different scholars.

Yet although the reader has a certain 'independence', this 'is not an arbitrary license. It is confined by the codes and conventions that govern the practices of a community.'[81] In order to think about how cultural forces affected readers and readings, I shall examine various contextual factors that bear on the Pindaric corpus in later antiquity, while also stressing the instability and openness of these 'codes and conventions'.[82] My main aim, however, will be to trace the textual forces Pindaric texts bring to bear on their readers, rather than to give a history of reading practices.[83] These textual forces are not confined to the denotative and connotative mechanisms of the texts themselves; the meanings, and wider cultural significance, of a given passage of Pindar are affected by its material form, and also by local factors such as the scholarly exegeses, literary receptions, and wider cultural and historical issues. My object in these readings is interpretation of texts in diachronic form, understood as a mode of textuality subject to interaction with multiple intellectual, material, and historical contexts.

The shifting meanings of the diachronic text are not primarily located in the consciousness of a particular ancient reader or in the discourses of a given interpretative community, but are the product of my own interpretative construction of the conditions in which Pindar's texts would have been encountered and of how they might be read in the light of those conditions. In assessing literary and scholarly responses to Pindar, for instance, my concern will not just be with the responses themselves and the sociohistorical and generic

---

[81] Chartier (1995) 136. His emphasis on the codifications of reading practices is influenced by Fish (1980) on the 'interpretative community' as a force which shapes individual acts of interpretation. Fish's model limits the degree to which texts can reconfigure their readers and give rise to experiences and meanings that alter the parameters of a given interpretative community.

[82] On the similar concept of the 'secondary poetic' cf. Heath (1989) 10, who admits that critical literature may only partially capture the meanings and effects of the texts at which it is directed. Cf. the remarks of Fowler (2000) 70–1. Heath (2002) 117–27 attempts to deal with these problems, suggesting the (critical) use of ancient literary criticism 'to inform our reconstruction of the assumptions about literary form and function underlying the composition of . . . texts' (p. 120). This is problematic in Pindar's case, given the lack of literary criticism contemporary with the poet's lifetime.

[83] Although these are certainly important: cf. Johnson (2010) 9–14 for an account of how reading practices are affected by sociocultural environments, and Ch. 4, pp. 170–1 for group reading as an influence on the construal of intertextual relationships.

pressures that informed their creation, but also with what they presuppose, the kind of reading positions they project, and their significance for readings of the Pindaric texts themselves. My interpretations
are aimed primarily at elaborating the kind of meanings and cultural
resonances to which we as modern readers might want to respond
when thinking diachronically about the Pindaric corpus. They also,
I hope, have an historical significance, in that they uncover some of the
ways in which Pindar's texts would have shown up to ancient readers
and the kind of interpretative potentialities that would have been open
to these readers even if they were not always understood by individual
readers in the ways I suggest.[84]

In order to examine the diachronic text more closely, we need to
elaborate the nature of the contextual influences to which it is subject.
Jauss's work on literature as a system of receptions gives useful
pointers in this direction. For him, a central task of interpretation
is to establish the 'horizon of expectations' against which a work is
initially understood, and which allows understanding of a work's
'artistic character';[85] this horizon consists of the salient cultural and
intellectual modalities with which readers understand a work and
which orientate their expectations of it.[86] The relationship between
works and the horizons in which they are received is dynamic; works
can only show up within a given set of cultural and interpretative
norms, but they also have the power to intervene in and alter these
norms by means of their mediation by individual readers. The
concern that this theory manifests with the relationship between
literature and history, and with the unique history of the institution
of literature itself, provides a corrective to ancient modes of literary
criticism examined earlier, where contextual factors were conspicuously

---

[84] There is a notable tension between the objection to positivism in reception
studies (for which see e.g. Martindale (1993) 2–10) and the avowedly 'positivistic'
character of much ancient Pindaric scholarship (demonstrated by the discussions
cited pp. 00–00). Any 'reception history' of Pindar in antiquity needs to take account
of, as it were, the positivistically articulated grounds of the intersubjectivity
manifested by ancient scholarship, or, put differently, the absence of 'reception-
consciousness' in ancient scholarly practice. Receptional literature is much more
aware of its own status however: see Ch. 4, pp. 181–5; Ch. 3, pp. 157–65.

[85] Jauss's discussion is indebted to that of Gadamer (2005) 299–306.

[86] Jauss (1982) 25.Cf. Martindale (1993) 1–34; (2006) 1–13 for elaborations of this
methodology in relation to classical scholarship. For further arguments about the
importance of contextual factors for reception-orientated readings see Gadamer
(2005) 335–6 with the remarks of Martindale (1993) 7.

absent. However, whereas Jauss is primarily concerned with establishing the cultural coordinates that determined the receptions that greeted a text's initial emergence,[87] my chief focus will be how changing historical and cultural circumstances affected the operation of Pindar's epinicians.[88] This analysis will need to be sensitive to how Jaussian horizons alter over time, and to the role of historical circumstances in mediating the self-positioning of communities of readers and in reforming the significance of works themselves. My readings will attempt to demonstrate that changing forms of political discourse, and changes in the distribution of political, military, and cultural authority play a significant part in mediating the significance of the Pindaric corpus. As such, my approach differs from reception studies that aim at elucidating the receptional texts rather than their models.[89]

The reception-based approach is grounded in an historicizing movement, but another strand of my argument is informed by critics who, while acknowledging the importance of contextual factors in literary production and reception, have sought to locate literature's capacity for determination *qua* literature in texts themselves.[90] These theorists insisted on the singular demands of literary texts, their capacity to generate particularized encounters and modes of reading specific to them.[91] Running through these works is an accent on the fragile, particularized space of the literary encounter that has the

---

[87] On the importance of generic considerations in Jauss's model cf. Jauss (1982) 25–8, and for the make-up of interpretive communities as formulated by the neopragmatists cf. Fish (1980). For an application to Jaussian thinking to Bacchylides cf. Stenger (2004).

[88] For remarks about this type of 'reception study' see Martindale (2007) 303.

[89] For such approaches to Pindar cf. e.g. Hamilton (2003); Rutherford (2012).

[90] Cf. especially Blanchot (1955) 207 for the argument that what threatens the distinctiveness of the particular text is the reader's insistence on attempting to accommodate the text to interpretative norms. Against this tendency, Blanchot advocated an attention to a text's irreducible particularity. Cf. McDonald (2006) 219–21 for an account of this tradition, and in general Clark (2005).

[91] Derrida (1992) 73 remarks that '[t]here is no assured essence or existence of literature. If you proceed to analyse all the elements of a literary work, you will never come across literature itself, only some traits which it shares or borrows, which you can find ... in other texts'. Elsewhere he argues for a double dynamic, focusing firstly on literary texts' deployment of certain 'movements of framing and referentiality' which constitute its difference from other such works, and such texts' ability to produce a type of reading distinctive to them (Derrida (1992) 213), and then on their appearance '*before the law*' of another, more powerful text protected by more powerful guardians', namely the critics, archivists, lawyers, and others entrusted with the task of regulating the literary (ibid. p. 214). Cf. McDonald (2006) 221–2.

advantage of affirming the uniqueness of individual works and consequently militating against their reductive assimilation into other
modes of discourse or, for that matter, their totalizing recuperation by
any given interpretation. This focus is particularly helpful, I shall
argue below, when thinking about Pindar's poetry in the context of
ancient Pindaric scholarship, whose strong emphasis on paraphrasing
exegesis both threatens and reinforces the particularity of the texts on
which it comments.

Yet this way of thinking about how literature is constituted is
vulnerable to the twin charges of essentialism and interpretative
reductionism. On the one hand, the quasi-sacral particularity of the
text and the space of reading projected by it looks rather like an
essence in another guise, a formalized state freed from ideological
determination. On the other, the insistence on the irreducible nature
of this space would seem to commit the critic to an acceptance of the
ultimate ineffability of the text, diminishing the potential for concrete
interpretations.[92] Another possible weakness in the approach under
discussion is the vagueness of its articulation of what counts as
literary self-determination: it could be argued that any text, regardless
of form, subject matter, genre, or any other local mark, could generate
its own literariness, therefore making the category 'literature' so fluid
as to be meaningless. Yet in mapping out literature's capacity to resist
interpretative determination, this approach opens a way of putting
contextual factors into conversation with an assertion of the dialogic
nature of the literary space and the capacity of this space to transform
its reader.[93]

One productive way of negotiating these issues is found in
Derrida's account of the singularity of the literary text. He is
committed to the uniqueness of the individual work, but recognizes
that this can only come about and be apprehended within a set of
cultural norms: '[a]n absolute, absolutely pure singularity, if there

---

[92] This problem is addressed by Clark (2005) 8, who rightly argues that '[t]oo
much of the standard defence of the literary as singular comes down to highlighting
our not being able to finally identify or fix the meaning of something...These
arguments should now be treated as truisms, starting places for thought and not
conclusions in themselves.'

[93] Cf. McDonald (2006) 220 on the differences between Blanchot's system and that
of Barthes (1973): against Barthes's emphasis on the productive role of class conflicts
in the formation of texts Blanchot's thinking of 'literature's inexhaustible capacity to
be other, its demanding singularity, made untenable any such epochal unities or hopes
of a grand historical synthesis'.

were one, would not even show up . . . To become readable, it has to be *divided*, to *participate* and *belong*.' Expanding on Derrida's description, Derek Attridge defines the singularity of a work as that which 'consists in its difference from all other such objects, not simply as a particular manifestation of general rules but as a peculiar nexus within the culture that is perceived as resisting or exceeding all pre-existing general determinations',[94] and that '[t]he experience of singularity involves an apprehension of otherness . . . in the mental and emotional opening that it produces'.[95]

These theoretical accounts are concerned with the instability of the category of the literary and how it might be defined and regulated, and are in large part responses to developments in modern literature and to a specific set of contemporary cultural conditions. As such they cannot be applied in any straightforward way to an analysis of ancient literature. It is a commonplace of classical scholarship that the ancients do not have a word or a conceptual apparatus which corresponds to 'literature' as named and conceptualized today,[96] and the kind of literary phenomena to which Derrida in particular pays attention are rarely prevalent in ancient texts. Nevertheless, the framework just elaborated has numerous methodological benefits for thinking about Pindar's poems. First, the focus on singularity sharpens sensitivity to the distinctiveness of the poems in their contemporary context and allows for an awareness of the ways in which epinicians make interpretative and ethical demands of their readers, foregrounding the textual specificity of these functions and the impossibility of entirely recuperating or translating them into other modes of discourse. I shall argue that Attridge's formulation of singularity as 'resisting or exceeding all pre-existing general determinations', while avoiding the cultural critical tendency to see literary texts as instances of general norms,[97] is less useful than Derrida's more general emphasis of the necessity of negotiating between the idiomatic aspects of a work and the various modes of its historical determination. Of particular importance here is a recognition of texts'

---

[94] Attridge (2004) 63. Clark (2005) 154 sees literature as '"founded"' in self-contestation, the tension between necessarily general norms of understanding and behaviour and the simultaneous claim of the singular work, impossibly and ineluctably, to be taken as an example of nothing but itself'.

[95] Attridge (2004) 67.

[96] Cf. Goldhill (1999) with the remarks of Martindale (2005) 32–3.

[97] See Clark (2005) 1–2 for a diagnosis of this position's shortcomings.

capacity to project the readers and readings suitable to them in unique ways, a process which in Pindar's epinicians comes about through a conjunction of specific occasionality and the particular relations devolved by individual poems between mythical narratives and interpretative situations.[98]

The theoretical models just discussed give us a useful set of tools for thinking about texts diachronically. Derrida, followed by Attridge, examines singularity as a general concept, and is not specifically concerned with the dynamics of reception. Consequently, his elaboration of singularity does not aim at an elucidation of how later texts can impact on previous ones. My particular interests here are in how the event of singularity is affected by the diachronicity of the text, and of the intertextual configurations that arise from this situation, and in how the text's own particular economy affects the contexts in which it is read.[99] We might question, however, whether singularity on this definition is susceptible of temporal extension; Attridge stresses that in bringing about the conceptual shifts necessary to apprehend it, a work's singularity works towards compromising its singular status: 'its emergence is the beginning of its erosion'.[100] On these grounds, it might be thought that the longer a work persists within a culture, the more fully it will be integrated into that culture's norms, and the more tenuous the 'apprehension of [its] otherness' will become. To an extent this is true; scholarship, critical engagements, teaching, and various types of cultural appropriation serve to assimilate a work to interpretative norms and furnish participants in that culture with various means of understanding it. These acculturative practices, however, treated by Attridge as essentially normalizing, can also have the effect of reconfiguring the otherness of a text, of bringing about interpretative situations in which the singularity of a text shows up in different forms from those possible in its previous cultural contexts. This observation also applies to literary receptions of

---

[98] Cf. Derrida (1992) 74 on 'the work which produces its reader, a reader who doesn't yet exist...a reader who would be "formed", "trained"... *invented* by the work... The work then becomes an institution forming its own readers, giving them a competence which they did not possess before.'

[99] Cf. Derrida (1982) 320 on the power of writing to 'engender infinitely new contexts in an absolutely non-saturable fashion'.

[100] Attridge (2004) 64. Following Derrida, Attridge stresses singularity's receptive status: 'singularity...is not a property but an event, the event of singularizing which takes place in reception...its emergence is the beginning of its erosion, as it brings about the cultural changes necessary to accommodate it' (ibid.).

'classic' texts. Studies of literary reception tend to focus on the uses made by later texts of their models, or on how later texts interact, agonistically, cooperatively, or both, with previous ones.[101] My method, however, will be (also) to reverse this practice and think about the ways later texts can resituate earlier ones and shift how they might be read. The potentiality for this mode of reading has been noted, in different forms, by various theorists, but many of its possibilities remain to be explored.[102]

Don Fowler's discussion of intertextuality, and the potential of that concept for enabling new ways of understanding the relations of literary (and other) texts, bears on this issue:

> It is the possibility of reversing the directionality of intertextual refer-
> ence—of accepting the influence of T. S. Eliot on Shakespeare—which is
> often seen as the worst of the horrors to which intertextuality can lead
> and even those who would be prepared to accept it tend to work
> wherever possible within a framework where source-texts precede tar-
> get texts. Where we do wish to see, for instance, Vergil's *Aeneid*
> differently in the light of later epic, our criticism will tend to be framed
> in terms of the later passages 'bringing out' something that was already
> 'there' in the *Aeneid*... If we locate intertextuality, however, not in any
> pre-existing textual system but in the reader, there is no reason to feel
> that it is in some way improper to acknowledge that for most profes-
> sional classicists today there *are* now traces of Lucan in Vergil, just as
> our Homer can only ever now be Vergilian... Are our views of the
> opposition between rationality and emotion in the *Aeneid* really the
> same after Captain Kirk and Mr Spock?[103]

What holds for contemporary scholars and students of Latin epic would also have held for Hellenistic readers of Pindar. Just as reading Virgil is a different experience when one has read Lucan from when one has not, so readings of Callimachus and Theocritus, particularly where they are responding to Pindaric models, have the potential to inflect how one subsequently approaches Pindar.[104] Fowler acknowledges that a chronological construction of intertextual reference 'is required for many of the constructions we wish to make about

---

[101] Cf. Fowler (1997) 15 for a schematization of differences between 'allusion' and 'intertextuality' as terms for orientating such relations.

[102] Cf. e.g. Jauss (1982) 35.   [103] Fowler (1997) 27–8.

[104] Cf. Fantuzzi (2014) 232–3 for comments on how Menander's dramatic practice may have influenced scholarly conceptions of classical tragedy.

antiquity', and it should be added that such a mode of reference is
often inscribed into texts' self-constructions; Theocritus *Id.* 16, which
I shall examine below,[105] is a celebrated instance of a text which uses
intertextual connections (with Pindar among others) to dramatize its
secondariness and belatedness within the tradition it constructs.
As I have previously argued, readings of Pindar which seek to understand texts in terms of their 'original' production and performance,
or as formative elements in a chronologically constructed literary
history, are always available to readers. But in order to take the
measure of some of the influences to which ancient readers would
have been subject, and to assess how we might want to construct the
cultural position of Pindaric texts in later periods, we need to take
account of other texts, and other cultural and historical developments, with which they interacted. Consequently, one of my central
focuses will be on the intertextual fields formed at particular times,
and which bear on interpretation of specific texts.

An intertextual field may provisionally be defined as a body of
discourses related to the reading of a particular text without any specific
role in and of itself.[106] Although later receptions of a text can have the
effect of bestowing cultural validation on it, this is by no means a
straightforward process, as receptions can also contribute to the texts'
resituation and to changes in how they are apprehended by readers.
Intertextual fields are not, or not wholly, structured by the purposes of
cultural producers but by the mediations of readers.[107] So both limbs of
my above definition, 'body of discourses' and 'related to a particular
text' are problematic. With regard to the former, each individual reader
will have read different texts and been exposed to different cultural,
social, and political experiences, and will hence be a unique cultural

---

[105] Cf. Ch. 3, pp. 157–65.

[106] A comparison might be made with the theorization of cultural fields in
Bourdieu (1993). This field is a structure primarily formed by cultural producers
and their actions in validating a particular artwork or articulating a particular mode or
model of valuation. The chief function of these cultural producers is to bestow value
on texts. He also addresses (p. 106) the temporality of the cultural field, arguing that it
is chiefly the product of ongoing struggles over authoritative legitimacy amongst
critics and other cultural producers: the creation of new positions in the field by
newcomers is productive of a differentiation that in turn produces a type of cultural
temporality which affects how previous works (and positions) within the field are
understood and valued.

[107] The situation is somewhat different in respect of the intertextual citations
found in ancient commentaries, for which see Ch. 4. Such citations would clearly
have formed part of a given 'field' without exhausting it.

aggregate; Attridge defines the reader in these terms as an 'idiocul-ture'.[108] Constructing an intertextual field for a given text will therefore always be an historically conditional exercise in relation to the application of that field to an historical reader. More importantly, just as texts construct implied readers,[109] contexts also project reader-positions in ways that require negotiation by historical individuals.

Here the second limb of my initial formulation, 'related to the reading of a particular text' comes into question. In confronting, for instance, poems by different authors about the same subject, readers have to judge if, and how, they are related to each other. There are established literary-historical methodologies for this practice, focusing on questions of influence, position within a given genre, and other similar author-based criteria. But when thinking about the place of a text within a looser diachronic configuration of intertexts, understood not only to refer to literary texts, but also to scholarly literature and cultural practices, different issues emerge. One such is the relationship that the primary text might itself explicitly or impli-citly impose on its intertexts by means of devices such as ethical standpoint, construction of narrative, and its figuration of narrator and reader. Siting a text within an intertextual field, therefore, is not an aggregative exercise of accumulating a set of meanings that might affect a primary text, but requires an attention to the specific relations that might arise between the primary text and its intertexts. The intertextual field is a space of (potential) conflict, differentiation, and tangential association that the reader needs to negotiate.[110] Nor should individual readerlyidiocultures be conceived as fixed; like texts themselves, they are dynamic systems open to reconstitution by different textual encounters. How these processes operate in the case of particular poems will be examined below; my point here is that implication in intertextual fields is not an incidental aspect but a constitutive factor of the reading process. Intertextual fields are both prereflectively determinative, albeit partially, in that they provide the frames through which a particular text is viewed, and interpretatively operative when made the subject of a reader's attention to his activity.

---

[108] Attridge (2004) 21–2, 67, 78.

[109] See in general Iser (1978) and the essays in Bennett (1995).

[110] Cf. the remarks of Gadamer (2005) 303 on the constitutive openness and changeability of interpretative horizons. On interactions between textual frames and historical horizons see Iser (1978) 96–9, and especially his comments p. 99 on the former's virtuality.

The two halves of my formulation are also mutually implicative, however, in that interpretative decisions about what relatedness consists of will affect the constitution of a particular intertextual matrix. Deciding on what counts and what does not count as a significant intertext for any given text is also problematic, and is connected to the problem of establishing demarcations of particular contexts. In theory, there are no limits to the number of texts, understood in the widest sense of the word, which could bear on a particularly readerly encounter; one might argue that, in the case of a Hellenistic reader's response to *O*.1, everything that that reader knew about epinician poetry, Hiero's place in Sicilian history and later literature, not to mention different versions of the Pelops myth, would have borne on his reading, in addition to whatever scholarly commentaries on *O*.1 he happened to have read.[111] Yet this selection of cultural data, even if recoverable, would only represent a part of that reader's intellectual constitution. Even if contexts are, in Derrida's terms, non-saturable, not susceptible of a totalizing empirical description, we may still attempt to sketch out in general terms what some of these contexts may have consisted of, as long as the provisionality of such constructions is borne in mind. In the following chapters, I shall examine a series of Pindaric receptions, both in literary texts and other cultural practices, and also some aspects of the scholarly reception of Pindar in the Hellenistic period. In doing so, I make no claim to exhaustiveness: my aim is to outline some episodes in the history of Pindaric reception with a view to thinking about their relations with the Pindaric corpus itself. These contexts are constructions of my interpretative procedures no less than my readings of individual poems or cultural data, and as historical accounts of influences on ancient reading practices are intended as no more than provisional guides. Establishing what counts as a context, considering how that context should be negotiated, and what intertexts are of value in informing a reading are always challenges for the individual reader.[112] In the case of Pindar's epinicians, these challenges extend the ethical demands made by the texts themselves. My analyses aim as much to reflect these interpretative processes as they do at establishing the conditions under which they occurred.

---

[111] These issues are discussed Ch. 3, pp. 131–2, 164–6.

[112] On the idea of value in reception theory see e.g. Jauss (1982) 30; Martindale (1993) 10; Clark (2005) 87–90.

In view of the preceding remarks, this is a convenient place for explaining my choice of contexts in which to examine Pindaric texts. I shall focus mainly on the Hellenistic period, beginning with the Pindaric (and other) literary and textual scholarship in the third century BC, and taking in a range of receptions down to the final decades of the first century BC. I shall also dwell briefly on the judgement of and allusions to Pindar in [Longinus] *On the Sublime*, although this text postdates (perhaps quite considerably) the Hellenistic period. This focus might appear to pose considerable problems for a study of material texts; although a number of Pindaric papyri are extant, there are none which date to the early Hellenistic period. My decision is dictated partly by considerations of space (a detailed literary analysis of Pindaric papyri and their readers would require a study of its own), but it is mainly based on the significance of the Hellenistic period as an epoch in the history of the Pindaric corpus. This period saw the growth of systematic Pindaric scholarship, important changes in the material presentation of texts, as *scriptio continua* was replaced by colometrized texts marked with critical signs, as well as numerous engagements with Pindar by poets such as Callimachus and Theocritus. Attention to a given context is justified, as I have argued, by the specificity of material and cultural conditions which constitute it, and the richness of the Hellenistic period in this respect makes it a valuable subject for such treatment.

SONGS OF PRAISES

Thinking about the functions and receptions of Pindar's texts in later antiquity brings into play numerous questions more or less remote from those with which Pindaric scholars have traditionally been concerned. However, my above discussion of the pragmatics of deixis showed that the hermeneutic disjunction between treating the texts as performance pieces and written documents should not be overstated.[113] Many of the issues prominent in analyses directed at the former continue to be important when thinking about written texts and their receptions, and effects created in the reading situation are often extensions of those that would have occurred in (re)performance scenarios.[114] Having discussed

[113] pp. 5, 14.
[114] See pp. Ch. 3, pp. 121–2. For further discussion cf. Barchiesi (2000).

some of the methodological questions which bear on analyses of the texts in later periods, I want to give a brief overview of recent trends in Pindaric scholarship relevant to my project, and outline my approach to some of the issues which bear on analyses of the poetic economy of the fifth century. My intention here is not to present a totalizing interpretative framework, but to raise some questions which have hitherto been neglected and to present a refocused view of issues previously formulated.[115]

Elroy Bundy's contributions to Pindaric scholarship in the early 1960s marked a turning point in the criticism of epinician poetry.[116] Pindaric studies had for some time previously been dominated by the biographical approach which reached its acme in Wilamowitz's *Pindaros*,[117] a methodology which sought to explain apparently obscurities by recourse to the events of the poet's life, and was happy to see Pindar as frequently employing allusions that could only be elucidated with reference to contemporary political situations.[118] As a corrective, Bundy advocated a study of the 'grammar of choral style', seeing the poems as 'the products of poetic and rhetorical conventions', attention to which allows an understanding of their encomiastic purpose.[119] While Bundy's formalist approach was beneficial in focusing on the functionality of the poems and dispelling the need for reliance on (unreliable) extratextual data to explain the poems' rhetorical procedures,[120] his monological conception of the poems' operation was flawed. For Bundy, epinician is 'an oral, public, epideictic literature dedicated to the single purpose of eulogizing men and communities'.[121]

---

[115] For the importance of pragmatic studies of deixis and other speech-acts see p. 14.

[116] Chiefly Bundy (1962). It should be noted that Bundy's formalist approach was anticipated by Schadewaldt (1928); cf. Kirkwood (1981) 13, 22 n. 4; Currie (2005) 11–12.

[117] Wilamowitz (1922); Bowra (1953), (1964) are more recent examples of the biographical approach.

[118] An approach exemplified by the attempts to read *P*.11 as a response to Theban politics: cf. p. 000. Some responses to this historicist approach: Bundy (1962) 35; Young (1970) 39; Lloyd-Jones (1973) 115–16; Carey (1981) 1–11; Kurke (1991) 9; Currie (2005) 12–13.

[119] Bundy (1962) 32, 35.

[120] On the structuralist aspects of Bundy's work cf. Currie (2005) 12–13.

[121] Bundy (1962) 35. An excessive focus on praise of the *laudandus* obscures more important dimensions of meaning: see Silk (2007) 196: 'praise is seldom the "point" of an ode. Pindaric odes . . . tend to assume the particular occasion of an athletic event and its societally approved outcome, and correlatively to *include* praise . . . but in the event, to offer a *celebration of value* arising from and *connected with* that outcome and that occasion' (emphasis in the original).

This formal approach was extremely influential,[122] but scholars have long recognized the necessity of putting rhetorical analysis into dialogue with contextual issues.[123] Perhaps the most influential study of this type has been that of Leslie Kurke, who conceptualized epinician performances as spaces of negotiation between poet, victor, and audience. Although some of Kurke's theses have been subject to considerable criticism and re-evaluation, her schema makes a useful starting point for considering issues pertaining to epinician's social setting.

A central preoccupation of the genre, on her reading, is the establishment of communal cohesion by means of a symbolic reintegration of the victor back into a society the stability of which his outstanding success might seem to threaten.[124] For Kurke, the threat of tyranny, actual or imaginary, is a prevalent concern which epinician works to counteract, alongside more general imbalances of power between victor and community:

> Within the space of epinikion, the poet negotiates with the community on behalf of the returning victor. To ease the victor's acceptance by various segments of the audience, the poet dramatizes shared representations, portraying the victor as an ideal citizen and ideal aristocrat. The audience, well trained to 'read' the poet's symbolic message, also plays its part in the 'communal drama', signaling approval by its participation in the festivities.[125]

---

[122] Cf. e.g. Race (1990), a study which highlights the benefits and limitations of the formalist approach: Race's analyses have the virtue of clearly articulating the formal structures of the poems, but have little to say about epinician's interaction with its historical circumstances and operate within in a limited conception of the poems' functionality. Thummer (1968) 11 sees the odes as made up of different categories of praise, but this classificatory approach is excessively reductive and fails to account for slippages across categories: for other criticisms cf. Carey (1981) 1–2. Cf. also Crotty (1982) for an attempt to see Pindar's poetics against a wider intertextual backdrop, and the more developed formulations of Pavlou (2008).

[123] Fearn (2013) 231 n. 1 offers a succinct synopsis of this issue.

[124] The staging and reinforcing of communal unity has been a major topos of criticism of archaic and classical Greek poetry: cf. e.g. Stehle (1997) 20. Goldhill (1991) 128–66. sees Pindar's epinicians as meditating on 'the limits of praise' and advocating awareness of human limitations, although his concern is mainly with the intratextual operation of such reflections.

[125] Kurke (1991) 258. Bourdieu's notion of symbolic capital forms an important part of Kurke's methodology, as that which both victory and its re-enactment in performance bestows on individual victors and, by extension, their communities. On the victor as (potential) tyrant cf. also Hubbard (2001) 389–90; Thomas (2007) 143; Carey (2007) 203 n. 20.

Central to this negotiation is the deployment of various topoi such as
'the loop of *nostos*',[126] the communally beneficial use of private
expenditure,[127] and the place of the victor's house within the city.

By means of the use of such topoi within the context of the
performance as a staging of communal interests, 'the poem enacts
the reintegration of the victor into his heterogeneous community'.[128]
Kurke sees this communal heterogeneity as an important feature of
epinician's social space. Pindar composed at a time of social flux, when
the premonetary economy was being displaced by the use of money,
democracies were flourishing in Athens and Syracuse, and traditional
aristocratic values were being challenged by a variety of cultural and
political developments. In Kurke's reading, Pindar mediates between
these different challenges, creating a form of poetry which responds to
contemporary developments while also asserting traditional values, 'a
kind of counterrevolution on the part of the aristocracy'.[129] Despite its
sophistication, however, this model risks homogenizing its subjects in a
manner that parallels the pitfalls of Bundy's formalism. The chief
problem here is that the tendency to think that all epinicians worked
in similar ways, obeying similar structural imperatives, obscures the
distinctiveness of individual poems, both in respect of the particular
contextual situations in which they emerged and the specific effects
they create. Partly in reaction to this danger, scholars have been
increasingly committed in recent years to relating Pindar's epinicians
to other types of contemporary cultural productions, and to understanding the importance of local socio-economic and cultural factors in
shaping the agendas of specific poems, and highlighted the varying
poetic strategies at work in poems for different types of victors.[130] The

[126] Kurke (1991) 15–34.

[127] For the motif of expenditure cf. Carey (2007) 203.

[128] Kurke (1991) 259.

[129] Ibid. 258–9. For some criticisms of her position from an historical point of view
cf. e.g. Thomas (2007) 141–4, 150.

[130] For contextual approaches see e.g. Krummen (1990), Hornblower (2004), Currie
(2005). The connections between epinicians and commemorative sculpture is discussed
by inter alia Steiner (1994) 91–9; Thomas (2007). For Pindar's epinicians as in dialogue
with contemporary architecture cf. e.g. Pavlou (2010); Athanassaki (2011b); Indergaard
(2011); Burnett (2005); see especially Fearn (2011) on the specificity of the poetic
strategies at work in the Aeginetan epinicians, emphasizing the sociocultural power of
the aristocracy on Aegina. Cf. also Carey (2007); Neumann-Hartmann (2009) for more
general treatments of contextuality. On the differences in poems for tyrants and for
aristocrats see e.g. Athanassaki (2009), (2011b).

notion of reintegration as a central aim has also been the subject of considerable modification, as scholars have emphasized the role of epinicians in articulating communal identity and asserting local identities in Panhellenic contexts.[131]

While I share the commitment to seeing epinician as a functional genre, I want in this study to bring other aspects of its operation into focus, dwelling especially on features that I believe can be illuminated by examining performance scenarios and reading situations in relation to one another. One important move in this respect is an increased attention to the role of readerly response. Cultural critical models tend to neglect the dynamics of the reading process, seeing it as a reflex of cultural and ideological norms. Kurke's emphasis, for instance, is on how 'the poet... transmitted a coherent message to his audience',[132] rather than on how these 'messages' were actually received.[133] Although we cannot tell how audiences responded to epinician performances, we can examine how interpretative responses are prefigured and demanded by the texts. I argue that Pindar's frequent meditations on the relationship between praise and envy, his idealization of victors, and the exemplary use of mythical narratives should be seen not as messages to be decoded, but rather as open–ended scripts requiring supplementation by readerly response.[134] Of central importance are the various ways in which they prompt readers to consider their own relation to the concepts deployed, and the wider validity of these concepts. While Pindar's poems frequently offer universalizing gnomic reflections, these are not simply 'asserted', but put into dialogue with particular ethical challenges which the reader must negotiate on his own terms.[135]

---

[131] Cf. e.g. Kowalzig (2007) 226–64 on O.7, which she sees as foregrounding a pan-Rhodian identity which subsumes and connects the individual Rhodian *poleis*. See also Olivieri (2011) on poetic interaction with Theban cult.

[132] Kurke (1991) 11. Mackie (2003) ch. 2 argues for the importance of audiences for shaping epinician's praise agenda, although she does not consider the idealizing and exemplary aspect of how victors are presented.

[133] Related is the variety of forms that 'praise' could take in individual poems: see Boeke (2007) 138 n. 108 and Ch. 6, pp. 242–55.

[134] I use 'reader' here, for the sake of convenience, to cover audience members as well as readers of books. On *paideia* in lyric poetry cf. Gentili (1988) 55–6. Instructive also are the remarks of Jaeger (1946) 216–19, who highlights *P*.6 and *N*.3 as examples of Pindaric *paideia*. It should be noted at this stage that the post-Bundyan focus on praise has often led scholars to diminish the importance of more cautionary aspects of Pindar's epinicians, the common strategy being to see them as forms of praise.

[135] On gnomai in Bacchylides see Stenger (2004) 52–5, and in Pindar Payne (2006).

In this sense, the reader's role is taken to be a more active one than that implied by Kurke in the above passage. In meditating on the indeterminacies and conflicts raised by epinician rhetoric, the reader undergoes a transformational apprehension of his interpretative, ethical, and social status.[136]

These modes of reading influenced, and were influenced by, the nature of the chorus. Choral identity and authority were crucial factors in how epinician's generalizing claims and mythical narratives were understood by audiences; this issue has received more attention in tragedy than it has in epinician,[137] although the tragic chorus is in many respects a problematic comparandum. Unlike tragic choruses, the epinician chorus did not wear masks or play characters,[138] but appeared *in propria persona*. Consequently, epinician choral utterance is closely linked to the performers' status as members of the community, although the ways in which this status is (re)constructed by the processes of rehearsal and performance are complex. The authority accrued to an epinician chorus is threefold, deriving partly from intertextual connections with previous literature and mythical traditions.[139] Important also are the chorus's status as a public body of selected and trained performers. The processes, largely opaque to modern scholars,[140] by which chorus members were selected and then trained by the poet, in the music and dance routine required by the poem as well as in the words, would in addition to their practical function in preparing the performers have had the additional function of bestowing legitimacy on the performance. At least in some cases, the poet himself would have served as the χορηγός or ἐξάρχων, leading the chorus during the performance.[141] As well as

---

[136] Relevant here is Iser (1978) 181–2 on the readerly negotiation of textual indeterminacies: in the Pindaric corpus, these take the form less of meanings which are not subject to fixing by the text than ongoing conflicts over the application of these concepts. For an overview of reader response theory cf. Bennett (1995) 1–19.

[137] Gould (1996); Goldhill (1996); Swift (2007). Cf. Fearn (2007) 305–15 for a comparison of Bacch. 15 with the choral dynamics of tragedy.

[138] Although cf. Fearn (2007) 307–12 on the mimetic aspects of dithyrambic performance.

[139] See e.g. Pavlou (2008); Indergaard (2011).

[140] The evidence is stronger for Athenian tragic choruses, for which cf. *DFA* pp. 87–92 and Wilson (2000), although cf. Currie (2011) on the funding of epinician choruses.

[141] Mullen (1982) 12–14, 17–19, 21, 158; Currie (2005) 16. For exceptions cf. *O*.6.87–92, *I*.2.47–8. For further discussion of the first person in Pindar see p. 7 n. 25.

being a means of personal self-projection for the poet, this feature of performance would have served as a representation and instantiation of the process of training and rehearsal, the symbolic climax of these previous processes. As a consequence, part of the chorus' legitimacy derives from an awareness on the part of the audience that a poem's didactic features such as gnomai and mythical exempla would have already been absorbed by the performers before the performance itself. In this sense, the chorus can be seen as (an) idealized reader (s) of epinician poetry, of human achievement and vulnerability, and a model for how its utterances should be understood, but the interpretative openness of many of Pindar's epinicians should caution against seeing this thematization as determinative. A crucial aspect of epinician, as argued above, is the participation of the audience in the poem's judgements and asseverations; consequently, choral authority emerges in part from its appeals to the reader as a relational process, gaining force from the reflections it opens up.

The interpretative demands made by epinician take various forms, and my readings are in no way exhaustive, but focus instead on their manifestations in particular forms across a range of poems. One such is the figuration of the *laudandus*. The distinction between the *laudandus* as an historical person and a textual figure has not been given sufficient weight: articulated as a relationship between these two aspects, the *laudandus* instantiates wider issues relating to the texts' referential status. Epinicians can in part be understood as relational matrices that map and reflect on the relational dynamics at work in the formation of social identities, but I shall argue that they also assert the particularity of the textual experience as an event that resists interpretative subsumption.[142] Several of my readings will trace the consequences of these interlocking aspects of epinician poetics and their production of specific encomiastic and ethical effects.[143] Idealizations of the *laudandus* are not simply self-contained responses to achievement, but open constructions constituted in part by the ethical demands they make both of the audience and, more and less implicitly, the *laudandus* himself. In this respect, paraenetic elements, which scholars have tended to subordinate to a principle encomiastic function, should be emphasized on their own terms, not only as exhortations to a particular victor to adhere to a code of behaviour,

---

[142] On literary texts as events see the comments of Iser (1978) 68.
[143] See particularly Ch. 3, pp. 155–8 and Ch. 6, pp. 255–6.

but also as a challenge to the wider community. Passages such as
O.1.30–5, *P*.2.58–96, *N*.7.23–4 and *N*.8.35–9 encourage readers to
assume an ethical pose in their reading, but they also foreground the
difficulties of doing so by dwelling on the prevalence of envy and other
destabilizing modes of behaviour. In this sense, epinicians often function as communal dramatizations not just of ethical ideals but the
problems involved in adhering to them.

The articulation of these problematics complements other more
overtly encomiastic elements such as the articulation of the divine
favour bestowed upon the *laudandus* and his community, reminding
readers of the necessity of appropriate responses to these interventions.[144] A related phenomenon is the deployment of negative
exempla, such as Ixion in *P*.2, Coronis in *P*.3, and the Apharetidae
in *N*.10: these figures, as has often been remarked, function as
illustrations of practices and ways of thinking which should be
avoided, and are usually taken as having the encomiastic function
of pointing up an opposition with the actual achievements and
conduct of the *laudandus*. In combination with the frequent
emphasis on $\phi\theta\acute{o}\nu o c$ and other types of human shortcoming, these
exempla also articulate the ongoing ethical and moral conflicts to
which individuals are subject.[145] Against the background of, for
example, late sixth- and early fifth-century epigrams commemorating
athletic success, which are markedly free of the kind of ethical
discourses prominent in Pindar, the ethical and paraenetic dimensions of Pindar's epinicians emerge as one of the central ways in
which Pindar articulates his poetic identity and the distinctiveness of
his texts.[146] While political and social changes undoubtedly played a
role in informing the deployment of these ethical discourses, I see
them not as primarily embodying an aristocratic reaction to

---

[144] For the importance of which see Bremer (2008).

[145] On ethical considerations as a motivating force in Pindar's structuring of myths
cf. Illig (1932); Goldhill (1991); Scodel (2001). See also D'Alessio (1994) on the
importance of the poet's social persona to his encomiastic authority. Fearn (2007)
312–15 argues for seeing Bacch. 15 in similar terms; the openness of the poem's
ending, together with Homeric intertexts and the parallels between the internal and
external audiences, prompt audience reflection on the moral issues raised by Menelaus' speech. Although Bacch. 15 is particularly marked in this respect, Pindar's poems
often, if more obliquely, pose similar interpretative questions.

[146] Thus Thomas (2007). A similar point could be made about Bacchylides, but he
tends to be less forthright in his ethical declarations than Pindar: see e.g. Hadjimichael
(2010–11).

democracy, or as a response to the threat of tyranny, but rather as promoting ethical generalities that are variously applicable to different groups of people in different contexts. Indeed, contextual variety is crucial here; we shall see that the ethical implications of poems composed for Hiero are different from those composed for, say, aristocratic victors in oligarchic societies.

A related issue is the function of mythical narratives. These are often taken as articulating a continuity between the present and the mythical past, relating an incident of athletic success to the timeless truths manifested in myth. While I do not disagree *tout court* with this line of thinking, I shall examine some cases in which discontinuity and difference are as important as continuity. I shall argue, for example, that *P.*11 dramatizes the disjunctions between mythical exemplum and encomiastic frame in order to produce an interpretative space in which the reader is drawn into a questioning of the applications of the mythical exempla. I shall also emphasize the plurality of these exempla's operation; as well as fulfilling an encomiastic function, they also encourage a recognition of human limitations and dependencies. A similar approach will be taken to figurations of performance, particularly in the cases of *O.*14, *P.*1, and *P.*12, where the differences between mythical acts of performance and those of the human sphere are central to how Pindar represents the function of his poetry.[147]

In the cases of *O.*14 and *P.*12 especially, the poems' metapoetic elements are deployed partly as a means of shaping readerly responses to wider ethical and interpretative issues. Running through these different focuses is a critical commitment to the singularity of the poems, their capacities to project particular modes of reading, to foreground the transformational aspects of the reading situations they demand, and to resist recuperative interpretation. While the intersections between idiom and normativity in epinicians are susceptible of pragmatic readings which focus on their communicative aspect,[148] they can also be understood as foregrounding the problematics of negotiating between general claims and their local functions. This negotiation is connected to the process by which any expansion

---

[147] For the prevailing view cf. e.g. Bakker (1997) 24; Athanassaki (2011a) 263, although note the useful discussion in Mackie (2003) ch. 2. Cf. Ch. 3, pp. 145–9; Ch. 5, pp. 213–16; Ch. 6, pp. 247–8 for further discussion of these issues.

[148] See e.g. Athanassaki (2009), (2011b).

of its meaning involves a displacement of the language of the text into an interpretative space not specified by the text itself, a process the limitations of which, I argue, are dramatized in Pindaric epinician's self-representational manoeuvres.

My exploration of these issues falls into two parts. The first consists of two chapters that analyse respectively the development of Pindaric scholarship during the Hellenistic period, and other features of Pindaric reception in antiquity such as the representation of the poet in epigrams and the biographical tradition. The latter chapter also reflects on how the materiality of books affected reading practices. These chapters aim to reconstruct, however provisionally, the salient features of the horizons within which ancient readers would have engaged with the Pindaric corpus. The second half of the book considers various poems in the light of these horizons. 'Edited Highlights' analyses *O*.1 and *P*.1 as opening poems in their respective books, and sets Pindar's representation of Hiero in relation to Theocritus' use of Pindaric models in *Id.* 16. 'Marginalia' takes both a broader and more local view of the Pindaric corpus, focusing on the microtextual interactions created by literary citations in the scholia. I analyse citations in commentaries on Pindar, focusing especially on how Homer is positioned as a literary model, and how Pindar himself is quoted in glosses on other authors; the latter is, I suggest, an under-examined feature of the processes by which Pindar's canonical status was affirmed and applied. The final two chapters elaborate readings of *O*.14, and *P*.11 and *P*.12. My reading of *O*.14 examines the poem as a performance piece, and argues that the text's distinctive metapoetic dimension reinforces its combination of celebration and mourning. I then consider how this metapoetic aspect would have operated in relation to the poem's closural role in the *Olympian* book and against the background of other literary representations of Echo. Similar considerations are at issue in my analysis of *P*.12, where I analyse the function of the poem's mythical narrative and its intersections with later stories about the invention of the *aulos*. This reading is preceded by a re-examination of *P*.11 that focuses on the disputed issue of how the narrative of Orestes and Clytemnestra relates to the poem's wider functions. Throughout these readings, I emphasize the importance of the literary strategies and effects I trace in the context of fifth-century performance culture, but I also suggest that they are brought to the fore and given new inflections by the material, diachronic status of the Pindaric corpus.

I

Contexts: To Alexandria
and Beyond

1

Texts and Metatexts

In Rudolf Pfeiffer's description of the situation in the last decades of the fourth century,

> the book is one of the characteristic things of the new, the Hellenistic, world. The whole literary past, the heritage of centuries, was in danger of slipping away despite the efforts of Aristotle's pupils; the imaginative enthusiasm of the generation living towards the end of the fourth and the beginning of the third century did everything to keep it alive. The first task was to collect and to store the literary treasures in order to save them forever.[1]

The projects of collecting, cataloguing, and explaining the texts of the past were crucial for how intellectuals in the Hellenistic period conceptualized their relationship with previous literature as well as their own activity. The growth of the Alexandrian library and the intellectual culture that centred on it,[2] as well as similar developments elsewhere, marked a new phase in Greek intellectual life.[3] These developments form the backdrop to my examination of how scholars, literary critics, and poets of the Hellenistic and early Imperial periods responded to Pindar.

---

[1] Pfeiffer (1968) 102.

[2] For which see e.g. de Vleeschauwer (1973), Jacob (1996); Bagnall (2002) offers a sensible corrective to the tendency to exaggerate the library's size based on (unreliable) ancient accounts. For further comment on the library as an institution see Ch. 4, pp. 208–10.

[3] For an overview of this process cf. Pfeiffer (1968) 87–104. The debate over the importance of performance in Hellenistic literature: Cameron (1995) with the response of Bing (2009) 106–15. The debate over the relative importance of reading and performance is connected to the question of the extent to which Hellenistic poetry should be seen as breaking with previous poetic traditions: stressing change Pfeiffer (1968) 88; Bulloch (1985); Bing (1988); Goldhill (1991); Fantuzzi and Hunter (2004). Hutchinson (1988) 1–7 and Cameron (1995) put the accent on continuity.

When the Hellenistic scholars began editing and glossing the classical lyric poets, and when readers of the period encountered their texts, they did so in a cultural landscape that differed in various respects from that in which the poetry had been composed. Dithyrambs, paeans, and other types of public poem continued to be composed and performed,[4] and we have ample evidence for the importance of drama in the fourth century and the Hellenistic period.[5] There is also evidence for continuing performance of 'classic' poets.[6] And yet reading had become as important a conduit of literary experience as performance, if not more so,[7] and the circumstances of reading were also subject to change. In the later Hellenistic period, encounters with classical texts were, for many readers, informed by scholarly commentaries, and by literary texts in which engagement with precursors was a central poetic mechanism. These influences, together with the greater time reading makes available for interpretative deliberation, enabled readers to bring to texts a different kind of attention from that which tended to be operative in performances. Notwithstanding the continuing importance of the *polis*, the political circumstances of the time were also distinctive; the great Hellenistic monarchies gave rise to forms of political behaviour and literary discourse that had their roots in, but also differed decisively from, those of the classical period.[8] These dialogues of continuity and difference will be central to my readings of Pindaric reception.

---

[4] See e.g. Dale (2009) 23–34.   [5] Lightfoot (2002).

[6] See e.g. Prauscello (2009) on the Hellenistic reception of Timotheus. Our knowledge of fourth century epinician is limited but suggestive: see e.g. Diod. Sic. 14.109 for the story of Dionysius I having his own poetry performed, somewhat less than successfully, at Olympia, and in general Hornblower (2012) 103–6. See further Ch. 3, p. 126 n. 17.

[7] Cf. Fantuzzi and Hunter (2004) 23 for the importance of reading in the Hellenistic period.

[8] For regal iconography, conceptions of monarchy, and their cultural effects see Préaux (1978) 181–294; Ma (2003), and on the connection between gods and monarchs in the Hellenistic period cf. Versnel (1990) 72–83 with further references. A striking instance of the intersection of human and divine is Theoc. *Id.* 17, for which see Hunter (2003) 8: 'just as both [Ptolemy] and his forebears move smoothly between levels of existence, so the poem in his honour slips between genres'. The employment of forms usually used for gods in songs for mortals was not precedented however; cf. Plut. *Lys.* 18 (= Douris, *FGrH* 76 F 71, 696 F 33c) for a paean to Lysander (*PMG* 867) written after the Peloponnesian war, with the comments of Hunter (2003) 24–5. Cf. also Hunter (1996) 79–82.

Scholarly practice is central to this dynamic, and generic classification epitomizes its complexities. Classifying 'classical' poetry by genre led to a heightened awareness of both the concept and practice of genre, as systematic, abstract reflection on generic norms and practices replaced an empirical understanding based on the lived experience of a performance culture.[9] This awareness in turn influenced literary composition.[10] As Marco Fantuzzi and Richard Hunter suggest, '[i]t is tempting to hypothesise that this work of cataloguing and establishing conventional norms in fact fostered a "reverse normativity"... that the Alexandrians ended up by composing the laws of the genres in order to violate them better'.[11] This double dynamic of defining and solidifying generic norms, and exceeding them in original compositions arises from a conflicted relation to previous literature:

> In short, an increased understanding of the nature and contexts of archaic and classical poetry led also to the realisation that such contexts were things of the past; the classification of the genre norms of archaic and classical poetry led almost automatically to an awareness of the impossibility of writing anything else in those genres, at least if the same norms, which included metrical and melodic norms, were to be followed... What remained was a heritage of linguistic and metrical conventions, which had often lost their functional contact with particular subjects and occasions: thus did the possibility of new combinations appear.[12]

The very preservation achieved by scholarly archives involves a distancing of what it preserves; Hellenistic scholars were furnished with an abundance of information about classical and archaic culture

---

[9] Critics have stressed the tension between the fluidity of how genre was conceived in the fifth century and the systematizing interests of the Hellenistic scholars: see e.g., on the relationship between encomium and epinician, Budelmann (2012), who, following Clay (1999), notes that the boundaries between the two were porous: epinicians could be performed at symposia, as well as at other types of celebratory occasion. On the 'generic indeterminacy' of epinician more generally cf. Currie (2005) 21–4.

[10] Creative engagements with the canonized lyric poets was likewise a doubly significant process, a matter of self-definition on the part of Hellenistic authors, which in turn had consequences for how the classical poets themselves were viewed. See generally Acosta-Hughes (2010). On metrical and stylistic choices as a means of differentiation from late classical lyric poetry see Dale (2009) 18–20.

[11] This idea goes back to Kroll (1924) 202–10; cf. also Rossi (1971) 83.

[12] Fantuzzi and Hunter (2004) 25–6.

which enabled close imaginative engagement, as texts arrived from all over the Greek world, and yet awareness of the specificities of place and performance also served to highlight the differences between the current situation and the past.[13]

A provisional formulation of this situation might be that the otherness of classical and archaic literature was reinforced by the very processes that enabled its continuance.[14] However, whereas Fantuzzi and Hunter's analysis is aimed at understanding the relationship between scholarly and poetic practice, my object is to explore the kinds of reading experience that may have confronted readers of Pindar's epinicians during this period, and how social, political, and intellectual developments may have shaped contemporary readers' approaches to these texts.[15] An instance of this dialogue is Hellenistic epinician: Callimachus and other poets composed poems celebrating athletic victories, and epigraphic commemoration continued to be as important a marker of athletic success as it had been in the classical period.[16] These texts, and the athletic culture of which they formed part, testified to Pindar's importance as a literary paradigm. Yet in differing radically from Pindar's victory odes in form, and in being aimed primarily at readers rather than composed for performance, the texts also highlighted the cultural shifts across and through which readers related to Pindar.

I shall begin by examining the evidence for editions of Pindar in the Hellenistic period and the growth of Pindaric scholarship as recorded by the scholia, before addressing critical responses to Pindar by authors such as Dionysius of Halicarnassus and Longinus. I shall address the scholarly approaches underlying the ordering of poems within editions, and consider the methodological problems involved in using the scholia. There are marked differences between

[13] Little is known of Pindaric scholarship in this period outside Alexandria. For Pergamene scholarship cf. Irigoin (1952) 61–3. Cf. Σ *P*.3.102b (ii 76 Dr = F 84 Broggiato) for Crates of Mallos' Pindaric criticism.

[14] For discontinuities in the performance tradition of Pindar's poetry see pp. 64–5 and p. 126 n. 17.

[15] Although epinician forms the focus of my study, it should be noted that for Hellenistic readers Pindar would not have been primarily an epinician poet: genres such as dithyramb and paean were clearly crucial in the formation of the view of Pindar as a 'religious' poet, for which see Ch. 2, pp. 97–100.

[16] For an overview of the evidence see Barbantani (2012). On Hellenistic athletic culture more generally see Van Bremen (2007). For a specific instance of Callimachean engagement with Pindar see e.g. fr. 384 Pf. and van Bremen (2007) 350; Phillips (2013c) 154–5 with further references; see in general Bona (1995).

these scholarly receptions, as the aims of literary critics sometimes differ considerably from those of the authors responsible for the ancient commentaries from which the scholia derive. Examining these strands of Pindaric reception alongside each other will give an impression of the various influences which mediated ancient readers' relations to the epinicians.

HELLENISTIC EDITIONS OF PINDAR

It is clear that Pindar was read and performed in the fourth century.[17] Aristotle and Plato are both familiar with his poetry, and cite him to exemplify general principles or rhetorical points, and as adjuncts to larger arguments.[18] Peripatetic scholars such as Chamaeleon were also responsible for biographies of the poets.[19] Unfortunately, however, it is unclear what sort of texts the fourth-century scholars had access to, and whether they began to edit or comment on Pindar's poems, or those of other poets, in the manner of their Hellenistic successors.[20] When we come to the Hellenistic period, however, our evidence for book culture improves somewhat. Although the details are sketchy, it is clear that a significant shift took place in the form and layout of poetic texts during the third century. Colometrized texts

[17] Telesias of Thebes performed both music in style of older poets such as Pindar and that of the New Musicians (fr. 76 Wehrli = [Plut.] *De mus.* 1142b–c): see LeVen (2014) 52–3 for analysis. For performances of Pindar's paeans see LeVen (2014) 16 and Ch. 3, p. 126 n. 17.

[18] Cf. e.g. Arist. *Rhet.* 1.1364a28, citing the beginning of *O*.1 to exemplify the principle that what is most often of use surpasses what is only seldom useful (τὸ γὰρ πολλάκις τοῦ ὀλιγάκις ὑπερέχει, ὅθεν λέγεται ἄριστον μὲν ὕδωρ). The phrasing of ὅθεν λέγεται suggests that the phrase had become a well-known saying detached from its poetic context: cf. also Pl. *Euth.* 304b. Aristotle also cites Pindar at *Rhet.* 2.1401a16–20 (fr. 96 S-M) to exemplify homonymy, and was clearly interested in questions of genre as they related to Pindar: Phld. *De poem.* 4.120 cites Aristotle comparing Pindar and the tragedian Dicaeogenes as part of a discussion of the difference between tragedy and the lyric genres: see Janko (2011) 355–6 for discussion.For Pindar in Plato see e.g. *Grg.* 488b, *Rep.* 365b, *Lg.* 690c, 715a, and *Scholies* p. 80. Cf. Carey (2011) 452–3 for Peripatetic and other pre-Hellenistic influences on canon formation, and Davies and Finglass (2014) 66–7 for Peripatetic scholarship on Stesichorus.

[19] See *Scholies* pp. 28–9.

[20] There is no compelling evidence to suggest that they did, although the possibility cannot be ruled out. For scepticism about Aristotle as editor of Homer see e.g. Pfeiffer (1968) 69–72.

accompanied by critical signs replaced ones predominantly written in prose, and the works of the canonical poets were arranged in books according to genre and metre, and grouped within these books according to a variety of typological principles. Although the main focus of this chapter will be on Aristophanes of Byzantium, any account must begin with Zenodotus, active earlier in the century, who is the first Pindaric scholar for whom we have evidence of editorial activity.

Σ *O.*2.7a (i 60 Dr) reports a Zenodotean reading: ἀκρόθινα πολέμου: Ζηνόδοτος μετὰ τοῦ ι γράφει ἀκροθίνια, ἅπερ κυρίως λέγεται παρὰ τὰς τῶν καρπῶν θῖνας ('first–fruits of war: Zenodotus writes it with ι, which is how heaps of fruit are commonly referred to') as does Σ *O.*6.92a (i 174 Dr), although there his reading is not cited by the scholia. Σ *O.*3.52a (i 120 Dr) reports Zenodotus' correction of the text on the grounds of biological verisimilitude: χρυςοκέρων ἔλαφον: Ζηνόδοτος δὲ μετεποίηςεν ἐροέςςης διὰ τὸ ἱςτορεῖςθαι τὰς θηλείας κέρατα μὴ ἔχειν, ἀλλὰ τοὺς ἄρρενας ('golden-horned doe: Zenodotus substituted "charming" because it is reported that the females do not have horns, but the males do'). There is also the possibility that some of the marginalia in *POxy* 841 and 2442 reflect Zenodotean readings.[21] Irigoin also sees a hint of Zenodotus' work in Σ *O.*5 inscr. a (i 138 Dr): αὕτη ἡ ᾠδὴ ἐν μὲν τοῖς ἐδαφίοις οὐκ ἦν, ἐν δὲ τοῖς Διδύμου ὑπομνήμαςιν ἐλέγετο Πινδάρου ('this ode was not in the older editions, as Didymus' commentaries on Pindar record'). He argues that the close study of *O.*5 and its authentication as one of the Olympian odes are the work of later scholars, particularly Aristarchus, and that the ἐδαφία ('manuscrits fondamentaux') 'représenteraient ... l'édition de Zénodote'.[22] This is possible, although given the fact that Σ *O.*5 inscr. a does not designate the ἐδαφία as referring to an edition by Zenodotus, it is equally likely that the term refers to the

---

[21] See Pfeiffer (1968) 118 n. 4 for Lobel's doubts as to whether the signs Z and Zη refer to Zenodotean readings; he argues that they are more likely to indicate ζήτει vel sim. Pfeiffer objects that ζήτει 'is never set in front of a simple variant reading' but always 'introduces a question about the subject matter', and thus concurs with Grenfell and Hunt's ascriptions of these variants to Zenodotus. For scepticism about ascription to Zenodotus see Ferrari (1992). See also D'Alessio and Ferrari (1988) 165–70 on the variants.

[22] Irigoin (1952) 32–3. For evidence of Aristarchus' work on *O.*5 see Σ *O.*5.1b, 20e, 27b, 29e, 54b (i 139, 145, 146–7, 147, 151 Dr). For his 'intertextual' scholarship see Ch. 4, pp. 173–4.

various manuscripts from different parts of the Greek world which Zenodotus drew on in the course of his textual studies.[23] Both Irigoin and Pfeiffer argue that Zenodotus was the first to make a critical edition of Pindar.[24] This is possible, but all of the readings recorded by the scholia could have come from a list of glosses rather than an edition.[25] Moreover, if we accept that Zenodotus did produce an edition of Pindar, we are not in a position to know what proportion of the corpus this covered. We could say on the basis of the above passages that it included the epinicians and paeans, but for the other poems we are in the dark.

We have considerably more evidence for Aristophanes of Byzantium's activity in the field of Pindaric scholarship.[26] The two most important pieces of evidence are the report of an athetization on metrical grounds at *Σ O*.2.48c (i 73 Dr = 380A Slater), and the notice in the *Vita Thomana* about Aristophanes placing *O*.1 first in the collection on the basis of its contents, namely because it included an encomium of the Olympian games and because of the narrative of Pelops who 'was the first to compete at Elis' (i 7 Dr). According to an ancient *Life* of Pindar, dated to the late second or early third century AD (*POxy* 2438.35), Aristophanes divided the Pindaric corpus into books in accordance with a system of generic classification. While

---

[23] For a different reading see Ruffa (2001), who argues that the ἐδαφία are Aristophanes' edition: on her reading, the scholium means 'l'ode non era (giudicata di Pindaro) nel testo di Aristofane, ma era detta di Pindaro nei commentari di Didimo' (p. 44).

[24] Pfeiffer (1968) 118; cf. Negri (2004) 12–13.

[25] For scepticism about the traditional view of Zenodotus as an editor of Homer see West (2001) 33–45, who argues that Zenodotus did not collate Homeric manuscripts, but simply annotated a rhapsodic copy of the text. A similar process may lie behind his Pindaric readings.

[26] For an overview cf. Negri (2004) 169–74. For Callimachus' editorial work, see Irigoin (1952) 33, Negri (2004) 13–15. Irigoin argues on the basis of *Σ P*.2 inscr. (where Callimachus is recorded as having classified *P*.2 as a Nemean) that Callimachus 'avait classé les œuvres de Pindare avec beaucoup de soin, distinguant les *Epinicies* des autres odes, distinguant aussi, dans le group des *Epinicies*, les *Néméennes* des odes ... écrites pour d'autres jeux', but the absence of any traces in the scholia of his textual work suggests that he did not produce an edition. However, Porro (2009) 186–8 is correct to point out that even the early stages of textual exegesis such as classification of poems by genre would have involved considerable interpretative reflection and debate, even if this is not reflected in later sources. Cf. Currie (2005) 23–4 on the problems caused by the 'Alexandrian filter' for scholars attempting to reconstruct the performance conditions of the fifth century, and Fearn (2007) 205–12 for Alexandrian classifications of Bacchylides' dithyrambs.

Irigoin and Nauck both take the above to indicate that Aristophanes produced a critical edition of Pindar, Slater in his commentary on Aristophanes' fragments has called this into question.[27] As part of this argument he cites the two passages from Dionysius of Halicarnassus' *De compositione verborum* which mention Aristophanes' colometrization of lyric poets:

κῶλα δέ με δέξαι λέγειν οὐχ οἷς Ἀριστοφάνης ἢ τῶν ἄλλων τις μετρικῶν διεκόσμησε τὰς ᾠδάς, ἀλλ' οἷς ἡ φύσις ἀξιοῖ διαιρεῖν τὸν λόγον καὶ ῥητόρων παῖδες τὰς περιόδους διαιροῦσι.

You must understand me to refer by 'cola' not to those groups into which Aristophanes or some other metrician arranged the odes, but to the divisions which nature sees fit to bring about, and into which the rhetorical schools divide their periods.

(Ch. 22 = 380B Slater.)

The second reference follows a series of quotations from lyric poets:

ἐκ δὲ τῆς μελικῆς τὰ Σιμωνίδεια ταῦτα· γέγραπται δὲ κατὰ διαστολὰς οὐχ ὧν Ἀριστοφάνης ἢ ἄλλος τις κατεσκεύασε κώλων ἀλλ' ὧν ὁ πεζὸς λόγος ἀπαιτεῖ.

This comes from the lyric poetry of Simonides. It has been written out in divisions which are those not of the cola arranged by Aristophanes or some other, but those which prose demands.

(Ch. 26 = 380B Slater.)

While Irigoin sees these passages as reinforcing Σ O.2.48c as evidence for an Aristophanic edition of Pindar with new colometry, Slater argues that the passages 'show only that Dionysius did not know who introduced the colometry, but thought that it could have been Aristophanes'.[28] This reading, however, neglects the argumentative context of the passages. Dionysius is opposing his own critical practice of analysing the rhythms and structures of texts in terms of the πεζὸς λόγος with what he sees as the artificial colometric divisions

---

[27] See Nauck (1848) 61–2; Irigoin (1952) 35–50.

[28] Slater (1986) 145. For further scepticism about Slater's scepticism cf. D'Alessio (1997) 52 n. 172; cf. also ibid. pp. 55–6 for comments on Aristophanes as the originator of the Pindaric colometry. We should be cautious, however, about positing too strong a distinction between classical and Hellenistic textual layout: the Lille papyrus of Stesichorus offers possible evidence for pre-Aristophanic colometrization. Moreover, as Haslam (1978) 34 points out, it is *prima facie* implausible that a single scholar should have been responsible for the colometrization of the entire lyric corpus.

practised by the metricians. The vagueness of Ἀριϲτοφάνηϲ ἢ τῶν ἄλλων τιϲ μετρικῶν is better seen as faintly derogatory, implying that this editorial intervention should not enjoy any particular authority, rather than expressing a decisive lack of knowledge on the part of Dionysius. The rhetoric of the passage also has a more defensive role: by not attributing the colometrization to a particular scholar, Dionysius also avoids directly opposing his own practices to those of Aristophanes, whose authority in such matters was clearly respected. Moreover, the fact that Dionysius mentions Aristophanes as the paradigm of such practices does suggest more strongly than Slater is willing to allow that he felt him to be if not necessarily the originator, then certainly an important figure in the history of colometrization.[29]

Slater also seeks to cast doubt on *POxy* 2438.35 as evidence for an Aristophanic edition, claiming that it implies cataloguing, rather than editorial activity. He notes that Aristophanes is not mentioned as part of the controversy over the classification of *P*.2 by *Σ P*.2 inscr. (ii 31–2 Dr), which he thinks implies that Aristophanes did not produce an edition. Furthermore, he suggests that the filling out of the Nemean and Isthmian books with poems which do not strictly belong there, such as *N*.11, composed to celebrate Aristagoras' appointment to the governing council of Tenedos, is not indicative of scholarly activity: '[t]he classification we have is . . . due primarily to consideration of book length, which suggests the attitude of a book publisher rather than a scholar.'[30] With regard to the *Vita Thomana*'s notice about Aristophanes placing *O*.1 at the head of the collection, he points to the fact that ἄριϲτον μὲν ὕδωρ contains the complete vowel spectrum,[31] and says that 'such a beginning could only have been created by Pindar

---

[29] Cf. Hdt. 2.23 on 'Homer or one of the other poets inventing the name [Ocean] and introducing it into their poetry' (Ὅμηρον δὲ ἢ τινα τῶν πρότερον γενομένων ποιητέων δοκέω τοὔνομα εὑρόντα ἐϲ ποίηϲιν ἐϲενείκαϲθαι). Irigoin (1952) 50 suggests that Aristophanes' edition became the basis for the vulgate; if this was the case, and was known to have been so, it would help to account for Dionysius' assumption that the colometric divisions originated with Aristophanes, in that any colometrized text would be seen to owe a debt to his scholarly activity. Tessier (1995) 13–34, esp. 22–4, argues for considerable colometrical variation in ancient papyri and is consequently sceptical about the extent of Aristophanes' influence on subsequent editions, but his claims are refuted by D'Alessio (1997) 46–8: see also Prauscello (2006) 82 n. 263; Ucciardello (2012) 126–7.

[30] Slater (1986) 146. For ancient controversy over the poem's generic status see *Σ N*.11.inscr.a–b (iii 184–5 Dr).

[31] Noted by Thummer (1968) 139.

himself, not by Aristophanes. Thomas Magister could easily have
misunderstood the papyrus observation [sc. *POxy* 2438.35] as a
reorganization by Aristophanes', before pointing out that Simonides'
poems are classified and organized on different grounds.

None of these arguments has much force. His opposition between
book publisher and scholar suggests an unrealistic division between
the two roles. Material factors such as the length of book-rolls certainly played a role in the arrangement of collections, in that they
provided physical limits, albeit variable, which shaped the potential
length, and hence contents, of an edition.[32] Scholars would also have
to have borne in mind the exigencies of the book trade if they wanted
their editions to serve as the basis of a widely disseminated text. In
terms of simple practicalities, it is hardly credible to expect even a
scholar such as Aristophanes to take eidographic precision to the kind
of lengths which would have required, for example, *N.*11 to have an
edition all to itself as the only example of its kind.[33] We should see
editorial practice in this period not as conforming to a monolithic
model but rather as involving 'multiple levels of grouping and ordering that implemented different taxonomic criteria at successive levels
of a hierarchy'.[34] Importantly, this activity was directed by the nature
of the corpus concerned and by the forms of material text available to
the editor, not simply by fixed categorizational rules.[35]

His argument that ἄριστον μὲν ὕδωρ constitutes 'a beginning [that]
could only have been created by Pindar himself' is also misleading, in
that it fails to distinguish between the different types of 'beginning'
at work. The poet is responsible for the words as beginning the
poem in performance, but the editor is responsible for their place at
the beginning of an edition.[36] Slater is right to point out that *POxy*

---

[32] See Irigoin (1952) 38; Van Sickle (1980); Lowe (2007) 175 on the influence of the
length of book-rolls on editorial and authorial activities. NB especially Lowe p. 172 on
the practicalities of the book-roll as a factor in editing: 'the form of the book-roll,
where poems at the front of a book were far easier and likelier to be consulted,
encourages a ranking of poems on a criterion of significance (or consultability) from
highest to lowest'.

[33] Cf. Negri (2004) 167.   [34] Lowe (2007) 170.

[35] See Negri (2004) 27–43, Lowe (2007) 170–5 for an analysis of eidographic
principles with respect to Pindar, Bacchylides, and Simonides. For classification of
lyric poetry more generally see Harvey (1955); Porro (2009) 186–90.

[36] Clay (2011) argues that *O.*1–3 were originally composed as a 'song cycle', and
that their placement in the edition responds to this: cf. Ch. 3, p. 143.

2438.35 does not necessarily indicate an Aristophanic edition, but it cannot be taken as evidence for classification exclusive of an edition either. His use of the absence of Aristophanes from the debate recorded at *Σ P.2 inscr.* about the correct classification of that poem is answered by Lowe, who argues that it probably indicates that 'the default classification as a Pythian in the standard edition was taken to represent [Aristophanes'] judgement'.[37] Equally, his suggestion that Thomas Magister may have misunderstood the papyrus as referring to 'a reorganization by Aristophanes' is rather arbitrary. We have no good reason to assume that a version of the *Life* contained on this papyrus was available to Thomas Magister, and even if it was, it seems unlikely that he would invent on the basis of this the reasons for *O.1* being placed first in the collection and attribute them to Aristophanes. Much more likely is that the *Vita Thomana*'s account of Aristophanes' editorial practice was based on sources now lost.

Certainty is elusive, but the combination of *Σ O.2.48c*, the references made by Dionysius of Halicarnassus, the list at *POxy* 2438.35, and the notice in the *Vita Thomana* strongly suggest that Aristophanes produced an edition of Pindar, almost certainly colometrized according to his understanding of Pindaric metre, and very possibly including lectional signs marking athetizations, ends of stanzas, and ends of poems.[38] Despite the historical importance of this edition, however, we should not be too rigid in our thinking about how it affected later editions. While the evidence indicates that Aristophanes' ordering of the poems served as the template for later editions, and while he clearly made important contributions to Pindaric scholarship, the nature of text production in the ancient world is such that we must allow for a good deal of variety in the constitution of individual texts; while the order of the poems is likely to have remained unchanged, the appearances of different texts will have

---

[37] Lowe (2007) 172.

[38] Cf. Lowe (2007) 169 who, in arguing for the existence of an Aristophanic edition, notes that 'it is hard to see how Aristophanes' arrangement and colometry could have been promoted in a mere ὑπόμνημα'. There may well have been other editions of Pindar made after Aristophanes, although cf. Irigoin (1952) 51–6 and Vassilaki (2009) on Aristarchus' Pindaric criticism. Irigoin notes the absence of Aristarchus' emendations from the manuscript tradition and argues on this basis that it is unlikely that Aristarchus produced an edition of Pindar: '[l]e sort résérve à ces corrections serait surprenant si Aristarque avait établi une edition qui, selon toute vraisemblance, aurait remplacé celle d'Aristophane' (p. 53).

varied considerably according to the different hands used by particular scribes, and each text will have had varying marginalia according to the learning and interests of its owner(s).[39] Regardless of the limitations of the evidence, however, we are justified in saying that the third and second centuries BC were a period of important changes in the constitution of books, as developments such as the formation of editions, and the use of colometry displacing older texts of lyric poetry written in prose, such as the fourth-century papyrus of Timotheus' *Persae*, changed the book into an object of scholarly construction, with significant consequences for readers.

SCHOLIA: AIMS AND METHODOLOGIES

One of the most important issues for thinking about the diachronic travels of the Pindaric corpus is how the scholarly literature written on Pindar in the Hellenistic period affected and interacted with the texts they commented on.[40] Central to this relationship will be the supplementary character of this literature. As well as providing exegesis of the text,[41] the scholia also give the reader historical and mythographical information which expands on that in the texts themselves;[42] as well as opening up new ways of looking at the texts, these supplementations emphasize the status of the Pindaric corpus as a means of accessing and reimagining the past. However, using the scholia as evidence for the scholarly texts of the Hellenistic period poses considerable evidential problems. The scholia in the Byzantine manuscripts are a collation of what was available in late antiquity, which was itself a collation of disparate texts from earlier

[39] This variation would also have encompassed the forms of critical signs, particularly coronides: see the remarks of Galen *De ind.* 14 on his methods in producing his own copies, and Ucciardello (2012) for glosses in papyri. See further Ch. 2, pp. 108–10.

[40] For a definition and discussion of hypomnemata cf. Pfeiffer (1968) 29. The term refers to a collection of glosses and interpretative comments on particular words and passages.

[41] These exegeses often take the form of paraphrase, but there are numerous places in which more advanced literary critical activity is in evidence. Cf. e.g. *Scholies* pp. 31, 287–8, 422–6 for analysis of Aristotelian influence on the critical concepts brought to bear by ancient commentators.

[42] Cf. *Scholies* pp. 18–21.

periods, and cannot therefore be treated as if they were all available to any individual reader.[43] Similarly, we must be wary of over-privileging the extant scholia, since the totality of Pindaric criticism in the Hellenistic and Imperial periods was far more voluminous.[44] We also need to acknowledge the impossibility of precisely dating scholia which do not refer to particular authors, and the differences that would have obtained between different hypomnemata and editions;[45] scholarly paratexts were open documents, subject to additions and alterations by any given reader or author, although it is clear from the remarks about Zenodotus, Aristophanes, and Aristarchus that these and other scholars had a canonical place in the corpus.

There are various ways in which the above problems can be negotiated. First, the question of dating and textual specificity. It is likely that there was little in the way of original scholarship on Pindar during the Imperial period that found its way into the scholia. Much of the scholarship that postdated this period was concerned with redactions of previous commentaries, with an emphasis on the type of exegesis suitable for use by schoolteachers.[46] This is indicated partly by the number of the scholia which provided exegetical para-phrases, and also by the fact that the vast majority of the sources cited in the scholia date from the Hellenistic period and before; Second Sophistic authors are cited very scarcely by the *scholia vetera*, and there is no trace of celebrated names such as Plutarch, Dio Chrysostom, and

[43] Still the best general account of the scholia's transmission is Deas (1931), who argues that Didymus' commentary, which collected much of the previous material, was the main source for the scholia (p. 22). Useful also are his remarks about the use of commentaries in schools (p. 28), which must have involved much abbreviation and compression. Cf. Irigoin (1952) 31–75 for an overview of early Pindaric scholarship.

[44] The differences between the surviving scholia to *P*.12 and the fragment of Theon's commentary on that poem (= *POxy* 2536) are a salutary reminder of the variations in the metatextual corpus: cf. below Ch. 6, pp. 274–5. Cf. also Deas (1931) 55–7 on the Byzantine manuscripts as imperfect representations of previous scholarly work; he points to phenomena such as the substitution of past tenses for the present tenses used in ancient scholarship to refer to customs and rituals; e.g. Σ *P*.4.338 (ii 143–4 Dr).

[45] For a definition and discussion of hypomnemata cf. Pfeiffer (1968) 29. The term refers to a collection of glosses and interpretative comments on particular words and passages, usually in the form of a separate book rather than marginalia; see further Deas (1931) 76–8 with bibliography, and more generally on the form of scholia Wilson (1967).

[46] Thus Deas (1931) 28. This does not mean, however, that readers commenting on their own copies of texts was not a significant practice: see n. 39.

Athenaeus.[47] The latter is not a conclusive demonstration of early dating of the material which comprise the scholia, since it would be possible for a commentator of, for example, the third century AD, to cite Hellenistic authors. However, the scarcity of Second Sophistic authors is suggestive when combined with the firmer evidence that most of the scholars named in the scholia and known to have worked specifically on Pindar date from the Hellenistic period down to the middle of the first century AD. Theon wrote a commentary on Pindar, and it is likely that Aristonicus did also,[48] but there is little to suggest that Hephaestion or Herodian did so, and Amyntianus certainly did not.[49]

---

[47] An exception being the five citations of the mythographer Apollodorus. The influence of Second Sophistic authors on other scholiastic corpora also seems to have been small: Plutarch's commentary on Hesiod is frequently cited, but there is only one citation of Plutarch in the Homeric scholia (Σ A *Il.* 15.625 = fr. 127 Sandbach).

[48] The *Suda* does not mention a work on Pindar by Aristonicus, focusing instead on his Homeric and Hesiodic scholarship, but this does not mean that he did not produce such a work; his Homeric scholarship was probably known to the compiler of the *Suda* through the so-called 'Four-Men Commentary', consisting of excerpts from Aristonicus, Didymus, Nicanor and Herodian, but his work on Pindar was probably lost by late antiquity. Σ *N.*1.37 (iii 17 Dr) (χρὴ δ᾿ ἐν εὐθείαις ὁδοῖς· Ἀριστόνικος· χρὴ καθ᾿ ἣν γεγέννηταί τις φύσιν, ταύτῃ ἀκολουθεῖν καὶ μὴ βιάζεσθαι αὐτὴν εἰς ἄλλα τρέποντα, μηδὲ τῷ φθόνῳ μάρνασθαι πρὸς τοὺς ἀγαθούς, ἀλλὰ συνασκεῖν ἅ τις ἔχει ἐκ φύσεως, '"one must on straight roads": Aristonicus: one must follow the nature which one was born with and not turn it by force in a different direction, nor rage enviously against good men, but discipline what one possesses by nature') suggests a commentary, as does the specifically literary nature of the comment recorded at Σ *O.*3.31a (i 113 Dr): οὐ θαυμαστὸν εἰ τὸ μήπω πεφυτευμένον ἄλσος εἶπεν. Ἀριστόνικος προληπτικῶς φησιν εἰρῆσθαι ('it is not of any moment if he says that the grove had not yet been planted. Aristonicus says that he speaks proleptically'). Less decisive are the comments recorded by Σ *O.*1.35c (i 28 Dr), *O.*7.154a (i 232 Dr), and Σ *N.*1 inscr.b (iii 7 Dr), all of which could have another provenance; the first two, for instance, could come from a response to Didymus rather than an independent commentary. Overall, however, a commentary seems the likely source. On Aristonicus in general cf. e.g. Pfeiffer (1968) 267–70; Montanari (1993) 279.

[49] Σ *O.*3.52a (i 120 Dr) refers to Amyntianus' περὶ ἐλεφάντων as the source of the citation. Both the citations of Herodian (Σ *O.*1.18a (i 23 Dr); *P.*3.65 (i 72–3 Dr)) concern accentuation and probably come from one of the grammatical treatises for which he was celebrated. Σ *I.*5 inscr.a. (iii 240 Dr) records Hephaestion's views on the placing of the poem (ταύτην τὴν ᾠδὴν Ἡφαιστίων μετὰ τὴν ἑξῆς φησι γεγράφθαι τὴν Θάλλοντος ἀνδρῶν, καὶ αὐτὴν Πυθέᾳ γεγράφθαι· ἐχρῆν οὖν καὶ προτετάχθαι, 'Hephaestion says that this ode was written after the one which follows it, which begins Θάλλοντος ἀνδρῶν [*I.*6.], and that it was written for Pytheas, so it should also be placed before it'), but this comment need not be taken from a commentary, and given the absence of any other references to Hephaestion in the scholia, such a work seems improbable (cf. Deas (1931) 29 for the identification of this author with the famous grammarian). The *Suda* does not mention a Pindaric commentary among his works, although it does refer to unnamed ἄλλα πλεῖστα among his œuvre.

Henry Thomson Deas and others are correct to argue for the role of an anonymous second-century AD redactor, who condensed the commentaries of Didymus, Theon, and others, after which point little new material entered the corpus.[50] On these grounds we can be reasonably confident that most of the material in the scholia would have been available in some form to readers of the later Hellenistic and early Imperial periods, and that passages containing extensive contextual, mythical, or literary–historical information would have been considerably more lengthy in the earlier commentaries. This observation brings with it an additional caveat; we should not think of the extant scholia, even in places where their comments are particularly extensive, as reflecting the dominant or prevailing ancient views of the passage in question, still less as reflecting the sum total of scholarship on a particular point. Awareness of this lends a certain provisionality to the readings offered below: our awareness of the scholia's supplementary dimension, for instance, would doubtless be enhanced by greater knowledge of scholars such as Artemon and Didymus, who were particularly interested in historical exegesis.[51] Nonetheless, for all their evidential limitations, they remain important witnesses of the debate that surrounded the Pindaric corpus.[52]

THE DATING GAME

One of the foundational manoeuvres of Pindaric scholarship is the dating of the epinicians according to the games at which the victory commemorated by a given ode was won. The scholia show that this was as important an issue for Hellenistic scholars as it has been for

[50] Deas (1931) 27–9; Lefkowitz (1985) 270–1, and cf. McNamee (2007) 98 for the paring away of scholarly material from later codices. Cf. also Porro (2009) 189–90; Montana (2011) on the formation of scholiastic corpora. On Didymus' Homeric scholarship see West (2001) 46–85, and for his commentary on Pindar see Braswell (2013).

[51] On Artemon see Ch. 4, pp. 175–7. Didymus is frequently cited as the source of historical discussions, as at Σ O.2.29d (i 68–70 Dr): cf. Irigoin (1952) 67–75, and in general Pfeiffer (1968) 274–9. Theon would also have been an important source for later school texts and private commentaries: cf. McNamee (2007) 33–5, Ucciardello (2012) 119–26.

[52] For remarks on the difficulties created by the scholia's citational practices see Slater (1989).

their modern counterparts: most of the *Olympians* and *Pythians* are accompanied by notices dating them to particular games,[53] and in some cases these dates were the subject of considerable debate.[54] The historical problems of dating have received copious attention, but the scholarly focus on establishing dates has tended to obscure the fact that not all of Pindar's ancient listeners would have had access to such information, and that knowing or not knowing the date of a poem's composition and the victory for which it was composed would have affected how a listener understood the poem's commemorative discourses.[55]

In the case of Pindar's first audiences, there will have been considerable variation in the contextual information brought to bear by individual listeners, even if many would have been familiar either through connection with the victor's family or through word-of-mouth report with the circumstances that gave rise to the poem's composition.[56] Once we move beyond the lifetime of those with first-hand experiences of the victories Pindar celebrated, listeners' awareness of context is likely to have been less strong. The poems themselves give little definite information about the victory they commemorate beyond mentioning the event,[57] and never connect themselves to a specific date. Families of victorious athletes will have preserved oral traditions about their victories, but these are likely to have been imprecise with respect to the dates when victories occurred, especially beyond the first generation after the victor concerned.[58] Such traditions will also have been dependent on

---

[53] The *Nemeans* and *Isthmians*, with the exception of Σ *N*.7.inscr., are not accompanied by notices of date, presumably because the victor lists for these festivals were more difficult for Hellenistic scholars to obtain.

[54] See e.g. Σ *O*.6.inscr.b (i 153–4 Dr), where the point at issue is whether or not the mule race was still part of the games at the suggested dates. For debate over the dating of the Panhellenic festivals see Negri (2004) 44–118.

[55] I employ 'listeners' at this stage for the sake of simplicity; I shall consider below possible disparities in perception of dating between readers and listeners.

[56] For further comments see e.g. Morrison (2011).

[57] Pindar never gives detailed accounts of the specific circumstances of a given victory, and does not try to represent the actual event as it occurred: for examples of his narration of victories see *O*.7.81–9, a catalogue in which the emphasis falls on how victories are recorded; see also *N*.5.43–9. Athletic imagery is, however, often used to refer to the poet's activities, as at *N*.5.19–21, *N*.6.26–7, *N*.9.55, *I*.1.24, *I*.2.35: see e.g. Lee (1983).

[58] See e.g. Thomas (1989) 126; Christesen (2007) 123. For reperformance centered on families see Currie (2004) 55–63; Hornblower (2012) 102–3.

circumstances; the forced evacuation to which Aegina was subject in 431, for instance, will have disrupted networks of guest-friendship and family ties, with presumably grave consequences for the reperformance environment.[59]

Written sources for epinician dates also seem to have been thin on the ground. Historiographical works based around Olympic victor lists began to be written in the early fourth century; the first systematic attempt to catalogue Olympic victors was that of Hippias of Elis,[60] and records of victors were kept at Olympia.[61] Commemorative epigrams from the period did not tend to include dates,[62] and although copies of texts in family archives may have been marked with dating information, the controversies over dating in the Hellenistic period suggest that such sources, if they existed, were not widely known.[63] We should reckon with the probability, therefore, that many who attended performances of Pindaric epinicians in the later fifth and fourth centuries would have had either a loose knowledge, or no knowledge at all, of the dates of the victories being commemorated. In the Hellenistic period, however, from about the

[59] Cf., however, Hornblower (2012) 94 on the possible continuing presence on Aegina of at least one family honoured by Pindar. For the circumstances of Pindaric reception on Sicily in the aftermath of the overthrow of the tyrannies see Ch. 3, p. 126 n. 17.

[60] Hippias' work was composed *c.*400 BC: for its contents, sources, and aims see Christesen (2007) 46–166. On early chronography in general see Feeney (2007) 16–20; Clarke (2008) 47–56. Timaeus also produced an *Olympic Victors*, for which see Baron (2013) 23–8. On Timaeus' wider chronographic significance see Feeney (2007) 92–5. Eratosthenes of Cyrene was a decisive figure in the development of chronography (see e.g. *BNJ* 241 F 1–3, 9–10), and also composed an *Olympic Victors* (*BNJ* 241 F 4–8). For Eratosthenes' establishment of the Olympiad dating system see Pfeiffer (1968) 163, Pownall on *BNJ* 241 F 1a, Clarke (2008) 65–70.

[61] Especially important is *IvO* 17, a bronze plaque from Olympia dated to the late fifth or early fourth century, which appears to have contained a list of victors from a particular iteration of the games as well as the number of the Olympiad: see Jeffery and Johnston (1990) 59; Christesen (2007) 135–6.

[62] For an overview of the evidence see Christesen (2007) 122–46. Surveying the evidence for inscriptions commemorating victories at local games, he concludes that 'most athletic victory inscriptions had no internal dating information and those that did contain chronological indicators could be placed in time only with difficulty. None of the extant inscriptions listing the victors in particular iterations of athletic contests provides a date based on one of the time-reckoning systems in general use in the Greek world . . . Internal dating information in the inscriptions of individual victor monuments is extremely rare, even at Olympia, even after numbered Olympiads became a standard means of reckoning time' (p. 145).

[63] On local and family archives see Introduction, p. 4 n. 16.

middle of the third century onwards, many readers would have had access to dates through commentaries, along with other paratextual information that would have helped them set the poems in context.[64]

These changes had consequences for the poems' reception. Dating, together with other contextual information, allows readers to place the poems historically: this is especially important in the cases of poems where dating bears dramatically on interpretation, but the poems offer no solid internal evidence of their dates. This is one of the points at which differentiation emerges between stages of Pindaric reception. Many listeners at reperformances, and probably numerous early readers, encountered texts undetermined by metatextual information, with the consequence that interpretative possibilities relating to historicization would not have been open to them in the same way as for later readers. To take the controversial example of *P*.11, a listener or reader who does not know the date of the poem is in a fundamentally different position from one who is informed that the poem dates to 474.[65] For the latter, providing that s/he trusts the dating, the poem cannot be read as alluding by authorial design to Aeschylus' *Oresteia*. For the former, however, the situation is considerably more fluid; s/he might on the basis of textual connections understand *P*.11 as a response to Aeschylus' trilogy, or as a precursor of it. Equally, s/he might assume an indeterminate position, noting the possibility of a connection but not feeling able to commit to a strong view of the texts' relationship. However s/he responds, the grounds of the response will differ from someone whose reading is mediated by definite information about the poem's date.

---

[64] A shift in modes of dating may also have been at work. The early dating of Pindar's epinicians, whether by paratextual information attached to copies of the poems or word-of-mouth information, may have been based on local calendars, usually structured by the use of named local officials: see the evidence collected by Christesen (2007) 122–46, and also Clarke (2008) 54–5 on modes of temporal organization in Atthidography. Given the Panhellenic nature of the major games, however, people may also have remembered victories by, e.g., Olympiads: even if no victory lists were available, reckonings based on personal experience ('two Olympiads ago') may have been prevalent. Perhaps the most likely scenario for the fifth century is a combination of the two modes. In the Hellenistic commentaries the poems are always dated by the games at which they took place. This form of dating emphasizes the poems' Panhellenic situation, and may well have been influenced by Eratosthenes' chronographical work: see above, n. 60.

[65] I assume this date here for the sake of argument: for more details about the controversy over the poem's date and its interpretative ramifications see Ch. 6, pp. 241–2, 252–3.

We should be cautious about strong periodizations, as it is certainly possible that epichoric traditions about dating and contexts may have influenced the poems' pre-Hellenistic reception to various extents. Nevertheless, it is possible to posit a shift in the perception of the poems' temporal localization attendant on the scholarly processes of dating the poems, with corresponding ramifications for how the poems were viewed contextually. How strong the shift was between the later classical period and that of the later third century is difficult to say, but it is likely that developments in chronography and historical scholarship enabled a more precise historicizing approach to the poems during this period than was possible before. In turn, the possibilities opened up by situating the poems historically were exploited at length by later scholars: Aristarchus and Didymus both included historical information and historical readings in their work on Pindar,[66] and other early Pindaric scholars elaborated historically grounded readings of the epinicians' rhetorical and narrative devices.[67]

Moreover, the variety of historicizing material included in early commentaries should also be emphasized. Scholarship on the scholia has tended to stress the strongly rhetorical character of their exegeses,[68] yet while the influence of rhetorical theory and practice on the scholia is indubitable, there are also numerous aspects of their exegetical activity that do not fall under this remit. Like their modern counterparts, ancient commentaries supplied their readers with a variety of contextual data, much of which does not relate to rhetorical analyses. Historiographical citations are especially important in this respect:[69] as well as being used to ground historicizing interpretations

---

[66] See respectively Vassilaki (2009); Braswell (2013) 113–16.

[67] See e.g. the reading of the narrative in *N*.1 by Chaeris, which seeks to explain why Pindar chose to narrate an episode from the very beginnning of Heracles' life (Σ *N*.1.49c, iii 19–21 Dr): ὁ δὲ Χαῖρίς φηςιν, ὅτι ὁ Χρόμιος πολλὰ cυμπονήcαc τῷ Ἱέρωνι κατὰ τὴν ἀρχὴν ἀμοιβῆc ἔτυχεν ἐξ αὐτοῦ, ὥcτε ἐκ περιουcίαc καὶ ἱπποτροφῆcαι· ὡc οὖν οὗτος ἔπαθλον πόνων ἔλαβε τὴν ἐπιφάνειαν, οὕτω καὶ Ἡρακλῆc πολλὰ ταλαιπωρήcαc ἔπαθλον ἔcχε τὴν ἀθαναcίαν καὶ τὸν γάμον τῆc Ἥβηc ('But Chaeris says that Chromius shared many labours with Hiero from the beginning and received requital from him, so that from his wealth he also raised horses. As he achieved distinction as a reward for his toils, so too did Heracles, who had endured much hardship, have as his reward immortality and marriage to Hebe'). For modern responses to Chaeris' view see e.g. Braswell (1992) 56 with further references, and cf. Bitto (2012) 104–5.

[68] Cf. e.g. Wilson (1980); Lefkowitz (1985); Bitto (2012).

[69] See Braswell (2012) 13–18; Phillips (forthcoming).

of Pindar's texts, they also supply the reader with a range of general information about matters ranging from the victor and his family, to historical events and epichoric myths. In some cases, the authors cited in the scholia take a radically different approach to mythical material from Pindar's, implicating readers in a variety of ways of thinking about the past.[70] These citations affect the terms on which a reading of Pindar takes place. Reading the epinicians with a commentary in the Hellenistic period was a multifaceted and exploratory exercise in which learning about local myths and traditions, situating a poem in an historical context, and comparing different versions of a given story were as important as engaging with the encomiastic premises of the poem concerned.[71] The historical interests of commentators also draw attention to the archival status of the poems themselves in a documentary context:[72] Pindar is often assimilated by the scholia to historiographical projects,[73] positioned as a recorder of myths and historical information. The poems' rhetorical conventions also foreground their status as traces of historical performance events. A crucial concern of my readings will be the provisionality and

---

[70] Glosses falling into each category are far too numerous for an adequate summary. The following are useful representative examples: information about victor and family: Σ *O*.7.152a–d (i 230–1 Dr); epichoric myth: Σ *N*.3.21 (ii Dr 45–6); historical narrative: Σ *O*.2.29d (i 68–70 Dr).

[71] Cf. Phillips (2013c) 161–6. For general comments on how the Pindaric commentaries pluralize and enrich the terms in which the primary texts can be read see *Scholies* pp. 18–20.

[72] On the archive see e.g. Derrida (1996) 1–3 and *passim*; Orrells (2010). Derrida's analysis brings out the doubleness of the archival process: the archive is a space of preservation and ordering, but in gathering books together, the archive cannot help but create new possibilities for how these texts might be related and read, and hence complicating its own attempts at instituting 'the unity of an ideal configuration' (1996: p. 3). The movement towards unification central to the formation of archival libraries, and reflected in the vocabulary of 'gathering' used in narratives of about libraries' foundation (e.g. Plut. *Mor.* 1095d, Πτολεμαῖος ὁ πρῶτος cυναγαγὼν τὸ μουcεῖον, and cf. cύνταξιν at Strabo 13.1.54.), is balanced by forces that contest such unification. Useful also in this respect is Foucault (1977) on the library as a heterotopic space, the structural and symbolic significance of which exceeds its purely architectural form. For the connection between libraries and commentaries see Ch. 4, pp. 208–10. On the 'archival' as a category cf. also the remarks of White (1999) 2, discussing the nature of historical knowledge as realized discursively: 'such information might better be called "archival", inasmuch as it can serve as the object of any discipline simply by being taken as a subject of that discipline's distinctive discursive practices'. This formulation captures the variety of uses to which 'information' about the past was put in the Hellenistic period.

[73] See Ch. 4, pp. 205–7 and Ch. 6, pp. 270–2.

variousness of the poems' status as records, and the dialogues that emerge in a documentary context between preservation and the proliferation of meaning.[74]

(META)TEXTS AND CONTEXTS

Another factor to be borne in mind when analysing the scholia as evidence for ancient reading practices is the variety of metatexts that they reflect. As well as commentaries and collections of glosses, there would also have been individual readers' marginalia, no doubt often influenced by or copied from commentaries to which they had access. Quite aside from the usual insecurities of textual transmission, we are confronted with a corpus subject to a process of constant modification which precludes pinning down any particular scholium's availability to a certain time and place. Moreover, hypomnemata and editions would have varied considerably; scholarly paratexts were open documents, subject to additions and alterations by any given writer or author. They were also open to excerption by individual readers: papyri show how readers drew on commentaries to form their own marginalia.[75] Consequently, the aim of the following readings is a diachronic sketching of some of the interpretative situations that arise from the scholarly texts of which the extant scholia are the descendants. Reading a text with a metatextual apparatus differs from hearing a performance or reading the text alone, and my analyses aim to articulate the kind of problems and questions that may have confronted ancient readers approaching the Pindaric corpus in this way. In doing so, I am dealing with a set of interpretative potentialities, the kind of formal questions and intertextual connections that the scholia prompt; in some cases these entail a certain amount of readerly elaboration, but in others the scholia direct readers quite firmly towards certain ways of construing the text and the data in

[74] I focus especially on *O*.14 and *P*.12 in this respect: see Ch. 5, pp. 223–8 and Ch. 6, pp. 263–81. Specific issues of dating are less important to my arguments, but see Ch. 6, pp. 252–3 for a discussion of *P*.11 from this perspective.

[75] Cf. e.g. the marginalia in *POxy* 841. For a full inventory of Pindaric papyri cf. Ucciardello (2012) 109–10, and for comment on annotations in Pindaric papyri cf. McNamee (2007) 305–49. For general comments see Johnson (2010) 185–90.

question.[76] What is at issue is not just what the scholia themselves say, but what is presupposed by such statements, and the potential readings they open up. While my readings will demonstrate that the scholia offer precious insights into the interpretative climate surrounding the Pindaric texts, the contexts in which they were read are crucial for interpreting their cultural significance. Crucial to these contexts were other types of literary critical texts, represented mainly by the stylistic treatises, and an examination of how this tradition relates to Pindar is indispensable for an understanding of the scholia's place in wider intellectual culture.

Dionysius of Halicarnassus is for us the most prominent representative of this stylistic critical tradition. In *On Literary Composition*, he gives definitions and examples of various compositional styles as part of a didactic programme ostensibly directed at the rhetorical training of his addressee Rufus Metilius (*De comp. verb.* 1).[77] As with much ancient 'literary criticism', *On Literary Composition* is designed primarily to offer instruction in the process of writing, and the question of how it may have affected reading practices is consequently not straightforward. Pindar, alongside authors such as Aeschylus, Antimachus, Empedocles, and Thucydides, is one of the representatives of the severe or harsh style (αὐcτηρόc), which Dionysius describes in the following terms (ch. 22):

τῆc μὲν οὖν αὐcτηρᾶc ἁρμονίαc τοιόcδε ὁ χαρακτήρ· ἐρείδεcθαι βούλεται τὰ ὀνόματα ἀcφαλῶc καὶ cτάcειc λαμβάνειν ἰcχυράc, ὥcτ' ἐκ περιφανείαc ἕκαcτον ὄνομα ὁρᾶcθαι, ἀπέχειν τε ἀπ' ἀλλήλων τὰ μόρια διαcτάcειc ἀξιολόγουc αἰcθητοῖc χρόνοιc διειργόμενα· τραχείαιc τε χρῆcθαι πολλαχῇ καὶ ἀντιτύποιc ταῖc cυμβολαῖc οὐδὲν αὐτῇ διαφέρει, οἷαι γίνονται τῶν λογάδην cυντιθεμένων ἐν οἰκοδομίαιc λίθων αἱ μὴ εὐγώνιοι καὶ μὴ

---

[76] Enquiring into readerly experiences of texts where those readings have not, as in the vast majority of cases, left evidential traces is difficult, and we have to extrapolate from the scholia's formal features and argumentative strategies the kind of experiences they could have induced. It is notable, however, that the practice of juxtaposing the views of different scholars and the use of the ἄλλωc . . . ἄλλωc structure encourages deconstruction of the commentator's authority and readerly adjudication; these structures were certainly common in later commentaries (2nd century AD onwards), and there is evidence that they formed part of earlier commentaries as well; cf. e.g. Σ *N*.1.3 (iii 9–10 Dr). We should not discount the possibility that the critical and comparative approach encouraged by such structures carried over into other aspects of readers' approaches to the material commentaries contained.

[77] For an overview of Dionysius' accounts of different textual effects cf. Bonner (1939); Damon (1991).

cυνεξεcμέναι βάcειc, ἀργαὶ δέ τινεc καὶ αὐτοcχέδιοι· μεγάλοιc τε καὶ διαβεβηκόcιν εἰc πλάτοc ὀνόμαcιν ὡc τὰ πολλὰ μηκύνεcθαι φιλεῖ· τὸ γὰρ εἰc βραχείαc cυλλαβὰc cυνάγεcθαι πολέμιον αὐτῇ, πλὴν εἴ ποτε ἀνάγκη βιάζοιτο.

The character of the harsh style is as follows: it requires words to be firmly fixed and take strong positions, so that each word may be seen clearly, and that the parts of the sentence should be distant from each other by considerable distances and separated by perceptible intervals. It makes use everywhere of harsh and dissonant collocations, such as those of picked blocks of stone laid together in buildings, not squared off and well polished, but unwrought and rough hewn. In general, it tends towards extension by means of long words which extend over a wide space, because restriction to short syllables is hostile to it, except when necessity compels.

He then characterizes various other aspects of the austere style: its rhythms are 'dignified and grand' (ἀξιωματικοὺc καὶ μεγαλοπρεπεῖc), its arrangement of clauses 'noble, bright, and free' (εὐγενῆ καὶ λαμπρὰ καὶ ἐλεύθερα); it 'wishes them to seem more like nature than art' (φύcει τ' ἐοικέναι μᾶλλον αὐτὰ βούλεται ἢ τέχνῃ), and is directed more at the expression of emotion than at character (κατὰ πάθοc λέγεcθαι μᾶλλον ἢ κατ' ἦθοc). Its periodic structures are not ornamented, but aim rather to give an impression of simplicity and absence of ornament (τὸ ἀνεπιτήδευτον ἐμφαίνειν θέλει καὶ ἀφελέc), and its overall stylistic effect is one which generates beauty through a 'patina of antiquity' (τὸν ἀρχαϊcμὸν καὶ τὸν πίνον ἔχουcα κάλλοc).[78] Dionysius' first example of the austere style is the opening passage of Pindar's *Dith.* 1, which he subjects to a microscopic stylistic analysis focused almost exclusively on the sound structures of the words and their sonic relations. For instance, his analysis of the poem's opening line (δεῦτ' ἐν χορὸν Ὀλύμπιοι) focuses on the juxtaposition of ἐν and χορόν, and the sonic effect thus created. Dionysius points out that the letters ν and χ form an unnatural union (ἀcύμμικτα δὲ τῇ φύcει ταῦτα τὰ cτοιχεῖα καὶ ἀκόλλητα), because ν never precedes χ in the same syllable; their juxtaposition therefore produces a pause between the letters and keeps the sonic structures of the two words separated (ἀνάγκη cιωπήν τινα γενέcθαι μέcην ἀμφοῖν τὴν διορίζουcαν ἑκατέρου τῶν γραμμάτων τὰc δυνάμειc).[79]

---

[78] Cf. τὸν ἀρχαῖον...πίνον used of Pindar's *Partheneia* at *Dem.* 39.
[79] Cf. Vaahtera (1997) for a critique of this critical practice.

In his definition of the austere style, as elsewhere in his critical discourse, Dionysius is drawing on an extensive tradition of conceptualizing literary texts in terms of their materiality,[80] whether as buildings or other types of objects, or as sound structures.[81] The above passage extends the rhetoric of *De comp. verb.* 6, where he compares writing to building, and develops the concern with euphonious sound structures that was important in Hellenistic criticism.[82] Although the definition and empirical account of literary styles in this passage works primarily as part of a *didaxis* of the reader-as-writer, the detailed verbal anatomizing of Dionysius' account also acts as a commentary on the process of voiced reading, drawing the reader's attention to the stylistic force of the sounds produced by this act. In common with numerous other ancient critics, Dionysius conceptualizes the process of reading as an uncovering of the (authorial) voice inscribed within it,[83] but there are passages where he acknowledges the historical specificity of such readerly recreations. At *Dem.* 22, he meditates on Demosthenes' greatness in terms of an opposition between performance and reperformance:

εἰ δὴ τὸ διὰ τοσούτων <ἐτῶν> ἐγκαταμισγόμενον τοῖς βυβλίοιc πνεῦμα τοcαύτην ἰcχὺν ἔχει καὶ οὕτωc ἀγωγόν ἐcτι τῶν ἀνθρώπων, ἦ που τότε ὑπερφυέc τι καὶ δεινὸν χρῆμα ἦν ἐπὶ τῶν ἐκείνου λόγων.

If the spirit with which his pages are imbued after so many years has such strength and moves men so much, how overwhelming and awesome a thing it must have been to have been present at the time when he delivered his speeches.

This passage tacitly acknowledges the non-identity of Demosthenes' performances (ἐπὶ τῶν ἐκείνου λόγων) and those readings of the present day which attempt to revivify the text's πνεῦμα. Nevertheless, the book is here imagined as an almost magical object, a receptacle for a spirit which is mixed into it (ἐγκαταμιcγόμενον); the passage

---

[80] Cf. Ch. 2, pp. 86–92.

[81] Cf. Porter (2010) 490–509 for an account of this tradition with further references. For the connection between this passage and [Long.] *De subl.* 40.4 cf. Porter (2001) 81. On Dionysius' metaphorical vocabulary in general cf. Lockwood (1937).

[82] Cf. Porter (2010) 494–5. Euphonism is a common critical motif in critics such as Quintilian, Cicero, and Plutarch, and is also frequent in the scholia: cf. Richardson (1980) 283–7; Meijering (1987) 42–3; Nünlist (2009) 215–17. For the importance of this mode of analysis in *De comp. verb.* cf. Damon (1991) 52–8.

[83] Cf. Porter (2010) 310–11.

registers the historicity of the book (διὰ τοcούτων <ἐτῶν> ... τότε), and its capacity to give the reader access to a πνεῦμα that is both a transhistorical remainder of the past, preserved intact and awaiting readerly excavation, and something dependent on the medium of its transmission.[84]

The vocabulary with which Dionysius describes the severe style and the monumental experiences to which it gives rise (e.g. μεγαλοπρεπεῖc, ὑπερφυέc, δεινόν) is common in critical assessments of Pindar, as in Quintilian's famous pronouncement (10.1.61):

> nouem uero lyricorum longe Pindarus princeps spiritus magnificentia, sententiis, figuris, beatissima rerum uerborumque copia et uelut quodam eloquentiae flumine; propter quae Horatius eum merito credidit nemini imitabilem.

> Pindar is certainly by far the pre-eminent figure among the lyric poets in his magnificence of inspiration, in his maxims, in his use of figures, in the happy wealth of his subjects and language, and in his torrent of eloquence. On account of these things Horace rightly believed him to be unsusceptible of imitation by anyone.[85]

Longinus' *On the Sublime* is the most thoroughgoing extant critical treatment of the sublime (ὕψοc) in literature,[86] and provides extensive analysis of the qualities dwelt on by Dionysius in his treatment of the severe style and mentioned by Quintilian in relation to Pindar. Somewhat surprisingly, Pindar does not feature much in *On the Sublime*,[87] although he is mentioned at 33.5 alongside Sophocles as authors praised for their inconsistent but overwhelming genius, who 'as it were set everything ablaze in their movement, but are often extinguished without reason and fall flat in complete failure' (ὁτὲ μὲν οἷον πάντα ἐπιφλέγουσι τῇ φορᾷ, cβέννυνται δ' ἀλόγωc πολλάκιc καὶ

---

[84] Cf. Porter (2001) 79–80 on the historicity of the Longinian sublime, which 'exists in a present experience of the past–or in its projection into the past ... the sublime exists only in a chain of citations'.

[85] Quintilian's *eloquentiae flumine* recalls Hor. *C*.4.2.5–8.

[86] The date of the treatise and the identity of the author are uncertain: some place him in the mid-third century AD (cf. Russell (1964) xxii–xxx), but a first-century AD date has found general favour: cf. e.g. Segal (1959); Russell (1964). For further references cf. Porter (2001) 63 n. 1. Discussion of sublimity is not confined to Longinus however: cf. Porter (2001) 67–76.

[87] A considerable amount of the text is lost, however, so this may be somewhat misleading. For Longinus on Bacchylides cf. Fearn (2007) 213–14.

πίπτουcιν ἀτυχέcτατα),[88] and who stand in contrast to the smooth perfection of, respectively, Ion of Chios and Bacchylides. However, [Long.] 35.4–5 includes a reminiscence of Pindar as part of a description of the sublime in nature:[89]

οὐδέ γε τὸ ὑφ᾽ ἡμῶν τουτὶ φλογίον ἀνακαιόμενον, ἐπεὶ καθαρὸν cῴζει τὸ φέγγος, ἐκπληττόμεθα τῶν οὐρανίων μᾶλλον, καίτοι πολλάκιc ἐπιcκοτου-μένων, οὐδὲ τῶν τῆc Αἴτνηc κρατήρων ἀξιοθαυμαcτότερον νομίζομεν, ἧc αἱ ἀναχοαὶ πέτρουc τε ἐκ βυθοῦ καὶ ὅλουc ὄχθουc ἀναφέρουcι καὶ ποτα-μοὺc ἐνίοτε τοῦ γηγενοῦc ἐκείνου καὶ αὐτομάτου προχέουcι πυρόc.

We are not astonished more by the little fire that we have lit for ourselves, since it keeps a steady light, than at the lights of heaven, even though they are often darkened, not do we think it more wondrous than the craters of Aetna, whose outpourings hurl rocks up from the depths and whole hills, and sometimes pour forth rivers of that earthborn and spontaneous fire.

The description of Aetna recalls, inter alia, Pindar's vignette at P.1.21–4:[90]

τᾶc ἐρεύγονται μὲν ἀπλάτου πυρὸc ἁγνόταται
ἐκ μυχῶν παγαί· ποταμοὶ δ᾽ ἁμέραιcιν
μὲν προχέοντι ῥόον καπνοῦ
αἴθων᾽ ἀλλ᾽ ἐν ὄρφναιcιν πέτραc
φοίνιccα κυλινδομένα φλὸξ ἐc βαθεῖ-
αν φέρει πόντου πλάκα cὺν πατάγῳ.

From its depths, purest springs of unapproachable fire belch forth; rivers pour forth by day a blazing stream of smoke, but in the darkness a rolling red flame carries rocks to the sea's deep plain with a crash.

Longinus' phrasing replays the Pindaric rocks (πέτρουc), rivers of flame (ποταμοὺc ... πυρόc), the depths of the mountain (ἐκ βυθοῦ), and the 'pouring forth' (προχέουcι). The interplay between text and referent forms an important part of the rhetoric of Longinus' passage: although the primary object of man's instinct to admire the sublime is

---

[88] Halliwell (2011) 334 n. 15 suggests that ἐπιφλέγουcι may echo Pindar's use of the verb at O.9.22, where the poet 'sets the city alight with blazing songs' (πόλιν / μαλεραῖc ἐπιφλέγων ἀοιδαῖc).

[89] As noted by e.g. Russell (1964) ad loc. Cf. Segal (1987) for the representation of the writer as hero in this and other passages.

[90] Description of Aetna was a popular topos in ancient literature: cf. e.g. [Aesch.] PV 367–72. Cf. Aul. Gell. 17.10 for a stylistic comparison between Pindar's description and Vir. Aen. 3.570–6. On the significance of the passage's 'cosmic' imagery cf. Halliwell (2011) 333–5, 353.

the great marvels of nature, the pointed allusion to literary treatments of Aetna such as Pindar's blurs the distinction between text and object, and suggests the extent to which perception of nature is in part shaped by engagement with literature.[91] As well as drawing on the equation between sublime texts and sublime subject matter, the Pindaric appropriations also instantiate Longinus' paedeutic theories: a central facet of his argument in *On the Sublime* is that exposure to and communion with sublime authors is the only means of achieving sublimity in one's own work. Here, the Pindaric intertexts enact this process, as the sublime force of the Pindaric passage spills over into Longinus' own writing, while Longinus' departures from the Pindaric model (e.g. τοῦ γηγενοῦς ἐκείνου καὶ αὐτομάτου... πυρός) enact the competitive nature of imitative engagement.[92]

Longinus repeatedly stresses the psychological effects of the sublime as part of his conception of reading as a dialogic process. After an initial loose definition of sublimity as a property of discourses at 1.3 (ὡς ἀκρότης καὶ ἐξοχή τις λόγων ἐστὶ τὰ ὕψη, 'the sublime is a consummate excellence and outstanding aspect of language'), he moves on at 1.4 to stress the transformational effects of great works: οὐ γὰρ εἰς πειθὼ τοὺς ἀκροωμένους ἀλλ᾽ εἰς ἔκστασιν ἄγει τὰ ὑπερφυᾶ· πάντη δέ γε σὺν ἐκπλήξει τοῦ πιθανοῦ καὶ τοῦ πρὸς χάριν ἀεὶ κρατεῖ τὸ θαυμάσιον ('the outstanding works move listeners not to being persuaded but to ecstasy; always that which is wondrous, with its power of amazement, prevails over the convincing and pleasing'). The experience of the sublime is uplifting (7.2–3), and occurs at the site of an informative dialogue with past authors; it is intimately connected to the greatness of an individual intellect (ὕψος μεγαλοφροσύνης ἀπήχημα, 'sublimity is the echo of greatness of mind' 9.2),[93] and 'imitation and emulation of past authors' (<ἡ>

---

[91] For similar vocabulary used of Demosthenes cf. *De subl.* 12.4.

[92] Cf. Walsh (1988) for the argument that *On the Sublime* both describes and embodies sublimity. Cf. particularly p. 252 n. 1 for his comments on 22.1, where in describing how emotion disturbs normal word order, the word for 'word arrangement' (τάξις) is placed in hyperbaton at the end of its clause (τῇδε κἀκεῖσε ἀγχιστρόφως ἀντισπώμενοι τὰς λέξεις τὰς νοήσεις τὴν ἐκ τοῦ κατὰ φύσιν εἱρμοῦ παντοίως πρὸς μυρίας τροπὰς ἐναλλάττουσι τάξιν).

[93] Cf. Walsh (1988) 260 for an assessment of the relation between this phrase and sublimity as a feature of texts: he argues that for Longinus 'there is no gap between thought and expression', and that the latter is an unmediated expression of the former. 35.4 can be seen in this light: the echoes of *P.*1 function as a textual correlative of the μεγαλοφροσύνης ἀπήχημα experienced when reading Pindar.

τῶν ἔμπροσθεν μεγάλων ϲυγγραφέων καὶ ποιητῶν μίμηϲίϲ τε καὶ
ζήλωϲιϲ, 13.2) is necessary in order for an author to achieve sublimity
in his own work.[94] At 13.2, Longinus employs the simile of the
Pythia's inspiration by Apollo to characterize how one may be influenced by previous authors, and follows this at 13.3–4 with an account
of authors such as Stesichorus, Herodotus, and Plato being inspired
by and engaging with Homer.[95]

   In the passages cited above, Pindar emerges as a distant and
somewhat forbidding figure, an impression enhanced by the infre-
quency with which he is mentioned or alluded to. At 33.5 both Pindar
and Sophocles are figured by an assimilation to powerful natural
forces which evade personalizing conception,[96] a mode of representation which seems to limit the possibilities for thoughtful engagement with these authors by foregrounding precisely how their work
makes such engagement difficult or even impossible; the expression
πάντα ἐπιφλέγουϲι, for instance, indicates such an effect.[97] Yet this
imagery may also be read as pointing up the force of the paradox
whereby the sublime is both an excessive, supra-rational experience
and something that can be captured, however provisionally, by critical comment and reproduced in one's own writing. The figurations
thus attempt to stretch what is meant by engagement with previous
authors by subsuming within it an experiential element beyond the
terms of semantic, or indeed semiotic, analysis. Reading becomes a

[94] For further remarks on this process cf. Halliwell (2011) 339–40.
[95] On the pervasiveness of *imitatio* in ancient literary culture cf. Russell (1979). Cf.
Whitmarsh (2001) 60–2 on the agonistic aspects of imitation in Longinus.
[96] Cf. the figuration of Homer as the Ocean at 9.13.
[97] Cf. particularly *De subl.* 1.4, where the sublime is correlated with the production
of wonder and amazement, with Porter (2001) 79–80; Hunter (2009) 130, 141–2.
Later in the same passage Longinus uses the image of the thunderbolt to describe the
effects of Demosthenes' writing. Porter (2001) 81–2 argues that the experience of the
sublime is intimately connected to the (potential) loss, disjunction, fragmentation,
and failure of the objects from which it arises, and cf. ibid., p. 83 on the sublime as a
force which emerges in particular sites and fragments the literary work of which it is
part (an effect imitated by the textuality of *On the Sublime* itself in its tissues of
citations): cf. also Whitmarsh (2001) 61 with further references. Cf. *De subl.* 20.3 on
the complex relationship between order and disorder in sublime works, and Innes
(1995) on the structural unity of *On the Sublime* itself, which she sees as illustrative of
the organic unity which Longinus attributes to the sublime, although cf. Halliwell
(2011) 351–4 for the tension between moments of sublimity and the structures of the
texts in which they emerge. Cf. also Whitmarsh (2001) 64–6 on the interplay between
(stylistic and conceptual) order and transgression. On the political dimension of the
treatise cf. Too (1998) 188–207; Whitmarsh (2001) 66–71.

mode of experience involving an openness to, and more detailed awareness of, the means by which sublimity overwhelms the subject.[98]

Assessing the possible effects of such critical models on ancient readers and their efficacy for explicating the functions of Pindaric texts, however, raises a different set of questions. For all their conceptual power and literary-historical interest, the critical positions articulated by Dionysius and Longinus should not be taken either as exhausting the potentialities of meaning and significance opened up by Pindaric texts in their diachronic situations, nor as providing a determinate critical horizon for readers. With regard to the latter, a pointed contrast emerges between the affective materialism of these two critics, with their focus on the emotive effects of stylistic devices, and the modes of analysis found in the scholia, which focus almost exclusively on questions of meaning and interpretation and frequently cite literary and historical comparanda. This is partly due to the fact that Dionysius and Longinus have writerly *paideia* and stylistic exemplification rather than interpretation or exegesis of Pindar as their primary goals, with the result that contextual, structural, and functional issues arising from his poetry are largely neglected. One possible effect of Longinus' elevation of the sublime over other formal features is a legitimization of a readerly fracturing of Pindaric texts in a way which duplicates Longinian citational and appropriative practices; the allusions to *P*.1.21–4 at *De subl.* 35.5, for instance, could be read as licensing a mode of reading which takes the sublime effect of this passage as the most striking and meaningful part of the poem.

Another approach to the possible influence of these critics on reading practices is to think about their potential interactions with the scholarly tradition represented by the scholia. Their influence on this branch of criticism seems to have been minimal; there are no passages in the scholia that reflect the kind of detailed euphonic analysis practised by Dionysius in the passage cited above, and despite the frequent use of ὕψος and its cognates,[99] the Longinian

---

[98] Cf. Porter (2001) 78: *On the Sublime* as 'a pragmatic manual in identifying sublime literature, in reading the signs of sublimity, and in reproducing the effects of sublimity in one's responses to the great canonical works of the past'. At p. 79 he suggests that 'the Longinian sublime captures the intensity of *the experience of canonicity itself*'.

[99] These are often used non-technically as synonyms for 'raise up' vel sim; cf. e.g. Σ *O.*9.31 (i 274 Dr) where ὑψοῦϲι glosses ἐπαείροντι.

sublime does not seem to have made much of an impression either. A possible exception to this is *Σ N*.3.143 (iii 62 Dr), which explains the phrase κραγέται δὲ κολοιοὶ ταπεινὰ νέμονται ('chattering crows range below') and the opposition between jackdaws and the eagle, in terms of the common theme of Pindar's poetic rivalry with Bacchylides:

οἱ δὲ ἀντίτεχνοί μου κολοιοῖς ἐοίκασι, κραυγάζοντες μόνον καὶ ταπεινὰ νεμόμενοι, οὐ δύνανται δὲ διαίρεσθαι εἰς ὕψος. δοκεῖ δὲ ταῦτα τείνειν εἰς Βακχυλίδην· ἦν γὰρ ὑφόρασις αὐτοῖς πρὸς ἀλλήλους. παραβάλλει δὲ αὐτὸν μὲν ἀετῷ, κολοιῷ δὲ Βακχυλίδην.

My rivals are like jackdaws, only chattering and 'staying close to the ground', and they are not able to rise to the heights. It seems that this is directed at Bacchylides, for there was mutual suspicion between these two. He compares himself to an eagle, and Bacchylides to a jackdaw.

In this metapoetic context, it might be possible to read οὐ δύνανται δὲ διαίρεσθαι εἰς ὕψος as reflecting the critical tradition surrounding ὕψος, but the absence of any specific articulation of such an argument urges caution: the phrase could simply be deploying ὕψος in its non-technical sense.[100] We should also note that cognates of ὕψος are relatively common in Pindar,[101] and the scholium's phrasing may be influenced by pronouncements such as *O*.1.115, where the poet prays for Hiero to 'walk on high' (εἴη σέ τε τοῦτον ὑψοῦ χρόνον πατεῖν) in a passage which correlates the achievements of poet and *laudandus*.[102] While it is difficult to make a case for *Σ N*.3.143 as being written under the influence of ὕψος-criticism,[103] still less that of any individual critic,

---

[100] For ὕψος used with prepositions to indicate 'on high' vel sim. cf. e.g. Hdt. 2.13; Eur. *Pho*. 404.

[101] The vocabulary of ὕψος also occurs in *Σ I*.5.56a–c (iii 246–7 Dr), which gloss the description of Aegina as a πύργος for 'high virtues to ascend' at *I*.5.44–5 (τετείχισται δὲ πάλαι / πύργος ὑψηλαῖς ἀρεταῖς ἀναβαίνειν); the scholia take ὑψηλαῖς as a transferred epithet referring to the tower, the fullest explanation given by 56c: οἷον ὑψοῦται αὐτῶν ἡ ἀρετὴ ὥσπερ τεῖχος· οὗτος γὰρ τὴν αὔξησιν πύργον καὶ τεῖχος εἴωθε λέγειν, ἀφ᾽ οὗ πυργοῦν τὸ αὔξειν καὶ ὑψοῦν λέγεται ('so their virtue is to be raised high like a wall. For he tends to speak of growth in terms of a tower or a wall, whence "to grow" is called "to build" and "to raise high"'). Here, however, there is no sense that ὕψος is being used in a technical, critical sense; the scholia's rhetoric expands on its use in the poem.

[102] Cf. Ch. 3, pp. 131–6.

[103] Cf. Russell (1964) xxi–xlii for the use of ὕψος vocabulary in critical texts, where it does not occur commonly until the late first century BC; Caecilius of Caleacte, against whom Longinus' treatise was directed, was clearly an important figure in the

both that scholium and O.1.115 are interesting test cases for thinking about how critical discourse may have inflected readings of Pindaric texts and engagements with Pindaric scholarship.

A reader familiar with Longinus might be tempted to see in εἴη cέ τε τοῦτον ὑψοῦ χρόνον πατεῖν a foreshadowing of the critical topos of sublimity and a marker of Pindar's own stylistic grandeur; similarly οὐ δύνανται δὲ διαίρεcθαι εἰc ὕψοc at Σ N.3.143 might touch off a connection with sublimity-criticism, even if it was not written with such a connection in mind. Given Longinus' approbation of Pindar, it is not unrealistic to think that use of ὕψοc vocabulary in texts such as the ending of O.1 and in scholarly metatexts might prompt a reader to see such passages in a Longinian light, although both present problems for such a viewpoint. O.1.115 refers to Hiero's past and future achievements rather than to poetry, and the sublime resonance of the passage cannot be readily divorced from its encomiastic specificity and its moralizing implications, both of which take on additional meanings in the context of written editions.[104] Similarly, Σ N.3.143 gives us a picture of Pindar's fraught and 'suspicious' relationship with Bacchylides which, although not completely incompatible with Longinus' picture of poetic activity (we might see a connection here between the two feuding poets and the φιλοτιμοτάτουc ἀγωνιcτάc of 35.2), points the reader towards the concrete sociopolitical contexts of such competition in a way that Longinus does not. Ancient readers of Pindar would have been taken in different directions by their encounters with these bodies of critical literature.

In part, the distinction between critical treatises and the scholia can be explained by their aims: the small-scale grammatical, textual historical, and rhetorical exegeses found in the scholia aim at explicating the texts and allowing them to be used as models for composition, whereas the analyses of Dionysius and Longinus aim at a larger and more conceptually elaborated treatment of compositional issues.[105] Yet strong dichotomizing of the two approaches would

development of this critical emphasis. For ὕψοc used of Aeschylus cf. AP 7.411. The relation between critical treatises and scholia is complicated further by the possibility of the technical use of ὕψοc in the former being influenced in part by glosses in commentaries.

[104] Cf. Ch. 3, pp. 139–42, 164–5. It should be noted that there is no trace of a sublimity-inflected interpretation in Σ O.1.185 (i 56 Dr), which takes the line to refer simply to 'happiness' (τῷ μὲν ὑψοῦ τὴν εὐδαιμονίαν ἠνίξατο).

[105] On the relationship between the scholia and Dionysius see Bitto (2012) 436–8.

be misleading; there is clearly a certain amount of overlap between their goals and frames of references, and many readers would have used both types of text side by side. The potential for such texts to interact and inform each other is illustrated by *Σ O*.1.5g (i 20–1 Dr):

ἔθος δέ ἐcτι Πινδάρῳ, μὴ οἷc προοιμιάζεται cυγκριτικοῖc, τούτοιc τὰ cυγκρινόμενα εὐθέωc ἐπάγειν, ἀλλὰ μεταξύ τινα εἰκόνα ἀποδεικτικὴν τῆc βελτιότητοc παρεντιθέναι καὶ οὕτω τὴν cύγκρicιν ἐπιφέρειν. ποιεῖ δὲ τοῦτο θερμόc τιc ὢν καὶ πολύνουc περὶ τὰ νοήματα.

It is characteristic of Pindar, not to bring in the comparanda immediately with the elements of comparison which he uses in his prooemia, but to introduce between them an image demonstrative of excellence, and thereby to increase the force of the comparison.[106] He composes in this way because he is inspired and profound in his use of ideas.[107]

This is the only occasion in the scholia where πολύνουc is used, and the only use of θερμόc meaning 'inspired'.[108] The distinctiveness of the terminology, at least in relation to the rest of the scholia, has occasioned discussion; it has recently been argued that the vocabulary should be seen not as discourse about Pindar as an inspired poet, but as rhetorical in emphasis, and concerned with constructing the poet's character.[109] The vocabulary used to described Pindar occurs in other types of critical literature, but has no close parallels elsewhere in the scholia.[110] Readers could also have understood the evaluation variously against the background of their wider reading: Pindar being

---

[106] This translation follows that of *Scholies* p. 189, but οὕτω ... ἐπιφέρειν could simply mean 'only then does he add the comparison'.

[107] I have provisionally followed LSJ in my translation of πολύνουc; for further comment on the meaning of this phrase see n. 111.

[108] See *Scholies* pp. 253–4, contrasting θερμόc with the pejorative use of ψυχρόc in stylistic evaluation (cf. e.g. Arist. *Rhet.* 3.1405b–1406b; Demet. *On Style* 114–27). For θερμόc as drawing on the language of inspiration familiar from texts such as Plato's *Phaedrus* and Longinus see *Scholies* pp. 254–5.

[109] On the rhetorical language of the scholium and its parallels in the scholia to Homer and Eustathius *Proemium* cf. Bitto (2012) 380. For previous discussion cf. Wilson (1980) 103; Lefkowitz (1985) 275–6, 280–2.

[110] The generalizing nature of the scholium may in be part be due to the popularity of the passage on which it comments. The number and complexity of scholia on the passage suggest that pedagogic use was often made of it, and the analysis in *Σ O*.1.5g may have programmatic force in this respect, alerting readers (and students) to the kind of terms in which Pindar's rhetorical approach is commonly couched.

πολύνους περὶ τὰ νοήματα,[111] for example, could be taken as the rhetorical correlative of Longinian μεγαλοφροςύνη,[112] and the prooemial technique described as a concrete example of the modes of affectivity elaborated in that treatise.

We also need to recognize the importance of context in determining the effects that such discourses could have produced: the scholium would, for instance, have been understood differently by a schoolboy reading his first commentary on Pindar and by an experienced reader able to understand πολύνους περὶ τὰ νοήματα in relation

[111] *Scholies* p. 256 argues that the combination of θερμός and πολύνους acts as implicit rebuttal of the Platonic critique of inspiration: for the scholiast, 'Pindare a tout à la fois le feu de l'inspiration, et la claire conscience des moyens nécessaires pour le mettre en oeuvre.' On this reading, πολύνους 'implique l'art d'exprimer beaucoup de pensées, d'images, d'impressions ou de sentiment en peu de mots', for which notion they compare the opposition between πολύνοια and πολυλογία employed at Pl. *Lg.* 641e. There are objections to this reading, however. The notion of expressive brevity in rhetoric is a common one (cf. e.g. Gorg. *Palam.* 37, Arist. *Rhet.* 3 1407b–1408a, Dion.Hal, *Ad Amm.* II.2), but does not seem to have been employed by ancient Pindaric scholars. It is notable that the discussion of ἐς δὲ τὸ πᾶν ἑρμηνέων χατίζει at Σ *O*.2.153a-c (i 98 Dr) contains no reference to expressive brevity, and in fact stresses the opposite: Σ 153c, for instance, argues that the need for interpretation arises from Pindar's inability to express the entirety of the subject matter (αὐτὸς γὰρ οὐ δύναται διὰ τὸ πλῆθος ἐξειπεῖν πάντα), and sees Pindar's statement about interpreters as paralleling *Il.* 2.488. Nor need πολύνους alone have the implication of 'exprimer beaucoup en peu': cf. e.g. Democritus B 65 D-K. At Dio Cass. 52.41.1 the term is used in a context where the emphasis falls on multiplicity of thought and expression (ὁ δὲ δὴ Καῖσαρ ἀμφοτέρους μέν ςφας καὶ ἐπὶ τῇ πολυνοίᾳ καὶ ἐπὶ τῇ πολυλογίᾳ τῇ τε παρρηςίᾳ ἰςχυρῶς ἐπῄνεςε); this conception parallels Quintilian's *rerum uerborumque copia* (*Inst. Orat.* 10.9.1). Moreover, it is not clear that εἰκόνα ἀποδεικτικὴν τῆς βελτιότητος implies multiplicity of expression: the emphasis rather seems to be on the greatness and power of the image's expressive force. Contemporary critical discourse also suggests another way of understanding νοήματα: at Dion. Hal. *Ad Amm.* II.2, νοήματα is used to denote 'arrangement of thoughts [in a sentence]': καὶ ἐφ' ὧν ἐνθυμημάτων τε καὶ νοημάτων αἱ μεταξὺ παρεμπτώςεις πολλαὶ γινόμεναι διὰ μακροῦ τὴν ἀκολουθίαν κομίζονται ('in his enthymemes and sentences there are often parentheses which delay the conclusion considerably'). The statement refers to a structural phenomenon similar to that described by the scholium, αἱ μεταξὺ παρεμπτώςεις paralleling μεταξύ . . . παρεντιθέναι. It is possible, therefore, that τὰ νοήματα in Σ *O*.1.5g refers to Pindar's 'arrangements of thoughts in sentences' rather than to 'ideas' more generally. I would therefore suggest understanding πολύνους περὶ τὰ νοήματα in a sense that approximates Dionyius of Halicarnassus' account of Thucydides' πολυτροπία ('versatility', *Ad Amm.* II.3), namely as referring to the sophisticated versatility with which Pindar handles prooemia. The reader is meant to understand that the poet inserts different images according to the particular context (cf. *Scholies* p. 256 on Pindar's 'nombreuses manières d'exprimer . . . pensées').

[112] Pindar's facility with ideas and his μεγαλοπρεπεία are two of the elements in respect of which he is to be admired at Dion. Hal. *De imit.* 31.2.5.

to other discourses about Pindar's role as a cult figure, and the biographical tradition about his inspiration by the gods.[113] The contexts in which Pindar was read are as significant as who was doing the reading. Schools were especially important in this respect as environments of debate and discussion that affected both the form in which the scholia have come down to us, and how we should understand their cultural significance.[114] In addition to paraphrasing commentary being driven by educational needs, the antithetical framing of debates between scholars may also have been influenced by how teachers conveyed scholarly material to their students.[115] The educational context also has more general consequences: I shall argue in more detail below that the scholia's readings, especially where intertextual relations are concerned, often constituted interpretative starting points rather than fully-formed readings.[116] In schools, these intertextual juxtapositions would have been openings for discussion, while for individual readers they would have served as prompts to interpretative reflection.[117] Reading the scholia therefore entails being aware of how contexts of use and reading may have allowed for interpretative elaboration, and of their potential for interaction with other types of literary criticism.[118]

While scholars have often criticized the limitations of the scholia's rhetorical analyses,[119] the limitations of Dionysius' and Longinus' critical perspectives are particularly marked in relation to contextual issues. At *Dem.* 26, Dionysius cites Pindar fr. 121 S–M as part of an argument about Plato being more concerned with the manner of his expression rather than the content (πλείονι κέχρηται φιλοτιμίᾳ περὶ τὴν ἑρμηνείαν ὁ φιλόσοφος ἢ περὶ τὰ πράγματα, *Dem.* 25), picking up on his expression of the common topos that praise of noble deeds can lead to their immortalization. There is nothing inherently unusual

---

[113] See Ch. 2, pp. 97–100.

[114] For use of commentaries in schools see n. 51.

[115] Cf. e.g. the scholia to O.1.1, where a 'philosophical' interpretation of the poem's opening phrase, that Pindar is 'following' Thales, is given alongside a more pragmatic view (humans cannot live without water), and a reading that draws on a Homeric parallel (*Il.* 14.201).

[116] See Ch. 4.

[117] Although group discussion was also important: cf. Ch. 4, pp. 170–1.

[118] Muckensturm-Poulle (2009) 91 argues that the scholia's citational practices are primarily 'scientifique et pédagogique'; such an exegetical conclusion should not obscure their more general supplementary functions.

[119] e.g. Lefkowitz (1985).

about this idea, and therefore in order to make it striking, Plato is forced to express it in an unusual way, and Dionysius suggests that this was true of Pindar as well: 'Pindar composed this [fr. 121 S–M] . . . with more thought for melody and rhythm than for expression' (Πίνδαρος τοῦτο πεποίηκεν εἰς Ἀλέξανδρον τὸν Μακεδόνα, περὶ τὰ μέλη καὶ τοὺς ῥυθμοὺς μᾶλλον ἢ περὶ τὴν λέξιν ἐσπουδακώς).[120] Aside from the questionable retrojection of authorial intent, such an approach diminishes the possibility for sensitivity to contextual variation in the use of such topoi. While Dionysius' analysis of sonic structures implicitly draws attention to the specificities of the reading process understood as a production of sound, the wider interpretative issues which emerge from Pindaric texts' configurations of ethical challenges, and the interplay between contextual specificity and diachronic dissemination, are largely elided in this account. Our notion of the materiality of texts, whether conceived as a document or as a structure of sound, has to be balanced by awareness of the other interpretative frames and intertextual connections available to Hellenistic readers.

   In addition to their minimal interest in the interpretative questions often privileged by the scholia, Dionysius and Longinus are also notable for their lack of attention to the book as a medium, a tendency shared with most other ancient critics: both work within the conceptual economy of the text-type, thinking the text as a verbal entity freed from the conditions of its material instantiations, this despite their attention to the materiality of language itself. The book becomes in these critical practices the effaced other of the very strategies of close reading its preservative function enables. In what follows, however, I shall examine some aspects of Pindaric reception, and of books themselves, which bring the materiality of the document and the interpretative issues surrounding it into the foreground.

---

[120] Cf. Porter (2010) 310–11.

2

Passing on the Garland: Receptions and Material Sites

Whereas the previous chapter was concerned with modes of discourse addressed specifically at directing and influencing reading practices, this chapter will address a group of texts and cultural phenomena that bear a more indirect relation to the Pindaric corpus.[1] I shall begin by looking at how books are described in epigrams, and the implications of these representational strategies for how readers might conceptualize their own practice, before considering how Pindar is characterized in epigrams about the canonized lyric poets. As well as being significant in themselves, these receptions of Pindar's character and poetry are an important part of the cultural background by which readers would have been influenced, even if the nature of this influence is at times complicatedly diffuse. Indeed, the complexities of how these texts relate to their subject(s) will be my primary focus: the epigrams in particular will be seen to manifest, and to encourage in readers, a high level of self-consciousness about the processes by which authorial figures are mediated and their texts understood.

The biographical tradition represented by the *Lives* of Pindar, and aspects of his commemoration at Thebes and Delphi, are two other strains of Pindaric reception that are in many respects remote from the scholarly discourses explored above, a difference largely shaped

---

[1] My focus is restricted to Greek texts: for Roman receptions of Pindar see e.g. Rutherford (2012). Considerations of space preclude engagement with the much-debated subject of Horace's reworking of Pindaric themes and motifs: for an overview see e.g. Race (2012). For a useful catalogue of material relating to Pindaric reception in the Hellenistic and Imperial periods see Kimmel-Clauzet (2013) 353–67.

by the specificity of their generic and cultic parameters. Nevertheless, I shall argue these phenomena also contribute significantly to the notion of Pindar as an historical individual, a conception that in turn feeds back into how readers relate to his texts and his authorial persona.[2] The chapter concludes with an analysis of how critical signs were used in ancient books to provide visual articulations of textual structures. In anchoring the reading experience in the material here-and-now of the material document, critical signs have connections with epigrammatic representations of books, and with the scholia's conception of writing as a determining feature of literary activity.[3] Like these discourses, they can be understood as creating a dialogue between books and performance culture, as well as adding a distinctive element to the reading experience.

BOOKS IN EPIGRAMS

The epigrammatic corpus is a particularly rich source for how ancient poets conceptualized and represented their forebears, and forms an important part of the cultural field within which readers of the later Hellenistic and Imperial periods would have encountered Pindaric texts. A central element of the representation of previous poems and poetry in this corpus is the interaction between the language of performance and references to the book, often mobilized in order to highlight the contextual and aesthetic differences between ancient and modern realizations of texts. In contrast to the critical literature examined above, it will become clear that these poems prompt attention to the book as a specific site of meaning, as well as reimagining the literary past.[4]

This conjunction of performance lexis and references to the book goes back to the early Hellenistic period. At Posidippus 17.5–6 GP

---

[2] The distinction drawn by Bitto (2012) 397–408 between the rhetorical exegesis of Pindar in antiquity, represented chiefly by the scholia, and 'receptional' responses, the images of Pindar that we find in the *Lives* and epigrams, designed to project an image of the poet as connected with the divine and consequently detached from the imitative practices, is misleading, in that it discounts the potential for interaction between these different receptive fields as mediated by individual readers.

[3] See Introduction, pp. 9–10.

[4] Cf. in general the comments of Bing (1988) 89–90.

(= 122 AB), the narrator references Sappho's 'speaking pages' (Σαπφῷαι δὲ μένουσι φίλης ἔτι καὶ μενέουσιν / ᾠδῆς αἱ λευκαὶ φθεγγόμεναι cελίδες) in lines which figure the book as a conjunction of materiality and performance, with φθεγγόμεναι in conjunction with ᾠδῆς hinting both at the trace of the living voice of the poetess contained within the book and the act of reading the poems aloud.[5] The polyptoton μένουσι ... ἔτι καὶ μενέουσιν highlights the book's preservative function, and registers the interaction between text and material form; the cελίδες 'remain and will remain' because of the quality of the poetry they contain, but their physical stability is also a condition of the poetry's survival. Notable also is the stress on the book's appearance given by λευκαί, which again gives rise to a slippage between material form and the aesthetic value of the text, suggesting both the visual beauty of the newly inscribed papyrus and the way in which the loveliness of the poetry contributes to its visual manifestation. The 'pages' are subordinated to the 'song' (ᾠδῆς) by functioning as its receptacle, but their status as an object of attention in themselves is strengthened by the application of Σαπφῷαι to them, which creates a strong connection between the author and the documents that represent her. The figuration of Sappho's λευκαὶ φθεγγόμεναι cελίδες captures the duality of the book as an object transformed by inscription into a trace of performance culture and something whose material specificity is also of importance. Moreover, the lines' redescription of the book, centring on the transformation of the mutely material cελίδες into things capable of being 'voiced', is itself mimetic of how texts are subject to change in different contexts.

The interrelation of performance and textual materiality which occurs in Posidippus 17 is a common generic topos in later authors. One notable example is Simias' epigram on Sophocles (5 GP, 929–34 = *AP* 7.21):[6]

> τόν cε χοροῖc μέλψαντα Σοφοκλέα, παῖδα Σοφίλλου,
> τὸν τραγικῆc Μούcηc ἀcτέρα Κεκρόπιον,
> πολλάκιc ὃν θυμέληcι καὶ ἐν cκηνῆcι τεθηλὼc
> βλαιcὸc Ἀχαρνίτηc κιccὸc ἔρεψε κόμην,
> τύμβοc ἔχει καὶ γῆc ὀλίγον μέροc, ἀλλ' ὁ περιccὸc
> αἰὼν ἀθανάτοιc δέρκεται ἐν cελίcιν.

---

[5] On Posidippus' conception of art in general see Prioux (2007) 19–74.
[6] Cf. Acosta-Hughes and Barbantani (2007) 432–3; Kimmel-Clauzet (2013) 176–7.

Sophocles, son of Sophillus, you who sang with choruses, the Cecropian
star of the tragic Muse, whose hair the flourishing, twisted ivy of
Acharnae often crowned in the orchestra and on the stage, a tomb
holds you, and a little measure of earth, but the rest of time beholds you
in immortal pages.

Whereas 3–4 figure Sophocles as part of the performance culture of
classical Athens, the end of the poem highlights the book as a space
of meaning.[7] The meaning of the last clause is disputed: Paton
follows Ellis in taking δέρκεται as meaning 'shines forth', and translates 'thy exquisite life shines yet in your immortal pages'. Others
suggest taking the ϲε of the opening line as the object of δέρκεται and
translating ὁ περισσὸς αἰών as 'the ages after your death'.[8] Yet the
ambiguity may be intentional, figuring the double function of
reception and reading in both bestowing value on its subjects and
being exposed to their singular economy. Similar is *AP* 7.46, an
anonymous epigram on Euripides in which the value of the monument, and implicitly the poem itself, derives from Euripides' 'reputation': οὐ ϲὸν μνῆμα τόδ᾽ ἔϲτ᾽, Εὐριπίδη, ἀλλὰ ϲὺ τοῦδε· / τῇ ϲῇ γὰρ δόξῃ
μνῆμα τόδ᾽ ἀμπέχεται ('this is not your memorial, Euripides, but you
are its; for this memorial is clothed with your repute'). However the
final lines of Simias' epigram are construed, the poem as a whole can
be seen to articulate a contrast between the performance economy
and the material context in which contemporary readers are involved,
in a way not dissimilar to Dionysius' description of reading Demosthenes examined earlier.[9]

Another epigram that foregrounds the opposition of writing and
performance is Antipater of Sidon 14 GP (3414–21 = *AP* 7.26) on
Anacreon:[10]

ξεῖνε, τάφον παρὰ λιτὸν Ἀνακρείοντος ἀμείβων,
  εἴ τί τοι ἐκ βίβλων ἦλθεν ἐμῶν ὄφελος,
ϲπεῖϲον ἐμῇ ϲποδιῇ, ϲπεῖϲον γάνος, ὄφρα κεν οἴνῳ
  ὀϲτέα γηθήϲῃ τἀμὰ νοτιζόμενα,
ὡς ὁ Διωνύϲου μεμελημένος εὐάϲι κώμοις,

[7] Contrast the different focus of *AP* 7.22, which focuses exclusively on Sophocles
as a performance poet.
[8] See e.g. Bing (1988) 59.
[9] Ch. 1, pp. 72–3 Cf. Kimmel-Clauzet (2013) 177–8.
[10] On representations of Anacreon in epigram cf. Rosenmeyer (1992) 24–7;
Acosta-Hughes and Barbantani (2007) 442–5.

ὡς ὁ φιλακρήτου cύντροφος ἁρμονίης
μηδὲ καταφθίμενος Βάκχου δίχα τοῦτον ὑποίcω
τὸν γενεῇ μερόπων χῶρον ὀφειλόμενον.

Stranger, passing Anacreon's simple tomb, if any benefit ever came to you from my books, pour an offering on my ashes, pour the glittering liquid, so that my bones may feel joy refreshed with wine, so that I who sang in Dionysus' well-voiced revels, I who was at home with wine-loving music, might not endure without Bacchus, even in death, the land which is owed to all the generations of men.

While the poem's opening line draws on the conventions of funerary epigram in addressing a passing stranger, the second sites the contemporary reader in relation to books (εἴ τί τοι ἐκ βίβλων ἦλθεν ἐμῶν ὄφελος), in contrast to Anacreon's status as a performer, strongly marked by repeated use of performance lexis (μεμελημένος εὐάcι κώμοις... cύντροφος ἁρμονίης).[11] This contrast again differentiates between present and past, but also shapes the imaginative response of the reader to Anacreon's poetry.[12] By remarking on the book's mediatory role, the poem encourages the reader to see Anacreon's books as a space of transformation which both allows for an imaginative engagement with the past and is also itself affected by that engagement.

Epigrams also participated more concretely in the processes of textual dissemination, as in the case of *AP* 9.186 by Antipater of Thessalonica, which was apparently written as an epigraph for an edition of Aristophanes:[13]

βίβλοι Ἀριστοφάνευς, θεῖος πόνος, αἷcιν Ἀχαρνεὺς
κιccὸς ἐπὶ χλοερὴν πουλὺς ἔcειcε κόμην·
ἠνίδ' ὅσον Διόνυcον ἔχει cελίς, οἷα δὲ μῦθοι

---

[11] Cf. *AP* 7.27 for Anacreon's revels in the underworld, and cf. 7.29, 30.

[12] This is not to say that such a response, seeing Anacreon as a particular type of performance poet concerned with wine and love, would not have occurred to readers independently, or as a result of reading critical literature, where such an assessement was common: cf. e.g. Cic. *Tusc.* 4.33.71. The poem does point the reader towards reading Anacreon with a particular conception of his poetry in mind, and given that much of Anacreon's poetry cannot be reduced to the stereotype of the drunken sympotic poet, the epigram can be seen as a deformational reading, but one which nevertheless leaves open the nature of the ὄφελος that might come from his poetry. On the artistic reception of Anacreon see Rosenmeyer (1992) 12–49.

[13] Although it would also have had resituational functions similar to those analysed here as a free-standing poem.

ἠχεῦcιν φοβερῶν πληθόμενοι χαρίτων.
ὦ καὶ θυμὸν ἄριcτε καὶ Ἑλλάδος ἤθεcιν ἶcε,
κωμικέ, καὶ cτύξαc ἄξια καὶ γελάcαc.

Books of Aristophanes, divine labour, on which the profuse ivy of
Acharnae shook its green locks. Look how much of Dionysus this
page contains, and how the stories sound out, filled with awesome
graces. O comic poet, best in heart and equal to the characters of Greece,
you hated and laughed at what deserved such treatment.

At 3–4 the book(s) are transformed by the cultural and performance
heritage whose traces they bear (1–2); as in the Posidippus passage
analysed above, the book's archival capacities are at issue (ἠνίδ' ὅcον
Διόνυcον ἔχει cελίc), and a contrast emerges between the grandilo-
quently synecdochic use of Διόνυcον to connote drama, as well as
dramatic effects and inspiration,[14] and the relative simplicity of the
documentary medium. The description of the 'stories' (οἷα δὲ μῦθοι /
ἠχεῦcιν φοβερῶν πληθόμενοι χαρίτων) references the specifically sonic
qualities of performance, but the double meaning of ἠχεῦcιν as
'sound' and 'echo' brings into play the idea of the μῦθοι in documentary form as an 'echo' of performance, as well as hinting at the role
of books in various kinds of reperformances of the plays.[15] If the
poem was used as an epigraph to an edition, this dynamic would
be strengthened by the role of the poem itself as positioning the texts
as part of a specific material form.

Moreover, the poem also plays on the continuity between epigraphic function and the materiality of the document; the phrasing
of ἠνίδ' ὅcον Διόνυcον ἔχει cελίc references the book's status as containing (ἔχει) its texts, but the poem itself, in marking the beginning
of the edition and directing the reader's attention in a particular way,
also participates in this containment. *AP* 9.188, an anonymous epigram on Plato, also dramatizes the conjunction of book and performance, although here the latter element is less marked, perhaps
reflecting the lesser generic importance of performance to the Platonic corpus: Ἀτθίδος εὐγλώccου cτόμα φέρτατον, οὗ cέο μεῖζον /

---

[14] Gow and Page (1968) 101–2 suggest 'dramatic inspiration' as the primary
meaning of Διόνυcον, but note that 'wine as the source of that inspiration need not
be excluded'. I would suggest that the vagueness of the synecdoche should be
preserved to give as wide a referential field as possible, particularly in view of the
multifaceted focus of the final line.
[15] On the metaliterary dynamics of Echo see Ch. 5, pp. 217–35.

φθέγμα Πανελλήνων πᾶϲα κέκευθε ϲελίϲ ('best voice of fair-speaking Attic, the whole page of all the Greeks hides no greater voice than yours', 1–2). Here as elsewhere, ϲελίϲ is used as a synecdoche for books in general, and the document is made to contain Plato's voice (ϲτόμα, φθέγμα) in terms not dissimilar from those we have seen deployed in relation to poets. The use of κέκευθε is also significant for the relationship between the book and its contents; the verb used in the perfect means 'contains',[16] playing on the archival dynamic common to the conceptualization of the book, but given the contrast between the document and a live reading, the verb's primary meaning of 'hides' is probably also to be felt, and imputes a double meaning to φθέγμα as both the unique, originary voice of the author himself and the voice of the reader who revivifies the text. The book both contains and hides Plato's φθέγμα, marking the disappearance of the author's voice, but also representing the text it contains as a material substrate (φθέγμα) open to recreation.

Several conclusions emerge. One is that epigrammatists were keenly aware of and interested in the materiality of the book, and in the process of relating to and reimagining past poetry through this medium. All of the above poems can, in different ways, be read as dramatizing the negotiations between material form and performance, understood as both the live events that took place in the past and the representation of performance within classical and archaic poetry. A correlative of the rhetorical strategies deployed in these epigrams is a readerly awareness of the negotiations just mentioned; unlike the critical literature examined above, the epigrams encourage attention to the book itself as a significant object. Although Pindar is not mentioned in relation to books in any of the extant epigrams, the figurations of the book in the poems just analysed would have been relevant to how readers of the period approached Pindaric texts, in that they would have played a role in constituting the broader cultural field by which such approaches would have been mediated.[17]

---

[16] Cf. LSJ s.v. a; NB. particularly Eur. *IA* 122 for its use of a book. Cf. also *AP* 9.192.1, where containment is more prominent. The phrase also draws on the epigrammatic topos of dust covering the deceased, as at *AP* 7.433 (Simonides 47 GP, 270–1): ἀντὶ δ' ἀκοντοδόκων ἀνδρῶν μνημεῖα θανόντων / ἄψυχ' ἐμψύχων ἅδε κέκευθε κόνις. The phrase as a whole suggests an equation between book and tomb, but the substitution of ϲελίϲ for κόνιϲ dramatizes the difference between them: the act of intertextual rewriting itself enacts the reconfigurative force of the book.

[17] The scholia's conceptualization of writing is also relevant to this process of mediation: see Introduction, pp. 9–10.

Nonetheless, we also need to be aware of the particular ways in which Pindar is represented in this corpus.

OTOBIOGRAPHIES: PINDAR'S EAR

When we come to epigrams specifically about Pindar,[18] we find that they focus on his relationship with the divine and his status as an ideal citizen, an aspect central to Leonidas 99 GP (2556–7 = *AP* 7.35): ἄρμενος ἦν ξείνοισιν ἀνὴρ ὅδε καὶ φίλος ἀςτοῖς, / Πίνδαρος, εὐφώνων Πιερίδων πρόπολος ('gracious to guests/strangers was this man and friendly/dear to his townsmen, Pindar, a servant of the fair-voiced Muses').[19] A funerary epigram by Antipater of Sidon 18 GP (3444–7 = *AP* 7.34) focuses more on the stylistic aspects of his poetry:

> Πιερικὰν cάλπιγγα, τὸν εὐαγέων βαρὺν ὕμνων
> χαλκευτάν, κατέχει Πίνδαρον ἅδε κόνις,
> οὗ μέλος εἰcαΐων φθέγξαιό κεν, ὡς ἀπὸ Μουcῶν
> ἐν Κάδμου θαλάμοιc cμῆνος ἀπεπλάcατο.

This dust holds Pindar, the Pierian trumpet, the heavily-smiting smith of well made hymns. If you were to hear his song you would say that a swarm of bees from the Muses fashioned it in Cadmus' bridal chambers.

The epigram's descriptive rhetoric plays on images from the Pindaric corpus:[20] the characterization of Pindar as a 'smith' (χαλκευτάν) recalls *P.*1.86 and *P.*3.113, while the image of the swarm of bees expands on Pindar's famous description of his own poetry as like a bee at *P.*10.53–4 (ἐγκωμίων γὰρ ἄωτος ὕμνων / ἐπ᾿ ἄλλοτ᾿ ἄλλον ὥτε

---

[18] For an overview of Pindar's representation in epigrams see Barbantani (1993) 14–28. Acosta-Hughes and Barbantani (2007) 435–8. Cf. Bergemann (1991) on the representation of Pindar in sculpture, which constructs a highly conservative image: '[d]as Bildnis zeigte den Dichter demnach als einen älteren Mann mit Denkerstirn und in dezidiert konservativem Habitus. Der Eindruck den die Barttracht Pindars bei den Zeitgenossen des Porträts hervorrufen müsste, war der eines altertümlichen, ja geradezu aristokratiken Wohlstandes' (p. 182).

[19] On this epigram see Barbantani (1993) 15–18, and below, Ch. 5, pp. 285–6. Kimmel-Clauzet (2013) 179–80 stresses the connection developed in the epigram between poet and locality. There is a parallel between the rhetoric here and the kind of eulogistic pairs Pindar himself employs in passages such as *O.*7.9, *O.*13.2, and *P.*3.71.

[20] Cf. Acosta-Hughes and Barbantani (2007) 436–7; Kimmel-Clauzet (2013) 182–3. Similar figurations are at work in Antipater of Thessalonica 75 GP (= *AP* 16.305), for which see Acosta-Hughes and Barbantani (2007) 437.

μέλιcca θύνει λόγον). Antipater's metaphor pluralizes the Pindaric model, and the odd conjunction of ἀπὸ Μουcῶν ... cμῆνοc, with no intervening information about how they are related, creates a sense of the miraculousness of the Pindaric μέλοc.[21] This sense is heightened by the cross-graining of the city and the natural world in ἐν Κάδμου θαλάμοιc cμῆνοc, in which Pindar's μέλοc is made to seem like a strange, if beautiful, irruption of one discursive order into another. Although the epigram does not dwell on the materiality of the book, a similar separation of present and past to those explored above is at work in οὗ μέλοc εἰcαΐων φθέγξαιό κεν, where the conditional optative puts the μέλοc doubly at issue, figuring it both as a unique and irrecoverable musico-poetic event of the distant past, and as an idealized form of the Pindaric poetic idiom open to partial recreation by individual voiced readings. This turns the emphasis towards the construction of Pindar's μέλοc in the epigram's semantic medium, which is presented as a means of reimagining the lost past of performance.

Pindar also appears in two anonymous epigrams which present catalogues of the nine canonized lyric poets. Both poems present miniaturized versions of the critical and archival culture which produced the canon, employing accepted critical judgements and forming an analogy between their own catalogic mapping and the wider archival processes upon which canonization depended. This strategy is signalled in *AP* 9.184 by the end of the poem coinciding with an enunciation of the 'limit' marked out by the lyric poets themselves (πέραc ἐcτάcατε); the poem participates in this delimitation by restating the poets' canonized status.[22] Pindar is mentioned first in both poems, befitting his status as the pre-eminent representative of lyric poetry (*AP* 9.184):

> Πίνδαρε, Μουcάων ἱερὸν cτόμα, καὶ λάλε Σειρὴν
> Βακχυλίδη Σαπφοῦc τ' Αἰολίδεc χάριτεc

---

[21] D'Alessio (2005) 122–3 points out that the epigram may refer to the song of the Muses at Cadmus' wedding, which he argues formed part of Pindar's first *Hymn*: on this reading, the final two lines of the epigram would be referring to Pindar's 'reproduction' (ἀπεπλάcατο) of the Muses' song in the *Hymn*. The image also picks up on the story of the bee settling on Pindar's mouth in the *Lives* (below, p. 98).

[22] The interaction of song/performance culture and book/reading culture is again at issue: the position of πέραc ἐcτάcατε draws attention to its specifically material mode of closure, marking the physical 'limit' of the poem, a meaning that contrasts with the (figurative) πέραc articulated by the canonized poets in performance.

γράμμα τ᾽ Ἀνακρείοντος, Ὁμηρικὸν ὅς τ᾽ ἀπὸ ῥεῦμα
ἔσπασας οἰκείοις, Στησίχορ᾽, ἐν καμάτοις,
ἥ τε Σιμωνίδεω γλυκερὴ σελὶς ἡδύ τε Πειθοῦς
Ἴβυκε καὶ παίδων ἄνθος ἀμησάμενε
καὶ ξίφος Ἀλκαίοιο, τὸ πολλάκις αἷμα τυράννων
ἔσπεισεν πάτρης θέσμια ῥυόμενον,
θηλυμελεῖς τ᾽ Ἀλκμᾶνος ἀηδόνες, ἵλατε, πάσης
ἀρχὴν οἳ λυρικῆς καὶ πέρας ἐστάσατε.

Pindar, holy mouth of the Muses, and garrulous Siren Bacchylides, and
the Aeolian graces of Sappho, and script of Anacreon, and Stesichorus,
you who drew the Homeric stream into your native labours; sweet page
of Simonides, and you Ibycus, who culled the sweet flowers of persuasion and love of boys, Alcaeus' sword, which often spilled the blood of
tyrants in defending the ordinances of his country, and Alcman's
nightingales which sing of young women, be kindly, you who set
down the beginning and the limit of lyric song.

As with the epigrams analysed above, this piece is notable for its
conjunction of different types of poetological diction. The opening
opposition of Pindar and Bacchylides employs evaluative and stylistic
terms (ἱερὸν στόμα and λάλε Σειρήν) which both reference the performance economy,[23] but Anacreon and Simonides are both
described in terms of the materiality of the book (γράμμα, γλυκερὴ
σελίς). These may reflect a stylistic appreciation through the language
of materiality, figuring them as more 'writerly', and equating this with
their well-known stylistic clarity and polish.

AP 9.571 is shorter, and less descriptive and accomplished, but
ends with a climactic stress on Sappho as the tenth Muse:

ἔκλαγεν ἐκ Θηβῶν μέγα Πίνδαρος· ἔπνεε τερπνὰ
ἡδυμελεῖ φθόγγῳ μοῦσα Σιμωνίδεω·
λάμπει Στησίχορός τε καὶ Ἴβυκος· ἦν γλυκὺς Ἀλκμάν·
λαρὰ δ᾽ ἀπὸ στομάτων φθέγξατο Βακχυλίδης·
Πειθὼ Ἀνακρείοντι συνέσπετο· ποικίλα δ᾽ αὐδᾷ
Ἀλκαῖος, κύκνος Λέσβιος, Αἰολίδι.
ἀνδρῶν δ᾽ οὐκ ἐνάτη Σαπφὼ πέλεν, ἀλλ᾽ ἐρατειναῖς
ἐν Μούσαις δεκάτη Μοῦσα καταγράφεται.

---

[23] For ἱερὸν στόμα cf. *AP* 7.75.1. Cf. also Barbantani (1993) 9 on the phrase's
religious connotations. On the 'Pindaric' epigrams in general see *Scholies* pp. 161–4.

Pindar cried out loudly from Thebes; joyously breathed Simonides' muse with sweetly melodious voice. Stesichorus and Ibycus shine out; Alcman was sweet; Bacchylides' lips spoke softly; persuasion attended Anacreon; Alcaeus, the Lesbian swan, uttered varied songs in the Aeolian mode. Sappho was not the ninth of men, but is counted as the tenth among the lovely Muses.

Again, the poem constructs a critical opposition between Pindar and Bacchylides, with the Pindaric sublime being contrasted with Bacchylides' lighter style. In *AP* 9.571 in particular, the exorbitance of Pindar's 'cry' (ἔκλαγεν ... μέγα) contrasts with both the material form and the catalogic containment to which 'Pindar' is subject.

All three poems subject Pindar to a form of cultural translation which emphasizes his elevated status, but also his cultural otherness. The poems insistently deploy the proper name Πίνδαρος with its literary–historical weight, and Antipater of Sidon's epigram focuses on the human life (and death) behind the name (κατέχει Πίνδαρον ἅδε κόνις). However, 'Pindar' is also represented with metaphors that reduce the historical figure to a poetic function (πιερικὰν cάλπιγγα, ἱερὸν cτόμα), a process that indirectly replays the conventionalized self-figurations of the epinicians, which likewise erase the actuality of the individual in order to project an authorial persona. Even at *AP* 9.571.1, where Pindar himself is made to 'cry out', the construction of the authorial figure is complex. The use of ἔκλαγεν plays on the verb's occurrences in the Pindaric corpus: it is used at *Pa.* 8a.10 (= fr. 52iA S–M) of mantic utterance, and at *P.*4.22–3 of Zeus' thunder.[24] The phrasing of ἔκλαγεν ἐκ Θηβῶν μέγα Πίνδαρος redirects Pindaric idiom, making a comparatively rare Pindaric usage into a synecdoche of his whole corpus and figuring 'Pindar' as the source of an utterance that verges on the superhuman.[25] The intertextual

---

[24] Cf. also fr. 169a.34 S–M: πικρο[τά]τạν κλάγεν ἀγγε[λία]ν.

[25] This sense is reinforced by other uses of κλάζω, which usually denotes sounds made by animals, objects, or inanimate forces: cf. LSJ *s.v.* 1–3. Its uses of human utterance tend to involve emotive situations; cf. e.g. Hom. *Il.* 2.222; Aesch. *Ag.*48. There is an important conflict between this mode of representation and the tradition that Pindar was 'weak-voiced' as recorded by Σ *O.*6.148a, which explains his sending of Aeneas as χοροδιδάcκαλοc with the datum that Pindar could not sing properly. This notice is best interpreted as a means of explaining the particular detail of the narrator's calling on Aeneas, and is historically implausible: Pindar was clearly an accomplished musical composer and would have been highly trained in the musical techniques of his day, even if he did not 'sing' in the sense of performing his poems himself. Related, and perhaps dependent, is an apophthegm attributed to Pindar (i 4 Dr): ἐρωτηθεὶς πάλιν ὑπό τινος διὰ τί μέλη γράφων ᾄδειν οὐκ ἐπίcταται, εἶπε· καὶ

situation of ἔκλαγεν grounds the critical articulation in Pindar's texts, but also entails relation to Pindaric language that is both deformational (κλάζω is never used by Pindar of authorial utterance) and aggregative, as the force of the Pindaric uses of the verb carries over into the present passage. This double relation lexically enacts the two-way dynamics of the receptive process.

The authorial figuration of ἔκλαγεν ἐκ Θηβῶν μέγα Πίνδαρος is typical of the process by which 'Pindar' is presented in these epigrams as a figure of otherness at a distant cultural and temporal remove from the present day, but also a figure with whom a certain cultural continuity can be achieved by means of various types of literary and scholarly appropriations.[26] Thus in the two catalogues cited, the descriptions of 'Pindar' mark him off, to a degree, from the other authors as a more difficult, less approachable figure, and we have seen how Antipater of Sidon 18 GP dramatizes the otherness of its subject. And yet the very process of writing (and reading) these epigrams is an act of cultural translation which makes its subject(s) available, which rehearses the cultural appropriations to which the authors have been exposed, and marks the extent of their inclusion within the Hellenic cultural tradition and their status as sources of cultural authority.[27] The othering of 'Pindar' that takes place in these epigrams is in part a response to the particular demands of the Pindaric corpus,[28] but it is also the creation of *virtualized* otherness which metaphorizes (the) Pindaric textual encounter(s).[29]

γὰρ οἱ ναυπηγοὶ πηδάλια κατασκευάζοντες κυβερνᾶν οὐκ ἐπίστανται ('on another occasion he was asked by someone why, as someone who wrote lyric poems, he did not know how too sing, and he replied 'Just as shipbuilders who make rudders do not know how to steer'). This is probably a post-classical text; the division between song (μέλη) and written composition (γράφων) reflects the post-classical conception of writing as central to the creative process. For comments on the apophthegm see *Scholies* pp. 122–9.

[26] This recapitulates a dynamic at work in some of Pindar's representations of poetic practice: see especially Ch. 6, pp. 255–63 on the role of music in *P*.12.

[27] A similar dynamic may be detected in Hor. *C*.4.2, for which cf. e.g. Harrison (1995).

[28] These should not be underestimated: linguistically Pindar would have been a challenging read, particularly for non-native speakers. Hor. *C*.4.2.10–12 (*seu per audacis nova dithyrambos / verba devolvit numerisque fertur / lege solutis*) and Stat. *Sil.* 5.3.151–2 (*qua lege recurrat / Pindaricae uox flexa lyrae*) attest to the metrical as well as verbal difficulties he posed.

[29] Cf. Porter (2001) 64 n. 4, who emphasizes the self-effacement of authors such as Longinus and Pausanias in their constructions of the past: they are constituted as

This dynamic of othering and appropriation is also at work in the
Lives and in the biographical accounts in authors such as Pausanias,
which likewise emphasize his qualities as a citizen and his close
relations with the divine. Similarly, the *Lives* in the Byzantine manuscripts are ultimately dependent on biographies by scholars such as
Chamaeleon and Istrus,[30] and this biographical tradition, like the
epigrams, formed an important part of the metatextual economy
which would have affected ancient readers' approaches to the
Pindaric corpus. Although it is likely that the biographies on which
this account is based were longer and somewhat more detailed than
the extant *Lives*,[31] they are unlikely to have contained much more
'factual' information, and we can still get a sense of the kind of
narratives with which readers in Hellenistic and Imperial periods
would have been confronted. Scholarship on biographies of the
ancient poets has tended to focus, rightly, on their fictional elements,
and on the various insights they can provide into how the poets were
understood in particular contexts.[32] Here, however, I want to examine the image of Pindar which emerges from biographical accounts
and cult practices,and the potential effects of these for orientating
readers in relation to his poetry.

Particularly important in this respect is the account of the *Dichterweihe* which follows the account of Pindar's genealogy (i 1 Dr):[33]

παῖς δὲ ὢν ὁ Πίνδαρος, ὡς Χαμαιλέων καὶ Ἴστρος φασί, περὶ τὸν Ἑλικῶνα
θηρῶντα αὐτὸν ὑπὸ πολλοῦ καμάτου εἰς ὕπνον κατενεχθῆναι, κοιμωμένου
δὲ αὐτοῦ μέλισσαν τῷ στόματι προσκαθίσασαν κηρία ποιῆσαι. οἱ δέ φασιν

viewers, for Porter, by what they behold: 'the monumental gaze...is...a gaze *of*
(i.e., *possessed by*) *the Other*'. I would stress, however, that this otherness is to an
extent a textual (re)production, and this is more markedly the case in the epigrams
under examination here.

[30] The latter a pupil of Callimachus, active in the mid-third century: see Jackson
(2000); *Scholies* p. 73.

[31] Pausanias' account of Demeter's appearance to Pindar (9.23.3–4) is considerably
longer and more detailed than that found in the *Vita Thomana*, and includes the
episode, not reported in the *Life*, of Pindar's posthumous appearance to an old woman
in a dream, and his recitation therein of his song for Demeter. It is likely that
Pausanias was drawing on earlier versions of the *Lives* for this narrative. Similarly,
the *Vita Thomana*'s account of Pindar setting up cult statues outside his house is a
much shortened version of the narrative found at *FGrH* 383 F 13 (= Σ *P*.3.137b,
iii 80–1 Dr).

[32] For the former mode of criticism cf. e.g. Fairweather (1974); Lefkowitz (1981);
and from a different perspective Kivilo (2010). For the latter, Graziosi (2002).

[33] On the topos in general cf. Kambylis (1965), *Scholies* pp. 96–7.

ὅτι ὄναρ εἶδεν ὡc μέλιτος καὶ κηροῦ πλῆρεc εἶναι αὐτοῦ τὸ cτόμα, καὶ ἐπὶ ποιητικὴν ἐτράπη.

According to Chamaeleon and Istrus, Pindar, when he was a child went hunting on Helicon and lay down to sleep, worn out by his exertions. While he was sleeping a bee landed on his mouth and made wax. Others say that he saw a dream vision in which his mouth was full of honey and wax, and he took up the path of poetry.

Unlike the narrative at Paus. 9.23.2 which sets the event at Thespiae, the *Life*'s siting of the *Dichterweihe* on Helicon recalls the famous passage in Hesiod's *Theogony* where the poet describes his encounter with the Muses. But whereas Hesiod was 'tending his sheep on holy Helicon' (ἄρναc ποιμαίνονθ' Ἑλικῶνοc ὕπο ζαθέοιο, Hes. *Th.* 23), Pindar is engaging in the aristocratic pursuit of hunting (θηρῶντα), and the language of 'toil' (ὑπὸ πολλοῦ καμάτου) can be read as reflecting, and being made proleptic of, the importance given in the epinicians to various types of labour and effort as prerequisites of athletic success.[34] The Muses' appearance and conversation with Hesiod is replaced by a purely symbolic event, which combines 'realistic' and 'mythical' elements by making the vision experienced by the poet (μέλιτοc καὶ κηροῦ πλῆρεc εἶναι αὐτοῦ τὸ cτόμα) an expansion of the real-world event of the bee settling on his mouth.[35] Pindar's poetic career is thus rooted in an event which straddles the quotidian and the symbolic, and dramatizes Pindar's intuitive relation to his world by making the decision to compose poetry immediately follow the dream experience.

The *Lives* register a similar dynamic of distancing and cultural continuity in their accounts of specific events in Pindar's life and of his continued historical significance. The *Vita Ambrosiana*'s accounts of Pan singing one of Pindar's paeans, and Pindar writing a song for him in recompense, and of Demeter's complaint to the poet leading to him composing a poem for her, both accentuate Pindar's semi-supernatural contact with the divine in a similar fashion to the *Dichterweihe*; Demeter's appearance in a dream (ἡ Δημήτηρ ὄναρ ἐπιcτᾶcα αὐτῷ ἐμέμψατο, 'Demeter stood by him in a dream and reproved him') recalls the significance of the dream vision.[36] The

---

[34] N.7.74, of athletic success: εἰ πόνοc ἦν, τὸ τερπνὸν πλέον πεδέρχεται.

[35] See *Scholies* pp. 74–5 for the connections between the episode and Pindar's own poetry, especially *P*.10.53–4.

[36] On Demeter and Pindar see *Scholies* pp. 87–90, emphasizing the poet's 'relation avec une prophétie divine'.

stories about the Spartans and Alexander the Great sparing Pindar's
house during their respective sacks of Thebes serve to index Pindar's
diachronic importance, as does the anecdote, also reported by
Pausanias, of Pindar's memorialization and cultic honours at Delphi
(*Vita Thomana* = i 5 Dr):

ἐτιμήθη δὲ cφόδρα ὑπὸ πάντων τῶν Ἑλλήνων διὰ τὸ ὑπὸ τοῦ Ἀπόλλωνος
φιλεῖcθαι οὕτως, ὡc καὶ μερίδα λαμβάνειν ἀπὸ τῶν προcφερομένων τῷ
θεῷ, καὶ τὸν ἱερέα βοᾶν ἐν ταῖc θυcίαιc· Πίνδαρον ἐπὶ τὸ δεῖπνον τοῦ θεοῦ.

He was so greatly honoured by all the Greeks on account of Apollo's
affection for him that he is given his share of the offerings brought to
the god, and the priest cries out during the sacrifice, 'Pindar comes to
the god's repast.'

This account and the practice it describes site Pindar within ongoing
Greek customs and draw attention to his privileged status within
them.[37] Pausanias adds another detail of Pindar's position at
Delphi, describing the dedication of 'Pindar's chair' in the temple of
Apollo:[38]

ἀνάκειται δὲ οὐ πόρρω τῆc ἑcτίαc θρόνοc Πινδάρου· cιδήρου μέν ἐcτιν ὁ
θρόνοc, ἐπὶ δὲ αὐτῷ φαcιν, ὁπότε ἀφίκοιτο ἐc Δελφούc, καθέζεcθαί τε τὸν
Πίνδαρον καὶ ᾄδειν ὁπόcα τῶν ᾀcμάτων ἐc Ἀπόλλωνά ἐcτιν.

Pindar's chair has been dedicated not far from the hearth. The chair is
made of iron, and they say that whenever he came to Delphi Pindar
would sit on it and sing whatever songs he had for Apollo.

These cult honours are paralleled at Thebes; Paus. 9.23.2 describes
Pindar's intramural burial in the stadium at Thebes, next to Iolaus'
heroon and gymnasium.[39] The cultic practices surrounding Pindar
and the biographical accounts have in common a relative absence of
focus on the specifics of Pindar's individual personality, knowledge of

[37] The ceremony is also likely to reflect a self-conscious notion of display, designed
in part to be recognized as an cultural enactment by its spectators. This is certainly
true of Pausanias' account: see Elsner (2001) 18–20. On the ritual aspect of the
ceremony see Kimmel-Clauzet (2013) 239–41.
[38] Paus. 10.24.5. On Pindar's cultic honours in general see Clay (2004) 76–7, 147–9;
Currie (2005) 147 n. 159, 302; Kimmel-Clauzet (2013) 230–41. NB Clay (2004) 77–8 for
artistic representations of Pindar. See also Rutherford (2012) 93 for Pindar as a cultural
icon, and 98–100 on Pindar cited as an authority on religious practices by Second
Sophistic authors. On Pindar at Delphi see *Scholies* pp. 112–13.
[39] See Clay (2004) 77; Kimmel-Clauzet (2013) 238. For Pausanias as a guide to
particular types of viewing practice cf. Elsner (2007) 1–20.

which doubtless did not long outlast his lifetime, and a corresponding idealization of him as a semi-divine figure.[40]

The generic variety of the representations I have examined, epigrams, biographies, and cult honours, alert us to the different ways in which the image(s) of Pindar were constructed and purveyed, and their correspondingly different demands on readers. The relations between these representations and readers' encounters with Pindar's texts themselves would have been correspondingly diverse, something which cultic honours exemplify particularly clearly. Going to Delphi and hearing the priest announce Πίνδαρον ἐπὶ τὸ δεῖπνον τοῦ θεοῦ and seeing Pindar's chair would have put the 'reader' into an intimate contact with traces of Pindar's cultural heritage, but at the same time the very concreteness of the chair and the priest's announcement is likely to have induced a sense of the absence of the poet himself and the distance between the present and the past. While these practices, and the textual accounts of them, serve to enact and sustain Pindar's cultural valuation, they also give rise to experiences which are in many ways remote from the practice of reading Pindaric texts. These memorializations and the stories told about them gesture to, and partially preserve, albeit in stylized form, the circumstances of Pindar's own time, requiring the individual 'reader' to reimagine the past, and imposing an awareness of that past's alterity in the act of commemorating it.

Pausanias' and the *Lives*' localizing accounts of Pindar can also be seen in the light of the wider dynamic between local and Panhellenic identities: although this interaction is represented as happening during the classical period, it may well have resonated strongly with later readers, given, for instance, the cultural importance of the negotiation between individual cities and Panhellenic notions of Greek identity, and of Greek relations with the Roman empire.[41]

---

[40] There is also tantalizing evidence for cultic activity connected to Pindar in Egypt: a statue of Pindar dating to the Hellenistic period was discovered in the Serapeion at Memphis, which may well have been connected either with cultic activity or the performance of Pindar's poetry: cf. Picard (1952), who emphasizes that the statue represents Pindar as an inspired poet, inclining his eyes to the heavens (pp. 10–13); see also Kimmel-Clauzet (2013) 237. For the report of Pindar sending a hymn to the temple of Zeus Ammon, which was later inscribed on a stele by Ptolemy Soter, cf. Paus. 9.16.1. See *Scholies* pp. 97–9 for discussion.

[41] Cf. Elsner (1992); (1994); Alcock, Cherry, and Elsner (2001); Hutton (2005) for Pausanias' role in the articulation of Greek cultural idenity, and on Pausanias' localism cf. Whitmarsh (2010) 1–3; Goldhill (2010) 57–68. Theban medism during

Pindar is a Panhellenic figure (ἐτιμήθη δὲ cφόδρα ὑπὸ πάντων τῶν Ἑλλήνων) but his cultural endurance is also connected to experiences and practices sited in and informed by particular locations. Such issues are particularly important in the *Lives*' anecdotes about the sparing of Pindar's house.[42] Both record that the Spartans' decision not to burn Pindar's house, and in the case of the *Vita Thomana* Alexander's decision as well,[43] was prompted by an injunction written on the building (Πινδάρου τοῦ μουcοποιοῦ τὴν cτέγην μὴ καίετε, 'do not burn the house of Pindar the lyric poet') the writing of which is described slightly differently by the two *Lives*: ἐπέγραψέ τιc τῇ οἰκίᾳ, 'someone wrote on the house',[44] *VA* (i 2 Dr); ἐπιγε-γραμμένον τὸν cτίχον τοῦτον, 'this line was written', *VT* (i 5 Dr).[45] The building's location makes it specifically Theban, and yet the command's implicit valuation of the building is expressive of Pindar's international importance (the house is τοῦ μουcοποιοῦ, not 'Theban' poet), and relies on an understanding of this by its intended reader in order to achieve its aim. The act of inscription is empowered by the cultural value of its subject, but also necessary for the survival of the building, which without the inscription or similar mediation by someone with local knowledge would, to the eye of a conquering Spartan, be just another house awaiting destruction. It is not much of a metaphorical stretch to see this anecdote as a kind of allegory for relations between poetry and history, Pindar's house standing for the cultural inheritance that outlives the uncertainties of historical processes, while also registering its fragilities: the anecdote in the *Vita Ambrosiana* gives this survival a political spin by recording that the house is now used as the Theban πρυτανεῖον. In making the survival of a Theban building dependent on its Panhellenic aspect and on the dynamics of its reception, the anecdotes stage in miniature the complexity of the relations between local and international cultures.

---

the Persian wars undoubtedly forms the backdrop to the (non-historical) variant of the Spartan sack: cf. *Scholies* p. 91.

[42] On which see Slater (1971); *Scholies* pp. 90–2; Kimmel-Clauzet (2013) 230–3.

[43] The latter is attributed by Dio Chrys. *Or.* 2.33 to Pindar's having written encomia for Alexander's ancestor of the same name: see further Hornblower (2012) 95–6. On the historicity of the anecdotes see Kimmel-Clauzet (2013) 230–1.

[44] On the 'accidental' nature of this inscription see *Scholies* p. 92.

[45] The sparing of Pindar's house was a common anecdote in the Imperial period: for a discussion of the sources see Kimmel-Clauzet (2013) 231.

INTERPRETING CRITICAL SIGNS

So far I have examined some aspects of Pindar's cultural reception in the Imperial period, focusing on how readers' encounters with Pindar may have been mediated by critical receptions of Pindar and his poetry in epigrams and biographical texts. We have seen that the book and the figuration of writing plays a varied role in these constructions, sometimes the object of considerable emphasis as in the scholia and the wider epigrammatic corpus, but mostly glossed over in critical discourses. I now want to look in more detail at some of the specific material factors involved in the form of ancient books, and their interpretative significance. I have already touched on the widespread implementation of colometry in lyric texts during the third century,[46] and it is worth considering the aims of colometrization and the effects that it had on readers.

While there is some evidence for pre-Hellenistic colometrization, it is clear that the editions of Aristophanes and Aristarchus in particular established a new paradigm in the appearance of lyric texts.[47] Some have suggested that the colometries given by the scholia closely approximate original performance practices,[48] but the grounds for this supposition are unconvincing.[49] More persuasive is the argument that the use of accents facilitated voiced reading, and were a means of enabling the reader to trace the 'voice' within the text itself.[50] Equally important is the recent observation that the colometric tendency towards incidence of cola and sense breaks 'highlights the syntactic structures of the first strophe, or helps [to] reconstruct it, helping readers who approach the text'.[51] This observation has a wider significance for how the rhetoric of programmatic openings might be understood in the context of a book. It is often noted that Pindar's poems open with statements of thematic significance;[52] the opening lines of O.7, for example, make the good-natured reciprocity of the

[46] See Ch. 1, pp. 53–7.

[47] It should also be noted that this process facilitated metrical emendation, and was presumably to some extent driven by an awareness of this issue: see e.g. the remarks of D'Alessio and Ferrari (1988) 167–8.

[48] e.g. Willett (2002), followed by Gentili (2002).

[49] Cf. the comments of Battezzato (2009) 14–18.

[50] Thus Nagy (2000) 14. Cf. also Porter (2010) 350–2. For the role of voiced reading in scholarship cf. West (2001) 55.

[51] Battezzato (2009) 18.

[52] For ancient awareness of this issue cf. Σ *O*.1.5g, discussed Ch.1, pp. 80–2.

symposium a model for the audience's response,[53] while the building metaphors at the beginning of *O.6* make claims for the poem's beauty and its ability to transmit the victor's fame (πρόcωπον / χρὴ θέμεν τηλαυγέc, 'one must place a far-shining frontage', 3–4).[54] The function of colometrization in mapping out syntactical structure translates these programmatic and metaphorical statements into the spatial architecture of the page. Thus in the case of *O.6*, the opening section's function as a πρόcωπον ... τηλαυγέc, in addition to its other resonances, now comes to describe the role of the passage in orientating the reader's understanding of the ode's metrical structure. In taking on a specific application to *readers'* realization of the text, the metaphor is made concrete by the appearance of the poem's cελίc on the page.[55] The distinctively spatial aspect of the book text interacts with the language of the poem to produce an effect distinctive to the written medium.

The factor on which I especially wish to dwell, however, is the use of critical signs, the marks that began to be appended to texts during the Hellenistic period, and which continued to be used throughout antiquity. In what follows, I shall argue that critical signs and other aspects of the materiality of the book are of considerable importance for thinking about the general function of books in this period and for gauging their interpretative demands. Critical signs fall into two broad categories. One group includes marks to do with accentuation, pronunciation, and sentence structure, and the other are those such as coronides, asteriskoi, and paragraphoi which serve to articulate the structures of poems.[56] I shall focus here on the latter, partly because little attention has been paid to these signs' interpretative significance, and partly because they are of particular importance in providing

[53] On the symposium in Pindar see e.g. Athanassaki (2009) 271–3.

[54] For an ancient reading of the passage cf. Σ *O.6.1a* (i 154 Dr): ἀλληγορεῖ ὁ ποιητὴc, ὡc ἐπὶ οἰκίαc μεγαλοπρεποῦc κατακευαcτὴc τὸν ἐπίνικον διατεθειμένοc. παραβάλλει δὲ προπυλαίῳ μὲν τὸ προοίμιον, τῷ δὲ ὅλῳ οἴκῳ τὸν ὕμνον, ἑαυτὸν δὲ τῷ κατακευάζοντι ('the poet is speaking allegorically, having constructed the epinician like the architect of a grand house. He likens the *prooemium* to the entranceway, the hymn to the whole house and himself to the architect').

[55] For sensitivity to the apertural force of opening passages cf. the citation of *O.6* at Σ Theoc. 1 arg. b (p. 23 Wendel) with discussion Ch. 4, pp. 202–5.

[56] On the distinction, not always accepted (cf. e.g. Tanzi-Mira (1920)), between coronides and paragraphoi cf. Schironi (2010) 10: 'the coronis, with its characteristic sinuous shape, is definitely a different sign from the paragraphos', and ibid. 78–9. Cf. Stephen (1959) 4 for the possible common origin of the two signs. It should be noted, however, that paragraphoi and coronides were frequently combined at the end of texts: cf. Schironi (2010) 70–2. On coronides in general cf. Turner (1987) 12–13.

visual articulation of the rhythmically and structurally complex texts of the lyric poets. Although the structural signs function differently from accents, they too are an important locus for thinking about the relations between reading practices and the performance culture from which the texts of the lyric poets arose.

Critical signs have a history that stretches back to the earliest extant papyri. Paragraphoi are employed in the Derveni Papyrus, while the fourth-century papyrus of Timotheus *Persae* is marked with a coronis. During the Hellenistic period critical signs were used extensively in the editorial process,[57] and were themselves the subject of critical treatises: numerous quotations survive from Aristonicus' treatise *On the Signs of Homer*, which considered lexical and etymological issues as well as the signs themselves.[58] More evidence for the use of critical signs in technical texts is provided by the Herculaneum papyri, especially the papyrus of Philodemus *De poematis* 4, in which various critical signs are employed.[59] The most relevant evidence for an assessment of Pindar, however, is Hephaestion's treatise *On Signs*, which is the only extant systematic account of the signs used in editions of the tragic, comic, and lyric poets.

The treatise opens with a marker of the limitations of its systematizing project, pointing out the variety of the signs discussed (τὰ σημεῖα τὰ παρὰ τοῖς ποιηταῖς ἄλλως παρ' ἄλλοις κεῖται): this statement is true not only of the different ways in which such signs were deployed, but of the various graphic forms they took, although Hephaestion is not concerned with the latter aspect.[60] Following this acknowledgement, Hephaestion goes on to give a brief account of the various different sign systems (*De sign.* 2–4):

2 παρὰ μὲν τοῖς λυρικοῖς, ἂν μὲν μονόστροφον τὸ ᾆσμα ᾖ, καθ' ἑκάστην τίθεται στροφὴν ἡ παράγραφος, εἶτα ἐπὶ τέλους τοῦ ᾄσματος ἡ κορωνίς.

---

[57] See Pfeiffer (1968) 115 on Zenodotus' use of critical signs as part of his editing of Homer.

[58] Cf. Pfeiffer (1968) 212–20 on signs used by Aristophanes, Aristarchus, and Aristonicus. Diog. Laert. 3.65–6 discusses the use of critical signs in Platonic texts.

[59] For a discussion cf. Janko (2011) 188–92.

[60] Hephaestion, however, is only concerned with their pragmatic effects and uses, rather than their aesthetic forms or interpretative significance. On the variation to which signs were subject cf. McNamee (1982) 130: '[t]he evidence of the papyri indicates that the use of text-critical signs in non-Homeric and non-Christian texts of the Roman period was in large part idiosyncratic if not actually capricious in many cases'. She notes (p. 131) that the ancora and antisigma are the only signs whose function seems not to have been subject to substantial variation.

ἐὰν δὲ κατὰ περικοπὴν τὰ ᾄσματα ᾖ γεγραμμένα, ὥστε εἶναι στροφὴν καὶ
ἀντίστροφον καὶ ἐπῳδόν, ἡ παράγραφος ἐπὶ μὲν τῷ τέλει τῆς τε στροφῆς
καὶ ἀντιστρόφου κεῖται, ἐπὶ δὲ τῇ ἐπῳδῷ ἡ κορωνίς·—καὶ οὕτως ἡ παράγραφος, ἣ διορίζει τά τε ὅμοια καὶ τὰ ἀνόμοια.—ἐπὶ μέντοι τῷ τέλει ὁ
ἀστερίσκος τίθεται, γνώρισμα τοῦ τετελέσθαι τὸ ᾆσμα, ἐπεὶ ἡ κορωνὶς ἐπὶ
πασῶν τίθεται τῶν ἐπῳδῶν. 3 καὶ μάλιστα εἴωθεν ὁ ἀστερίσκος τίθεσθαι,
ἐὰν ἑτερόμετρον ᾖ τὸ ᾆσμα τὸ ἑξῆς· ὃ καὶ [μᾶλλον] ἐπὶ τῶν ποιημάτων
τῶν μονοστροφικῶν γίνεται Σαπφοῦς τε καὶ Ἀνακρέοντος καὶ Ἀλκαίου·
ἐπὶ δὲ τῶν Ἀλκαίου ἰδίως κατὰ μὲν τὴν Ἀριστοφάνειον ἔκδοσιν ἀστερίσκος
ἐπὶ ἑτερομετρίας ἐτίθετο μόνης, κατὰ δὲ τὴν νῦν τὴν Ἀριστάρχειον καὶ ἐπὶ
ποιημάτων μεταβολῆς. 4 ἡ δὲ διπλῆ ἡ ἔξω βλέπουσα παρὰ μὲν τοῖς
κωμικοῖς καὶ τοῖς τραγικοῖς ἐστι πολλή, παρὰ δὲ τοῖς λυρικοῖς σπανία·
παρὰ Ἀλκμᾶνι γοῦν εὑρίσκεται· γράψας γὰρ ἐκεῖνος δεκατεσσάρων
στροφῶν ᾄσματα [ὧν] τὸ μὲν ἥμισυ τοῦ αὐτοῦ μέτρου ἐποίησεν ἑπτάς-
τροφον, τὸ δὲ ἥμισυ ἑτέρου· καὶ διὰ τοῦτο ἐπὶ ταῖς ἑπτὰ στροφαῖς ταῖς
ἑτέραις τίθεται ἡ διπλῆ σημαίνουσα τὸ μεταβολικῶς τὸ ᾆσμα γεγράφθαι.

In the lyric poets, if a song is monostrophic the paragraphos is placed by
each strophe, and the coronis at the end of the song. If the pieces are
written in sections so that they consist of a strophe, an antistrophe and
an epode, the paragraphos falls at the end of both the strophe and the
antistrophe, and the coronis at the end of the epode. Thus the paragraphos divides both the like and the unlike. The asteriskos, however, is
placed at the end, marking the fact that the song has come to an end,
since the coronis is placed by all the epodes. The asteriskos is most
commonly employed when the following song is in a different metre.
This is common in the monostrophic poems of Sappho, Anacreon, and
Alcaeus. In Aristophanes' edition of Alcaeus, the asteriskos is used to
mark a difference in metre, but in the edition current today based on
Aristarchus it is also used to mark a change in poems. The outward-
facing diplē is common in comedy and tragedy, but rare in the lyric
poets. It is found in Alcman, though, because he wrote songs in fourteen
strophes, writing one seven strophe half in the same metre, and the
second half in another. Because of this the diplē is placed against the
seven strophes written in the second metre, indicating that the song has
been written with a change of metre.

Several important historical points emerge from this synopsis. Firstly,
the sign systems used are dependent on the metre and structure
of the poems to which they are attached. The account also testifies
to the importance of the Hellenistic scholars in establishing the
sign systems on which later ones were based, or from which
they diverged: he regards the present edition as 'based on' that of

Aristarchus (κατὰ δὲ τὴν νῦν τὴν Ἀριστάρχειον), a comment which points to a relative conservatism in the use of a particular system, however much variation there may have been between systems marking different types of poetic structures.[61] However, the extant papyri follow the system outlined in § 2, rather than those attributed to Aristophanes of Byzantium and Aristarchus in § 3.[62] It seems that Hephaestion mentions these latter systems because of their unusualness, as well as because they derive from two seminal figures in the scholarly tradition. Hephaestion does not mention Pindar, but on the basis of this account we would expect the signs employed for Pindar's poems to follow the models outlined in § 2, and the system for triadic poems described here is indeed attested in the prefatory *scholia recentiora* to Pind. *O*.1, *O*.3, *O*.4, *O*.6, *O*.7, *P*.1 and *P*.2; the monostrophic system at *Σ P*.6.metr.b also follows the pattern described in § 2. The extant papyri, however, show that there was variation. In *Pa.* 5 (= *POxy* 841 col. 19–22), a monostrophic piece, coronis is used as well as paragraphos to mark strophe end, and an asteriskos is used between *Pa.* 5 and 6.[63] There are, however, numerous instances in Pindaric papyri of a coronis marking the end of a strophic system in the manner described by Hephaestion.[64]

[61] For discussion of this reference see Slater (1986) 146–7, and Ch. 1, pp. 56–7 above. It is unclear whether in his edition of Alcaeus Aristophanes also followed the procedure outlined in § 2, using a paragraphos to mark each strophe, a coronis at the end of each poem, and an asteriskos in addition to the coronis to mark a difference of metre. None of the extant papyri of monostrophic poems of Sappho adheres to the Aristarchean model, but follows the system of paragraphos and coronis; see e.g. *POxy* 1231 fr. 1 col. i 12–13 and Lobel 1925: xvi–xvii.

[62] Cf. Slater (1986) 147, who cites as an example *SLG* S 295 (= *POxy* 2878 fr. 10), tentatively attributed to Sappho or Alcaeus, which has remains of a coronis and asteriskos together. *SLG* S 232 (= *POxy* 2637 fr. 30) has paragraphoi after vv. 1 and 3 and what seems to be a small coronis as well as a paragraphos after v. 6. Lobel ad fr. 30.1–2 remarks that 'there is an upright rising at a right-angle from the inner end of the *paragraphos*, for which I cannot account'. This may be no more than a scribal peculiarity; the paragraphos below v. 6 has a downward stroke descending in a leftward diagonal from just inside the outer end of the horizontal. Other instances of such critical marks in lyric poetry include *SLG* S 209 (= *POxy* 2735 fr. 45), although the traces here are very slight. NB also *SLG* S 133 (= *POxy* 2803 fr. 1 col. ii 12–13), where Lobel identified two antisigmas; Barrett proposed that they were traces of a coronis. It is unclear whether the poems from which these fragments come were monostrophic.

[63] Cf. Rutherford (2001) 139–40 for the debate over whether this marks the end of the preceding poem or the beginning of the next.

[64] Pind. *Parth.* 2 in *POxy* 659 (= *P.Lond.Lit.* 44) i 5–6; ii 35–6; iii 57–8; iv 64–5; 79–80; similar signs are also found in the *Paeans*: *POxy* 841 e.g. vi 73–4; xvii 31–2, and

The existence of *On Signs* testifies to the importance of critical signs for readers. There is an additional pointer to their significance and usefulness in Diogenes Laertius' account of the critical signs used in editions of Plato, citing Antigonus of Carystus for the information that when editions of Plato with critical signs were first produced, their owners charged readers to view them (ἅπερ [sc. the editions] Ἀντίγονός φησιν ὁ Καρύστιος ἐν τῷ Περὶ Ζήνωνος νεωςτὶ ἐκδοθέντα εἴ τις ἤθελε διαναγνῶναι, μιςθὸν ἐτέλει τοῖς κεκτημένοις, Diog. Laer.Vit. Phil. 3.66). If true, this anecdote sheds interesting light on the intellectual value these signs had for readers.[65] We might deduce from its relatively specialized subject that *On Signs* was written chiefly for the attention of a highly educated audience, but the treatise is notable, as mentioned above, for its acknowledgement of the variousness of critical signs and for its attempt to impose a certain order on the field by specifying the normative systems used for particular types of poetry and in its quasi-canonization of Aristophanes and Aristarchus. In setting out these normative systems, in marking generic distinctions between different types of signs, and in recording, however minimally, their historical genealogy, the treatise functions as an empirical account of actual practices, but could also have been read as a model of correct, or at least prevailing, usage. It may therefore have been employed as a reference point for scribes seeking to use the 'correct' systems in their copying, or by readers in making their own copies of a text or in giving directions to a scribe relating to the type of critical signs they wanted them to employ. Hephaestion's systematizing approach goes hand in glove with a disregard for the particular visual forms critical signs took, and apart from the opening phrase there is not even a hint at this variety. Rather, his account abstracts a set of functional operations that signs carry out from the mass of particular forms; as well as having pedagogic and systematizing point, this strategy also reflects something of the formulaic ideality of critical

see also *POxy* 2440, 2441, 2442, and *P.Louvre* E 7733 and 7734 with D'Alessio (2000). Cf. Schironi (2010) 17 n. 43 for further examples.

[65] Their wider intellectual significance is particularly important in the case of Plato: Diog. Laert. 3.65–6 makes clear that as well as having the textual critical and stylistic functions common in other authors, signs were also used in Platonic texts to draw attention to specific philosophical issues: cf. e.g. διπλῆ πρὸς τὰ δόγματα καὶ τὰ ἀρέσκοντα Πλάτωνι ... ἀςτερίςκος πρὸς [ie. 'indicates'] τὴν cυμφωνίαν τῶν δογμάτων (3.65–6). Cf. also the distinction drawn by Galen *De ind.* 29–30 between books for his own use and those 'adapted' for use by others.

signs, which combined functional standardization with considerable visual individuality and variation.

The negotiations between particular form and standardized function are at work in the epigram of Meleager placed at the end of his *Garland* collection. The epigram describes the coronis' form and closural function, and is a pointer towards the importance of the sign's visuality, and offers hints about its interrelation with texts (*AP* 12.257):

ἁ πύματον καμπτῆρα καταγγέλλουσα κορωνίς,
οἰκουρὸς γραπταῖς πιστοτάτα σελίσιν,
φαμὶ τὸν ἐκ πάντων ἠθροισμένον εἰς ἕνα μόχθον
ὑμνοθετᾶν βύβλῳ τᾷδ᾽ ἐνελιξάμενον
ἐκτελέσαι Μελέαγρον, ἀείμνηστον δὲ Διοκλεῖ
ἄνθεσι συμπλέξαι μουσοπόλον στέφανον.
οὖλα δ᾽ ἐγὼ καμφθεῖσα δρακοντείοις ἴσα νώτοις,
σύνθρονος ἵδρυμαι τέρμασιν εὐμαθίας.

I, the *coronis* that announces the final turn, a most trustworthy guardian of written pages, declare that Meleager has drawn to a close, having gathered the labour of all poets rolled up into one in this book, and has woven for Diocles from flowers a garland that serves the Muses and that will always be remembered. I sit enthroned at the limit of his learning, curled tightly like a snake's back.

The metaphor of the coronis as a coiled snake (οὖλα ... καμφθεῖσα) is connected to the book's form as a 'rolled-up' (ἐνελιξάμενον) object,[66] as the visuality of the coronis comes to metaphorize the process of gathering and rolling up involved in the constitution of the book. This institutes a two-way movement of meaning, in which the visual appearance of the coronis is marked by the form of the book, and the coronis as a unifying mark signals the closural function of the poem itself. As such, the metaphorical force of the coronis is an instance of a wider interrelation between visuality and textuality, and can be read as a generalizing comment on coronides' literary role(s). The description of the coronis as resembling a snake (δρακοντείοις ἴσα νώτοις) points to the visual status of this sign as being somewhere between the non-representational signs such as diplai and obeloi and

---

[66] For this and other metaphors cf. Gutzwiller (1998) 281. Gigante (1978) proposed οἰκουρός, which if correct induces a connection with the snake which guarded Athena's house on the Acropolis, of which οἰκουρός was the standard epithet (cf. Ar. *Lys.* 759). The coronis' 'guarding' thus takes on a quasi-sacral function.

the illustrations often found in papyri.[67] The poem exploits this indeterminate status by referencing both the coronis' (semi-)representational and significatory aspects.

The act of placing this poem beside (an instance of) that visual sign inscribes this interrelation and prompts further interrogation of the sign's function. This coupling of text and critical sign responds to and instantiates the duality of the coronis' role as both independent of and dependent on the text it marks. By having the coronis 'announce' (καταγγέλλουϲα) the end of the collection and Meleager's authorship (ἐκτελέϲαι Μελέαγρον), the speaker imputes a certain functional independence to the coronis, a sense strengthened by its function as a 'most trustworthy guardian' (οἰκουρὸϲ ... πιϲτοτάτα), a phrase which figures its role of signalling the completion of the book as extraneous to the contents of the texts to which it relates.[68] At this point we might compare Hephaestion's description of the paragraphos, ἢ διορίζει τά τε ὅμοια καὶ τὰ ἀνόμοια; according to this formulation, the paragraphos not (only) *marks* a metrical division, but *performs* it (διορίζει). Similarly in the poem, the coronis does not simply mark an independent closure, contained in the text itself, but plays a part in instituting that closure. Yet this reading is complicated by the fact that the coronis' putative independence is being constructed by the poem itself; while this does not preclude coronides having, and being felt to have, an independent function, it does draw attention to the complexities of the (textual) relations in which they are involved. In its closural role, the poem blurs referentiality and function, itself operating as a kind of coronis in closing the book, while also drawing out various meanings from the visual sign it stands beside. The poem and the coronis are also functionally interrelated, in that the poem's description of the sign intervenes in its operation; by drawing out its significational potentiality, as in the connection between the coronis and the book described above, the poem makes *this particular* coronis operate at a specific intersection of text and visuality.

---

[67] For the ornamental function of the coronis cf. Schironi (2010) 83. Cf. Eidinow (2009) for Horace's metaliterary manipulation of critical signs.

[68] Its role as a 'guardian' also has the practical aspect of preventing, or at least making more difficult, non-authorial additions to the collection. Cf. *P.Lit.Lond.* 11.136, where a similar coronis poem has been appended to an Homeric papyrus; here the coronis is called 'guard of letters' (γραμμάτων φύλαξ): cf. Wifstrand (1933) 468 for comment.

These considerations are also relevant when we think about the diachronic situation of copying and reproduction to which Meleager's book was subject. In this situation, an interaction emerges between the text and the multiplicity of forms that coronides could take.[69] In describing the coronis as a coiled snake, the epigrammatic speaker imposes his authorial authority on the processes of textual reproduction. The poem may have encouraged copyists to fashion a coronis in imitation of the description, and even if this did not happen the specifying figuration of the poem would still have been operative, marking in advance the poem's reproduction: regardless of the precise form of the coronis in subsequent texts, the reader would have been prompted to 'read' the coronis' appearance in the light of the poem.[70] Against this contextual background, the description can also be seen as an attempt on the part of the speaker to impose a standardizing control on the potential plurality of visual forms by which the text could be articulated, by specifying the functionality which any coronis would have in this position regardless of its particular visuality. The coronis' status as an οἰκουρὸς . . . πιϲτοτάτα derives from the conventionality with which such signs were employed, but also from the text's (re)description of its role.

Meleager's coronis epigram is a useful starting point for thinking about the more general issues involved in the function of critical signs, and its dramatization of the intra- and extratextual duality of the coronis can be read as a generalizing comment on the role of coronides and other structural markers. In order to explore this duality more fully, it should be recognized that such critical signs are not merely extraneous appendages, but that they intervene in the ontology of the books on which they are inscribed. When a reader comes across a line in a poem marked with an obelus (–) in order to indicate its spuriousness, s/he is involved in a series of interpretative situations which affect the constitution of the text to which he relates. First, in addition to its primary significational function, the mark sites the text as an object produced in a particular way, and as the outcome of processes of aesthetic valuation and scholarly judgement.

---

[69] For a selection of images cf. Tanzi-Mira (1920).

[70] This would not have been the case in a coronis which was in no way snake-like, but by the Imperial period most coronides took a form which would approximate to Meleager's description, which is sufficiently generalizing to admit of considerable visual variation in the signs it describes. My analysis here is confined to coronides in book-rolls: for coronides in codices cf. Schironi (2010) 80.

Furthermore, the notion of spuriousness at work in this case situates the text in a relation to an ideal original text or utterance, which in turn implies a criterion of judgement capable of assessing this relation. More importantly, there is at stake in the use of the critical sign a conceptual system which grounds such a relation, based on notions of authorial intention, textual authenticity, and wider canons of stylistic and historical understanding of textuality. The use of critical signs assumes readerly competence in these areas, and brings the conceptual apparatus of scholarly debate into the reading processes; the text thus becomes, in part, a space of critical debate where the reader is invited to think about and potentially contest the judgements marked by the critical signs. Signs having to do with authenticity mark the text with the concept of an author as the ultimate source of meaning and authenticity, pointing back to and presupposing a text's point of origin in authorial utterance or composition, but they also mark the absolute division of (a particular material instantiation of) the text from its authoredness, which can only now be figured as the grounding principle of editorial activity. These signs implicate the text in a significational economy of presence and origin, while simultaneously attesting to the text's status as the scene of a radical break with the systems of presence and intention which presided over its inception.

Hephaestion's account of the critical signs used of the lyric poets focuses on signs which articulate the structures of poems. As such, these signs implicitly mark aspects of performance; the signs demarcating a triadic structure, for instance, form a kind of visual correlative for the structuring effects of dance movements and the positioning of the chorus that would have articulated such a performance's scenic aspect. They do so, however, in a way which marks an abstract structure rather than referring explicitly to the specificities of performance, which the reader is left to imagine according to his own knowledge, and which were in any case only dimly understood in later antiquity.[71] This conceptualization is clear in Hephaestion's account of the outward-facing diplē used to mark Alcman's fourteen-stanza poems; its role is to indicate change of metre alone (διὰ τοῦτο ἐπὶ ταῖc ἑπτὰ cτροφαῖc ταῖc ἑτέραιc τίθεται ἡ διπλῆ cημαί-νουcα τὸ μεταβολικῶc τὸ ᾆcμα γεγράφθαι) rather than any changes in the musical setting or choreography that such changes may have

---

[71] I refer especially to the music and choreography of Pindar's performances, of which little detailed understanding is shown in the scholia and other critical texts.

entailed. The structural articulation which these critical signs mobilize is also inflected by their physical form; coronides in particular, because of the variations that could be practised on the basic form, operated as signatures for the scribe, marking the particular copyist's craftsmanship.[72] As such, they are instances of a general feature of book production in the ancient world, whereby each copy of a text was a unique instantiation of it, realizing the text in a material idiom according to conventionalized parameters. But the visual forms of coronides are not simply an ornamental feature of texts; in working as a scribal signature, and as a stylistic marker of the text's provenance, coronides participate in a visual economy which is separate from textuality, even though the *functionality* of individual coronides is closely involved with the texts they mark.

Having considered some aspects of how critical signs are distinguished as outside the processes of textuality, I want to consider their significational operations in more detail, focusing particularly on the structural signs discussed by Hephaestion. Coronides and paragraphoi mark structures internal to the text itself, but are also connected, as we have seen, to extratextual scholarly discourses, as well as partaking of conventions of visuality strictly extraneous to the texts themselves.[73] When thinking about the particular modes of closure and separation that paragraphoi, asteriskoi, and coronides instantiate, we might be tempted to say that they simply signal structural features without taking part in them, features inherent in the text itself and independent of institution by any extratextual mark (γνώρισμα τοῦ τετελέσθαι τὸ ᾆσμα, Heph. *De sign.* 2). However, while there is a degree of truth in this position, it does not take account of the distinction between the functional ideality of the critical signs and the particularities of individual endings of poems, and movements

---

[72] Cf. Stephen (1959).

[73] Coronides and paragraphoi were also frequently combined with end-titles: cf. Schironi (2010) 61–70. The interrogation of the differences between cημεῖα and λόγοι go back at least to Heraclitus' fragment about the Delphic oracle (DK B 93): ὁ ἄναξ, οὗ τὸ μαντεῖόν ἐcτι τὸ ἐν Δελφοῖc, οὔτε λέγει οὔτε κρύπτει ἀλλὰ cημαίνει ('the lord whose shrine is at Delphi neither speaks nor conceals but gives signs') on which see Kahn (1979) 123 '" [g]iving a sign" means uttering one thing that in turn signifies another'. He notes that in the rhetoric of the Delphic oracle the sign can take various forms, for instance image, metaphor, or ambiguous wording. Heraclitus' use, where the act of giving a cημεῖον confronts the interpreter with a confusing multiplicity which they need to negotiate in order to work out the true meaning, contrasts with other uses where the cημεῖον conveys information directly and clearly, for which see *Il.* 23.358; *Od.* 12.26; Hdt. 2.38; Pl. *Rep.* 614c.

within them. This might be provisionally formulated as a distinction between a marking of *the fact that* a poem ends (τοῦ τετελέϲθαι τὸ ᾆϲμα) and the actualities of *how* a poem ends.

This can be illustrated by thinking about the sign system described in the Pindaric *scholia recentiora* for, e.g., *O*.1: ἐπὶ τῷ τέλει ἑκάϲτηϲ ἐπῳδοῦ κορωνὶϲ καὶ παράγραφοϲ, ἐπὶ δὲ τῷ τέλει τοῦ ᾆϲματοϲ ἀϲτερίϲκοϲ. If we assume that the rest of the poems in most ancient editions of Pindar's Olympians followed this system,[74] as outlined by Hephaestion in § 2, we face a situation where the identical forms of the asteriskoi which mark the end of each poem contrast with the texts' verbally different endings. The asteriskoi and coronides perform the practical function of assisting the reader's navigation of the text, as well as providing ornamentation, but they also draw attention to the significational and thematic variation at work in the collection, and to the differences between closural movements within poems at the ends of strophic systems and the ends of poems as a whole. Similarly, the closural articulation of poems within the book also shapes how the ending of the book as whole might be viewed, assimilated as it is to other closures in being marked by an asteriskos, but also differentiated by its position.

Such effects are particularly noticeable in the case of tonally different endings. At *O*.6.103–5 the narrator calls on Poseidon to favour his project:

> δέϲποτα ποντόμεδον, εὐθὺν δὲ πλόον καμάτων
> ἐκτὸϲ ἐόντα δίδοι, χρυϲαλακάτοιο πόϲιϲ
> Ἀμφιτρίταϲ, ἐμῶν δ᾽ ὕ–
> μνων ἄεξ᾽ εὐτερπὲϲ ἄνθοϲ.

Lordly ruler of the sea, husband of Amphitrite of the golden spindle, may you give a direct voyage free from hardships, and make burgeon the pleasurable flower of my songs.

Somewhat different in tone is the end of *O*.7, which concludes with a request for Diagoras' family's continuing renown, followed by a gnomic statement about the instability of human fortune (*O*.7.92–5):

> μὴ κρύπτε κοινόν
> ϲπέρμ᾽ ἀπὸ Καλλιάνακτοϲ·

---

[74] Not an excessive speculation given the apparent influence of the Hellenistic editions, but cf. Ucciardello (2012) 113–15 on the different forms books of Pindar could take.

Ἐρατιδᾶν τοι σὺν χαρίτεσσιν ἔχει
θαλίας καὶ πόλις· ἐν δὲ μιᾷ μοίρᾳ χρόνου
ἄλλοτ᾽ ἀλλοῖαι διαιθύσσοισιν αὖραι.

Do not conceal the common seed which hails from Callianax: the city
also holds festivals at the celebrations of the Eratidae. But in a single
portion of time, the winds blow now here, now there.

Marking these two passages with an *asteriskos* points up their tonal
and significational differences in contrast to the formulaic, contentless ideality of the critical sign.

POxy 841, which contains an edition of Pindar's *Paeans*, is marked
with numerous critical signs and gives us the opportunity of examining some concrete examples of the effects they create. One striking
instance occurs in *Pa.* 5, a paean written for an Athenian procession
to Delos, of which only the last two stanzas survive intact.[75] A coronis
occurs beside the end of each:

> ἰήϊε Δάλι᾽ Ἄπολλον·
> καὶ σποράδας φερεμήλους
> ἔκτισαν νάσους ἐρικυδέα τ᾽ ἔσχον
> Δᾶλον, ἐπεί σφιν Ἀπόλλων   40
> δῶκεν ὁ χρυσοκόμας
>   Ἀστερίας δέμας οἰκεῖν·
> ἰήϊε Δάλι᾽ Ἄπολλον·
> Λατόος ἔνθα με παῖδες
> εὐμενεῖ δέξασθε νόῳ θεράποντα   45
> ὑμέτερον κελαδεννᾷ
> σὺν μελιγάρυϊ παι–
>   ᾶνος ἀγακλέος ὀμφᾷ.

Ieie Delian Apollo. And they founded homes in the scattered islands
rich in flocks, and they held Delos of wide fame, when golden-haired
Apollo gave them the body of Asteria to dwell in. *Ieie* Delian Apollo.
There may you, Leto's children, receive me as your servant, with kindly
thoughts, with the honey-sounding, ringing voice of a glorious paean.

The poem seems to have described the Ionian colonization of the
Aegean: 35 describes the 'taking' and settling of Euboea, the penultimate

---

[75] Wilamowitz (1922) 327–8 argues that the singers were Euboeans on the basis of
the scholium to 45, which glosses with θεράποντα 'Pandorus, son of Erectheus, Aiclus';
he suggests that the scholiast may have interpreted the final stanzas as spoken by the
original colonists. Rutherford (2001) 297 suggests an Athenian chorus.

stanza the settlement of various other islands, and the final stanza the settlement of Delos.[76] It is structurally and metrically straightforward, consisting of monostrophic dactylo-epitrites. In such a setting, the coronides are not so obviously required as a guide to structure, but their role in articulating the poem as a material construct is all the more noticeable as a result. The coronides at strophe end balance the repeated ἰήϊε Δάλι' Ἄπολλον in the strophe's first line, creating a congruence between visual and verbal structures. This is an instance of a more general pattern in which paeanic refrains and visual markers often coincide; we may compare *Pa.* 2.35–6, 71–2, and 107–8 where the epode ending refrain ἰὴ ἰὲ Παιάν, ἰὴ ἰέ· Παιὰν / δὲ μήποτε λείποι coincides with coronides marking the end of the strophe system. At *Pa.* 6.121–2 the coronis marking epode end falls beside a similar refrain (<ἰὴ> ἰῆτε νῦν, μέτρα παιηό- / ν]ων ἰῆτε, νέοι).[77] In each case, the conventionality and repetition of the signs emphasizes the particular stylistic force of the cited invocations and refrains.[78] This is particularly marked at *Pa.* 6.121–2 where the coronis interacts with μέτρα παιηό- / ν]ων ἰῆτε to reinforce the distinction between the ἰῆτε cry as a performance marker and as a part of a material text. In punctuating the space of the text on the page, the coronides emphasize the visual medium in which the poem's verbal articulations now function.[79]

Also observable in *Pa.* 5 is a visual articulation by the critical signs of the text's thematic structure. As mentioned above, the poem maps out the processes of colonization, and may well have been performed processionally.[80] The coronides reinforce this process of mapping by acting as visual points on the page between which the poem moves. The linearity of the poem's movement, given a specifically spatial aspect by the coronides, contrasts with the more complex movements of the colonizations, which take in Euboea (35–6), and then various unnamed islands (38–9), before concluding at Delos (40–2). The description of these islands as 'scattered' (σποράδας) emphasizes the

[76] Cf. Rutherford (2001) 295.
[77] This invocation is not used to end all the epodes however: cf. *Pa.* 6.60–1 and Rutherford (2001) 70.
[78] For the closural and transitional functions of paeanic refrains cf. Rutherford (2001) 71–2 with further examples, and for refrains more generally cf. e.g. Cannatà Fera (1990) 124–9.
[79] For μέτρα used of spatial distances cf. LSJ s.v. § 3.
[80] So Rutherford (2001) 294.

migration's reach, but also the force of subordination and collection implicit in the text's linear narrative, a feature reinforced by the coronides' spatial articulation. The coronides beside 35–6 (*Eὔ-*] / βοιαν ἕλον καὶ ἔνασσαν) and 41–2 (δῶκεν ὁ χρυσοκόμας / Ἀστερίας δέμας οἰκεῖν) stress the connection between Euboea and Delos as points within the onward movement of colonization, but the visual and functional identity of the coronides also highlight the significational differences between the lines. This interplay extends to how we might 'read' the coronides themselves, allowing them to be marked by a different closural sense in the case of each stanza despite their visual identity. This distinction is particularly important at the end of the poem, as the contentless structural mark given by the coronis contrasts as a closural feature with the specificity of the paeanic signature, linked as it is to a particular performance location and voiced by a particular choral speaker.[81] Genre is also at issue: the visuality of coronides was not dependent on the genre of the poem of which they were used, and as a result their use creates a contrast between the poem's genre-specific closural constructions and their own transgeneric and purely structural operation.

From these examples we can see something of the multiplicity of how critical signs function. Asteriskoi and coronides articulate the constructedness of the collection and the book, but they also draw attention to its internal differentiation by marking poems off from each other and heightening the reader's sensitivity to thematic differences between poems, drawing attention to generic specificities, and inviting the kind of comparisons I elaborated above between *O*.6 and *O*.7. Moreover, critical signs are also of consequence for the relations I have explored between performance referentiality and the written text. In highlighting the material specificity of the document and providing a structural articulation supplementary to that of the text itself, critical signs encourage a recognition of the interactions between this materiality and performance references within the text itself. A relation, or sets of relations, also emerges between the functionality of the structural signs and the intratextual networks

---

[81] Rutherford (2001) 296 suggests that the end of the poem gives a relatively weak sense of closure on the grounds that appeals to the gods can also be used at the beginnings of paeans (cf. e.g. *Pa*. 6.1), and wonders whether this may be to allow for the chorus 'to sing the song over again from the beginning, as might have been required if they were performing it while processing along the Sacred Way from the harbour at Delos to the sanctuary'.

which arise in the book, as the contentless ideality of the signs is opened up to being marked by individual poem (and strophe system) ends, and by the relations between them.

These interactions mirror those at work in the epigrams explored earlier, and, more obliquely, the dynamics of Pindar's reception in cult and biography. Running through them is a sense of the importance of the specific material circumstances that inflect literary experience. This is explicitly foregrounded by the epigrammatic tradition, and by the scholarly economy within which critical signs were used. The *Lives* and cult practices, on the other hand, aim at creating and fostering a sense of contact with the historical individual behind the poetry and the traces of his existence, however fictionalized these may be. In comparison to the subject-matter of my previous chapter, these readings articulate the rich variegation of the horizons within which ancient readings of Pindar would have taken place. In the remaining chapters, I shall analyse a selection of Pindar's epinicians in the light of these horizons.

II

Singing Pages

3

Edited Highlights

The rest of this book will be devoted to close readings of Pindar's epinicians against the background of the cultural contexts examined in the previous two chapters, beginning with a group of poems that include some of Pindar's most celebrated literary achievements, and upon which the processes of recontextualization exerted a particular influence. My subject in this chapter will be interactions between individual poems and the book as a whole, and how the placing of poems within a book can affect their meaning. I shall also consider how some of Pindar's poems for Hiero of Syracuse may have appeared in the light of changing structures of governance and conceptions of political leaders in the Greek world, and how these poems interacted with some of the Hellenistic poetry for which they served as models. Although my analyses are directed specifically at Pindar, they also have resonance for the situations of other classical poets and their readers during this decisive periodin the history of the book.

A distinction needs to be made clear at the outset between the types of textual experiences at which my readings are directed. My primary aim is to think about the experiences that would have confronted Hellenistic readers when they read Pindar's epinicians in book form. Although I shall be discussing phenomena related to editorial and scholarly activity that are particular to the reading situation, some of my arguments, especially those that relate to effects created by temporal and spatial deixis, could also be made in adjusted form about reperformance scenarios.[1] I am not claiming, however, that readers have a unique relation to these effects, or that such spatio-temporal

---

[1] Cf. Introduction, pp. 13–15, 37–8.

disjunctions are solely dependent on the interaction between text and book: rather, such effects are extensions of phenomena that would also have been at work in performance situations.[2] Nonetheless, I shall argue that in some cases these 'extensions' are in themselves important, and contribute to texts' changing cultural significance.[3] With this dynamic in mind, I turn first to an examination of *O*.1 and its function as the opening poem of the Olympian book.

OLYMPIAN 1: AETIOLOGY AND EXEMPLARITY

The opening of *O*.1 was celebrated in antiquity: Lucian has Micyllus, while praising gold, refer to Pindar's praise of gold and water 'at the beginning of the most beautiful of all his songs' (ἐν ἀρχῇ εὐθὺς τοῦ καλλίστου τῶν ἀϲμάτων ἁπάντων, Luc. 19.7). As discussed above, however, *O*.1 was not always the first poem in editions of the Olympians, its position being the result of an editorial decision by Aristophanes of Byzantium.[4] The notice from the *Vita Thomana* that reports this decision is a helpful insight into Aristophanes' editorial policies, and also raises a series of questions about the influence of the structures of editions, and the thinking behind them, on reading practices (i 7 Dr):

ὁ δὲ ἐπινίκιος οὗ ἡ ἀρχή· Ἄριστον μὲν ὕδωρ, προτέτακται ὑπὸ Ἀρις-
τοφάνουϲ τοῦ ϲυντάξαντοϲ τὰ Πινδαρικὰ διὰ τὸ περιέχειν τοῦ ἀγῶνοϲ
ἐγκώμιον καὶ τὰ περὶ τοῦ Πέλοποϲ, ὃϲ πρῶτοϲ ἐν Ἤλιδι ἠγωνίϲατο.

---

[2] It is possible, for example, that some of the connections between *O*.1 and *P*.1 that I explore below (pp. 142–5) could have been generated by reperformance of these odes as a pair. Such performances could have taken place in Syracuse from soon after their composition, and at later dates (cf. p. 126 n. 17). This point could also be extended to include earlier Pindaric books: the two poems may have been grouped together with other 'Sicilian Odes' (and perhaps poems for Hiero in other genres) in pre-Alexandrian editions. However, I am not claiming that only readers of the Hellenistic period would have been able to engage with reading the poems in parallel, but simply that such connections would have formed part of the reading experience during this period. The distinctiveness of the Hellenistic reading situation rests not only on the possibility of making such connections, but on the wider cultural backdrop within which these connections emerge. For instance, the programmatic status of *O*.1 as an opening poem adds a dimension to the relationship between the poems that would not have been present in earlier editions.
[3] Cf. e.g. my remarks about the status of the written text in relation to the description of the Muses in *P*.1 (pp. 145–50).
[4] Ch. 1, pp. 55.

> The epinician which begins 'Water is best' was placed first [in the collection] by Aristophanes when he ordered Pindar's poems, on account of its containing an encomium of the games, and because of the matter relating to Pelops, who was the first to compete at Elis.

We do not know the source for the above notice, and there are various contexts in which the argument recorded here could have affected a reading of the epinicians.[5] The comment could have formed part of a marginal note in Aristophanes' autograph, although such marginalia were unlikely to be copied into commercial texts.[6] More likely sources for the wider dissemination of this critical comment are its place in a ὑπόμνημα and oral dissemination.

The comment draws attention to the status of the text as a material document, and opens up a new way of seeing O.1 in relation to its material context.[7] Now, the 'praise of the games' has become a reason for placing the poem at the head of the collection, indicating the paradigmatic quality not just of the Olympian festival but of this particular poem and its 'encomium of the games' (τοῦ ἀγῶνος ἐγκώμιον). The comment also suggests that the edition of the Olympian odes is similarly paradigmatic for the epinician project as a whole.[8] Pelops, because of his status as the first competitor at Elis, now becomes a paradigm not only for the games but for the edition which describes them. Aristophanes' reading broaches a parallelism between the games and the edition; just as Pelops began the games, so the poem which memorializes him begins the collection. Although the nature of the contents of the other poems prevent this from becoming a totalizing editorial or reading strategy, in the light of the gloss reading O.1 becomes, however provisionally, a means of simultaneously beginning the collection and returning to the origins of the games.[9]

By referring to the constitution of the book, the Aristophanic comment draws attention to the document as itself a meaningful construct, something dictated by its contents but which also affects

---

[5] Aristophanes' ordering of the poems formed the template for later texts of the epinicians: for the evidence for editions prior to Aristophanes, cf. Ch. 1, pp. 53–5.

[6] Cf. Irigoin (1952) 53.

[7] For the exegetical strategies of the scholia to O.1 as in some respects conditioned by its place in the book cf. Ch. 1, p. 80 n. 110.

[8] Cf. Negri (2004) 27–43.

[9] This does not mean, however, that we should see Pelops as the *founder* of the games: for the historical problems with such a position cf. McLaughlin (2004).

how the reader approaches them. Taking this comment as a starting point, I shall now explore how the material document interacts with the text's enunciative situations in relation to the passages of *O*.1 that are of particular importance to the Aristophanic reading. I begin at the beginning:

ἄριστον μὲν ὕδωρ, ὁ δὲ χρυςὸς αἰθόμενον πῦρ
ἅτε διαπρέπει νυκτὶ μεγάνοροc ἔξοχα πλούτου·
εἰ δ᾽ ἄεθλα γαρύεν
ἔλδεαι, φίλον ἦτορ,
μηκέτ᾽ ἀελίου cκόπει   5
ἄλλο θαλπνότερον ἐν ἁμέρᾳ φαεν–
      νὸν ἄcτρον ἐρήμαc δι᾽ αἰθέροc,
μηδ᾽ Ὀλυμπίαc ἀγῶνα φέρτερον αὐδάcομεν·
ὅθεν ὁ πολύφατοc ὕμνοc ἀμφιβάλλεται
cοφῶν μητίεccι, κελαδεῖν
Κρόνου παῖδ᾽ ἐc ἀφνεὰν ἱκομένουc   10
μάκαιραν Ἱέρωνοc ἑcτίαν.

Water is best, and gold like fire blazing at night shines pre-eminent among lordly wealth. But if you wish to sing the games, my dear heart, do not look for any star shining more warmly by day than the sun in the empty heaven, nor let us declare a contest superior to Olympia. From there the renowned song encompasses the wits of the wise, who have come to sing the son of Cronus at Hiero's rich and blessed hearth.

In the context of a material document, the phrasing of ὁ πολύφατοc ὕμνοc ἀμφιβάλλεται / cοφῶν μητίεccι involves the reader in a division between the projected enunciative situation, whether conceived as a chorus or a monodist performing before an audience, and the experience of reading. The material text draws out and expands on the denotational vagueness implicit in the reference to the cοφῶν.[10]

---

[10] Gerber (1982) 28–9 sees in cοφῶν a generic reference to poets: for a discussion of the use of this terminology see Gianotti (1975) 85–109. This reading, however, is too restrictive. cοφῶν μητίεccι literally means 'the divisings of wise men', and although Pindar undoubtedly uses cοφόc and its cognates to refer to poets and poetry (cf. e.g. *O*.2.86), we should allow the double resonance of both specific and literal meanings here. Gerber's interpretation of cοφῶν μητίεccι relies on his reading as 'not so much "song" as "subject for song"' (ibid. p. 26, citing *P*.6.7–8 and *N*.6.33 as parallels), but this again is too restrictive and elides the literal meaning of ὕμνοc. The lines refer both to Olympia as a subject of song for poets and more literally to the effect of song on listeners more generally. For a summary of the debate about the possible meta-phoricity of ἀμφιβάλλεται see Gerber (1982) 26–8 and e.g. Nisetich (1975), and for

A question that arises here is whether the reference can be restricted to 'poets', or whether it is more generally applicable, for instance to the visitors to Hiero's court whose happy revels are described at 10–17, or to people watching the performance (who are at least metaphorically 'coming to Hiero's blessed hearth'), or more broadly to readers or people encountering the poem in other types of performance scenarios, such as symposia.[11] While the primary reference in the projected enunciation is doubtless to the visitors of 10–17, the rhetoric is deliberately capacious, gesturing to the possibility, and indeed the desirability, of the poem's wider impact.[12] The reading context replays and extends this construction of poetic dissemination; in the context of the book the reader also finds himself incorporated in the text's self-figuration.[13]

The poetic self-references at 3–4 and 7 can also be read differently depending on whether they are seen in terms of performance or a later reading situation. The apostrophe εἰ δ' ἄεθλα γαρύεν / ἔλδεαι, φίλον ἦτορ is self-referential in the projected enunciation, but at the beginning of a poem which begins a collection which will be all about ἄεθλα, wherein the reader has anticipated and acceded in advance to the conditional 'wish' (ἔλδεαι) by opening the roll and beginning to read, there is a connection, albeit indirect, between the situation referenced by these lines and the reading experience. This dynamic is picked up again in line 7; the first person plural of αὐδάσομεν draws the reader towards the narrator, an enunciation in which the individual reader is subsumed into a wider communality. Simultaneously, however, the reader's awareness of the distinction between his/her situation and that of the poem in performance complicates this appropriation, serving to distance the reader from the text in the

ambiguity in Pindar more generally see Renehan (1969); Hummel (1992) 289–90, (2001); Pfeijffer (1999a) 23–34; Griffith (1999).

[11] Vetta (1983) xxv–xxviii suggested that the performances at Hiero's court could have taken the form of large symposia; cf. also Krummen (1990) 155–216. For performances of epinicians at symposia cf. also Currie (2004); Athanassaki (2009) 244 n. 12.

[12] Cf. Goldhill (1991) 144–5; Athanassaki (2009) 271–3.

[13] Explicit references to readers are rare in the scholia. An exception is Σ *P*.3.198b, in which the first person plural is used to describe a subject position articulated by the primary text: ἀνθρώπων δὲ φάτις περιφραστικῶς, ἡμεῖς οἱ ἄνθρωποι ('[the phrase] "men's speech" is periphrastic, [since] we [are] the men'). The scholium thus references, albeit obliquely, the role of contemporary readers in maintaining the poem's transhistorical force.

same movement as he is drawn towards it. The material document is a space of mutual appropriation, the reader being appropriated by the text, being metaphorically elided into a wider enunciative situation, while also recreating its enunciative strategies.[14]

The contextual shift in the sense of the adjective πολύφατος ('much-spoken'/'renowned') focuses this dynamic, indicating the text's capacity for multiple reinscription. The history of the text, its diachronic exposure to a variety of readers, instantiates the rhetoric of the enunciation.[15] The divided situation of reading is refocused in 10–11 (ἱκομένους / μάκαιραν Ἱέρωνος ἑστίαν) in terms of an opposition between signified spatiality and text space. Here the image of 'arriving' might point up a distinction between the solitary, cerebral experience of reading and the sensuous, communal experience of performance. At this point, however, we need to be wary of a straightforward opposition between performance and solitary, silent reading. Reading aloud to oneself, solo declamation, or singing, to a small group, or a sympotic performance before a larger audience would have each created different enunciative situations. A solo performance before a small group, for example, would have the effect of indirectly applying ἱκομένους / μάκαιραν Ἱέρωνος ἑστίαν to the audience, drawing a connection between the empirical audience of the reperformance and the implied audience of the projected enunciation.[16]

Moreover, this is not a matter of a simple opposition between two empirical situations. Even in the projected enunciation, ἱκομένους / μάκαιραν Ἱέρωνος ἑστίαν is not straightforwardly denotational, in that it metaphorizes, by means of the broader referentiality described above, the position of an audience who are being figuratively welcomed to Hiero's hearth.[17] These lines, together with 14–17, can be

---

[14] On the poem's use of prepositions see Griffith (1991).

[15] On the meaning of πολύφατος see Gerber (1982) 25–6 and Hummel p. 651. Gerber argues that only the passive meaning should be felt here, citing *P*.11.47 and *N*.7.81. Cf., however, Hummel (1992) for the etymological doubleness of πολύφατος as derived from both φημί and φαίνω. On the ancient interpretations of the word see *Scholies* pp. 267–72.

[16] For the citation of Pindar's poetry in a symposium and its capacity to rearticulate that context cf. p. 234.

[17] Our lack of knowledge of the original performance scenario, which would have been shared by a Hellenistic reader, complicates matters here. There are various different performance scenarios which might be conceived for this poem, and we cannot dismiss the possibility of a public performance space being metaphorized by

interpreted as a nod to future reperformance, and as constructing Hiero as an idealized symposiastic figure.[18] But they also construct a *virtualized* sympotic space which marks the text's reception. The performance and the sympotic songs of 14–17 are not identical, and while the reference does invite the reader to see the performance of *O*.1 as a space in which the whole of Syracuse is transformed into a symposiastic domain with Hiero as implicit *arbiter bibendi*, the poem's ethical and narrative complexity imposes the impossibility of a radical equation in these terms. Later readers are also drawn into this metaphorical system. The reader, or the audience of the reperformance, finds his/her approach to the text metaphorized in terms of a metaphor that has already been applied, creating both a displacement of the reader from the scene of reading and a filiation with previous audiences (and readers) appropriated by the metaphor.[19]

The capacity of performance references such as those at 10–11 to generate a multiple applicability depending on the context of their enunciation is something which should be borne in mind throughout the following reading. Another example of this phenomenon is the mention of the jealous neighbours at *O*.1.47–51 as the source of the story about Pelops' dismemberment. In a performance context, the specification of the neighbours as 'grudging' (ἔννεπε κρυφᾷ τις αὐτίκα φθονερῶν γειτόνων, 47) makes them a negative paradigm for citizens who do not share in the *laudandus*' success, a figuration which is extended by textual dissemination.[20] Much attention has

---

the text as μάκαιραν Ἱέρωνος ἑστίαν; the phrase could have referred metaphorically to the city as a whole. For possible performance and reperformance scenarios see Morrison (2007) 57–65. The performance history of Pindar's poems for Hiero is also likely to have been rather chequered: it is hard to imagine, for instance, any large-scale public performances of these odes being put on by the post-466 democracy, although sympotic reperformances by aristocrats are certainly possible. On the other hand, the tyrannies of Dionysius I and Hiero II offer possible reperformance contexts: both modelled themselves on their tyrannical predecessors, and were keenly engaged in the use of poetry and performance to project public images: see e.g. Duncan (2012) on Dionysius I's uses of tragedy. Cf. also Timaeus *FGrH* 566 F 32, which gives an account of rival performances of 'classic' paeans, including those of Pindar, and Dionysius' own compositions: for analysis see LeVen (2014) 15–17.

[18] Cf. Athanassaki (2009) 261–2. The symposiastic element is commented on by Σ *O*.1.24d (i 25–6 Dr).

[19] Felson (2004) 388 argues that deixis (in *P*.9) encourages readers to identify with the earliest audience, but deixis also has the effect of inscribing spatial differentiation, and hence of accenting the imaginative effort necessary to make such identifications.

[20] Cf. Scodel (2001) 128.

been devoted to the myth of *O.*1, and specifically to the ways in which Pindar (may have) revised the better-known account(s) of Tantalus feeding Pelops to the gods.[21] Replacing this story with Poseidon's love and consequent assistance for Pelops has a marked encomiastic force,[22] but the act of revision is itself ethically programmatic, projecting a mode of interpreting myths, and more generally of viewing the world, that foregrounds the narrator himself and his intellectual comportment as exemplary. The poem's readers are assisted in negotiating a world full of deceptive stories (30–2) and deceptive speakers (28–9).[23]

Similarly, Aristophanes' use of Pelops' status as the first competitor at Olympia to justify *O.*1's place at the head of the edition allows a connection to be made between the commemoration of Pelops at Olympia at 90–6 and the monumentalizing function of the text:

νῦν δ᾽ ἐν αἱμακουρίαιc   90
ἀγλααῖcι μέμικται,
Ἀλφεοῦ πόρῳ κλιθείc,

---

[21] On the myth of *O.*1 cf. Köhnken (1974); Sicking (1980); Howie (1984); Griffith (1989); Howie (1991), esp. 101–4. Cf. Cairns (1977) 129 for the parallelism between Hiero and Pelops. Nagy (1990) 116–35 argues that Pindar's version is also traditional, but this relies on a forced interpretation of *O.*1.36.

[22] e.g. Howie (1984) 281–6.

[23] The disputed lines 25–7 about Clotho taking Pelops from the 'pure cauldron' (ἐπεί νιν καθαροῦ λέβητοc ἔξελε Κλωθώ) 'equipped with his shoulder shining with ivory' (ἐλέφαντι φαίδιμον ὦμον κεκαδμένον) flag up Pindar's intervention into the myth. For some interpretations, cf. e.g. Dissen (1830) 10, who argues that the mention of Clotho refers to Pelops' birth rather than to his revival after dismemberment, and Howie (1984) 284 for criticism of this position, with further references. Kakridis (1930) 475 takes ἐπεί (26) as causal, followed by e.g. Lloyd-Jones (1973) 133 n. 125, and hence interprets Poseidon as falling in love with Pelops as a result of his ivory shoulder: for objections cf. Gerber (1982) 55. Howie (1984) 285 argues that the lines 'are intended to resemble a summary of the traditional story and be mistaken for it'. This relies on an ambiguity between the λέβηc as implement for cooking or bathing after birth, which is then resolved by Clotho's role, which makes clear that Pindar has revised the story to make it an account of Pelops' birth (cf. however, Gerber (1982) 56–7 for the argument that λέβηc is unlikely to mean 'birth vessel'). On this reading, the ivory shoulder then becomes 'a special sign', either to be understood as actually made of ivory, or merely appearing similar to it (pp. 286–7). He compares other revisions of myths where figural and literal meanings are at issue, and in which a literal meaning has displaced a figurative (e.g. Hecataeus, *FGrH* 1 F 27, Hdt. 1.122, Pl. *Phaedr.* 229b–d, pp. 287–9). Paus. 5.13.4–6 records the story that Pelops' shoulder blade was recovered at sea, identified by the Delphic Oracle, and kept at Olympia where it had sacral status. Parke (1933) suggests that the relic was on display during Pindar's lifetime. For a different approach see Griffith (2000).

τύμβον ἀμφίπολον ἔχων πολυξενω–
τάτῳ παρὰ βωμῷ· τὸ δὲ κλέος
τηλόθεν δέδορκε τᾶν Ὀλυμπιάδων ἐν δρόμοις
Πέλοπος, ἵνα ταχυτὰς ποδῶν ἐρίζεται   95
ἀκμαί τ᾽ ἰσχύος θρασύπονοι·

Now he has a share in the splendid blood-sacrifices, leaning at rest
beside the ford of the Alpheus, and having there a much-frequented
tomb beside an altar that many strangers visit. And the fame of the
Olympian festivals has shone from afar, won in Pelops' racecourses
where there are contests in swiftness of foot and the heights of boldly
toiling strength.

The stress on the cultural importance of Pelops' cult site (τύμβον
ἀμφίπολον ἔχων πολυξενωτάτῳ παρὰ βωμῷ) inscribes a contrast
between the signified space, with its emphasis on the physicality of
the rites (αἱμακουρίαις) and pilgrimage, and the scene of reading.
Aristophanes' critical comment, however, involves a redescription
of Pelops' exemplarity in the poetics of the edition. Just as he was
the hero ὃς πρῶτος ἐν Ἤλιδι ἠγωνίσατο, and thus exemplary not only
for Hiero but for competition at Olympia generally, so the inscription
of the Pelops narrative at the beginning of the edition adds the notion
of Pelops as exemplary for the reader's engagement with the rest of
the poems in the collection, as he becomes a paradigmatic model
against which other heroes can be read.[24] The material context of
reading prompts reflection on exemplarity and of the parallelism and
differences between reading and cultic pilgrimage as ways of performing and perpetuating cultural memory.

The expression of Pelops' fame at 93–5 (τὸ δὲ κλέος / τηλόθεν
δέδορκε τᾶν Ὀλυμπιάδων ἐν δρόμοις / Πέλοπος) is also picked up and
expanded by the material context of reading, and the scholia on the
passage may reflect the influence of Aristophanes' placement of O.1
and his argument for doing so. At Σ O.1.151b (i 50 Dr) we find the
comment τὸ τηλόθεν χρονικῶς ἀκουστέον ('"from far off" should be
taken temporally').[25] As it stands this is a rather odd reading, given
that firstly, Pindar never elsewhere uses τηλόθεν to denote temporality,

---

[24] For Pelops used paradigmatically in the Homeric scholia see Ch. 4, pp. 194–7.
[25] For discussion of this group of scholia see *Scholies* pp. 415–16.

and secondly that the spatial reading makes perfectly good sense.[26] This reading would be perfectly comprehensible, however, in terms of Aristophanes' stress on Pelops' temporal priority. The temporal interpretation of τηλόθεν could derive from a reading, either that of Aristophanes himself or of someone responding to his comments at some stage in the exegetical process, which stresses the temporal structure of Olympia's fame, stressing its glory as something which emanates from an event in the distant past.[27]

The phrase τηλόθεν δέδορκε connotes both the brightness of Olympia and its being seen, picking up the imagery of brightness in the first stanza.[28] The action of looking implied by δέδορκε, as a figural projection of the action of the verb, is not focalized by a given individual, projecting instead a generalized viewing position. The generality of this projection also subsumes the reader of the material text, who also 'looks' at Olympia, or rather a particular textual figuration of Olympia, from far away. The rhetoric of the text again stresses the reader's distance from the signified space, but this

---

[26] Σ O.1.151d and f (i 50 Dr) both take the phrase in a spatial sense (e.g. 151f τουτέστι πανταχῇ βλέπεται καὶ βοᾶται ὁ Ὀλυμπιακὸς ἀγών, 'that is, the Olympian competition is noticed and talked about everywhere'), as do modern commentators, e.g. Gerber (1982) 146–7. τηλόθε(ν) is also found at N.2.12, N.3.81, and N.6.48, each time with a purely spatial sense. In its uses in other literature it is always spatial; see e.g. Il. 5.651 (and cf. Il. 1.30 τηλόθι πάτρης); Soph. Aj. 1318 (NB that other adverbs from the τηλ- root are normally spatial, although see τηλοῦ used temporally at POxy 1015.13; IG 5 (2) 173.1, and perhaps also Od. 17.253). It is notable that the scholia do not gloss τηλόθεν in its other Pindaric occurrences, which suggests that the word's meaning was uncontroversial. This contrasts with the extensive exegesis at Σ O.1.151a–f (i 50 Dr), where the glosses may reflect a debate over the meaning of τηλόθεν precipitated by Aristophanes' argument for O.1's place in the addition; the stress placed on the spatial sense of τηλόθεν suggests an attempt to rebut the temporal reading. Cf. n. 28 below.

[27] Another scholium that may reflect the influence of Aristophanes' editorial decision is Σ O.1.142a (i 47 Dr) ἕλεν δ' Οἰνομάου: ἐνίκησεν (' "he took Oenomaus": he defeated him'), where the gloss is not exactly synonymous with the lemma. Given the obvious epinician connotations of ἐνίκησεν, the gloss may have been influenced by Aristophanes' stress on Pelops as the first Olympian victor. There are of course no grounds for attributing the gloss to Aristophanes himself.

[28] Cf. Snell (1953) 2–3 who shows that δέρκεσθαι 'refers not so much to the function of the eye as to its gleam as noticed by someone else.' The scholia emphasize the passive force of δέδορκεν: see e.g. Σ O.1.151c (i 50 Dr) τὸ δὲ δέδορκεν, ἀντὶ παθητικοῦ τοῦ δέρκεται· ἵν' ᾖ, ὁρᾶται (' "shines out" is used instead of the passive "is viewed", so as to mean "is seen" ') Σ O.1.151d (i 50 Dr) τουτέστι πανταχῇ βλέπεται καὶ ὁρᾶται ὁ Ὀλυμπιακὸς ἀγών. ἰδίως δὲ τὸ δέδορκεν ἐξενήνοχεν ἀντὶ παθητικοῦ τοῦ βλέπεται ('that is, the Olympian competition is noticed and talked about everywhere. He employs "shines out" idiomatically instead of the passive "is seen" ').

distancing involves the reader in a metaphorical redescription of his activity by which s/he is preceded. The text's rhetoric, both context-bound and context-transcendent, interacts with new contexts of meaning, with the result that the reader is confronted by a textual situation involving a series of imaginative dislocations. The passage as a whole becomes a site for the interaction between the poem's rhetoric and its material condition: the concept of distancing in τηλόθεν inscribes one of the conditions of fame, the necessity of its travelling and diffusion, and whereas the perfects μέμικται and δέδορκε connote endurance and continuity, naming something whose establishment has continued into the present, the material context draws attention to κλέος as something still being disseminated and added to by readerly activity.[29]

The closing lines of the poem also acquire a changed and expanded force from their place in the material document:

> τὸ δ' ἔ-
>
> σχατον κορυφοῦται
>
> βασιλεῦσι. μηκέτι πάπταινε πόρσιον.
>
> εἴη σέ τε τοῦτον ὑψοῦ χρόνον πατεῖν,   115
>
> ἐμέ τε τοσσάδε νικαφόροις
>
> ὁμιλεῖν πρόφαντον σοφίᾳ καθ' Ἑλ-
>
> λάνας ἐόντα παντᾷ.

The summit is crowned by kings.[30] Do not look beyond it. May you walk on high for this time's course, and may I likewise associate with victors, conspicuous for skill among Hellenes everywhere.

O.1 was composed for a performance in 476. Ten years later, Hiero was dead, his brother and successor Thrasybulus exiled, and after a brief period of civil strife the Syracusans instituted a democracy which was to last into the fourth century.[31] Hiero became a figure

---

[29] See Gerber (1982) 142 on μέμικται: 'Pelops' worship is viewed as continuous from the time of his death to the present.' See ibid. 145–6 on the debate over whether τὸ κλέος should be taken with Ὀλυμπιάδων or Πέλοπος and the weak personification connoted by δέδορκε. He suggests that the syntax is purposively opaque, connoting the elision of Pelops with Olympia as a whole.

[30] My rendering of this phrase follows Race, and reflects the interpretation current in antiquity, which emphasizes the distinction between kings and ordinary men: τὸ δὲ τελευταῖον καὶ τὸ πλῆρες, οὗπερ οὐκ ἔστιν ὑπερβολὴν τοῖς ἀνθρώποις εὑρεῖν, ὑψοῦται καὶ ἔστι τοῖς βασιλεῦσιν ('that which is final and complete, which it is not possible for men to surpass, is exalted and belongs to kings', Σ O.1.181, i 56 Dr).

[31] See Finley (1979) 58–60.

of debate for later authors seeking to interrogate the nature of absolute rule and explore its problems. Xenophon's *Hiero*, for instance, is a fictional account of a conversation between the tyrant and the poet Simonides, in which the former complains about the problems, political and personal, that beset him. For an educated Hellenistic reader, reading the end of *O*.1 could well have involved a negotiation between the text's idealizing and laudatory strategies and the historical events which succeeded it. Likewise, its representation of tyranny could have been read in the light of ongoing debates about the nature of monarchic authority and its intellectual implications. I shall return to these possibilities below; for the moment, I want to focus on how the end of the poem construes relations between poet and *laudandus*.

The wider historical and literary context points up the conditionality of the wish expressed in εἴη σέ τε τοῦτον ὑψοῦ χρόνον πατεῖν. It could be argued that in maintaining his rule until the end of his life, not to mention winning further success at the games, Hiero succeeded in fulfilling this hope, a reading strengthened by taking τοῦτον . . . χρόνον as referring to Hiero's lifetime,[32] but this reading is offset by knowledge of the disease that afflicted him in his final years, and of the failure of his dynasty. This historical perspective mediates the text's celebration of kingship as the ultimate state of human achievement (τὸ δ᾽ ἔσχατον κορυφοῦται / βασιλεῦσι). Furthermore, one might wonder about the disjunction between the idealized image of kingship expressed here and its attempted instantiations by individual rulers; reflection on the problems encountered by Hiero during the course of his reign might incline a reader to see an irony (unintended by the author) in these lines, particularly in relation to the more problematizing discussions of tyranny in *P*.1 and *P*.2. The complication of the poem's rhetorical strategies by the historical perspective also affects the injunction μηκέτι πάπταινε πόρσιον. The situation of this address emphasizes the transcontextual nature of the paraenesis, and the exhortation to observe the limits of human endeavour gains additional point from the reader's awareness of the qualified nature of Hiero's success.[33] Read in the light of these historical changes and the reader's wider

---

[32] Thus Gerber (1982) 176.
[33] Cf. Payne (2006) on the transcontextual nature of Pindaric gnomai.

knowledge, the text reflects human frailties and limitations as well as celebrating success.[34]

The metapoetic aspect of the poem's conclusion is also highlighted by its place in the edition. The poem ends by orienting itself outwards, towards a future it attempts to delimit by means of a wish for the author's future success. But this openness to the future also entails the text's exposure to circumstances it cannot control, to the contingencies of its reception and of the various critical and intellectual contexts by which it can be appropriated. Again, this situation instantiates the text's rhetoric, functioning as a realization of the statement ἀμέραι δ' ἐπίλοιποι / μάρτυρες σοφώτατοι ('days to come are the wisest witnesses', 33–4). In the context of the projected enunciation, this appeal to 'future days' acts as a bulwark against false and exaggerated stories, specifically those about Pelops which Pindar rejects in favour of his own version (28–32 and 47–51).[35] But the statement also suggests the reliance of the text itself on such judgements; lines 33–4 combine with the ending of the poem to defer judgement of the poem and its subject to the future, while also framing the ethical terms in which those judgements should be couched. A similar dynamic is at work in the divided addressee of εἴη σέ τε τοῦτον ὑψοῦ χρόνον πατεῖν. In the projected enunciation, this remark is addressed to Hiero, albeit in a public context. In a context of reading, the reader, as it were, overhears this address, as well as literally being addressed him/herself. This divided address again emphasizes the reader's distance from the space of the projected enunciation, but the programmatic context also licenses an application of the phrase to the reader's activity. Reading epinician poetry is a way, albeit in secondary and indirect terms, of 'walking on high', of sharing in the glory that epinician poetry bestows on great achievements. This resonance replays the application in a performance scenario of 116–17 to the chorus, and the wider citizen body which they represent, who like the poet participate in Hiero's success.

The final lines yoke poet and *laudandus* together, but the exact nature of this relationship is complex, and becomes more so when the

---

[34] A similar point might be made about a reader's experience of odes for Aeginetan victors in the light of that island's subsequent defeat at the hands of Athens, and about the status of Orchomenos in O.14. for which cf. Ch. 5 p. 211 n. 3.

[35] For discussion cf. Gerber (1982) 68–9; Scodel (2001) 127–8, who suggests that the phrase implies that 'time provides evidence the audience should use to recognize that [the rejected story of Pelops] is false'. Cf. also Fisker (1990) 40–1.

poem is read against a wider historical and literary context. The problem of the relationship hinges on the meaning of τοccάδε, which can be taken in either a quantitative ('and may I, as much as you . . . ') or a temporal sense ('and may I, for as long as you . . . ').[36] The word can bear both meanings, and deciding between them has consequences for the way we see the relationship between poet and his patron. The quantitative reading would seem to draw a connection between the poet's achievement and the nature of the *laudandus'* continuing success, although this is couched in terms of the maintenance of a general social status (νικαφόροιc / ὁμιλεῖν, 'to associate with victors', 116–17) as well as a broader reputation for poetic and intellectual excellence (πρόφαντον coφίᾳ καθ᾽ Ἕλλαναc ἐόντα παντᾷ, 117). The temporal reading, on the other hand, would make the poet's social and intellectual success temporally coextensive with that of the *laudandus.*

Yet neither of these readings clarifies the dynamics of power involved in praising, leaving vague the precise nature of interdependency of victor and poem, whether the latter derives its authority from the former or vice versa.[37] The structure of the sentence implies that the poet is dependent on the victor, his secondariness indicated by a qualifying adverb antecedent to the noun (χρόνον) applied to the tyrant. The grammatical structure, however, disguises problematic questions as to how this relationship is played out. These questions are sharpened by the material context of reading, in which the enunciative situation is altered; instead of being performed in the presence of its (primary) addressee and pointing up its relation to a living man with many potential glories, athletic and military, awaiting him, the text now names, in naming 'Hiero', a temporally diffuse space of conflicting meanings and narratives gathered under the proper name. The text's naming of Hiero (μάκαιραν Ἱέρωνοc ἑcτίαν, 11) is a paradoxical gesture; the proper name is destined to outlive the individual it names, and thus inscribes the finitude of that individual in the same movement as it bestows an identity. Inscribed within this bestowal of identity is a depropriation of the 'self' that it announces,

---

[36] Gerber (1982) 176 reads τοccάδε as temporal, while Slater p. 509 interprets it as qualitative. For the temporal sense cf. Aech. *Ag.* 860; Soph. *OT* 1212; for the quantitative cf. *Od.* 21.253; Soph. *El.* 403.

[37] See Goldhill (1991) 116–19 for an examination of this problem with regard to the disputed ending of Ibycus' poem for Polycrates (*SLG* S 151.46–8).

and, more important for our purposes, the possibility of its reconstitutive iteration.[38]

The reader again confronts a doubled discursive frame. The text's diachronic situation instantiates the wish of the narrator to 'be conspicuous for wisdom among Hellenes everywhere', and thus reconfigures the projected temporality of the utterance. If τοccάδε is read as temporal, it comes to reference the diachronicity of the text and the various readings and receptions that have guaranteed the author his status as πρόφαντον; correlatively, the τοῦτον . . . χρόνον would now name not Hiero's lifetime, but likewise his role as a figure in the history of the text. This scenario reverses the rhetoric of the projected enunciation. The grammatical structure may indicate the poet's dependence on the victor, but in the diachronic situation of the text's dissemination, the victor is dependent on his textual realization. A quantitative reading of the phrase would have similar implications. In the context of the edition the phrase has a strong programmatic force, a fact picked up by the comments recorded by Σ O.1.186 (i 86 Dr), which reads the phrase as assimilating other possible victors to Hiero: τοccάδε νικαφόροιc: ἀντὶ τοῦ, τοcούτοιc νικηφόροιc ὁμιλεῖν, οἷοc εἶ cύ. χαίρω δὲ γράφων τοιάδε, καὶ ἔcται τοιαῦτα οἷα ἐπὶ cοῦ ("'likewise with victors": instead of "to associate with so many victors of your sort. I enjoy writing things such as this, and they will be such as they are in your cast"').[39] This reading sees the text as figuring Hiero as a paradigmatic victor. There is no hint that the scholiast sees this paradigm as functioning in terms of the edition; instead, the reading is retrojected onto the historical situation of the poem's origin and performance, and Hiero's paradigmatic quality is imagined as applying to the poet's future writings (γράφων τοιάδε, καὶ ἔcται τοιαῦτα οἷα ἐπὶ cοῦ). Nevertheless, the movement from the unspecific mode of paradigmatic function broached by the scholiast and a specific paradigmatic function within the edition is suggested by the role of the opening poem in shaping generic expectations of the collection. At the very least, the poem's placement obliges readers to mediate between the specific and the general paradigmatic functions attributable to Hiero, and to the poet.[40] Reading O.1 in the light of its

---

[38] Cf. Derrida (1985) 3–38.   [39] Cf. *Scholies* pp. 450–1.

[40] For the poet as exemplum see e.g. Lefkowitz (1980) 34, 38; Goldhill (1991) 141–2 discussing *N*.8.35–9.

place in the edition and in relation to the Aristophanes' editorial comments therefore involves a series of questions about aetiology and exemplarity and the relations that obtain between them, about the nature and sources of poetic authority, and about the role of the reader in negotiating the various frames of reference devolved by the material transcription of a performance text, and multiple levels of exemplarity.[41] Hiero functions as an historical exemplum for other victors within the collection, Pelops as a mythical exemplum both for Hiero, and for other victors. Similarly, the self-construction at 117 is also mediated by its *Nachleben*: the process of canonization fulfils the narrator's claim while also participating in the processes by which its operation is altered.

Yet as mentioned above, Hiero himself had a textual afterlife that further complicates how Pindar's poems for him may have been understood and approached by later readers. Fourth-century texts about tyranny form an important part of this background,[42] and Xenophon's *Hiero*, a fictional dialogue between Hiero and Simonides set at the tyrant's court,is a particularly intriguing text in this respect. As well as participating in the contemporary climate of political debate,[43] the treatise can also be understood as a creative reading and expansion of epinician political discourse. Both Hiero's complaints about the misfortunes he suffers as a result of his position and Simonides' responses rework motifs common in epinician poetry such as the importance of victory to the community, the role of envy, the necessity of beneficial expenditure, and the function and nature of praise itself.[44]

Simonides' advice in particular bears a complex relation to its epinician precursors.[45] At 11.5–8, for instance, Simonides opposes

[41] Goldhill (1991) 149.

[42] Although these texts do not seem to have exerted an influence on the scholia's glosses on passages concerned with tyranny.

[43] For the background see Gray (2007) 4–14, and for ironic readings of *Hiero* and *Cyropaedia* see Strauss (2000), Tatum (1989), Nadon (2001), with the responses of Gray (2007) 14 with further references.

[44] See in general Sevieri (2004).

[45] The act of rewriting a poet as a speaker in a philosophical dialogue itself expresses the dynamics I explore here: *qua* fictional figure, Simonides charts the (imagined) philosophical subtexts of the poems he and his contemporaries composed. Xenophon thus positions his text as (imaginatively) expressing the presuppositions of epinician culture, while also acting (historically) as a secondary reconfiguration of them. Cf. Sevieri (2004) 278–9.

expenditure by a tyrant on himself and on the city as a whole, suggesting that the latter will bring him greater praise.[46] It will be better for Hiero, the poet argues, if the greatest number of competitors at the games are seen to come from his city rather than for Hiero to send the greatest number of racing teams himself (11.5). Competing against other states is more befitting of a tyrant than competition against private individuals (11.6–7), leading to a situation of greater benefit (11.8):

καὶ πρῶτον μὲν εὐθὺς κατειργασμένος ἂν εἴης τὸ φιλεῖσθαι ὑπὸ τῶν ἀρχομένων, οὗ δὴ σὺ ἐπιθυμῶν τυγχάνεις· ἔπειτα δὲ τὴν σὴν νίκην οὐκ ἂν εἷς εἴη ὁ ἀνακηρύττων, ἀλλὰ πάντες ἄνθρωποι ὑμνοῖεν ἂν τὴν σὴν ἀρετήν.

And first of all you will have secured that which you really wish to achieve, to be loved by your subjects. And then it won't be just a single person who announces your victory, but all men will sing your excellence.

This passage implicitly criticizes the athletic and commemorative culture of which fifth-century epinician was a part, on the grounds that it focused too much on the individual at the expense of the community. The criticism is pointed by the allusion to the announcement of the victor's name at the games (εἷς εἴη ὁ ἀνακηρύττων), and the phrasing of πάντες ἄνθρωποι ὑμνοῖεν τὴν σὴν ἀρετήν appropriates from epinician the function of praising great men. In transferring this role to the wider community, Xenophon articulates the difference between a tyrant praised simply for his achievement and one praised as having won success as a 'beloved' representative of his community.

And yet the relation of the passage to epinician discourse is not one of simple opposition. Epinician aims to win for its subjects precisely the kind of Panhellenic fame gestured to in the last clause, which could also be taken as hinting at the practice of reperformance.[47] Moreover, the kind of fame Simonides advises Hiero to aim at, based

---

[46] There are numerous other points of contact between the texts: *Hiero* 8.3–4 expands on the enunciation of the ruler's importance at *P*.1.87, while the criticisms of traditional choregic and competitive practices at 9.4 and 9.11 act as an implicit critique of fifth-century practice. The latter passage in particular, focusing on the cost of athletic success, answers the motif of expenditure in epinician (e.g. *P*.1.90) with the criticism that the μεγάλας δαπάνας invested 'in horse racing, and gymnastic and choral competitions' (ἐν ἱππικοῖς καὶ γυμνικοῖς καὶ χορηγικοῖς ἀγῶσιν) are not worth the μικρὰ ἆθλα that result.

[47] Gray (2007) 143 compares the songs sung for Croesus at the end of *P*.1.

on affection and respect, is similar to that advocated by Pindar's epinicians, which frequently warn against φθόνος and advocate good conduct on the tyrant's part.[48] The final phrase of the dialogue, εὐδαιμονῶν γὰρ οὐ φθονηθήςῃ ('you won't be envied in your happiness', 11.15), reinforces this dialogic relationship. Xenophon's phrasing employs two terms central to Pindaric discourse, and gives them a force that expands on their role in Pindar.[49] This expansion occurs partly through the greater detail with which Xenophon elaborates his arguments for an ethically inflected tyranny, and is given point by the position of φθόνος in the dialogue's final stages. Unlike at *P*.1.84, where φθόνος is the preserve of the envious townspeople, a fact of life that the poet is forced to deal with, Xenophon's dialogue enables the tyrant to act in such a way as to (at least notionally) make φθόνος impossible. This manoeuvre takes agency away from the poets who might speak on the tyrant's behalf and reattributes it to the tyrant himself. A metaliterary mechanism is also at work, as Xenophon redirects control of φθόνος from the dynamic action of public performance to his own argumentative and advisory strategies.

The phrase also has a specifically intertextual dimension. The use of εὐδαιμονῶν, for example, recalls τὶν δὲ μοῖρ' εὐδαιμονίας ἕπεται ('a share of happiness attends you') at *P*.3.84, the only time the noun or its cognates are used in poems for Hiero. A markedly appropriative dynamic is at work here, however: the context of *P*.3.84 is a somewhat gloomy one, as the poet consoles Hiero for the suffering inflicted on

---

[48] e.g. *P*.1.94, mentioning Croesus' φιλόφρων ἀρετά. The good repute at which the *laudandus* aims (εὖ δ' ἀκούειν, *P*.1.99) is understood to be in part conditional upon his character. On φθόνος in Pindar generally see Bulman (1992). Simonides' role in the dialogue would lead us to expect particular engagement with his poetry, a greater knowledge of which might reveal more about Xenophon's strategies. But Simonides' arguments engage with epinician discourse in general, and hence can be read (at least in part) as a response to Pindar.

[49] Gray (2007) 145 argues that the phrase εὐδαιμονῶν γὰρ οὐ φθονηθήςῃ 'subverts the idea that it was better to be hated as a ruler than pitied as a subject', comparing *P*.1.85 (κρέσσον γὰρ οἰκτιρμοῦ φθόνος), but this is somewhat inaccurate. 'Hated' is too strong a translation of φθόνος: Pindar's point here is that Hiero should not cease to aim at successes (μὴ παρίει καλά, 86) because of 'townsmen being grieved in their hidden hearts when they hear of others' successes' (84): see further *Pitiche* p. 359. In other words, it is Hiero as a competitor rather than generally as a ruler that is at issue in these lines: being envied for successes is better than being pitied for failures. Moreover, the poem clearly aims at transmuting possible resentment at Hiero into more positive feelings, as well as encouraging the tyrant to behave in a way that would take away some of the possible grounds for such resentment (86–100).

him by his illness.[50] Whereas the final stanzas of *P.*3 dwell on the immortal renown bestowed by poetry as a consolation for suffering, Xenophon's argumentative practice promises (in addition) happiness during one's lifetime. Moreover, by referring to a 'happiness' untroubled by the existential threats faced by the Hiero of *P.*3, Xenophon emphasizes the status of his Hiero as a textual figure and model freed from the limitations to which historical, flesh-and-blood individuals are subject. This intertextual nexus underscores both Xenophon's debt to Pindar, and his reconfiguration of the terms he has appropriated from epinician.

These dialogues, among other things, encourage a particular way of reading Pindar, as both a precursor and model for how tyranny is conceived by later authors, and as a set of discourses requiring supplementation and additional argument. I shall return to these issues below, but in the meantime I want to dwell briefly on another strand of Hiero's reception in ancient historiography. While Xenophon's discourse about tyranny can be seen as continuing and expanding on Pindar's, the tradition of criticism aimed at Hiero poses a challenge to the reader of epinician. Perhaps the most strongly critical assessment is that of Diodorus Siculus, who calls Hiero φιλάργυρος καὶ βίαιος καὶ καθόλου τῆς ἁπλότητος καὶ καλοκἀγαθίας ἀλλοτριώτατος ('avaricious and violent and a complete stranger to sincerity and gentlemanly behaviour', 11.67.4).[51] Nor is this the only such account: Aristotle relates a tradition of Hiero's use of female informants at public meetings as a means of consolidating his power.[52] These accounts raise the question of how troubled ancient readers of epinician may have been by attacks on the historical premises on which Pindar's poems for the tyrant were based.

---

[50] For the ancient tradition about this illness (gallstones) see e.g. Σ *P.*3.inscr.a (ii 62 Dr).

[51] Timaeus is a possible model for Diodorus' account, but cf. Baron (2013) 13, 215–18. For more positive versions of Hiero see Ael. *VH* 4.15 with *Scholies* pp. 286–7.

[52] Arist.*Pol.* 5.1313b11–15. Hints of this negative tradition in the scholia to Pindar are rare, but cf. Σ *N.*1.inscr.a (iii 6 Dr), which prefaces an account of Hiero's founding of Aetna with Ἱέρων γὰρ οἰκιστὴς ἀντὶ τυράννου βουλόμενος εἶναι, phrasing that by specifying desire to be seen as a founder *instead of* a tyrant implies sensitivity to the latter's (potential) negative associations. It is unclear whether this represents the scholiast's assessment or a retrojection onto Hiero of an assessment of popular perception.

A pessimistic reading might hold that this alternative tradition, providing that it is taken as historically reliable, exposes the fragility of encomiastic discourse: the brutal realities of how Hiero exercised power compromise the claims made by Pindar on his behalf, and show up the hollowness of Pindar's attempts at paraenesis. Such a position is complicated, however, by the presence of a tradition that saw Hiero as a more positive figure,[53] and by texts such as Xenophon's *Hiero* that project him as a (semi-)fictional figure around which debates about tyranny can be orientated. One response to the critical tradition would be to emphasize the disjunction between text and history, the historical realities being of secondary importance when compared to how Pindar constructs the *laudandus*. What matters, on this account, are the text's representational modes and the interpretative, ethical, and socio-political demands they make on audiences and readers. Another, related, approach would be to see the Pindaric corpus as a stage in an ongoing process of debate about, and attempts to regulate, the means by which tyranny is exercised. In the light of the contested historical status of Hiero and his regime, the most meaningful interpretative manoeuvre would be to scrutinize hisliterary receptions for approaches to socio-political phenomena that continue to resonate in changing circumstances. This approach most closely approximates the positioning of Pindar's poems for Hiero by their reception in Xenophon, allowing for a juxtaposition of literary and political history; however limited and compromised might have been the success of Pindar's epinicians *qua* political utterances in 470s Syracuse, their influence on the literary tradition testifies to their capacity to articulate the terms within which subsequent debates have been played out.

It could be argued that these approaches to the texts, in terms of the problematic receptions of tyranny, are inherently unfaithful to epinician poetry's demands. By reinscribing Pindar's Hiero in a network of debates about tyranny, and by underwriting it with a historicity in which tyranny emerges as a problematic figure, exposed to historical vicissitudes and literary contestation, the above readings disregard the way in which the text seeks to shape its reception. This approach, in effect, would be taking the position of the envious neighbours of O.1.47 who tell false tales about Pelops, rather than responding to

---

[53] Plut. *Mor.* 551f compares Hiero with Peisistratus as promoters of civic virtue, and cf. also Athen. 1.3b with comments below, Ch. 6, pp. 283–5.

the text under the constraints of φιλία.[54] The diachronic mode of reading, however, should not be seen as displacing or rendering defunct the text's modes of self-figuration, still less of making, for instance, the end of *O*.1 into (simply) an ironically charged and denigratory reflection on the shortcomings of tyranny. Rather, I have sought to acknowledge the multiple resonances the diachronic text takes on as the poem's strategies are recontextualized and the challenges they pose to readers. The mode of reading broached by the φιλία/φθόνος opposition does not lose its force, but is complicated by other modes of authorization such as editorial activity in its role of mediating access to the text, and the expanded intertextual relations against which the text is situated. In relation to Xenophon's *Hiero* and the other intertexts examined above, the φιλία/φθόνος opposition broached by *O*.1, *P*.1 and other poems operates at a more generalized, theoretical level; instead of being used to regulate the reactions of determinate audiences to a contemporary political situation, these terms operate as part of a transcontextual discourse that tests the force of the poem's ethical modalities against new historical and intellectual contexts.[55]

My reading also prompts attention to the role of an editor in shaping the reader's approaches to a poem and to an edition. Such a comment opens up various ways of seeing the text in relation to its material context, but also suggests questions about whether Aristophanes was justified in placing *O*.1 first,[56] and about how Pelops' exemplarity as first Olympian competitor fits with Heracles' role as founder of the games in *O*.3 and *O*.10.[57] Whether or not we find Aristophanes' reasons satisfying is less important than the extent to which the process of relating the *Vita Thomana* notice to *O*.1 prompts us to take note of and question editorial authority. In shaping the form and contents of a book, the editor reauthors the text, opening up new connections between poems.[58] His authority,

---

[54] Goldhill (1991) 161 argues that reading epinician 'against the grain' is a violation of the principles of φιλία and works in accordance with φθόνος. Such a mode of reading not only goes against the ethical model of epinician, but also denies the possibility of the poem's efficacy.

[55] See further below pp. 157–65.

[56] Cf. Negri (2004) 32–4 on the programmatic qualities of *O*.2.

[57] See Negri (2004) 36–8.

[58] For the significance of the poetry book as an aesthetic form in the Hellenistic period see e.g. Kerkhecker (1999) 282–90 arguing for Callimachus editing his *Iambi*; NB particularly pp. 288–9 for Callimachus' editorial activity as a scholar as a probable influence on his poetic activities, and cf. Gutzwiller (1998) 183–5.

however, is open to questioning by the reader, a process that in its turn entails a reflection on the reader's own relation to the text. In order to explore these issues further, I now consider some other aspects of the poetics of the edition.

BEGINNINGS AND ENDINGS: SHAPING EDITIONS

The questions raised above about the programmatic functions of *O*.1 and its relation *qua* opening poem to the rest of the Olympian odes and to the epinician collection as a whole require us to think about what actually constituted an 'edition' of Pindar's epinicians in antiquity.[59] Ancient readers would have had access to a collection of individual rolls, each one probably containing a single 'book' of poetry, such as the Olympian odes or one book of the *Partheneia*.[60] This allows for a situation in which, as William Race points out, 'the rolls . . . must have been freely rearranged' by different editors and readers.[61] Although this general observation does not affect my above remarks about the internal organization of particular books, it does entail consideration of what is meant by a programmatic function when considering how that function might span different books. Moreover, we must also consider the extent to which modes of storage, cataloguing, and titling may have mediated access to the texts and hence helped to shape the reader's experience of them. There is no *a priori* reason, for example, for a reader to pick up the *Olympians* before the *Pythians*, and hence be drawn into the programmatic dynamics that I have been exploring.[62] If, however, the reader came to the text in a library wherein the epinician books had been ordered in such a way as to place the *Olympians* first, his/her

[59] For the programmatic functions of the openings of poetry books see e.g. Van Sickle (1980) 13; Rutherford (2001) 159; Negri (2004) 31; D'Alessio (2007) 101–2.

[60] However, a third-century *sillybos* from Antinoopolis (*P.Ant.* 21) bears the inscription Πίνδαρος ὅλος, which indicates a 'complete' edition. This presumably consisted of a group of book-rolls stored together. Cf. *Scholies* p. 106.

[61] Race (1987) 409; see ibid. for a doxography of the debate about the order of Pindaric books and the attempts to square the competing claims of the order in the *Vita Ambrosiana* with that given by *POxy* 2438.35. Race's position is anticipated by Deas (1931) 49.

[62] Although the status of Olympia as the older, more prestigious festival may have influenced such a decision.

decision to start a reading with that book would be shaped in large part by the institutional and critical context of his activity. This is of course only one of a potentially innumerable series of different reading contexts which could have framed an individual's approach to the texts; the point of the example is to bring into focus the importance of material, institutional, and socio-historical frames for the reading experience.

The formation of editions also opens up the possibility of comparing different poems and seeing them in relation to each other, and of seeing groups of poems as thematically connected. *O*.1–3 and *P*.1–3 are particularly promising candidates in this respect because of their positions in their respective books, their shared *laudandi*, and the various thematic connections between them. It has been plausibly argued, for example, that *O*.1–3, all composed for victories in 476 by Hiero and Theron, were designed to be performed as a 'song cycle' attended by overlapping audiences who would have picked up on connections between the poems.[63] Whatever the historical truth of this argument, it is certainly the case that the grouping of the poems in the edition, and the 'ring composition' of *O*.3.42 (εἰ δ' ἀριστεύει μὲν ὕδωρ, κτεάνων δὲ χρυςὸς αἰδοιέστατος, 'if water is best and gold the most revered of possessions') recalling *O*.1.1 (ἄριστον μὲν ὕδωρ), encourages attention to them as a configuration. Similarly, *P*.1–3, all composed for Hiero, can be approached as a self-contained group, articulating a particular poet–patron relationship.

In this section, however, I shall focus on the relationship between *O*.1 and *P*.1 as documentary texts. Despite their formal and structural differences, there are numerous parallels between the poems. Both are addressed to Hiero, and have openings with strong idealizing elements, which can be read in terms of their implications for the individual poem and for the collection as a whole. Both end with figurations of tyranny. The envious neighbours at *O*.1.47 parallel Zeus' enemies at *P*.1.13–14 as negative paradigms for response to poetry, while the Phalaris/Croesus dyad at the end of *P*.1 can be read as interacting in various ways with the end of *O*.1. On the other hand,

---

[63] Cf. Clay (2011), who argues that *O*.1–3 are designed to connect the achievements of Hiero and Theron, and that the editor who ordered the poems as they stand in the edition 'showed a sensitivity to Pindar's design and...preserved what the Theban poet had conceived of as a Sicilian triptych': see further Morrison (2012) 123–4. On the issue of overlapping audiences for these poems cf. Morrison (2007).

the opening of *P*.1 is more overtly concerned with performance than anything in *O*.1, and this, together with its marked position at the beginning of the Pythian book, makes the opening of *P*.1 an interesting test case for exploring the intersection of performance rhetoric and documentary textuality.

Signs that ancient scholars were concerned with connections between these groups of poems are few and far between; given that ancient commentaries frequently cited Pindaric passages in relation to others, it is somewhat surprising that the scholia preserve no recognition of or comment on the echo of *O*.1.1 at *O*.3.42, nor on the similarity of phrasing at *O*.1.114 and *P*.3.22.[64] An exception is the comparison between the openings of *O*.2 and *P*.1 made at Σ *O*.2.1a (i 58–9 Dr):

> ἀναξιφόρμιγγες: ἤτοι <οἱ> τῶν φορμίγγων ἀνάccοντεc· ἕπονται γὰρ τοῖc ὕμνοιc καὶ φόρμιγγεc, δι᾽ οὓc καὶ ἀπεδείχθηcαν· ἢ οἱ ἀναccόμενοι ὑπὸ φορμίγγων ὕμνοι· πρότερον γὰρ ἐνδίδωcι <τὸ> μέλοc ὁ κιθαριcτήc, ἔπειτα ἡ ᾠδὴ λέγεται· ὡc καὶ ἐν Πυθιονίκαιc· χρυcέα φόρμιγξ Ἀπόλλωνοc καὶ ἰοπλοκάμων cύνδικον Μοιcᾶν κτέανον.

'Lyre-ruling': this means 'those which rule over lyres'; for lyres follow hymns, by means of which they have been shown forth. Alternatively, [it means] hymns which are commanded by lyres; for first the citharist strikes up the melody, then the poem is enunciated. So also in the Pythians: 'Apollo's golden lyre and just possession of the violet-coiffed Muses'.

The extant reference to *P*.1.1 is somewhat elliptical, as it is *P*.1.2–4 which provide the parallel for 'the citharist striking up the melody' and the song following. Although no extended appreciation of the link between the two openings is extant, we cannot discount the possibility that scholars and readers dwelt further on the interpretative possibilities marked by the elliptical ὡc καὶ ἐν Πυθιονίκαιc.[65] At the very least, the comment demonstrates an awareness of a connection betweeen the roles played by the image of the φόρμιγξ in the two openings. Neither this scholium nor those on the opening of *P*.1 make

---

[64] μηκέτι πάπταινε πόρcιον (*O*.1.114), ἔcτι δὲ φῦλον ἐν ἀνθρώποιcι ματαιότατον, / ὅcτιc αἰcχύνων ἐπιχώρια παπταίνει τὰ πόρcω ('there is a most fruitless tribe among men who scorning what lies close gazes on distant things', *P*.3.21–2). The latter passage dwells on Coronis' misdeed in sleeping with Ischys when pregnant by Apollo.

[65] For further analysis of ancient citational practices and their interpretative environment see Ch. 4, pp. 188, 209–10.

explicit the connection between the φόρμιγξ as opening a song and
the image of the φόρμιγξ opening the poem, although this connection
is implicit in Σ *P*.1.3c (ii 8 Dr), which offers an alternate explanation
of why the *cithara* is said to be Apollo's possession: ἢ Ἀπόλλωνος, διὰ
τὸ τὸν Ἀπόλλωνα προκατάρχειν τοῦ χοροῦ τῶν Μουςῶν ('Or it is
Apollo's because he leads the Muses in the dance').[66] This reading
is expanded in *P*.1.3d (ii 8 Dr), according to which ὁ μὲν Ἀπόλλων τῇ
κιθάρᾳ τῶν ᾠδῶν προκαθηγεῖται τῶν Μουςῶν, αὗται δὲ χορεύουςιν
('Apollo leads the Muses in their singing with the *cithara*, and they
dance in a chorus').[67] These explications facilitate attention to the
parallel between Apollo's role in leading off the Muses and the poet
guiding his chorus,[68] and to the apertural role of the description itself
within the poem.

As in the case of *O*.1, the vocabulary of performance can take on
new resonances as part of a material text. The description of the βάςις
ἀγλαΐας ἀρχά 'hearing' the lyre (2) has a double application to the
beginning of a signified performance and, metaphorically, to the
beginning of a reading. The mention at 3 of ἀγηςιχόρων ὁπόταν
προοιμίων is also assimilable to its material context, figuring *P*.1 as
the προοιμίον of the book as a whole:

χρυςέα φόρμιγξ, Ἀπόλλωνος καὶ ἰοπλοκάμων
ςύνδικον Μοιςᾶν κτέανον· τᾶς ἀκούει
  μὲν βάςις ἀγλαΐας ἀρχά,
πείθονται δ' ἀοιδοὶ ςάμαςιν
ἀγηςιχόρων ὁπόταν προοιμίων
  ἀμβολὰς τεύχῃς ἐλελιζομένα.
καὶ τὸν αἰχματὰν κεραυνὸν ςβεννύεις   5
αἰενάου πυρός. εὕδει δ' ἀνὰ ςκά-
  πτῳ Διὸς αἰετός, ὠκεῖ-
αν πτέρυγ' ἀμφοτέρωθεν χαλάξαις,
ἀρχὸς οἰωνῶν, κελαινῶπιν δ' ἐπί οἱ νεφέλαν
ἀγκύλῳ κρατί, γλεφάρων ἀδὺ κλάϊ-
  θρον, κατέχευας· ὁ δὲ κνώςςων
ὑγρὸν νῶτον αἰωρεῖ, τεαῖς

---

[66] At Σ *P*.1.3b (ii 8 Dr) Pindar is argued to be countering the notion that Hermes
invented the instrument.

[67] Cf. Σ *P*.1.5a. (ii 9 Dr).

[68] Although such a connection would have been available to readers without the
assistance of commentaries.

ῥιπαῖϲι καταϲχόμενοϲ. καὶ γὰρ βια-
τὰϲ Ἄρηϲ, τραχεῖαν ἄνευθε λιπών   10
ἐγχέων ἀκμάν, ἰαίνει καρδίαν
κώματι, κῆλα δὲ καὶ δαιμόνων θέλγει φρέναϲ ἀμφί τε Λατοΐ-
δα ϲοφίᾳ βαθυκόλπων τε Μοιϲᾶν.

Golden *phorminx*, just possession of Apollo and the violet-coiffed
Muses, to which the footstep listens, the beginning of splendour. The
singers obey the signs whenever you strum and strike up the openings
of chorus-leading preludes. You douse the spearing lightning of ever-
flowing fire. The eagle slumbers on Zeus' sceptre, having slackened his
swift wings on both sides, the lord of birds; for you have poured a dark-
visaged cloud over his curved head, a sweet seal for the eyelids. Slum-
bering, he ripples his supple back, caught by your notes. And even
violent Ares, putting aside his sharp-pointed spears, delights his heart in
drowsing, and your darts bewitch the gods' minds thanks to the skill of
Apollo and the deep-bosomed Muses.

The opening lines ground the utterance in a relation to the physicalities of performance. The invocation of the χρυϲέα φόρμιγξ, the
description of the 'step listening' (ἀκούει μὲν βάϲιϲ), the vivid 'striking
up' (ἐλελιζομένα) of the φόρμιγξ, followed by the detailed description
of music's bewitching effects, all emphasize the poem's place in a
performance economy. In describing an idealized mode of performance on Olympus in which Apollo and the φόρμιγξ represent and
embody music's enchanting and ordering effects, the narrator creates
an analogue for (the) historical performance(s) which functions at
several levels, and which has numerous consequences for interpretation of the poem in a book.[69]

Apollo and the Muses in this passage form an idealized analogy for
the activities of the poet and his chorus, and as such are part of a
wider system of analogies; critics have noted, for instance, the parallelism between Zeus' suppression of Typhos and Hiero's victory over
the Carthaginians and Etruscans (71–2).[70] Both actions involve forces
of disorder being subordinated and controlled. However, the opening
passage also exemplifies the interpretative challenges posed by
Pindar's epinicians. In a performance setting, these challenges project

[69] On the opening of *P*.1 in the context of reperformance see Morrison (2012)
128–9.
[70] Cf. e.g. Too (1998) 19–22.

the listener as a particular type of interpretative agent, and in the context of the book have the additional effect of being programmatic for the reader's engagement with the rest of the collection. Central to these dynamics are the relations and differences between the human and divine choruses. As Lucia Athanassaki has pointed out, Hiero and the human chorus find themselves in a situation of greater social and political complexity than those of their divine counterparts. Unlike Apollo, the human singer has to contend with the contingencies of particular concrete situations when deciding what and how to compose, issues which are to the fore in the fourth and fifth triads (61–100).[71] Connected to this is the disparity between the origins and subjects of the respective songs; while Apollo's music seems to arise spontaneously, the Pindaric *persona loquens* emphasizes the situation of his performance in an environment of poetic competition (45) and social negotiation (81–6). The absence of any reference to the semantic content of Apollo's performance further emphasizes this difference. While there is certainly an agonistic and self-validating element in the poet/Apollo, chorus/Muses, Hiero/Zeus diptychs, each of which serves as a validation of poetic practice,[72] the comparisons also have a paraenetic force in emphasizing the greater difficulties facing the human singer and, by extension, the *laudandus* and his citizens.

For the moment, I want to emphasize how the very fact of the performing chorus being put into relation with an idealized precedent is significant for shaping response to the poem as a whole. In addition to the functions just mentioned, this feature dramatizes the poem as a relational mode in which referential categories are connected with each other in ways different from those prevalent in ordinary speech. This relationality pertains to language as well as to the group of performers who take on some of their identity from their connection with the performing Muses. The χρυcέα φόρμιγξ invoked in the opening line, for instance, is simultaneously a signifier and concrete referent to which the human audience gains only a mediated access, but which also operates as an idealized symbol of performance

---

[71] Athanassaki (2009) 252: 'unlike the impact of divine song, the appeal of human song is not unconditional. It is neither universally nor eternally irresistible nor inescapable'. Cf. also ibid. pp. 258–9

[72] Poetic competition is more directly referenced at *P.*1.45, where the javelin simile ends with the request that Pindar may outshoot his rivals (μακρὰ δὲ ῥίψαιc ἀμεύcαcθ' ἀντίουc, 'and with a long cast surpass my opponents').

practice.[73] This figuration makes the audience aware of a break between signifier and referent which is reinforced by the extended specification of the instrument's role on Olympus. Yet this differentiation grounds both the force of the analogy and the language used to convey it: without the differentiation, neither the symbolism of the φόρμιγξ nor the mediatory role of language would come about. As a consequence, response to the poem calls for a negotiation of various interpretative complexities, and as such is very different from the somnambulant response of Ares and Zeus' eagle to Apollo's music (εὕδει, ἰαίνει καρδίαν / κώματι) and the 'bewitching' (θέλγει φρένας) effect it has on the unnamed other gods.[74] The reference at 97–8 to songs commemorating tyrants has a similar effect. The idealizing reference to (sympotic) performance culture in general and a nod to future reperformances of the poem combine to underscore the poem's place within, and dependence on, a wider culture of performance and critical judgement.

Another relation emerges in this passage between language as the substrate for transcontextual ideality, and the provisionality and momentariness of that language's realization in a given performance or reading.[75] The use of present tenses in the opening strophe and antistrophe (e.g. ἀκούει, πείθονται, and ὁπόταν . . . τεύχῃς) signify the continual nature of the event described.[76] Consequently, there is a conflict between the transcendental, continuous nature of the present as experienced by the gods and the temporality of its signification, which occurs as part of a chain of discrete significations. In registering the permanence of the Olympian scene, the language of the opening stanzas dramatizes its status as an archival medium, while the fact that this function is a reflex of the referent's distinctive temporality (the language can only register the gods' experience as such because of the nature of that experience) points up the interdependency of referent and sign. This issue can in turn be connected to performance and writing. No easy opposition of the two is possible, in that the

---

[73] Cf. Krischer (1985) for the representation of divine performance here and in previous texts. For the debate over whether the instrument should be seen as referred to one realm or the other cf. Athanassaki (2009) 246 nn. 19–20. Segal (1998) 13 sees the two performances as blended together.

[74] For this effect cf. *Pitiche* pp. 332–3.   [75] See Payne (2006).

[76] Cf. *Dith.* 2.1–17 with Furley and Bremer (2001) ad loc., and Athanassaki (2009) 248.

opening of the poem dramatizes itself as a rhetorical archive; unlike in passages which record factual details, such as athletic victories or political successes (e.g. *P*.1.32, 71–2), here the archival function is instantiated by the text's temporal structure.[77]

The formation of an historical Pindaric archive through collections of the texts and the supplementary scholarship devoted to them extends this structuring. But while the opposition between the text written and performed may not be absolute, there are ways in which apprehension of the two modes differs. On the one hand, a comparison can be made between the particularity of a performance and that of the material document. Practices of copying in the ancient world meant that, like a performance, each book was a unique, non-reduplicable entity, notwithstanding the conventional use of certain writing styles, and the standardized deployment of lectional signs.[78] The text's idealizing description of performance, however, highlights the supplementarity of writing as a something absent from what the text itself describes. In order to clarify this issue, we may compare the figuration of writing in texts written specifically for inclusion within a book, where a self-consciousness often emerges about the interaction between writing and text. One example is the passage of Callimachus' *Aetia* in which the narrator prays to the Graces in terms that relate specifically to the materiality of the book: ἔλλατε νῦν, ἐλέγοιϲι δ' ἐνιψήϲαϲθε λιπώϲαϲ / χεῖραϲ ἐμοῖϲ, ἵνα μοι πολὺ μένουϲιν ἔτοϲ ('Come now, wipe your shining hands on my elegies, so that they may abide for many a year'). As discussed above,[79] this invocation highlights the specifically material aspect of the readers' encounter with poetry.

When thinking about *P*.1 as a documentary poem, we are faced with a different interpretative situation. Because writing is not mentioned by the text, the documentary medium is extrinsic to the text's

---

[77] This structure is modelled on the description of the Muses at Hes. *Th.* 2–4, where present tenses are used in a similar way to denote continuous activity (αἵ θ' Ἑλικῶνοϲ ἔχουϲιν ὄροϲ μέγα τε ζάθεόν τε, / καί τε περὶ κρήνην ἰοειδέα πόϲϲ' ἁπαλοῖϲιν / ὀρχεῦνται καὶ βωμὸν ἐριϲθενέοϲ Κρονίωνοϲ, 'who hold the great and holy mountain of Helicon and dance around the dark spring with tender feet, and the altar of Cronus' mighty son'). Thereafter, however, there is a switch to aorists and imperfects (χοροὺϲ ἐνεποιήϲαντο 7, ἐπερρώϲαντο δὲ ποϲϲίν 8, ἐννύχιαι ϲτεῖχον, 10). On the conventionality of this shift, its possibly injunctive nature, and possible antecedents in earlier poetic traditions see West (1989). Eschewing such a temporal shift, the opening of *P*.1 emphasizes the continuousness of its referents to a greater extent.
[78] For the last see Ch. 2 pp. 108–10. [79] Introduction, pp. 11–13.

referential economy, and functions in relation to it as a purely supplementary and external mode. The references to performance and the descriptions of the instrument's sound also have the effect of situating writing as the other of the text, as a medium different from performance, or the performance of this particular text. Moreover, unlike in the case of Callimachus' passage, where the interplay of text and medium is the result of authorial design and narratorial self-figuration, the equivalent interplay in *P.*1 emerges from the conjunction of text and medium, unmediated by any explicit textual formulation and therefore not articulated by authorial control. The unlocalizability of the point at which the relation between writing and text emerges is important: in *P.*1 writing appears to intrude onto the text as the ground of the reader's access to it, but as a medium ungrounded in the strategies of the text itself. Yet this approach to writing as the text's supplementary other is only made possible by the text's existence in written form, and it might be suggested that the supplementary relation can be reversed, so that the notion of the text as a performance piece becomes the supplement to the written text, as the latter forms the basis of an imaginative engagement with the text as realized in performance.[80] The text's capacity to cause its written medium to appear as its supplementary other, and the simultaneous necessity of the written medium to the book's function is emblematic of the other interactions I have discussed. In bringing about an *othering of the written itself* by exposing the documentary medium to a textual construct whose rhetoric excludes it, *P.*1 evinces the transformational aspect of the literary text even as it is itself resited by its material aspect.[81]

Another passage which bears on the relation between the performed and the written text is 25–6, where the narrator rounds off the description of Typhos buried under Aetna with a description of how the mountain and its hidden villain appear:

---

[80] For the scholiasts referring to Pindar 'writing' his poems see Introduction, pp. 9–10.

[81] A similar point could be made about numerous passages in Pindar, and other early poets, in which performance is at issue. The relationship between text and medium has particular force in this case, however, because of the extent of the emphasis on chorality, and because of the poem's programmatic position at the beginning of the book. The latter role gives a dimension to the choral self-reference that it would not have had in performance.

κεῖνο δ᾽ Ἀφαίστοιο κρουνοὺc ἑρπετόν
δεινοτάτουc ἀναπέμπει· τέραc μὲν
θαυμάciον προcιδέcθαι,
θαῦμα δὲ καὶ παρεόντων ἀκοῦcαι...

That creature sends up Hephaestus' most terrible springs, a portent marvellous to behold, and a wonder even to hear of from those present...

These lines dramatize the importance of the notions of immediacy and immediate experience (τέραc μὲν θαυμάciον προcιδέcθαι), but stress that hearing about Aetna second hand is also a θαῦμα. There is likely to be a difference in meaning between τέραc and θαῦμα, the former referring to the visual process of interpreting a sign, in this case inferring from the Ἀφαίcτοιο κρουνούc the presence of the creature hidden beneath the mountain, and the latter more neutrally to the sense of 'wonder' felt on hearing the description.[82] This difference, however, is not registered by Σ *P*.1.47c (ii 14–15 Dr), the only extant ancient interpretation of the line, which instead equates the two experiences: ὁ δὲ νοῦc· ἐκεῖνο δὲ τὸ τοῦ Ἡφαίcτου ἑρπετὸν κρουνοὺc πυρὸc δεινοτάτουc ἀναδίδωcι, θαυμαcτὸν μὲν ἰδεῖν, θαυμαcτὸν δὲ καὶ τῶν παρόντων καὶ ἑωρακότων <u>ἀκοῦcαι</u> ('the meaning: this creature of Hephaestus sends up most terrible streams of fire, a wondrous thing to see, and a wondrous thing to hear about from those who were present and have seen it').

As well as describing the marvellousness of the mountain and the spread of its fame, these lines also implicitly refer to the circumstances of the performance. In this sense, θαῦμα δὲ καὶ παρεόντων ἀκοῦcαι references the situation of the audience, who are hearing about the eruptions second hand.[83] Many of the audience at the first performance, and indeed the chorus, living near the volcano, would doubtless have seen the eruptions for themselves, although visitors from beyond the immediate area may not have done. Audiences at later reperformances elsewhere in the Greek world may likewise have only heard about Aetna. Regardless of the precise resonance of the phrase for a given individual or group, however, θαῦμα δὲ

---

[82] Cf. *Pitiche* p. 338.
[83] The vocabulary of wonder recalls ecphrastic discourse: cf. *Il.* 18.377. Hellenistic readers would have been additionally sensitized to the metapoetic force of Pindar's θαῦμα by passages such as Theoc. *Id.* 1.56, Ap. Rh. *Arg.* 1.767, Mosch. *Eur.* 49.

καὶ παρεόντων ἀκοῦcαι describes the force of the poem itself; its verbal recreation of Aetna is a θαῦμα to be admired.[84]

Similarly, the use of προcιδέcθαι carries a secondary reference to the visuality of the description at 21–4, with its vivid pictures of belching flames and rocks rolling to the sea; reading the text is a (re)creative moment of *enargeia*.[85] Engagement with choral performance is represented in these lines not as a purely immediate experience, but rather as entailing fictive recreation and the intervention of the various subjective experiences of individual listeners. These lines also apply to the experience of reading, wherein παρεόντων ἀκοῦcαι takes on the added resonance of 'hearing about'/(re)imagining a performance by people who had been 'present' to see the eruptions. Significantly for the poem's documentary status, the line legitimizes second-hand dissemination as a means of access to the text.[86]

The poem ends with a passage which highlights the importance of ethics as a constituent part of readerly response to epinician, a feature thematically programmatic for the rest of the collection. The mention of 'witnesses' for Hiero's deeds at 87–8 is important for setting up the ode's paraenetic finale:

> εἴ τι καὶ φλαῦρον παραιθύccει, μέγα τοι φέρεται,
> πὰρ cέθεν. πολλῶν ταμίας ἐccί· πολλοὶ
> μάρτυρες ἀμφοτέροιc πιστοί.

If something slight leaps out from you, it is taken as great. You are steward of many things. There are many faithful witnesses of both.

---

[84] Cf. Morrison (2012) 131.*P*.1.26 draws on the description of Typhoeus at Hes. *Th*. 821–52, and reduplicates the lexis of ἄλλοτε δ᾽ αὖ cκυλάκεccιν ἐοικότα, θαύματ᾽ ἀκοῦcαι (834). There are other significant points of contact between the passages: the description of Aetna's flames resituates the flames that in Hesiod's version glow from the monster's eyes (ἐν δέ οἱ ὄccε / θεcπεcίηc κεφαλῇcιν ὑπ᾽ ὀφρύcι πῦρ ἀμάρυccεν, 825–6). By involving the listener in a tradition of representations, these intertexts draw further attention to the distinction between Etna/Typhos as referent and significational structure.

[85] The visual 'realism' of the poem is registered at Σ *P*.1.17b (ii 11 Dr), glossing the description of the eagle: ὑγρὸν νῶτον· τὸν εὐδιάχυτον ὑπὸ τῆς ἡδονῆς. γραφικώτατα δὲ cυνδιατιθέμενον τῇ ᾠδῇ καὶ θελγόμενον τὸν ἀετὸν ὑπετύπωcεν (" "Rippling back": made fluid by pleasure. He produces a most vivid impression of the eagle's bewitchment and its disposition to the song'). For comment on this scholium see Wilson (1980) 105–6, who notes that this is the only occasion in which such an equation between verbal and visual arts is made in the scholia.

[86] Cf. Morrison (2012) 131.

Ancient and modern commentators have debated what ἀμφοτέροιc refers to. The scholium on the second line interprets ἀμφοτέροιc alternatively as referencing 'the true and the false' (presumably things done by Hiero, with the previous ἀψευδεῖ δὲ πρὸc ἄκμονι, 86, in mind) or 'you and your son', and records Dionysius Sidonius' interpretation of the phrase as referring to 'you and your associates'. None of these readings is particularly convincing; it is preferable rather to take it as referring both to good and bad deeds, a sense which looks forward to the dichotomy of Phalaris and Croesus in the final passage.[87]

Such a reading is paralleled in Σ P.1.169 (ii 27 Dr), which comments that 'rulers' errors are great' because of their social position:

εἴ τι καὶ φλαῦρον παραιθύccει· λείπει ὁ γάρ· ἐὰν γάρ τι καὶ εὐτελὲc παρὰ coῦ λεχθῇ καὶ ὁρμήcῃ, καὶ τοῦτο μέγα καὶ διὰ πάντων φέρεται. φηcὶ δὲ μεγάλα εἶναι τὰ τῶν ἀρχόντων ἁμαρτήματα, κἂν εὐτελῆ τυγχάνῃ. εἰ καί τι οὖν εὐτελὲc ἁμάρτῃc, τοῦτο μέγιcτον ἔcται.

'If something slight leaps out': He leaves out something like the following: for if something small is spoken by you and you drive it on, it will be taken as important by everyone. He says that rulers' errors are great, even when they do something small. If you err in something small, it will be important.

In modern scholarship, however, 87–8 have usually, like the ending of *O.1*, been interpreted encomiastically, their implication being that Hiero's deeds are to be assessed positively.[88] Although such an encomiastic element is at work, the lines' paraenetic force should also be registered. This passage dramatizes the audience, and the wider citizen body, as 'witnesses' who hold their ruler to account. The specification of the witnesses as 'faithful' demands that they respond in a way which fits the nature of what is being responded to, and concomitantly the ability to distinguish between legitimate and illegitimate forms of behaviour.[89] Hiero emerges from these lines as a figure overseen by his audience. The passage validates his power by constructing it as the outcome of popular co-operation and legitimization; like the chorus at the beginning of the poem, his position is relational, dependent in part on how he is perceived. Within the

---

[87] So *Pitiche* p. 360.   [88] Cf. Race (1986) 48.

[89] This may be accentuated if the lines are heard to recall 'days to come are the wisest witnesses' at *O.1.33–4* (see above p. 133): this connection would further underline the role of listeners' interpretation in the text's reception.

poem, 87–8 anticipate the Phalaris/Croesus dyad, both of whom are subjects for the kind of judgement referenced here. Within the collection, the lines also recall O.1.33–4 and the dynamic at work there between the poem's own judgement and the openness of its future. Later readers are also put in the position of μάρτυρες, weighing, from different vantage points from those open to the poem's first audiences, the *laudandus'* achievements and thereby participating in the construction of his fame.

The end of the poem continues this ethical thrust, and also gains programmatic force from its place in the book:

μὴ δολωθῇς,
ὦ φίλε, κέρδεσιν ἐντραπέ-
λοις· ὀπιθόμβροτον αὔχημα δόξας
οἶον ἀποιχομένων ἀνδρῶν δίαιταν μανύει
καὶ λογίοις καὶ ἀοιδοῖς. οὐ φθίνει Κροί-
σου φιλόφρων ἀρετά.
τὸν δὲ ταύρῳ χαλκέῳ καυτῆρα νηλέα νόον   95
ἐχθρὰ Φάλαριν κατέχει παντᾷ φάτις,
οὐδέ νιν φόρμιγγες ὑπωρόφιαι κοινανίαν
μαλθακὰν παίδων ὀάροισι δέκονται.
τὸ δὲ παθεῖν εὖ πρῶτον ἀέθλων·
εὖ δ' ἀκούειν δευτέρα μοῖρ'· ἀμφοτέροισι δ' ἀνήρ
ὃς ἂν ἐγκύρσῃ καὶ ἕλῃ, στέφανον ὕψιστον δέδεκται.   100

Do not be deceived, my friend, by shameful gains. The acclaim of renown that survives a man is all that reveals the way of life of departed men to chroniclers and singers. The kindly excellence of Croesus does not perish, but Phalaris, with his pitiless mind, who burned men in a bronze bull, is encompassed everywhere by a hateful reputation; lyres that resound beneath the roof do not welcome him in gentle fellowship with boys' voices. Successfulness is the first of prizes, being well spoken of the second; but a man who encounters and wins both has received the highest garland.

Within a reading process dictated by the hierarchy of the epinician books, reading the *Pythians* after the *Olympians*, this passage works as a recapitulation and expansion of the programmatic and exemplary functions of O.1. The deployment of Croesus and Phalaris as a double exemplum of the positive and negative aspects of tyranny expands on the reflection on tyranny's benefits and limitations at O.1.114. In O.1 the transgressive potentialities of monarchic rule remain largely implicit; the stress of the Tantalus narrative, for instance, falls on his relations with the gods, and his inability 'to digest his great good fortune' (καταπέψαι / μέγαν ὄλβον οὐκ ἐδυνάσθη, 55–6) rather than on his political position within his kingdom. In the final passage of *P.*1, however, relations between tyrant and community are to the fore.

Croesus is praised for his φιλόφρων ἀρετά, a phrase which, given the poem's Delphic connections, probably connotes his renowned gifts to Apollo as well as his kindliness as a ruler. Phalaris, however, is figured as a paradigm of cruelty, his burning of men in a bronze bull (τὸν δὲ ταύρῳ χαλκέῳ καυτῆρα) emblematic of a transgressiveness that denatures the natural world by using the image of an animal as an instrument of torture, and violates the laws of human communities. Hiero's position relative to these two exempla is marked by a difference in temporal figuration. Whereas Croesus and Phalaris are described using present tenses (οὐφθίνει 94, κατέχει 96, δέκονται, 98), Hiero is addressed with an optative (καιρὸν εἰ φθέγξαιο, 81), imperatives at 86 (μὴ παρίει καλά. νώμα δικαίῳ πηδαλίῳ στρατόν· ἀψευδεῖ δὲ πρὸς ἄκμονι χάλκευε γλῶσσαν, 'do not put aside good deeds. Guide your people with a just rudder. Forge your tongue on an anvil free of falsehood'), a conditional followed by an imperative at 90 (εἴπερ τι φιλεῖς ἀκοὰν ἀδεῖαν αἰεὶ κλύειν, μὴ κάμνε λίαν δαπάναις, 'if you wish always to hear pleasant reports, do not weary of too much expenditure') and a hortatory subjunctive at 92 (μὴδολωθῇς). This creates a contrast between the fixed, determined state of Croesus and Phalaris, and the figuration of Hiero, whose conduct is still in the process of being defined. The shift to the perfect tense in the final line (στέφανον ὕψιστον δέδεκται) complicates this opposition; the grammatical subject of this verb is the indefinite ἀνήρ / ὅς, but Hiero is clearly the implied subject, as a victor who has earned both success at the games, and good repute through the poem. While the perfect tense connotes a completed process, the indefiniteness of its subject and the conditionality implied by the preceding imperatives and subjunctives imply a figuration which is still uncompleted.[90]

---

[90] Race (1986) 47–8 comments on the encomiastic function of paraenetic speech, following Arist. *Rhet.* 1 1367b37 (cf. also Pernot (1993) 710–24). I differ from Race in seeing Hiero as a textual figure as well as an historical individual, with the effect that the text creates a simulacrum of real-world power relations. Cf. Athanassaki (2009) 254–59: she argues (p. 259) that 'posthumous inclusion in the sympotic repertoire was ... the ultimate challenge for tyrants', and sees this passage as 'portraying the human side of the tyrant' so as to win him aristocratic favour (cf. ibid. p. 272). While

So while Croesus and Phalaris are denoted as figures who have assumed a fixed place in the poem's projected system of values, Hiero is in the process of being constructed, his finitude deferred by the demands made on him by the text's moral imperatives. These demands resist textual closure in that they point beyond the text to the horizon of an empirical history. Hiero as a textual figure connotes, by means of an oscillation between the negative and positive courses exemplified by Phalaris and Croesus, the challenge of respecting and maintaining the laws of human conduct and avoiding excess. At this point, it is worth thinking again about the reception of Pindar in Xenophon's *Hiero*, a text which, as we saw above, casts poems such as *P*.1 as (contested) models for its own discourses.[91] I suggested that Xenophon's rewriting of (Pindar's) Hiero emphasized the tyrant's status as a textual figure, positioning Pindar's poems as reference points in an ongoing dialogue about how tyranny should best be exercised. We are now in a position to see more clearly that this manoeuvre extends modes of reference already at work in Pindar's texts, especially the final stanzas of *P*.1. Although, as my reading has made clear, the poem itself stresses the distinctiveness of Hiero's textual status, this feature would have been given further emphasis by its relation to the use made of it by Xenophon.

Alongside, and in co-operation with, the poem's celebration of success, Hiero's textual figuration reminds readers and listeners of the difficulties of correct social conduct. As in the case of *O*.1, the material document and the intertextual connections later literature establishes with it significantly recapitulate the text's rhetoric. The book participates in Hiero's fame, enshrining the celebration of his success in a transhistorical form, while also enforcing his suspended figuration. Reading *P*.1 as programmatic for the *Pythians* as a whole therefore involves the reader in an intertextual relation with *O*.1, from which emerges a juxtaposition of different figurations of a single character, and hence a reconfiguration of the exemplary modality. Both poems likewise entail encounters with a series of ethical imperatives to

---

symptic reperformance was doubtless important, her focus on this as a means of posthumous dissemination is rather narrow; other types of 'performances', such as private readings, would doubtless have played a part. For *P*.1.97–8 as potentially anticipating reperformance cf. Budelmann (2012) 178–9, and 179 n. 18 for the suggestion that it may anticipate the performance of Bacch. fr. 20c, an encomium composed for the same victory.

[91] See above, pp. 136–9.

which the reader is also subject. The openness of these formulations stresses their continuing importance.

RECEPTION AND REREADING

So far I have focused on the role of material and metatextual factors in shaping approaches to the book, and tried to account for the potential impact on readings of Pindar of changing historical circumstances. I want now to consider the consequences of Hellenistic literary reception of Pindar for readerly engagement with these poems by examining the possible relations between Theocritus' *Idyll* 16, written for Hiero II, and Pindar's poems for the tyrants.[92] Theocritus' description of the difficulties of the contemporary poet contains a tissue of Pindaric references which position Theocritus in relation to his epinician predecessor.[93] In particular, his critique of miserly patrons at 5–21 depends in part on Pindar's figuration of the ideal relation between patron and poet, as at *P*.1.89–92:[94]

> εὐανθεῖ δ' ἐν ὀργᾷ παρμένων,
> εἴπερ τι φιλεῖς ἀκοὰν ἀδεῖαν αἰ–
> εὶ κλύειν, μὴ κάμνε λίαν δαπάναις·   90
> ἐξίει δ' ὥσπερ κυβερνάτας ἀνήρ
> ἱστίον ἀνεμόεν πετάσαις. μὴ δολωθῇς,
> ὦ φίλε, κέρδεςιν ἐντραπέλοις·

Abiding in a flourishing temper, if indeed you wish always to hear pleasant reports, do not grow too weary of expenditure, but like a helmsman let out the sail and spread it to the wind. Do not be deceived, my friend, by shameful gains.

---

[92] On the dating of Theoc.16 cf. Gow (1950).

[93] Cf. e.g. Clapp (1913); Perrotta (1925); Hunter (1996) 82–90, (2014) 72–4. González (2010) stresses the importance of civic elegy as a model. Hunter (1996) 87 points out the possibility of a connection between *P*.1 as written to celebrate Hiero's founding of Aetna and *Id*. 16's celebration of Hiero II having recently come to power. This, however, depends on a date for *Id*. 16 early in Hiero's reign, which is by no means certain. González (2010) 69 finds difficulties with the notion of *P*.1 as a model for *Id*. 16 but overstates the case, particularly in his view that Theocritus' sarcasm has no Pindaric precedent (cf. *P*.2.72–96); while it is true that *Id*. 16 departs from its Pindaric models in various ways, his assessment (pp. 70–1) of *Id*. 16 as an ethicizing intervention into Syracusan society could equally well describe, with the requisite historical and generic adjustments, Pindar's own poetry.

[94] Hunter (1996) 86 n. 26 notes that ὡς πάρος at 14 signals the reworking of a previous passage.

Theocritus' complaint at 15 about patrons who 'have been vanquished by acquisitiveness' (νενίκηνται δ᾽ ὑπὸ κερδέων) is also modelled on a common Pindaric topos,[95] and the repeated injunction not to hoard wealth recalls, for instance, *I*.1.67–8:

> εἰ δέ τις ἔνδον νέμει πλοῦτον κρυφαῖον,
> ἄλλοισι δ᾽ ἐμπίπτων γελᾷ, ψυχὰν Ἄϊδᾳ τελέων
> οὐ φράζεται δόξας ἄνευθεν.

If someone hoards secret wealth within, and attacks others with laughter, he does not consider that he is paying his soul to Hades without repute.

But there are also important differences between the rhetorical stances of Theocritus' complaint at 5–21 and Pindar's advice to Hiero in *P*.1. As argued above, Pindar's imperatives and subjunctives construct the poem as a dialogue whose subject is in the process of being constructed, whereas Theocritus' questions meet with a glum answer (14), and 14–21 consist of a description of a fixed state of affairs. There are also structural differences; unlike Pindar, Theocritus never addresses his (prospective) patron directly. Theocritus' treatment of Pindar in *Id*. 16 is complicated further by the fact that the latter is one of three main models, the more important, at least ostensibly, being Homer, directly referenced at 20 as the miserly patron's catch-all poet of choice and the subject of the exemplum of the bestowal of poetic fame on Odysseus at 51–7.[96] Another important predecessor is Simonides, the poet responsible at 34–47 for the immortalization of the Thessalian nobles.[97] With regard to readerly perception of Pindar, a certain relativization is at work, as Pindaric texts are constructed as one set of positions among others within the corpus of texts that preserve and transmit fame.

Theocritus' self-differentiation is perhaps most apparent in the poem's conclusion, a passage replete with Pindaric allusions, as the narrator calls on the Graces to accompany him and assist him in his project (104–9):

> ὦ Ἐτεόκλειοι Χάριτες θεαί, ὦ Μινύειον
> Ὀρχομενὸν φιλέοισαι ἀπεχθόμενόν ποτε Θήβαις,   105
> ἄκλητος μὲν ἔγωγε μένοιμί κεν, ἐς δὲ καλεύντων

---

[95] Cf. *P*.3.54, *N*.9.33.   [96] Cf. also 74–5, and Hunter (1996) 90–7.

[97] Cf. Hunter (1996) 97–109; Acosta-Hughes (2010) 179–86.

θαρσήσας Μοίσαισι σὺν ἁμετέραισιν ἴοιμ' ἄν.
καλλείψω δ' οὐδ' ὔμμε· τί γὰρ Χαρίτων ἀγαπητόν
ἀνθρώποις ἀπάνευθεν; ἀεὶ Χαρίτεσσιν ἅμ' εἴην.

O Graces, Eteoclus' goddesses, O you who love Minyan Orchomenos that is hated by Thebes, when unsummoned I shall stand fast, but I shall take heart and go to those that call on me together with our Muses. I shall not leave you behind. For what is desirable to men without the Graces? May I always be with the Graces.

Theocritus signals his relationship with Pindar by siting the Graces at Orchomenos (105), alluding to that city's prominence as a cult centre of the Graces but also to Pindar's depiction of Orchomenos in *O*.14. A more specific echo occurs at 108–9, where τί γὰρ Χαρίτων ἀγαπη-τόν / ἀνθρώποις ἀπάνευθεν; recalls *O*.14.5–7, where Pindar describes the Graces' role in human civilization (σὺν γὰρ ὑμῖν τά τε τερπνὰ καί / τὰ γλυκέ' ἄνεται πάντα βροτοῖς, / εἰ σοφός, εἰ καλός, εἴ τις ἀγλαὸς ἀνήρ, 'with your favour all sweet and pleasant things are accomplished by mortals, if a man is wise, or fair, or famous'). The final phrase of the poem also echoes Pindar, as the Theocritean narrator's wish to be 'always with the Graces' recalls Pindar's wish to associate with victors and be conspicuous for his wisdom at *O*.1.116–17 (ἐμέ τε τοσσάδε νικαφόροις / ὁμιλεῖν πρόφαντον σοφίᾳ καθ' Ἕλ- / λανας ἐόντα παντᾷ). But the Theocritean narrator's claims are different from those of his model; whereas Pindar claims the right to associate on equal terms with victors, and is unabashed about making claims for intellectual respect, the Theocritean speaker, in the straightened circumstances described through the poem, eschews Pindar's grand social claims, and instead claims a more direct relationship with the Graces, picking up on the proximity signalled by Μοίσαισι σὺν ἁμετέραισιν ἴοιμ' ἄν.[98]

Generic differentiation may also be at issue if we detect in ἁνίκα τέττιξ ... ἀχεῖ ἐν ἀκρεμόνεσσιν (94–6) an allusion to Pindar's use of Echo in *O*.14. Although ἠχή is a common word for 'sound'/'echo', the poem's general engagement with Pindar and the close relations between *O*.14 and the ending, as well as the metapoetic dimensions of Theocritus' τέττιξ and Pindar's Echo, strengthen the connection. On this reading, the intervention of the bucolic τέττιξ into the higher

---

[98] The Muses and the Graces are equated here, unlike in Pindar; cf. Hunter (1996) 84.

genres of hymn/encomium is emphasized by its displacement of Pindar's Echo.[99] The mention of Eteoclus at 104, and the close association formed between him and the Graces (ὦ Ἐτεόκλειοι Χάριτες θεαί) caps *O.14* by including a detail not found in Pindar's version, and also prefigures the close relationship between the poet and the Graces elaborated in the final line.[100] One might also read ἀπεχθόμενόν ποτε Θήβαις as metonymically signalling an agonistic relationship with the Theban Pindar via the vehicle of Theocritus' rewritten Orchomenos: the exaggerated hostility of the metapoetic ἀπεχθόμενον conflicts ironically with the narrator's pose of power-lessness earlier in the poem.[101]

As Richard Hunter has pointed out, however, the meaning of Χάριτες is put into question by the intertextual networks in which the poem involves itself.[102] The word itself can refer to 'pay', 'honour', 'favour', and poems themselves, and the conceptualization of the Χάριτες is complicated by the relationship with Simonides and the traditions surrounding him. At 16.8–12 Theocritus envisages his Graces as papyrus rolls trapped in a chest:

> αἳ δὲ σκυζόμεναι γυμνοῖς ποσὶν οἴκαδ᾽ ἴασι,
> πολλά με τωθάζοισαι, ὅτ᾽ ἀλιθίην ὁδὸν ἦλθον,
> ὀκνηραὶ δὲ πάλιν κενεᾶς ἐν πυθμένι χηλοῦ   10
> ψυχροῖς ἐν γονάτεσσι κάρη μίμνοντι βαλοῖσαι,
> ἔνθ᾽ αἰεί σφισιν ἕδρη, ἐπὴν ἄπρακτοι ἵκωνται.

They come home complaining on naked feet, and reproach me heavily for their vain journey. Timid, they rest again in the bottom of an empty coffer, bending their heads over their cold knees. Their seat is always there when they return unsuccessful.

---

[99] See below, Ch. 5, pp. 217–23 for Echo as a metapoetic figure in *O.14* and Germany (2005) on Echo in the *Homeric Hymn to Pan* as (possibly) a symbol of intertextuality.

[100] For the story of Eteoclus cf. Paus. 9.38.1, who says that the three stones representing the Graces fell from heaven 'for Eteoclus', and Σ *O.14.inscr.c* (i 390 Dr), which cites Hesiod for the story.

[101] The historical reference is to Thebes' sack of Orchomenos in 364 BC.

[102] Hunter (1996) 105. A similar negotiation is at work in the use of κέρδος and ὄνασις and their cognates; at 15, the former refers to the purely monetary and material 'gains' to which misers are in thrall (νενίκηνται δ᾽ ὑπὸ κερδέων), but at 22 it is used to question the value of the 'gain' which comes from stored wealth; the polyvalent meanings of ὄνασις as both 'benefit' and 'profit' are at issue at 23, and again at 57 where the Ionian bards 'benefit/profit' their subjects (εἰ μή σφεας ὤνασαν Ἰάονος ἀνδρὸς ἀοιδαί).

It has long been recognized that this passage alludes to a well-known anecdote which forms part of the tradition about Simonides' avaricious personality, recorded by Stobaeus 3.10.38:

Σιμωνίδην παρακαλοῦντος τινὸς ἐγκώμιον ποιῆσαι καὶ χάριν ἕξειν λέγοντος. ἀργύριον δὲ μὴ διδόντος "δύο" εἶπεν οὗτος "ἔχω κιβωτούς, τὴν μὲν χαρίτων, τὴν δὲ ἀργυρίου· καὶ πρὸς τὰς χρείας τὴν μὲν τῶν χαρίτων κενὴν εὑρίσκω, ὅταν ἀνοίξω, τὴν δὲ χρησίμην μόνην".

Someone asked Simonides to compose an encomium and said that he would have recompense for it. When they did not give him money he said 'I have two coffers, one for graces, the other for silver. I find the one empty of graces for practical purposes whenever I open it, and only the other is of any use.'

Gow comments that whereas in the anecdote χάριτες means 'thanks', in Theocritus 'the symbolism is less clear. His χηλός is apparently a receptacle for books and money alike'.[103] In using a poet as a means to criticize the miserliness of patrons, Theocritus deploys Simonides 'as both a positive and a negative exemplum for both poet and patron'.[104] But this passage also has consequences for how we might read Theocritus' engagement with Pindar in the poem's concluding passage. The sense of Χάριτες as documents in 8–12 carries over into the final passage as well, creating a polyvalent set of meanings: the Graces are personifications, material rewards, and material documents. This gives rise to the possibility of reading ἀεὶ Χαρίτεσσιν ἅμ' εἴην as 'may I always be with my [Graces in the form of] documents', realizing the image of the poet who is bound up with his compositions, and hence a disjunction between the flesh and blood author and the literary identity inscribed within the material document. On this reading, ἐς δὲ καλεύντων / θαρσήσας Μοίσαισι σὺν ἀμετέραισιν ἵοιμ' ἄν points not to the wandering poet arriving at his patron's home but to the book-based manifestation of a purely textual figure. The final lines of the poem therefore stage a conflict between the figuration of a close personal relationship between the poet and the personalized Graces, and that of the author as a disembodied adjunct to the material manifestations of his texts.

---

[103] Gow (1950) 308. The Graces are also multivalent in epinician: cf. MacLachlan (1993) 87–123, Currie (2011) 283. On the interpretation of the Graces in the scholia see Pontani (2013).

[104] Hunter (1996) 105.

The conflicted implications of these two figurations of poetical activity testify to the complexity of the poet's role in mediating competing models of poetic activity.

The multiplicity of Theocritus' Χάριτες extends to their generic aspect; Reinhold Merkelbach has shown that they are fashioned to represent a band of children going from house to house, who would sing songs in exchange for food or small gifts.[105] As such, they provide an index for the generic complexity of the poem as a whole; this process highlights the constructedness of the literary discourses in which the negotiations of patronage are played out, forming part of what Hunter terms Theocritus' project of 'expos [ing] the realities of poetic patronage'.[106] These various strategies turn up different ways of rereading the Pindaric texts on which they draw. On one level, the criticism of contemporary patrons at 5–21, and the validation of Simonides at 34–47, implicitly constructs the Pindaric and Simonidean past as an idealized locus wherein the relations between poets and patrons were played out according to the demands of reciprocal φιλία. Similarly, the generic and conceptual complexity of Theocritus' Χάριτες raises the possibility of an opposition between a generically complex, text-based, Theocritean poetics and a relatively more simple Pindaric model. The self-consciousness with which Theocritus explores the realities of patronage and the constructedness of its discourses could be read as retrospectively undermining Pindar's discourse by exposing its fictionality and inscribing a multiplicity of meanings into the Pindaric model, or as doing the opposite, emphasizing the intimacy of Pindar's relations with the tyrants by highlighting the conversational directness of his paraenetic discourses. But these oppositions, and the modes of reading predicated on them, quickly break down, partly in the light of the complexities of Pindar's construction of praise I considered in my readings of O.1 and P.1, and partly because the Theocritean situation (re)alerts the reader to these complexities. The treatment of τιμή at 66–7, for example (αὐτὰρ ἐγὼ τιμήν τε καὶ ἀνθρώπων φιλότητα / πολλῶν ἡμιόνων τε καὶ ἵππων πρόσθεν ἑλοίμαν, 'I would have honour and men's love before many mules and horses') which refers to

---

[105] Merkelbach (1952). González (2010) 85–7 sees the Graces as also metaphorizing the figure of the poet travelling from performance to performance, but the symbolism also encompasses the peregrinations of material documents.
[106] Hunter (1996) 109.

both the 'honour' and 'pay' demanded by the poet,[107] plays on the complexity of the relation between material and symbolic capital already explored by Pindar, whose injunction to Hiero at *P*.1.90 to spend money on self-glorification (εἴπερ τι φιλεῖς ἀκοὰν ἀδεῖαν αἰεὶ κλύειν, μὴ κάμνε λίαν δαπάναις) cannot be divorced from the ethical imperatives that follow; no amount of songs would save a tyrant who behaved like Phalaris from infamy.

Much of the above analysis of *O*.1 and *P*.1 focused on the effects created by the diachronic recontextualization of poems written for specific occasions, one aspect of which was the recalibration of elements such as addresses and advice to the victor, which in the diachronic situation operate as virtualized discourses rather than stylized dialogues with a living person. This situation shifts the terms of the interaction between poet and patron, both of whom become purely textual figures, and whose power relations are no longer anchored in a real set of historical circumstances. The invocation of the Graces at *Id*. 16.104–9, with its absence of any address to Hiero and its implicit emphasis on the materiality of the book, dramatizes precisely such a break with the conditions of patronage as is brought about by the text's diachronicity. It may also be possible to detect a more specific material aspect of this passage, namely a connection between the closural role of the invocation of the Graces in *Id*. 16 and the place of *O*.14 at the end of the Olympian book. In the light of our ignorance of Pindaric editions in the 270s–260s this must remain speculative, but it is possible that some early Hellenistic books of the *Olympians*, or another similar grouping, had *O*.14 as their final poem, allowing the end of *Id*. 16 to be read as an allusion to a particularly material form of closure which expands on the conceptualization of the Graces as books at 8–12. And whatever the situation of Pindaric editions in Theocritus' time, the editions of the late third and second century, and indeed later antiquity, would certainly have opened up the possibility of such a reading whether or not Theocritus originally intended such an allusion.[108]

---

[107] Cf. Hunter (1996) 105, who reads the lines as playing on the double sense of τιμή in order to represent 'the doubleness of the patronage relationship, both its "theory" and its reality'. For González (2010) 88–90, the rejection suffered by the Theocritean narrator at the outset of the poem is indicative of a breakdown in the social order and reciprocity represented by the Graces.

[108] *O*.14 is not the only Pindaric poem in the background here: there is also a verbal correspondence between Theocritus' passage and fr. 155 S-M (τί ἔρδων φίλος σοί τε,

The construction of the Graces in *Id.* 16 as both personifications and documents, and the poem's recycling and problematization of the terms of panegyric poetry, are part of the way the poem constitutes itself as a reading of the panegyric tradition. The contextuality of this reading, so strongly emphasized in, for example, the critique at 5–21, prompts a consideration of the contextuality of the reading practices more generally. Certainly, a model of reading epinician which privileges the context of the original performance as a site of meaning, and which focuses on the text as authorially constructed, is an important tool for enabling some of the critical discourses we wish to construct about Pindar, but it is important to acknowledge that these are not the only nor necessarily the most important readings possible. Awareness of this issue is strengthened by the strategies of *Id.* 16. In probing the discourses of patronage and in juxtaposing different registers (hymn, epinician, children's song), *Id.* 16 participates in the possibility, also manifest in the editorial realizations of the texts described above, of a shift in perceptions of Pindaric texts, away from seeing them as performance pieces, and towards (also) seeing them as formalized diachronic structures capable of serving as generic models. In this sense, for example, the Theocritean reinterrogation of what it means to be a good patron can be read as picking up on the openness of the paraenesis in *P.*1, continuing the negotiations dramatized in that poem.

The belatedness which forms such an important part of Theocritus' narratorial stance in *Id.* 16, albeit mediated by other factors, also has consequences for perceptions of Pindar. Richard Hunter argues that the poem stages an 'ironic acknowledgement that the language of patronage has been preserved, but its meaning irretrievably altered in the march of time and circumstance: the attempt to recreate the archaic relationship of Pindar and Hiero I must always remain an imaginative, literary *mimesis*'.[109] But the gap that Hunter points to here between present and past also applies to Pindar's poetry itself in a Hellenistic context, where the depiction of poet–patron relations serves as an index for historical changes as well as a record of previous

---

καρτερόβρεντα / Κρονίδα, φίλος δὲ Μοίcαιc, / Εὐθυμίᾳ τε μέλων εἴην, τοῦτ' αἴτημί ce). Theocritus' closural use of the Graces may also have been influenced by passages such as *N.*5.50–4. The material aspect of the Graces would also have been strengthened for subsequent readers by their figuration at Call. *Aet.*fr. 7 Harder.

[109] Hunter (2003) 45.

times. Theocritus' ironized attempt 'to recreate the archaic relationship of Pindar and Hiero I' prompts consideration of the secondariness of the epinician text as constituted by the material document
which, although it is born out of 'the archaic relationship of Pindar
and Hiero I', can also be viewed as a mimesis or trace of an original
performance. Moreover, the use of Pindar's poetry as a generic model
also affects readers' relations to it, instantiating its claims of authority
by means of a supplementation that highlights the texts' dependence
on reception and reading for their efficacy.[110]

Pindar's status as both a privileged model and as a corpus open to
contestation leads, as we have already seen, to a complex intertextual
situation where later receptions can be variously, and simultaneously,
understood as co-operating with strategies already at work in the
texts, as shifting our understanding of concepts important to the
Pindaric corpus, as both validating and relativizing Pindar's status
as a generic and stylistic exemplum, and as accentuating the specifically diachronic aspects of the text as a material document. We are
also now in a position to see more clearly that some of the most
distinctive features of Hellenistic poetics, such as the dramatization of
the tensions between present and past, song and writing, socially
embedded and disembedded poetic modes, were also at work in the
encounters that Hellenistic authors (and readers generally) would
have had with texts of the classical period. From this angle, the Graces
of *Id.* 16, simultaneously goddesses and books, singers and simulacra,
can be seen as an allegory of the experience of confronting a material
instantiation of a performance poem. I shall return to some of these
phenomena when reading *O.*14 in the context of the Hellenistic
edition, but in my next chapter I shall turn my attention to a different
group of intertextual encounters. Classical scholars have tended, as
I have just done, to ground discussion of intertextual matters primarily in the relations between primary texts. Yet while this is a perfectly
justifiable strategy, it has had the consequence of marginalizing the
fact that, just as for their modern counterparts, much of ancient
readers' conception of intertextual relationships would have been
formed, or at least influenced, by literary citations in commentaries
and the microtextual encounters thus generated. My next chapter
takes this issue as its central focus.

---

[110] Cf. further Phillips (2013c) 170–5.

4

Marginalia: Textual Encounters in the Scholia

It is now generally agreed that scholarly activities such as editing and commenting on texts, as well as events such as lectures and discussions, played a crucial role in articulating the sites of literary encounter within and through which readers of the Hellenistic period encountered 'classic' texts. Recent scholarship has done much to illuminate trends in ancient thinking about literature,[1] the role of commentaries in education and intellectual life,[2] and the importance of scholarship for poets' creative engagements with literary traditions.[3] The corpora of ancient scholia have also been subjected to increased and much-needed scrutiny.[4] This chapter aims to contribute to these trends by examining a feature of the scholarly environment that has received comparatively little attention,[5] namely how intertextual relationships were conceptualized, how literary citations operated in scholarly commentaries, and the role they played in articulating the ancient reading experience.

Some preliminary remarks are in order on the historical and theoretical challenges this analysis entails. I have already discussed the general problems involved in using the scholia as historical evidence for intellectual practices,[6] and the nature of the evidence imposes methodological limitations specific to discussion of citations.

---

[1] Foundational is Pfeiffer (1968); for more recent treatments see the essays in Montanari and Pagani (2011), and Matthaios, Montanari, and Rengakos (2011).

[2] Cribbiore (2001); McNamee (2007). On education more generally see Morgan (1998).

[3] See e.g. Wilson (1980); Lefkowitz (1985); Bitto (2012); *Scholies* pp. 15–31.

[4] Nünlist (2009); David et al. (2009); Braswell (2013).

[5] Although cf. Braswell (2012) 19–26; Phillips (2013c). On Didymus' use of literary citations see Braswell (2013) 116–18.

[6] See Ch. 1, pp. 60–1.

The following readings are necessarily provisional, not least because the evidence available to us does not reflect the total amount of scholarly information potentially available to readers in the period under discussion.[7] Contextual specificities such as who was reading a particular text, when and where such a reading took place, and in what wider intellectual setting, could all make a difference to the readings I elaborate, but with the exception of a few cases such details are beyond our knowledge.[8] Taking this into account, my readings attempt to sketch out the kind of interpretative scenarios generated by Hellenistic scholarship without making claims for their historical completeness. Another important qualification relates to the provenance of the citations. With a few exceptions, the citations that I shall discuss are not connected with a particular scholar. It is likely that some or indeed many of these intertextual connections were discussed by well-known Hellenistic scholars, but it is impossible to tell if and when this was the case, and when they were first used in commentaries.[9] It should also be emphasized that I am not claiming that fifth-century listeners would have been incapable of engaging intertextually with Pindar's poems, or that readers' intertextual engagement is dependent on the existence of commentaries. My aim here is rather to give an account of the evidence for how readers' intertextual approaches were mediated. As in the case of, for example, deictic references,[10] the situation of reading a text with a commentary extends and recontextualizes phenomena that would have occurred in different ways during performance.[11] What is distinctive about the reading situation, however, is the greater time it affords readers for considering intertextual relationships and exploring their complexities.

---

[7] It should also be noted that some of the material I discuss may date to the Imperial period: cf. Ch. 1, pp. 60–1.

[8] One such issue relates to the title of this chapter: some citations were, as ancient papyri show, literally 'marginalia', written in the margins of the primary text, but separate commentaries (ὑπομνήματα) would also have been a source for such quotations.

[9] Ammonius' 'On the Material Plato Took Over From Homer' demonstrates Hellenistic interest in intertextual relationships: cf. [Long.] *de Subl.* 13.3 and Hunter (2012) 44 for discussion. Cf. also Σ A *Il.* 1.219a for Aristarchus comparing Plato and Homer's speech-writing techniques, with the remarks of Nünlist (2009) 318, Hunter (2012) 5.

[10] See Ch. 3, pp. 121–2.

[11] Pavlou (2008) 533–41 makes a strong case for seeing intertextuality with specific texts as an important feature of Pindar's poetics; see further Morrison (2011), (2012), and for intertextuality in Bacchylides e.g. Fearn (2007) 122–43.

The scholia frequently cite poets for exegetical and comparative purposes, but usually without much qualification.[12] The work from which the citation comes is often not mentioned, and citations are usually introduced by simple phrases devoid of contextualizing comment.[13] Occasionally, a slightly more specific form of citation is employed to elucidate a similarity between the text being commented on and the cited text,[14] and I shall examine below various instances of a particular intertextual relationship being specified between Pindar and his predecessors. In general, however, relationships between texts are not elaborated. Equally, there is little evidence of generic or chronological distinctions in the vocabulary used of different poetic utterances: verbs such as μνημονεύει and μαρτυρεῖ are used equally of Homer and Hesiod, the classical and Hellenistic poets, and indeed Pindar himself.[15] Although this may partly be the result of redaction, the practices of other scholiastic corpora, and papyrus commentaries such as that of Theon's on *P*.12 (*POxy* 2536),[16] in which Euripides' *Oedipus* is cited, and the discussion of the provenance of the phrase κύκνος ὑπὸ πτερύγων at *POxy* 2737 fr. 1 col i 20–6, support the notion that citations tended to be accompanied by only minimal comment.

It should not be assumed, however, that the form of citations was conditioned by an absence of critical reflection. It is also worth bearing in mind that readers of the Hellenistic period would have been familiar with the densely intertextual literature of their own time, that created many of its most telling effects through self-conscious engagement with its poetic models.[17] Such texts cannot but have sensitized readers to intertextual complexities, and we shall

---

[12] For a fuller discussion of this issue cf. Phillips (2013c) 155–61.

[13] The author's name alone (Σ *O*.3.19b = i 110 Dr, Σ *O*.3.50c = i 119 Dr); ὡς (καὶ) φησίν (Σ *P*.2.18a = ii 34 Dr); καὶ φησίν (Σ *P*.4.122 = ii 116 Dr); ὁ δὲ . . . λέγει (Σ *O*.1.40a = i 30 Dr); ὡς with author's name (Σ *O*.4.31a = i 135 Dr); καί with author's name (Σ *P*.4.253c = ii 133 Dr); ὡς καί with author's name (Σ *O*.7.4 = i 200 Dr); καθὰ καί with author's name (Σ *I*.6.10a = iii 251 Dr); ὅμοιον τῷ παρα with author's name in the dative (Σ *O*.1.129b = i 46 Dr); καὶ τὸ παρά with author's name in the dative (Σ *O*.3.50b = i 119 Dr); οὕτω/οὕτως καί with author's name (Σ *P*.2.132c = ii 54 Dr); καθὼς καί (Σ *N*.4.5 = iii 64 Dr); ὥσπερ with author's name and name of text (Σ *P*.3.177b = ii 87 Dr); καθάπερ καί with author's name (Σ *I*.8.17b = iii 271 Dr).

[14] Cf. e.g. Σ *I*.4.39a (iii 228 Dr) τῷ αὐτῷ τρόπῳ καὶ Εὐριπίδης κέχρηται ('Euripides uses the same trope').

[15] Cf. Phillips (2013c) 157–8.   [16] Cf. Ch. 6, pp. 274–5.

[17] For an overview see Fantuzzi and Hunter (2004) 3–17, and in more detail Acosta-Hughes (2010).

encounter below some instances in which contemporary poetic practice has influenced views of Pindar's engagements with his predecessors. The contexts in which commentaries were often used are also of
crucial importance. Much of the material contained in the Pindar
scholia derives from commentaries designed for use in schools, and in
such a setting literary citations are often likely to have served as
starting points for discussion or elaboration by the teacher. We also
have ample testimony about the reading of texts, and specifically the
practice of inter- and intratextual comparison, as an important feature of elite social life. Plutarch relates that Alexander the Great and
his companions engaged in 'comparison of Homeric verses at symposia or as a way of passing the time' (τῶν Ὁμήρου cύγκριcιc ἐπῶν ἐν
ταῖc διατριβαῖc ἢ παρὰ τὰ cυμπόcια, Plut. *Mor.* 331c), a vignette that
functions in part as a model for the social dimension of such practices
in Plutarch's own time.[18] More immediately relevant to my analysis
here is the detailed picture given by Aulus Gellius of a group of
educated friends comparing passages in Theocritus and Virgil's
Eclogues at a dinner party (*aput mensam cum legerentur utraque
simul Bucolica Theocriti et Vergilii, NA* 9.9.4). Of particular issue for
the discussion are effects created by Theocritus that are idiomatic and
not susceptible of translation: the phrase τὸ καλὸν πεφιλημένε (*Id.* 3.3)
is described as *uerba . . . non translaticia* (*NA* 9.9.8), and Virgil has
done well to avoid it in his 'translation' at *Ec.* 9.23–5. The chapter
ends with the narrator recalling an extended comparison of *Od.*
6.102–8 and *Aen.*1.498–502 by the grammarian Valerius Probus,
who censures Virgil for imitating Homer ineffectively.[19] Although
they are not mentioned in this passage, commentaries would often
have played an important role in articulating the grounds of such
discussions.[20]

---

[18] See Johnson (2010) 128 n. 53 for further references. While our best evidence for
such reading communities comes from the second century AD, it is likely that some of
their dynamics would have been shared with similar social groups during the Hellenistic period.

[19] See e.g. Austin (1971) 167 for discussion. Probus' account of the passage was not
universally accepted in antiquity: Servius (on 497) comments *uituperant multi* [sc. the
simile], *nescientes exempla uel parabolas uel comparationes adsumptas non semper
usquequaque congruere, sed interdum omni parte, interdum aliqua conuenire.*

[20] The minimalism of glosses can partly be explained by their contexts of use, but it
is also significant that the modern practice of gathering multiple parallels for a given
word or topos is not found in ancient commentaries, whose authors aimed at
'apposite illustration' of usages by the quotation of a single passage: see Braswell

The sociocultural aspects of this readerly activity have been much discussed in recent scholarship: group readings and discussions were spaces for elite competition, the performance of social identity, and formed a key part of the practices by which reading communities defined themselves as custodians of their cultural inheritance.[21] Nor should reading alone be considered as undetermined by these sociological factors: reading literature was for Greeks of the Hellenistic and Imperial periods in part an exercise in constructing cultural identities and performing one's status as a Greek.[22] Commentaries articulated some of the norms and procedures which underlay this process, and we should be aware of the wider resonances that intertextual connections could have in this respect. My chief interest here, however, is in the meanings generated by the textual conjunctions upon which such concrete reading situations would have been based. My readings therefore interrogate not only the terms in which the scholia's intertextual combinations are couched but also the interpretative potentialities they create. As in the cases explored in the previous chapter, my aim is not only an historical exegesis of the relevant texts, but a consideration of their interpretative demands on readers and the lines of thought that they imply or assume.

Such discussions entail limitations of scope. In addition to the numerous passages in the scholia in which historians and other authors are quoted, there are hundreds of citations of poets ranging from Homer to the tragedians and the Hellenistic poets, and a thoroughgoing examination of this body of material would be far beyond the remit of this chapter. I shall focus instead on two particular types of citations, first of Homer and Hesiod in the Pindar scholia, and then some instances of how Pindar himself is cited in scholia on other poets. A picture will emerge from this analysis that, while far from exhaustive, will contribute to a better understanding of the processes of reception and canonization, and of the encounters through which ancient readers' conceptions of textual relationships

---

(2012) 22. This practice may well have been influenced by the difficulties of consulting texts (thus Slater (1989) 45), but it also has interpretative consequences, creating a situation in which a reader can focus on the relation between two texts without being distracted by others.

[21] See Johnson (2010) 98–136 on Aulus Gellius' construction of readerly communities.

[22] See e.g. Gleason (1995), Whitmarsh (2001) 90–130, esp. 116–29.

were mediated. Examining literary citations in scholarship allows us to form a better idea not only of readers' engagements with Pindar, but also of the frames of reference and readerly habits that they would have brought to bear on reading the poetry of their own times. Furthermore, I shall argue that citations of Pindar form an important conduit of reception, rehearsing and making concrete his status as a 'classic' poet by deploying his statements as part of authoritative exegesis and using his texts as exemplary models and sources of information. Consideration of how Homer is cited in the Pindar scholia, on the other hand, also allows us to scrutinize how Pindar's literary antecedents were perceived by ancient commentators, and to assess how commentaries contributed to readers' conceptions of literary history.

POETIC PRECURSORS

Unsurprisingly, Homer is cited more often in the Pindar scholia than any other author. There are around three hundred occasions on which the Homeric texts are quoted or referenced, and this body of texts is of central importance for thinking about how textual relationships were constituted in ancient Pindaric scholarship. I shall not attempt a compendious treatment of these metatexts; my focus instead will be directed at citations which have particular bearing on the literary relationship between Homer and Pindar as envisaged by Hellenistic commentators, and at uncovering how the mechanics of citation contributed to the interpretative horizons open to readers of the period.

As a prelude to this discussion, I want to sketch out the picture of the Hellenistic scholarly background with reference to three instances of named scholars discussing Pindar's use of poetic models.[23] The first shows that interest in intertextual connections dates to a relatively early period in Hellenistic scholarship. Given his extensive scholarship on Homer, one would expect Aristarchus to be sensitive

---

[23] *Σ I*.4.63a–b (iii 232 Dr), where Chrysippus is quoted as discussing why Pindar claims at *I*.4.27–9 that Homer has honoured Ajax, also testify to scholarly discussion of intertextual issues in the Hellenistic period.

to verbal connections between the two poets, and *Σ P.*4.14 (ii 98 Dr) shows that this was indeed the case:

ἀργινόεντι μαστῷ· Ἀρίσταρχος μὲν τὸ Ὁμηρικὸν οὖθαρ ἀρούρης παράγειν αὐτόν φηcι πιθανῶc, ὑπαλλαξάμενον τὸν μαστόν· Ἱεροκλῆc δέ φηcι τὴν πόλιν κεῖcθαι ἐπὶ λόφου μαcτοειδοῦc λευκογείου. μᾶλλον δὲ ἀπὸ τῆc εὐτροφίαc, ὡc Ἀρίσταρχοc· καὶ γὰρ ὁ ἀργινόειc cυνᾴδει τούτῳ μᾶλλον, ἀπὸ γάλακτοc.

'On the shining white breast of a hill':[24] Aristarchus convincingly suggests that the poet is modifying the Homeric phrase 'udder of the earth', substituting the word 'breast'. Hierocles explains that the city stands on a white hill resembling a breast; but according to Aristarchus the phrase is more to do with the land's fertility, and in fact the use of 'shining white' accords better with this interpretation, as having to do with milk.[25]

Perhaps the most striking feature of Aristarchus' observation is that the phrases he compares are conceptually rather than verbally linked.[26] While it is not much of a leap to move from seeing Pindar's ἀργινόεντι μαστῷ as connoting fertility (ἀπὸ τῆc εὐτροφίαc) to seeing it as reworking Homer's phrase,[27] the gloss demonstrates not only that Hellenistic scholars were capable of noticing such subtle connections,[28] but also that they could win the approval of later readers (φηcι

---

[24] I follow Race's translation of the phrase.

[25] For the adjective used of 'springs of milk' cf. *AP* 7.23.3.

[26] For Aristarchus' use of the *Cypria* for textual critical purposes cf. *Σ N.*10.114a (iii 179 Dr): ὁ μὲν Ἀρίσταρχοc ἀξιοῖ γράφειν ἤμενον, ἀκολούθωc τῇ ἐν τοῖc Κυπρίοιc λεγομένῃ ἱcτορίᾳ· ὁ γὰρ τὰ Κύπρια cυγγράψαc φηcὶ τὸν Κάcτορα ἐν τῇ δρυῒ κρυφθέντα ὀφθῆναι ὑπὸ Λυγκέωc ('Aristarchus thinks that "him sitting" should be written, following the account given in the *Cypria*. For the author of the *Cypria* says that Castor was seen by Lynceus when concealed in the tree'). For Didymus' reading of the passage see Braswell (2013) 240–3.

[27] Aristarchus' stress on fertility parallels that of the Homeric scholia, which gloss the phrase with τρόφιμον τῆc γῆc (*Σ* T *Il.* 9.141b1) and τῆc γῆc τὸ τροφιμώτερον (*Σ* b *Il.* 9.141b2).

[28] Cf. *Σ I.*6.58a (iii 256 Dr) for Aristarchus understanding a cup 'bristling with gold' (φιάλαν χρυcῷ πεφρικυῖαν, *I.*6.40) as 'a metaphor involving boars' (Ἀρίσταρχοc ἐκ μεταφορᾶc τῶν κάπρων φηcὶν εἰρῆcθαι), citing the phrase φρίξαc εὖ λοφιήν from *Od.* 19.446. The explanation is that ὡc ἐξοχὰc ἐχούcηc τῆc φιάλης καὶ τετραχυμμένης τῇ ποικιλίᾳ τοῦ χρυcοῦ, καθαπερανεὶ πεφρικότα κάπρον ('just as the cup is elevated and roughened with the decoration of gold, in a like fashion the boar raised his bristles'). Aristarchus therefore sees Pindar as combining a concern with verisimilitude with an artful adaptation of Homeric language. Other commentators offered more straightforward readings of the passage: cf. e.g. *Σ I.*6.58c (iii 256 Dr) διὰ τὴν ἀπόcτιλψιν λέγει ('he says this because of its emission of light').

174   *Marginalia*

πιθανῶc). It is also significant that the phrase οὖθαρ ἀρούρηc only occurs twice in Homer, at *Il.* 9.141 and in Odysseus' repetition of the speech at *Il.* 9.283 (εἰ δέ κεν Ἄργοc ἱκοίμεθ᾽ Ἀχαιϊκὸν οὖθαρ ἀρούρηc);[29] ἀργινόειc likewise occurs only twice.[30] Pindar's reworking of one unusual Homeric phrase with another recalls a common phenomenon in Hellenistic poetry, whereby poets allude to rare or disputed passages in Homer in order to parade their erudition and create striking poetic effects. While the primary aim of Aristarchus' gloss was clearly to explain the metaphorical function of Pindar's phrase in its immediate context, it is also possible that Aristarchus saw Pindar's subtle reworking as a precursor of the poetic techniques of his own time.

Another, later, example is a scholium on a line from Pindar's account of the death of Amphiaraus in *O.*6, where Talaus is made to declare 'I dearly miss the eye of my army, capable as seer and spear-warrior' (ποθέω cτρατιᾶc ὀφθαλμὸν ἐμᾶc ἀμφότερον μάντιν τ᾽ ἀγαθὸν καὶ δουρὶ μάρναcθαι, *O.*6.16). This is glossed with a quotation from Asclepiades of Myrlea (Σ *O.*6.26 = i 160 Dr): ὁ Ἀcκληπιάδηc φηcὶ ταῦτα εἰληφέναι ἐκ τῆc κυκλικῆc Θηβαΐδοc (fr. 8 B). As modern scholars have noted, the phrase ἀμφότερον μάντιν τ᾽ ἀγαθὸν καὶ δουρὶ μάρναcθαι is very close to a hexameter,[31] and Asclepiades may have pointed this out. Although we cannot tell whether Asclepiades explored the relationship between the passages further, the fact that he is cited is itself significant.[32] It may in part testify to the *Thebaid* being a relatively *recherché* text or one with which readers were not expected to be familiar, especially if the gloss derives from a commentary intended for school use. But the citation may also indicate that the act of making the connection between the texts was itself of importance and deserving of comment.[33]

---

[29] Although cf. its occurrence at *Hom.h.Dem.* 450.   [30] *Il.* 2.647, 656.

[31] Cf. e.g. Hutchinson (2001) 384. For other approaches see Davies (2014) 122–3.

[32] For a discussion of Pindar's possible indebtedness to the *Thebaid* in the passage as a whole see Davies (2014) 121–7. The lexis is often used of literary 'borrowings': cf. e.g. Σ Ap. Rh. 1.1085–87b (= p. 96 Wendel) εἴληφε δὲ τὰ περὶ τῶν ἀλκυόνων παρὰ Πινδάρου ἐκ Παιάνων.

[33] Instances of references to scholarly predecessors in the scholia are comparatively rare, but cf. Σ *O.*8.70c (i 255 Dr), where the discussion is introduced with the phrase διάφοροι τῶν παλαιῶν ἐξηγήcειc περὶ τοῦτο γεγόναcι τὸ ῥητόν. The use of παλαιῶν, with its stress on different groups of interpreters and their historicity, indicates a self-consciousness about scholarly genealogy that may have been more widespread in unredacted commentaries.

A more developed intertextual reading is found in a gloss on Pindar's account of Apollo finding out about Coronis' adultery at *P*.3.27–9 (οὐδ' ἔλαθε σκοπόν· ἐν δ' ἄρα μηλοδόκῳ Πυθῶνι τόccαιc ἄϊεν ναοῦ βαcιλεύc / Λοξίαc, κοινᾶνι παρ' εὐθυτάτῳ γνώμαν πιθών, / πάντα ἰcάντι νόῳ, 'But she did not elude the watcher. For although he happened to be in Pytho where sheep are sacrificed, Loxias the lord of the temple perceived it, convinced by the surest confidant, his mind that knows all things'). The scholia on the passage record the judgement of Artemon on Pindar's handling of the Hesiodic narrative (*Σ P*.3.52a = ii 70–1 Dr, fr. 60 M–W = *FGrH* 569 F 5):

ὁ δὲ Ἀρτέμων τὸν Πίνδαρον ἐπαινεῖ, ὅτι παρακρουcάμενοc τὴν περὶ τὸν κόρακα ἱcτορίαν αὐτὸν δι' ἑαυτοῦ ἐγνωκέναι φηcὶ τὸν Ἀπόλλωνα· ἱcτορεῖται γάρ, ὅτι τὴν Ἴcχυοc μίξιν ἐδήλωcεν αὐτῷ ὁ κόραξ, παρὸ καὶ δυcχεράναντα ἐπὶ τῇ ἀγγελίᾳ ἀντὶ λευκοῦ μέλανα αὐτὸν ποιῆcαι· τοῦτον δὴ τὸν μῦθον διωcάμενόν φηcι τὸν Πίνδαρον τῷ ἑαυτοῦ νῷ καταλαβεῖν τὸν Ἀπόλλωνα τὰ πεπραγμένα τῇ Κορωνίδι· παράλογον γὰρ τὸν ἄλλοιc μαντευόμενον αὐτὸν μὴ cυμβαλεῖν τὰ κατ' αὐτοῦ δρώμενα. χαίρειν οὖν φράcαc τῷ μύθῳ τέλεον ὄντι ληρώδει αὐτόν φηcι τὸν Ἀπόλλωνα παρὰ τοῦ νοῦ πυθόμενον ἐπιπέμψαι τὴν Ἄρτεμιν τῇ Κορωνίδι. τὸν δὲ περὶ τὸν κόρακα μῦθόν φηcι καὶ Ἡcίοδον μνημονεύοντα λέγειν οὕτωc·

> τῆμοc ἄρ' ἄγγελοc ἦλθε κόραξ ἱερῆc ἀπὸ δαιτόc
> Πυθὼ ἐc ἠγαθέην, καί ῥ' ἔφραcεν ἔργ' ἀΐδηλα
> Φοίβῳ ἀκερcεκόμῃ, ὅτι Ἴcχυc γῆμε Κόρωνιν
> Εἰλατίδηc, Φλεγύαο Διογνήτοιο θύγατρα.

Artemon praises Pindar for rejecting the story of the raven and saying that Apollo found out [about Coronis] by himself. The story goes that the raven told him about her affair with Ischys, whereupon Apollo, enraged by the report, changed its plumage from white to black. He [sc. Artemon] says that Pindar rejected this story and had Apollo grasp Coronis' deeds with his own mind. For it is unrealistic that one who gives prophecies to others should not know the things that are done in relation to himself. So having dismissed the myth as completely absurd, he [sc. Pindar] says that Apollo sent Artemis against Coronis having made the discovery with his own mind. He [sc. Artemon] says that Hesiod, who also tells the story of the raven, speaks as follows:

At that time a raven came as a messenger from the sacred feast to holy Pytho, and told long-haired Phoebus the hidden deeds, that Ischys, Elatus' son, had slept with Coronis, the daughter of Phlegyas who was born of Zeus.

The nature of Artemon's work, and consequently the context of the above remarks, is unclear.[34] What does emerge from the scholium, however, is a strong sense of the literary critical parameters being brought to bear. He 'praises' (ἐπαινεῖ) Pindar's 'avoidance' (παρα-κρουσάμενος) of the Hesiodic story on the grounds that it is unrealistic to think that Apollo, as the god of prophecy, would need to learn from others about things that intimately concerned him. He also infers that Pindar's treatment correlates with a disdain for the 'silliness' of the Hesiodic story (τῷ μύθῳ τέλεον ὄντι ληρώδει). This is not explicitly stated by Pindar, unless we think that the strong phrasing of κοινᾶνι παρ᾽ εὐθυτάτῳ γνώμαν πιθών, / πάντα ἰσάντι νόῳ is meant to be understood as implying a concomitant disdain for Hesiod's version. Given that Pindar sometimes expresses explicit opposition to previous versions of myths, as in his narrative of Pelops in *O*.1 or his disagreement with Homer in *N*.7, it may be that Artemon's judgement here was influenced by these poems, and reflects a general apprehension of Pindar's agonistic engagement with his literary predecessors as being an important part of his poetic idiom.

The evaluative criterion here is that of plausibility rather than generic or pragmatic considerations. More explicitly than in the case of Aristarchus' comment at *Σ P*.4.14, this approach is clearly indebted in part to the literary practice and literary critical principles expressed by authors such as Callimachus in his *Hymn to Zeus* (*H*.1.59–64):

> δηναιοὶ δ᾽ οὐ πάμπαν ἀληθέες ἦσαν ἀοιδοί·
> φάντο πάλον Κρονίδῃσι διάτριχα δώματα νεῖμαι·
> τίς δέ κ᾽ ἐπ᾽ Οὐλύμπῳ τε καὶ Ἄϊδι κλῆρον ἐρύσσαι,
> ὃς μάλα μὴ νενίηλος; ἐπ᾽ ἰσαίῃ γὰρ ἔοικε
> πήλασθαι· τὰ δὲ τόσσον ὅσον διὰ πλεῖστον ἔχουσι.
> ψευδοίμην, ἀΐοντος ἅ κεν πεπίθοιεν ἀκουήν.

The poets of long ago were not entirely truthful. They say the lot assigned Cronus' sons their three separate dwellings, but who save a fool would draw lots for Olympus and Hades? Lot drawing is for things equally matched, but these things are as far apart as can be. When I tell lies, may they be such as to convince a listener.

---

[34] On Artemon cf. Broggiato (2011); Phillips (2013c) 159–60. Artemon's approach parallels the rationalizing critiques of myth found in thinkers such as Hecataeus and Hellanicus in the fifth century, and common in the Hellenistic period: cf. Winiarczyk (2013) 46–68.

Like Artemon's Pindar, Callimachus takes a critical approach to myths, weighing up the plausibility of the details reported in canonical versions.[35] Artemon's interpretation of the mythopoeia in *P*.3 makes Pindar a precursor of this approach. Significantly, what is at issue for Artemon is not the ethical force of the narrative, or its place within the poem's system of generically inflected aims and effects, but the intellectual coherence of the fabula. As Artemon frames it, Pindar's passage does not allude to Hesiod, but practises a kind of negative intertextuality, dismissing the story (τοῦτον δὴ τὸν μῦθον διωcάμενόν) upon which the Hesiodic text is based.

In this reading, what is chiefly at issue is not the relationship between the texts but the difference between the stories they tell. As such, this critical intervention is symptomatic of the fact that during the Hellenistic period no theoretical framework seems to have been elaborated for textual comparison directed at aesthetic ends. We shall see, however, that commentators were capable of seeing Pindar as engaged in various different relations with his poetic predecessors ranging from simple borrowing to outright contestation, often but not always with generic concerns in mind, even if these do not seem to have been welded into a general theory of 'Pindaric intertextuality'. Contemporary notions of poetic quality and practice were sometimes retrojected onto Pindar, but the scholia also occasionally manifest a sense of Pindar's cultural and historical otherness. These considerations are important not just for the scholia under discussion, but for our sense of how readers may have responded to them, and for the interpretative manoeuvres glosses may have suggested. The examples discussed below show that intertextual competitiveness and generic self-definition were part of the interpretative horizons that readers could have brought to bear,[36] and consequently even when extensive glosses containing such interpretations do not survive for a particular passage, we should not assume either that such views were never represented in scholarly commentaries, or that individual readers

---

[35] Other instances of the critical approach to myth can be cited from Pindar, most famously the revision of the Pelops myth in *O*.1. Pindar's approach is shaped primarily by his use of myth as a means of ethical and encomiastic communication: see e.g. Scodel (2001).

[36] This is another point at which the influence of the Hellenistic poets' intertextual practices may have been felt: for intertextual competition with 'classic' authors see e.g. Call. *H*.1.54–65 with Phillips (2013c) 170; for intertextuality in the *Aetia* see e.g. Acosta-Hughes and Stephens (2002); Harder (2002).

could not have developed such views themselves. The analysis that Artemon applies to Pindar's Apollo, for example, could easily provide a basis for thinking about numerous other passages where Pindar interacts with his poetic predecessors.

This basic orientation holds for all the glosses I shall discuss, ranging from references to small-scale Homeric borrowings to more developed general reflections. Representative of the former is the gloss on ἔρεισμ᾽ Ἀκράγαντος at *O*.2.6: ἕδρασμα ὄντα καὶ τείχισμα τῆς Ἀκράγαντος. καὶ Ὅμηρος ἕρκος Ἀχαιῶν ('being a seat and fortification of Acragas. And Homer [says] "bulwark of the Achaeans"', Σ *O*.2.12a = i 61 Dr).[37] The aim of the scholium is simply to point out the similarity of Pindar's phrase with Homer's, without going into detail about the literary effect of such parallelism. We also find instances where Homer is cited as a comparandum for a more extended topos, as at Σ *O*.8.16 (i 241 Dr).[38] The scholium glosses the following passage, in which Pindar reflects on the variety of ways in which men can win success with the gods' help (*O*.8.12–14):

ἄλλα δ᾽ ἐπ᾽ ἄλλον ἔβαν
ἀγαθῶν, πολλαὶ δ᾽ ὁδοί
σὺν θεοῖς εὐπραγίας

To different men come different blessings, and many are the paths to god-given success.

The scholium glosses as follows, with reference to the following lines in which Timosthenes' victory at Nemea is referenced alongside the Olympian victory of his brother (Σ *O*.8.16):

οὐ πάντες τὰ αὐτὰ ἔχουσιν ἀγαθά, ἀλλὰ ἄλλος ἄλλα. λέγει ὅτι αὐτὸς ὁ Ἀλκιμέδων Ὀλύμπια νενίκηκεν, ὁ δὲ ἀδελφὸς Τιμοσθένης Νέμεα· διὸ οὐ πάντες πάντων κοινωνοῦσι τῶν ἀγαθῶν.

---

[37] Cf. also e.g. Σ *O*.1.19d (i 24 Dr), Σ *O*.1.26h (i 27 Dr), Σ *O*.2.19c (i 65 Dr), Σ *O*.4.3d (i 130 Dr).

[38] Comments about Homeric influence on Pindar's narrative technique are rare, but cf. Σ *P*.4.124a (ii 116 Dr), where the scholiast notes that the phrase τίς γὰρ ἀρχὰ δέξατο ναυτιλίας ('what beginning took them on their voyage?') is a question addressed to the Muse, who is not named in Pindar's text. The scholiast goes on to comment that in following the question with an answer, Pindar is employing an Homeric technique: εἶτα Ὁμηρικῷ ζήλῳ μετὰ τὴν ἐρώτησιν ἐπάγει τὸ αἴτιον ('then in Homeric style he gives the cause after the question'). A similar explanation is found in Σ 124b (ii 116 Dr).

Not everyone enjoys the same success, but each <succeeds> differently. He says that Alcimedon himself won at Olympia, his brother Timosthenes at Nemea. So not everyone partakes in all successes.

This comment is followed by a citation of *Il.* 4.320 (ἀλλ᾽ οὔ πως ἅμα πάντα θεοὶ δόcαν ἀνθρώποιcιν), which illustrates the scholium's point about the uneven distribution of successes, and picks up on Pindar's cὺν θεοῖc.

The Homeric citation is drawn from a passage in which Nestor, replying to Agamemnon's wish that his intellectual capabilities were matched by physical prowess, remarks that despite his age, he will participate in the battle and direct his troops. The contextual differences between the passages are marked; whereas Pindar speaks of different victories, Nestor reflects on the difference between youth and old age (εἰ τότε κοῦρος ἔα νῦν αὖτέ με γῆρας ὀπάζει, 4.321). The scholium does not mention this wider context, and the immediate exegetical aim of the gloss does not require reference to it. At the same time, however, the looseness of the phrasing (the Iliadic quotation is introduced simply by Ὅμηρος) does not preclude a reader considering the more general relationship between the two passages, and the possibility of Pindar having reworked the Homeric statement in order to give it encomiastic point.[39] The problems and possibilities created by the citational practice on show in this scholium exemplify the issues we shall encounter elsewhere.

Another way in which the scholia refer to the relationship between Homer and Pindar is by use of the verb παραφράζειν, which denotes a reworking of material, an expression in different terms of the same or a similar concept, or narrative datum. The final lines of *P.*11 refer to the Dioscuri's particular mode of immortality (61–4):

> ... καὶ Κάcτορος βίαν,
> cέ τε, ἄναξ Πολύδευκες, υἱοὶ θεῶν,
> τὸ μὲν παρ᾽ ἇμαρ ἕδραιcι Θεράπναc,
> τὸ δ᾽ οἰκέονταc ἔνδον Ὀλύμπου.

and mighty Castor, and you, lord Polydeuces, sons of the gods, you who spend one day in your homes at Therapne, and the next day dwelling on Olympus.

These lines are glossed at *Σ P.*11.95 (ii 263 Dr) with the phrase τὸ τοῦ Ὁμήρου παραφράζει, and a reference to *Od.* 11.303–4 (ἄλλοτε μὲν

---

[39] Cf. also *Σ O.*9.158b–c (i 304 Dr) for a citation of a similar Homeric statement.

ζώους᾽ ἑτερήμεροι, ἄλλοτε δ᾽ αὖτε / τεθνᾶcιν). There is, however, an important difference between the two passages: in Homer's account the Dioscuri live in the underworld and are dead one day and alive the next, whereas Pindar specifies that they spend alternate days on Olympus. This gloss demonstrates the elasticity of παραφράζειν, and the variety of textual relationships it can illustrate is confirmed by Σ O.10.47b (i 322 Dr), where Pindar's lines (νεῖκος δὲ κρεccόνων / ἀποθέcθ᾽ ἄπορον, 'strife with the stronger cannot be put aside', O.10.39–40) are glossed with παραφράζει τὸ Ὁμηρικόν and a citation of *Il.* 1.80 (κρείccων γὰρ βαcιλεὺς ὅτε χώcεται ἀνδρὶ χέρηι, 'for a king is mightier when he is angry with a lesser man'). The previous scholium, however, introduces the same quotation with the phrase καὶ Ὅμηρος, which shows that παραφράζει could be understood as having no more specific denotational force than the modern 'cf.'[40] This in turn raises the question of who was responsible for the latter gloss, and whether it provides evidence for citational practices during the early Hellenistic period, or whether it is the result of later synopsis. The state of the evidence does not allow for certainty, but given the number of minimal glosses in both manuscripts and papyri, we should be wary of supposing that these were always or even predominantly the result of redaction.[41]

There are also cases in which the wider context of a cited text bears on its interpretative function, even if this relationship is not made explicit. One such is the debate over the opening line of *N.*3, which centres around the question of why Pindar addresses the Muse as 'our mother' (ὦ πότνια Μοῖcα, μᾶτερ ἁμετέρα). The first interpretation is that it refers to poetic inspiration (ὡc ἂν ἐπιπνεόμενος ἐκ τῶν Μουcῶν, 'because [he is] inspired by the Muses', Σ *N.*3.1a, = iii 41 Dr), a view buttressed by a citation from Hesiod (ἐκ γάρ τοι Μουcέων καὶ ἑκηβόλου Ἀπόλλωνος / ἄνδρες ἀοιδοὶ ἔαcιν, 'poets come from the Muses and far-shooting Apollo' *Th.* 96–7). The second reading is a variant of the topos of composing for money: Pindar calls the Muse a mother because she is a 'nurse', because he lives off his poems (ἢ τροφὸν, διὰ τὸ ἀποζῆν αὐτὸν ἐξ ὧν ἔγραφεν ἐπινίκων). This interpretation is

---

[40] Cf. e.g. Σ Aesch. *Sept.* 200, where the verb is used of the lines μέλει γὰρ ἀνδρί, μὴ γυνὴ βουλευέτω, / τἄξωθεν recalling Hector's words to Andromache at *Il.* 6.490–1 (παραφράζει τὸ cὺ μὲν τὰ c᾽ αὐτῆς ἔργα κόμιζε ἱcτὸν ἠλακάτην τε καὶ τὰ ἑξῆc). The notion of expressing the same sentiment or concept in different terms may in part be influenced by the importance of the principle of *imitatio* in rhetorical training.

[41] Cf. pp. Ch. 1, p. 60 n. 39.

opposed by another, 'better' (ἄμεινον) according to the compiler, according to which 'mother' is used 'because the Muse was kind to him, just as Athena [was] to Odysseus' (ὅτι προσηνὴς ἦν αὐτῷ ἡ Μοῦσα, ὥσπερ Ὀδυσσεῖ ἡ Ἀθηνᾶ). There follows a quotation of *Il.* 23.783: μήτηρ ὣς Ὀδυσσῆϊ παρίσταται ἠδ᾿ ἐπαρήγει ('she [Athena] stands by and helps him like a mother').

In formal terms, the citation is decontextualized. The line is spoken by Ajax after Odysseus has bested him in wrestling with the goddess's help; the use of μήτηρ by Ajax therefore has an indignant bite remote from the tone of Pindar's invocation.[42] But the wider context of Athena's relationship with Odysseus is also crucial to understanding the point being made by the citation. Although the use of μήτηρ is the hinge around which the comparison turns, the citation is also deployed in opposition to the more limited readings recorded earlier in the scholium. Local and wider intertextual contexts are at work; as with Athena's assistance in the games, the citation implies, the Muse's kindness helps Pindar in a competitive environment. The ἢ τὸ πάρος περ of the previous line of Ajax's speech also makes it clear that παρίσταται ἠδ᾿ ἐπαρήγει describes a prolonged relationship. This wider framework would have been apparent even to a reader who did not consult or remember the *Iliad* passage, however, on account of the fame and paradigmatic quality of Athena and Odysseus' relationship. Unlike the readings that see μᾶτερ ἁμετέρα as connoting poetic inspiration or the social utility of the 'nurse', the comparison with Athena and Odysseus suggests a longer lasting, more complex relationship of kindness (προσηνής), proximity (παρίσταται), and assistance (ἐπαρήγει), of which the quotation from the *Iliad* is a compressed expression.

There are, however, numerous examples of glosses in which the mode of interaction between the texts is more specifically denoted, and examination of these reveals that ancient scholars were possessed of a richly suggestive system of terms for discussing intertextual matters, even if these did not receive extensive theoretical elaboration.[43] Intertexts are occasionally mobilized as part of a qualitative

---

[42] According to Σ T *Il.* 23.783b, this utterance was a reason for Athena's hatred for Ajax, 'because he compared the maiden to a mother' (ὅτι τὴν παρθένον εἴκασε μητρί).

[43] For vocabulary used of a phrase derived from Homer cf. Σ O.7.6d (i 200 Dr): ἐξ Ὁμήρου τοῦτο παρέξεται φάσκοντος· τῷ κτέρας οὐδὲν ὅμοιον. Cf. Σ O.9.46 (i 278 Dr) for the notion that Pindar has 'misinterpreted' an Homeric detail (ὅτι παρακήκοεν Ὁμήρου λέγοντος).

judgement,[44] and there are also cases in which Pindar is noted to be departing from or opposing an Homeric treatment of the same material. One example of this is a scholium that comments on Pindar's portrayal of Peleus' making his own spear at *N*.3.32–3 (παλαιαῖϲι δ' ἐν ἀρεταῖϲ / γέγαθε Πηλεὺϲ ἄναξ, ὑπέραλλον αἰχμὰν ταμών, 'lord Peleus took pleasure in achievements of ancient days, having cut his matchless spear'). The scholium emphasizes Pindar's departure from the Homeric version of the story (*Σ N*.3.57 = iii 51 Dr):

ἀναφέρει δὲ ἐπὶ τὰ Ὁμηρικά Πηλιάδα μελίην, τὴν πατρὶ φίλῳ τάμε Χείρων. ἀντιτάττεται δὲ τοῖϲ Ὁμήρου· ὁ μὲν γὰρ ὑπὸ Χείρωνόϲ φηϲι τμηθῆναι αὐτὴν καὶ δοθῆναι Πηλεῖ, οὗτοϲ δὲ ὑπὸ Πηλέωϲ φηϲὶν αὐτὴν τμηθῆναι. δόξει δὲ ὁ Πίνδαροϲ διὰ τὸν Αἰγινήτην χαρίζεϲθαι τῷ Πηλεῖ· οὐ γὰρ μόνοϲ εἷλε τὴν Ἰωλκόν, ἀλλὰ μετὰ Ἰάϲονοϲ καὶ τῶν Τυνδαριδῶν, ὡϲ ἱϲτορεῖ Φερεκύδηϲ.

He makes reference to the Homeric 'the ash spear of Peleus, which Cheiron cut for his [sc. Achilles'] father' (*Il.* 19.390). <Pindar's verses> are set against Homer's.[45] For [Homer] says that the spear was cut by Cheiron and given to Peleus, but [Pindar] says that it was cut by Peleus. Pindar will appear to be paying a compliment to Peleus because of the Aeginetan victor (?).[46] For he did not capture Iolcus alone, but with Jason and the Tyndaridae, as Pherecydes records.

---

[44] At *Σ I*.4.110c (iii 238 Dr) we find a criticism of Pindar's phrasing, in which the smoke from a sacrifice is described as 'kicking against the heavens' (αἰθέρα κνιϲάεντι λακτίζοιϲα καπνῷ, *I.*4.66) combined with a citation of Homer: ϲκληροτέρᾳ δὲ κέχρηται μεταφορᾷ· ἐχρῆν γὰρ εἰπεῖν ψαύουϲα ἢ θιγγάνουϲα τοῦ αἰθέροϲ ἡ κνῖϲα τοῦ καπνοῦ. ἄμεινον Ὅμηρόϲ φηϲι· κνίϲη δ' οὐρανὸν ἷκεν ἑλιϲϲομένη περὶ καπνῷ ('he has employed a rather harsh metaphor. It would have been better to say that the savour of the smoke "reaches" or "touches" the heavens. Better is Homer's 'the savour reaches the heavens twisting around the smoke' (*Il.* 1.317)).
[45] There is a slippage here between 'Pindar' and 'Pindar's words'. My translation takes ἀντιτάττεται as referring to Pindar's words rather than Pindar's relationship with Homer, on the grounds that when ἀντιτάϲϲομαι is used to mean 'draw oneself up against', the object takes the dative; that Homer's verses and not Homer himself are the object suggests that the relationship envisaged is between the two texts rather than the authors. Given the compression of the Greek, however, it is not implausible that ἀντιτάττεται should refer to Pindar himself. This is the only occurrence of the verb used to describe textual relationships in the Pindar scholia.
[46] The use of the future tense refers to a meaning that will become clear once the reader has read 34, in which Peleus' solo capture of Iolcus is narrated. This use of δόξει is unparalleled in the scholia to Pindar, but cf. *Σ Nic. Ther.* 9a. Comparable also is the use of the future ἔϲται at *Σ O*.10.83a (i 331 Dr), and cf. also *Σ* bT *Il.* 2.199a for a more explicit mapping out of the interpretative process.

The gloss combines different types of intertextual lexis (ἀναφέρει, ἀντιτάττεται), suggesting that the reader is meant to recognize a two-stage process of filiation and antagonism.[47] Significantly, the intertext is made part of a genre-specific rewriting of the myth, which is connected to the poem's encomiastic function and Pindar's desire to 'pay a compliment to' (χαρίζεϲθαι) Peleus and, by extension, his Aeginetan audience.[48]

Even in cases where no particular literary point is being made by the scholia, the terms in which they cast the relationship between the two authors can be revealing. At *O*.7.23, Pindar claims that Tlapolemus was Heracles' son by Astydameia, rather than Astyoche as at *Il.* 2.658. Several scholia on the passage survive, and they deal variously with the difference between the Pindaric and the Homeric genealogies. The first scholium on the line notes that Pindar gives an account of the genealogy that is 'contrary' to Homer (ἐναντίωϲ τῷ ποιητῇ τὰ περὶ τῆϲ μητρὸϲ Τληπολέμου ἱϲτορεῖ ὁ Πίνδαροϲ, Σ *O*.7.42a

---

[47] For more explicitly military imagery used of reading, specifying the moral dimension of the reading experience, cf. Plut. *Mor.* 14f with Whitmarsh (2001) 95, and Hunter and Russell (2011) 74–5.

[48] For other contradictions of Homer cf. e.g. Σ *O*.1.91a (i 37 Dr), which cites *Od.* 11.582–3 as an example of one of the accounts of Tantalus' punishment that differ from Pindar's, and also Σ *N*.9.104c (iii 161 Dr), *I*.7.30a (iii 265 Dr). Homer is sometimes represented as a norm to which Pindar's text needs to be accommodated: cf. e.g. Σ *I*.1.43a (iii 204 Dr), where an apparent contradiction of Homer's description of Therapne (Pindar's phrase ὑψίπεδον Θεράπναϲ οἰκέων ἕδοϲ seems to contradict *Od.* 4.1 οἳ δ' ἷξον κοίλην Λακεδαίμονα κητώεϲϲαν) is resolved by taking ὑψίπεδον as metaphorical (ἢ ὑψίπεδον αὐτήν φηϲι διὰ τὰϲ τῶν οἰκούντων ἀρετάϲ τε καὶ εὐδοξίαϲ). Pindar's statements are also sometimes interpreted as evidence for how he understood particular passages of Homer. One example is *N*.2.14, where 'Hector heard from Ajax at Troy' (ἐν Τροΐᾳ μὲν Ἕκτωρ Αἴαντοϲ ἄκουϲεν). The scholia on the passage take this phrase as referring to the content of the previous phrase, which asserts Salamis' capacity for producing brave warriors (καὶ μὰν ἁ Σαλαμίϲ γε θρέψαι φῶτα μαχατάν δυνατόϲ). In explaining precisely how Hector could have 'heard' about Salamis from Ajax, one scholium takes Pindar's ἄκουϲεν literally, and suggests that Pindar must have understood Ajax' mention of Salamis at *Il.* 7.198–9 (ἐπεὶ οὐδ' ἐμὲ νήϊδά γ' οὕτωϲ / ἔλπομαι ἐν Σαλαμῖνι γενέϲθαι τε τραφέμεν τε) as 'spoken to Hector' (ἔοικε δὲ ὁ Πίνδαροϲ τὸ παρ' Αἴαντοϲ ῥηθὲν πρὸϲ Ἕλληναϲ ὑπονενοηκέναι εἰρῆϲθαι πρὸϲ Ἕκτορα, Σ *N*.2.22a, iii 37 Dr). It is unclear whether the scholiast thought that the whole speech, or only the quoted lines were directed at Hector. Given that Ajax begins by addressing his 'friends' (ὦ φίλοι, 191), the scholiast is likely to have understood Pindar as thinking that the speech was addressed to Hector *as well as* to the Greeks, although this is not made explicit: presumably the scholiast imagined Hector as near enough to the Greeks to hear what was being said. Nevertheless, it is significant that the commentator(s) responsible for this gloss felt the need to connect Pindar's statement to a particular incident in the *Iliad*, rather than taking it as a general statement about Hector's two encounters with Ajax.

= i 210 Dr), but the precise terms of this difference are variously explained. One (group of) commentator(s) anachronistically claim(s) that Pindar must have 'come across' his version in the historiographer Achaeus (ἔοικε δὲ ὁ Πίνδαρος ἐντετυχηκέναι τῷ Ἀχαιῷ ἱστοριογράφῳ, Σ Ο.7.42a = i 210 Dr), whereas another suggests that the difference is due to Pindar having access to a copy of the *Iliad* that included a textual variant (Σ Ο.7.42b = i 210 Dr): Ὅμηρος ταύτην Ἀστυόχην φησὶν, οὐκ Ἀστυδάμειαν. εἰκὸς δὲ τὸν Πίνδαρον ἀπαντῆσαι ταύτῃ τῇ γραφῇ· ὃν τέκεν Ἀστυδάμεια βίῃ Ἡρακληείῃ ('Homer says that this was Astyoche not Astydameia. It is likely that Pindar encountered this reading (*Il.* 2.658) "… whom Astydameia bore to mighty Heracles"'). This account presents a picture of Pindar following a particular version of the Homeric text rather than producing a version deliberately 'contrary' to Homer, a scenario which implies deliberate differentiation.

Later in the scholium, after an enumeration of mythological variants, it is suggested that it is 'likely' (εἰκός) that Pindar obtained his information about the Amyntoridae's descent from 'learned' Rhodians (παρὰ τῶν κατὰ τὴν πόλιν λογίων ἤκουσεν Ἀμυντορίδας εἶναι Ῥοδίους μητρόθεν). This conception of Pindar's composition, involving 'fieldwork' on Rhodes and dealing with oral sources (ἤκουσεν), differs markedly from the notion of him following the account in Achaeus, and may reflect a scholarly argument about Pindar's methods: one of these interpretations may have been developed specifically in order to rebut the other, and the uses of ἔοικε and εἰκός suggest competition to produce the most plausible account of Pindar's working methods.[49] The two positions also relate differently to the practices of Hellenistic poets. The account of Pindar following Achaeus produces a situation that parallels that of the learned Hellenistic poet engaging with historical sources,[50] while the 'fieldwork' interpretation may reflect a conception of Pindar's practices based on the Herodotean model of historiographical inquiry involving autopsy and reporting of oral accounts.[51] At stake would be a

[49] The role of 'likelihood' in the argument about Pindar using a certain variant may also presuppose the idea that fewer texts were available to fifth-century authors than to their modern counterparts.

[50] Cf. e.g. Callimachus' reference to Xenomedes of Ceos at *Aetia* fr. 75.54–5 Harder. See also West (2011) for the conception of 'Pindar as a man of letters'.

[51] The phrasing of παρὰ τῶν κατὰ τὴν πόλιν λογίων recalls, whether by design or not, the 'learned Persians' (Περσέων … οἱ λόγιοι) of Hdt. 1.1. Herodotus frequently mentions visiting the places he writes about, but cf. Priestley (2014) 21–2, 25–6 on ancient traditions about Herodotus' travels.

distinction between a Pindar conceptualized in terms of contemporary norms and projected as a precursor of contemporary poetic activity, and an image of the poet developed through comparison with his (younger) contemporaries.

The rejection of Odysseus' superiority over Ajax in *N*.7 has a strong claim to be the *locus classicus* of Pindar's engagement with Homer,[52] and the scholia on the poem are a valuable instance of ancient reflections on intertextual contact. Pindar's rebuttal of Homer's canonical account is sustained by reflections on the deceptive power of Homer's poetry (*N*.7.20–30):

> ἐγὼ δὲ πλέον᾿ ἔλπομαι
> λόγον Ὀδυccέος ἢ πάθαν
> διὰ τὸν ἀδυεπῆ γενέcθ᾿ Ὅμηρον·
>
> ἐπεὶ ψεύδεcί οἱ ποτανᾷ <τε> μαχανᾷ
> cεμνὸν ἔπεcτί τι· coφία
> δὲ κλέπτει παράγοιca μύθοιc. τυφλὸν δ᾿ ἔχει
> ἦτορ ὅμιλοc ἀνδρῶν ὁ πλεῖcτοc. εἰ γὰρ ἦν
> ἓ τὰν ἀλάθειαν ἰδέμεν, οὔ κεν ὅπλων χολωθείc   25
> ὁ καρτερὸc Αἴαc ἔπαξε διὰ φρενῶν
> λευρὸν ξίφοc· ὃν κράτιcτον Ἀχιλέοc ἄτερ μάχᾳ
> ξανθῷ Μενέλᾳ δάμαρτα κομίcαι θοαῖc
> ἂν ναυcὶ πόρευcαν εὐθυπνόου Ζεφύροιο πομπαί
>
> πρὸc Ἴλου πόλιν . . .

I expect that the account of Odysseus became greater than his sufferings because of Homer's sweet words, since there is a certain majesty in his fictions and winged artfulness; poetic skill deceives, seducing with tales. The greater part of men have a blind heart. For if they had been able to see the truth, then mighty Ajax, in anger over the arms, would not have planted in his chest the smooth sword, he who was the most powerful in battle, except for Achilles, of those whom the escorting breezes of straight-blowing Zephyr conveyed in swift ships to Ilus' city, to bring back the wife of golden-haired Menelaus.

As in the case of *Σ N*.3.57, the engagement with Homer here is seen as generically inflected. In glossing the opening lines of the above passage, the scholia comment δυνατοὶ γάρ εἰcιν οἱ ποιηταὶ τὰ τυχόντα ἔργα μεγαλύνειν καὶ αὔξειν. διὸ καὶ cὺ φρόντιζε τοῦ ὑμνεῖcθαι ('poets are capable of making great and amplifying what actually happened.

---

[52] See e.g. Most (1985a) 148–56; Sotiriou (1998) 147–8.

Therefore you should give thought to being commemorated in song',
Σ N.7.29a = iii 121 Dr). Alert to the passage's possible encomiastic
resonances, some scholars at least understood the lines as a covert
address to the *laudandus*.

Other scholia on the passage take a greater interest in its intertextual aspect. At Σ N.7.39b (iii 122 Dr) we find a quotation of *Il*. 2.768–9
(ἀνδρῶν δ᾽ αὖ μέγ᾽ ἄριστος ἔην Τελαμώνιος Αἴας, / ὄφρ᾽ Ἀχιλεὺς
μήνιεν), which emphasizes that Pindar's ὃν κράτιστον Ἀχιλέος ἄτερ
μάχᾳ is supported by Homer, and perhaps implies that in pressing
Ajax' claim Pindar is using Homer's text against him. Moreover,
Pindar's use of the phrase ποτανᾷ <τε> μαχανᾷ recalls the Homeric
ἔπεα πτερόεντα, and acts as a gloss both on the power of poetry and
on his appropriation of Homer.[53] Both modes of signification are
registered in Σ N.7.29b (iii 121 Dr):

> ποτανὴν δὲ μηχανὴν τὰ ποιήματα εἶπε, καθὸ ὑψοῖ καὶ μετεωρίζει τὰς
> ἀρετὰς τῶν ὑμνουμένων, ἢ καθὸ τὰ ἔπη κοινῶς λέγεται παρ᾽ Ὁμήρῳ
> πτερόεντα, ἢ διὰ τὸ οὕτω μεμηχανῆϲθαι ὥϲτε κατὰ πᾶϲαν χώραν πέτεϲθαι
> καὶ διϊκνεῖϲθαι.

> He calls the [sc. Homer's] poems 'winged artfulness', because they exalt
> and raise aloft the excellences of their subjects, or because words are
> commonly called 'winged' in Homer, or because they are so constructed
> as to fly and journey through every country.

Although presented as alternatives (ἤ . . . ἤ), the three explanations
are not mutually exclusive. The second interpretation implicitly
acknowledges the influence and power of Homeric language and
ideas, and although the textual interaction envisaged here is not
elaborated, the gloss does not obstruct a reading that would emphasize the agonistic aspect of the relationship being constructed. As
I have suggested above in relation to other passages, there may also be
traces of critical literature about sublimity (ὕψος) here, especially in
the phrasing of καθὸ ὑψοῖ καὶ μετεωρίζει, which recalls the language
of sublimity most famous from Longinus. This scholium may well
pre-date *On the Sublime*, but even if this was the case, this passage and

---

[53] On the ambivalence of οἱ in 22, which could refer to either Homer or Odysseus,
see Most (1985a) 150–1. He concludes that 'Pindar seems to have written deliberately
in a way that makes it impossible to distinguish whose lies and winged device are
meant . . . The primordial deception at Alcinous' court [sc. Odysseus' narrative of his
travels] was the condition and first instance of the deception which, according to
Pindar, was to characterize the whole Greek reception of the *Odyssey*'.

its scholia are a useful test case for considering the possible interrelations of commentaries, literary criticism, and primary texts.

Competition between authors and emulation of poetic models is a
central feature of Longinus' approach to literature, and the two are
often paired as related aspects of the literary endeavour (<ἡ> τῶν
ἔμπροςθεν μεγάλων cυγγραφέων καὶ ποιητῶν μίμηςίς τε καὶ ζήλωςιϲ,
13.2).[54] The process of emulation is a means by which an individual
writer's character and style are formed: ἔϲτι δ' οὐ κλοπὴ τὸ πρᾶγμα,
ἀλλ' ὡϲ ἀπὸ καλῶν ἠθῶν ἢ πλαϲμάτων ἢ δημιουργημάτων ἀποτύπωϲιϲ
('such borrowing is not theft, but is rather like the reproduction of
good character in sculptures or other works of art', 13.4).[55] Perhaps
even more important for our passage is the notion that 'the meaning
of a discourse and its mode of expression are frequently interrelated'
(ἡ τοῦ λόγου νόηϲιϲ ἥ τε φράϲιϲ τὰ πλείω δι' ἑκατέρου διέπτυκται,
30.1). In these terms, it is easy to see Pindar's alteration and
development of Homeric phrasing (ποτανᾷ τε μαχανᾷ and ἔπεα
πτερόεντα), giving it wider conceptual application as a generalization
about poetry, as an instantiation of their literary relationship that
simultaneously testifies to Homer's power and contests the model
bequeathed by his text. Pindar's verbal alteration stands in miniature
for the agonistic dynamics of the passage as a whole.

At this point it is important to recognize the limitations of this set
of scholia. Any reader educated enough to read Pindar would have
noticed the connection between ποτανᾷ... μαχανᾷ and ἔπεα πτερόεντα without assistance from the scholia. Similarly, a reader familiar
with Longinus could have engaged in the kind of reading I have just
elaborated whether or not the scholia's ὑψοῖ καὶ μετεωρίζει reflects the
influence of this type of literary criticism. Nevertheless, we need to
take account of what sort of interpretative starting point a commentary on the passage may have provided for readers, and how reading
with a commentary may have informed responses. The scholia's
multiple interpretations are suggestive in this respect; whereas
the second interpretation sees ποτανᾷ... μαχανᾷ as an Homeric
reference, the first and third of the alternatives countenanced in

[54] Cf. his description of Plato and Homer in terms redolent of military engagement
(13.4): Plato is an ἀνταγωνιϲτὴϲ νέοϲ who οὐκ ἀνωφελῶϲ δ' ὅμωϲ διηριϲτεύετο· "ἀγαθὴ"
γὰρ κατὰ τὸν Ἡϲίοδον "ἔριϲ ἥδε βροτοῖϲι".
[55] Cf. Ch. 1, p. 77 for the didactic functions of the text and their relations to
reading.

Σ 29b see the phrasing as exercising a connotative force independent of the Homeric intertext. Although, as noted above, the interpretations are not mutually exclusive, in that the phrase could reference poetry's disseminatory aspect (τὸ οὕτω μεμηχανῆϲθαι ὥϲτε κατὰ πᾶϲαν χώραν πέτεϲθαι καὶ διϊκνεῖϲθαι) while also recalling Homer, the alternatives may reflect a debate over whether to see the phrase intertextually, and if so what emphasis to place on the intertextual relation. The first and third readings also raise the possibility of seeing the phrase as breaking away from Homeric influence by means of verbal differentiation.

In presenting readers with these interpretative possibilities, the alternating form of which encourages readerly participation in the construction of meaning, the commentary creates a situation that is qualitatively different from that which obtains when a reader encounters the text without any kind of metatextual apparatus. By giving the reader a precise reference to Homer's depiction of Ajax, and prompting consideration of the various intertextual shadings that the passage might take on, the scholia serve to initiate interpretative activity on a particular set of grounds and direct it in a particular way. Rather than providing a definitive reading, the scholia create a frame for reading that sharpens the contours of which such a reading might consist. Just as importantly, the citations above *implicitly legitimize* the connections they make, the very act of citation carrying with it the premise that the links suggested are in some way important and worth noting.[56]

With these issues in mind, I shall now discus some citations of Homer and other authors in which the relations between the poems, and their articulation by the scholia, are less clear. My first such example comes from the narrative of the first Olympian games in O.10, in which Pindar gives the reader snapshots of several victors. One is Niceus, who won the discus (O.10.72–3):

μᾶκος δὲ Νικεὺς ἔδικε πέτρῳ χέρα κυκλώϲαιϲ
    ὑπὲρ ἁπάντων, καὶ ϲυμμαχία θόρυβον
παραίθυξε μέγαν

Niceus cast the stone from his circling arm far beyond all the others, and his fellow soldiers raised a great din.

---

[56] Citations also implicitly include readers in a wider reading community by communicating textual connections that have been made, and legitimized, by previous readers/scholars. As such, the process of citation asserts the historicity of individual textual encounters by connecting them to previous readings.

There are numerous scholia on the passage, explaining why a stone is used with the support of a quotation of *Od.* 8.190 (*Σ O*.10.86a = i 333 Dr), and comparing the phrasing of χέρα κυκλώcαιc with *Od.* 8.189 (τόν ῥα περιcτρέψαc ἧκε cτιβαρῆc ἀπὸ χειρόc, *Σ* 87 b (i 334 Dr), 'whirling it around he threw it from his mighty hand'.[57]

The scholium I wish to focus on here, however, draws on the same passage of the *Odyssey*, but provides a somewhat more elaborate interpretation (*Σ O*.10.87c = i 334 Dr):

τὸ δὲ καὶ cυμμαχία θόρυβον, καὶ τοῖc παρεcτῶcιν αὐτοῖc cυμμάχοιc ἔκπληξιν καὶ τάραχον ἐκίνηcε μέγαν διὰ τὸ ὑπερβεβλημένον τῆc βολῆc θαῦμα. καὶ τοῦτο παρὰ τὸ Ὁμηρικόν·

κατὰ δ' ἔπτηξαν ποτὶ γαίῃ
Φαίηκεc δολιχήρετμοι, ναυcίκλυτοι ἄνδρεc.

'Alliance . . . din'; and he stirred up amazement and great disturbance in the allies who stood around with the overwhelming wonder of his throw. This is like the Homeric 'They cowered down onto the earth, the Phaeaceans with their long oars, men famed for ships' (*Od.* 8.190–1).

The vagueness of the terms in which the comparison is couched will by now be familiar, and rather belies the contextual differences between the passages, to which I shall return below.[58] For the moment, however, I want to stress that the emphasis on the shock and wonder of the crowd occurs in more than one gloss. At *Σ O*.10.87c ἔκπληξιν καὶ τάραχον . . . μέγαν ('amazement and great disturbance') are mentioned, vocabulary which also occurs in *Σ* 88a (= i 334 Dr, θαυμάcαν ἀνεβόηcεν, 'they cried out in wonder'), 88c (i 334 Dr, διαταραχθῆναι . . . ἀποθαυμάcανταc ἐπὶ τῷ τῆc βολῆc μήκει, 'they were thrown into confusion, wondering at the length of the discus cast') and 88d (i 334 Dr).[59] These readings are somewhat surprising given that θόρυβοc does not necessarily have to connote shock or wonder but may indicate a more neutral 'noise'. It is possible that an early commentator made the comparison with the passage in

---

[57] For a comparison of the passages see Sotiriou (1998) 217–18.

[58] For the use of παρὰ τὸ Ὁμηρικόν indicating similarity cf. e.g. *Σ O*.2.128 (i 94 Dr), *Σ O*.7.168c (i 234 Dr), *Σ O*.9.74a (i 284 Dr), *Σ P*.3.119 (ii 78 Dr), *Σ N*.7.76 (iii 127 Dr), *Σ I*.8.95a (iii 276 Dr). Cf. also *Σ N*.1.36 (iii 17 Dr).

[59] This may be another instance of mutual influence between the Pindaric and Homeric glosses: cf. the description of at *Σ Od.* 8.190 of the Phaeacians ducking 'in shock' (δύναται δὲ καὶ ἔνευcαν πρὸc τὴν γῆν, ὅπερ οἱ ἐν καταπλήξει ποιοῦcιν).

the *Odyssey*, reading Pindar's crowd's reaction as one of shock under the influence of this comparison, and that this reading held sway over later writers.[60] Odysseus' cast of the discus takes place in a particular context of display and competition, as he responds to being goaded by Euryalus about his (apparent) lack of athletic prowess (*Od.* 8.159–64). Moreover, the scholia as they stand do not quote the full sentence from the *Odyssey*, missing out the phrase which specifies that the Phaeacians were 'cowering on the ground...under his cast of the rock' (ἔπτηξαν ποτὶ γαίῃ / ...λαὸς ὑπὸ ῥιπῆς), thus giving the misleading impression that their 'cowering' (ἔπτηξαν) is solely a consequence of their shock at Odysseus' throw, when in fact they are avoiding the discus. There is no hint in Pindar's narrative of the kind of conflicted atmosphere that prevails in the games of *Od.* 8, and since the scholia do not make explicit the reasons for the comparison, it could be argued that the relation between the passages has little interpretative significance.

Such a response, however, would overlook the importance of this set of scholia, however questionable their readings, for the ancient reception of the passage. The large number of scholia on this line indicates that its exegesis was felt to be important, and that the assembled scholia probably derive from a number of different commentaries. Even if individual readers did not accept the scholia's views, their responses to the passage would have at least in part been shaped by their awareness of them: contesting the intertextual connection would itself have been a critically significant gesture. From another angle, the scholia can be seen as opening up a potentially significant allusive dimension, inviting the reader to see Pindar as reworking the *Odyssey* passage and lending Niceus a further glory by means of the comparison with Odysseus. This relation heightens the reader's sense of the aetiological boldness of the poem, involving as it does a comparison which makes a mythologically prior figure (Niceus) relate to a more recent one (Odysseus) in an older text. The Niceus–Odysseus comparison thus inverts the chronological relationship between Homer and Pindar, with Pindar's poem retrojecting the

---

[60] The use of ἔκπληξις in literary criticism (for which see e.g. [Long.] 1.4) to denote the affectivity of texts may also have suggested to readers a connection between the reaction of the crowd and the wonder and amazement that the text itself (may) aim(s) to elicit. For the connection between spectators and readers in ancient criticism cf. e.g. Σ bT *Il.* 23.362–72 on the spectators watching the funeral games, discussed below, pp. 200–2.

dynamics of the *Odyssey* passage onto a pre-Odyssean mythological period.[61] Moreover, Pindar's narrative can be read as erasing the conflicts of the *Odyssey* narrative in order to represent a more united homosocial group, and as positioning the Olympian games as outdoing those of the *Odyssey*.

The language of ἔκπληξις is again at work in a gloss on the passage in *N*.1 where Amphitryon discovers Heracles wrestling with the serpents (*N*.1.55–9):

> ἔcτα δὲ θάμβει δυcφόρῳ
> τερπνῷ τε μιχθείς. εἶδε γὰρ ἐκνόμιον
> λῆμά τε καὶ δύναμιν
> υἱοῦ· παλίγγλωccον δέ οἱ ἀθάνατοι
> ἀγγέλων ῥῆcιν θέcαν.

He stood stunned with wonder both painful and joyous, for he saw the extraordinary determination and power of his son, and the immortal gods had reversed the messengers' report.

At *Σ N*.1.85a (= iii 24–5 Dr), glossing the phrase ἔcτα δὲ θάμβει, the passage is compared with two moments of equally powerful emotion in Homer:

> ἔcτη δὲ ὁ Ἀμφιτρύων ἐκπλήξει βαρυτάτῃ καὶ τέρψει πολλῇ cυγκραθείς. Ὅμηρος· δακρυόεν γελάcaca. καὶ ἐν ἄλλοις· τὴν δ' ἅμα χάρμα καὶ ἄλγος ἕλε φρένα.

Amphitryon stood affected by the most grievous shock and great pleasure. Homer (*Il.* 6.484): 'laughing tearfully'. And elsewhere (*Od.* 19.471): 'joy and grief together seized her mind'.

Pindar's lines attracted comment in part because of the complex nature of the emotional reaction they express,[62] to the explication of which the Homeric citations contribute. We may compare the detailed elaboration of the emotion at *Σ N*.1.85b (iii 25 Dr, ὅτι μὲν δρακόντων ἦν ἔφοδος ἐπὶ νεογνὰ τὰ τέκνα, δύcελπις ἐγένετο· ἐπεὶ δὲ εἶδεν αὐτοὺς ἀγχομένους ὑπὸ Ἡρακλέους, ἐτέρφθη, 'because the snakes had access to the newly-born baby, he became despondent, but when he saw them being strangled he was delighted') with *Σ* AbT *Il.* 6.484:

---

[61] For such 'fracturing of time' as a feature of Hellenistic poetry cf. Hunter (1993) 165–6.

[62] On shifts of mood and emotional effects in Pindar generally see e.g. Pfeijffer (1999a) 45–7.

δυνατῶc ῥηθὲν ἀνερμήνευτόν ἐcτιν· οὐ γὰρ ἁπλοῦν τὸ πάθοc, ἀλλὰ
cύνθετον ἐξ ἐναντίων παθῶν, ἡδονῆc καὶ λύπηc· εἰc γέλωτα μὲν γὰρ
αὐτὴν προήγαγε τὸ βρέφοc, εἰc δάκρυον δὲ ἡ περὶ τοῦ Ἕκτοροc ἀγωνία
('it is powerfully expressed and indescribable. For the emotion is not
simple, but a compound of opposed emotions, pleasure and grief.For
the child brings her to laughter, but the struggle over Hector brings
her to tears').[63]

As in the other examples we have discussed, the intertextual
juxtapositions invite the reader to see Pindar reworking Homeric
antecedents, but they also powerfully exemplify the affective traits
of their respective texts. Hector and Andromache's conversation was
recognized in antiquity as a memorable instantiation of the *Iliad*'s
emotive power and its commentary on the intersection between the
worlds of warfare and family.[64] The citation from the *Odyssey*, drawn
from the scene in which Odysseus is recognized by his nurse, is an
instance of a structurally crucial motif famously highlighted by Aristotle in his comment about the central role played by recognition in
the *Odyssey* (ἡ δὲ Ὀδύccεια πεπλεγμένον (ἀναγνώριcιc γὰρ διόλου) καὶ
ἠθική, '. . . and the *Odyssey* is complex (it is pervaded by recognition)
and character-based', *Poet.* 1459b). *Σ N.*1.85a thus has a distillatory
force, juxtaposing three passages in which affectivity intersects with
rhetorical aims and ideational traits that distinguish their respective
genres. As well as drawing attention to a transgeneric trope, the
comparison also implies differentiation. This is especially marked in
relation to the context of the *Iliad* citation; Astyanax' vulnerability
and the shadow cast by Hector's eventual fate contrasts with Heracles'
λῆμά τε καὶ δύναμιν, his extraordinary deeds (*N.*1.62–9), and his
deification (69–72).Over and above a simple rhetorical contrast, the
scholium stimulates reflection on the relationship between microtextual effects and macrotextual structures,and encourages recognition
of how Pindar has reworked his Homeric antecedents in the light of
his encomiastic project. Amphitryon's 'shock and delight' (both as
enunciated by the text and the scholium) scripts that of the reader,
an effect that would have been especially apparent in the light of

---

[63] This is the only use of ἀνερμήνευτον in the Homer scholia. In view of the
succeeding analysis, it clearly refers to the emotion being inexpressible by a single
word rather than per se.

[64] Cf. e.g. Soph. *Aj.* 500–4: for further comment on the ancient reception of the
scene see Graziosi and Haubold (2010) 47–52. For the importance of 'suffering' in the
Iliad cf. Arist. *Poet.* 1459b: ἡ μὲν Ἰλιὰc ἁπλοῦν καὶ παθητικόν.

Aristotle's formulations of textual affectivity, but the scholium's comparisons also help to clarify the connection between Amphitryon's paradoxically compound emotion and Heracles' power. The juxtapositions underline how 'extraordinary' (ἐκνόμιον) Heracles' feat is by enabling comparison of the reaction it provokes; whereas Homer's characters react with 'tearful laughter' and 'joy and grief', it is 'wonder' (θάμβει) that forms the hinge of Amphitryon's response. The comparisons, with their generic articulation, help to establish the centrality of this 'wonder' in the audience's reaction to the poem as a whole.

Certain trends can be seen running through the scholia I have examined. As well as drawing attention to various Homeric borrowings and sketching out an agonistic relation between the two poets, the scholia position Pindar's texts in relation to contemporary canons of rhetorical and aesthetic practice.[65] In the case of Artemon's analysis of *P*.3, Pindar is made both to conform to contemporary notions of poetic practice and to function as a forerunner of them. Significant also are the conceptual grounds against which specific intertextual relationships are articulated; little attempt is made to see intertextual relations as contextually inflected beyond the simple move of relating a particular intertext to the poem's encomiastic strategy. This partly reflects the commentators' lack of interest in the poems' occasionality,[66] but it also testifies to the primary texts' transhistorical force. The intertextual space thus created is relatively free of generic and epichoric inflection, and there is little in the way of generalizing interpretative orientation to guide readers in construing the wider significance of particular intertexts. Although there are cases in which a borrowing is seen as having a particular function, readers are often left to fill out the significance of intertextual connections themselves. As the next part of my analysis will demonstrate, the challenges that attend this interpretative freedom are no less pressing in cases where Pindar is cited in scholarship on other poets. Involving the reapplication of Pindar's texts in a variety of exegetical and comparative contexts, such citations, no less than the type just examined, constitute an important conduit through which views of and approaches to Pindar's texts would have been channelled.

---

[65] Cf. Wilson (1980); Lefkowitz (1985); Bitto (2012).
[66] See e.g. Bitto (2012) 91–7.

PINDAR VIATOR

There are numerous citations of Pindar in the scholia to Homer, Apollonius Rhodius, and Theocritus. Pindar is often quoted as a source of mythological details or variants,[67] and as a purveyor of gnomic statements.[68] As in my previous analysis, however, my chief focus here will be a series of scholia in which the texts' rhetorical effects and wider literary significance are to the fore. As will become clear, many of the issues that arose when considering the intertextual dynamics of citations in the Pindaric scholia will also be of importance here, albeit from a different angle. These citations, I shall argue, constitute an important conduit of Pindar's literary and scholarly reception, through which his status as a canonical poet is established and opened to contestation through particular intertextual connections. The dynamics of citation are themselves significant in shaping notions of literary history; whereas in the Pindar scholia, a consciousness of Pindar being influenced by earlier poets was often manifest, driven in part by the desire to diagnose Homeric and Hesiodic precursors for Pindar's poetic methods, in the scholia on Theocritus and Apollonius, Pindar is mentioned as a literary model. As we shall see in the case of the Homer scholia, however, and as has already become clear with regard to citations in Pindaric commentaries, citations accompanied by only minimal determination coexist with those in which the terms of influence and chronology are more clearly spelled out. When examining this body of material, then, we need to be sensitive to the variety of intertextual relationships that emerge between different poets, and the corresponding multiplicity of interpretative situations that ancient readers would have negotiated in their scholarly explorations.

My starting point is a pair of scholia in which the intertextual relationships envisaged by ancient scholars are made explicit. The first is a gloss on the end of Achilles' speech at *Il.* 18.120–6, in which he insists to his mother that he will not remain withdrawn from the fighting:

> ὣc καὶ ἐγών, εἰ δή μοι ὁμοίη μοῖρα τέτυκται,
> κείcομ᾽ ἐπεί κε θάνω· νῦν δὲ κλέοc ἐcθλὸν ἀροίμην,

---

[67] Cf. e.g. Σ A *Il.* 3.243, citing Pindar as a source for the story of the Apharetidae; Σ *Il.* A 21.194 on Pindar's story about the Achelous; Σ *Od.* 21.303 on Pindar as a source for the narrative of Ixion and the Centaurs' birth.

[68] e.g. Σ T *Il.* 13.636, glossing πάντων μὲν κόρος ἐcτὶ καὶ ὕπνου καὶ φιλότητοc with *N.*7.52–3: κόρον δ᾽ ἔχει / καὶ μέλι καὶ τὰ τέρπν᾽ ἄνθε᾽ Ἀφροδίcια.

καί τινα Τρωϊάδων καὶ Δαρδανίδων βαθυκόλπων
ἀμφοτέρῃςιν χερςὶ παρειάων ἀπαλάων
δάκρυ' ὀμορξαμένην ἀδινὸν ϲτοναχῆϲαι ἐφείην,
γνοῖεν δ' ὡς δὴ δηρὸν ἐγὼ πολέμοιο πέπαυμαι·   125
μὴ δέ μ' ἔρυκε μάχης φιλέουςά περ· οὐδέ με πείςεις.

And so I too shall lie low when I am dead, if the same fate has been crafted for me. But for now, may I seize fine fame, and make the Trojan women and the Dardanian women with their deep dresses wail ceaselessly, wiping tears from their delicate cheeks with both hands, and may they know how long I have been absent from the fighting.[69] Do not hold me back from the battle, though you love me. You will not persuade me.

The glosses on the final line of the speech run as follows (Σ 18.126):

μηδέ μ' ἔρυκε <μάχης φιλέουςά περ· οὐδέ με πείςεις>: τὸν πλείω λόγον αὐτῆς περιτέμνει ὡς ἐμποδίζοντα τῇ ςπουδῇ. bT ἔςτι δὲ ὅμοιον <τῷ> Πινδάρου· 'ἀλλ' ἐμοὶ μὲν ἄεθλος οὗτος / ὑποκείςεται.' T ὅλος δὲ ὢν πρὸς τῇ ἐκδικίᾳ τοῦ φίλου οὐδὲ ἐπιλογίζεται τὸ κατὰ τὰ ὅπλα ὅτι ἄπορος αὐτῷ νῦν ἡ ἔξοδος. bT

'Don't hold me back from the battle, though you love me. You will not persuade me.' He cuts off her whole speech as it is holding him back by its earnestness. bT It's the same as Pindar's 'But for me this contest awaits' (O.1.84–5). T He is wholly set on avenging his friend and does not consider, in relation to his weapons, that going out [sc. to fight] now is impossible for him. bT

Whereas the first and third scholia explicate the statement against the background of Achilles' rhetorical stance and personal feelings, the T scholium offers a comparison with a statement from Pelops' speech to Poseidon which precedes his victory over Oenomaus. Similarity is the hinge of the comparison (ἔςτι δὲ ὅμοιον <τῷ> Πινδάρου): the scholiast identifies a connection between Achilles' eagerness for battle, and Pelops' determination to test himself against Oenomaus. The comparison is significant for setting Pindar's text within a continuum of Homeric influence, suggesting that Pindar's portrayal of Pelops may have drawn on Homer's Achilles, and opening up the possibility of seeing Pelops as (at that moment at least) an

[69] This translation attempts to capture the generalizing force of the movement from singular (τινα) to plural (γνοῖεν).

Achilles-like character, similar to his Homeric forebear in the magnitude of his ambition.[70]

The similarity between the passages applies narrowly to the sentiments of the individual statements at issue. Yet while the immediate aim of the gloss is to note this similarity, readers may also have been prompted to think about the differences between the wider contexts in which the two statements are made. Even within the gloss itself, there are pointers to this disparity. The lexis of ἀλλ᾽ ἐμοὶ μὲν ἄεθλος οὗτος insinuates a differentiation from the Homeric πολέμοιο ... μάχης, which hints at the distinction between Achilles' feats on the battlefield fighting against a large number of enemies and Pelops' encounter with a single opponent, and also points to the generic specificity of Pindar's text as a celebration of athletic success.[71] Awareness of these differences opens the way to reflection on the wider distinctions between Pelops and Achilles, the former's success and marriage contrasting with Achilles' eventual fate.[72] Their respective relations with the gods are likewise at issue: both the above passages precede gifts bestowed by the gods, Hephaestus' armour and Poseidon's golden chariot and winged horses (O.1.87).[73] Yet while Pelops wins a swift success (ἕλεν δ᾽ Οἰνομάου βίαν παρθένον τε σύνευνον, O.1.88), Achilles' armour is part of a longer narrative of greater moral complexity.

Seen in these terms, the gloss has interpretative implications beyond its explication of the texts' rhetorical and conceptual similarity.The juxtaposition of the two texts instantiates Pindar's canonical status by implicitly equating his phrasing with Homer's,but the juxtaposition is also suggestive of differences between the texts that heighten readerly awareness of their particular aims.Pindar's encomiastic project, and his use of Pelops as an exemplar of beneficial relations between gods and men, stand in pointed contrast to Achilles' ultimately tragic career. The tension between the gloss's assertion of 'similarity' and the contrasts just elaborated is an important reminder of how open such citations could be to interpretation by

---

[70] On the presentation of Pelops in O.1 see e.g. Köhnken (1974), Howie (1991) 101–4, and Ch. 3, this book, p. 128 n. 3 for further references.

[71] ἄεθλος is of course commonly used in Pindar of athletic contests.

[72] Σ O.1.134a–b (i 47 Dr) both stress that marriage is the goal of Pelops' 'contest'.

[73] The differentiation is also reflected in their respective relations to their addressees: Achilles' relations with the Olympian gods are mediated through Thetis, whereas Pelops speaks directly to Poseidon.

individual readers. Assertion of interpretative authority also opens a space for its contestation, and in this case, where a gloss with a limited exegetical function gives rise to multiple interpretative possibilities, such a dynamic is especially prevalent. This productive instability is written into the analytical terms employed: the imprecise nature of the 'likeness' (ὅμοιον) indicated by the scholium creates a situation in which the reader is drawn into elaborating precisely what is at stake in the comparative manoeuvre.

A very different dynamic is found in the scholium on *Il.* 13.20, which glosses Homer's description of Poseidon's journey to Aegae:

> αὐτίκα δ' ἐξ ὄρεος κατεβήσετο παιπαλόεντος
> κραιπνὰ ποσὶ προβιβάς· τρέμε δ' οὔρεα μακρὰ καὶ ὕλη
> ποσσὶν ὑπ' ἀθανάτοισι Ποσειδάωνος ἰόντος.
> τρὶς μὲν ὀρέξατ' ἰών, τὸ δὲ τέτρατον ἵκετο τέκμωρ   20
> Αἰγάς, ἔνθα δέ οἱ κλυτὰ δώματα βένθεσι λίμνης
> χρύσεα μαρμαίροντα τετεύχαται ἄφθιτα αἰεί.

And straight away he came down from the rugged mountain, moving swiftly on his feet. The great mountains and forest trembled under Poseidon's immortal feet as he went. Three times he strode, and on the fourth stride he reached his goal, Aegae, where his famous palace stands built in the depths of the lake, imperishable always, glittering golden.

Poseidon's swift journey (τρὶς μὲν ὀρέξατ' ἰών, τὸ δὲ τέτρατον ἵκετο τέκμωρ) is glossed with the paraphrasing explanation that he reached his destination 'with three steps' (τρισὶ βήμασι, Σ bT 13.20). The T scholium on the line takes a rather different tack, comparing Pindar's description of Apollo rescuing his unborn child from Coronis' pyre at *P.*3.43–4: ὑπερβαλέσθαι δὲ τοῦτο θελήσας Πίνδαρος εἰς ὑπόνοιαν ἧκεν ψεύδους· 'βάματι δ' ἐν πρώτῳ κιχὼν παῖδ' ἐκ νεκροῦ / ἅρπασε' ('wishing to outdo this <passage>, Pindar has come to suggest a falsehood: "in the first stride he reached his child and seized him from the corpse"'). The relationship between the passages is also noted in the Pindar scholia, where a textual dispute is mentioned (Σ *P.*3.75 = ii 73–4 Dr):

> βάματι δ' ἐν πρώτῳ: ἐὰν μὲν γράφηται ἐν πρώτῳ, ὡς νῦν γέγραπται, ἔσται
> ἑνὶ βήματι ὁ Ἀπόλλων ἀπὸ τῆς Πυθῶνος ἐληλυθὼς εἰς τὴν Θεσσαλίαν· ἐὰν
> δὲ, ὡς ἔν τισι, βάματι δ' ἐν τριτάτῳ, ἔσται παραφράζων τὸ τρὶς μὲν ὀρέξατ'
> ἰών. ἔστι δὲ σεμνότερον καὶ πρέπον τῷ θεῷ τὸ ἅμα τῷ πρώτῳ βήματι
> ῥύσασθαι τὸν παῖδα, ἔστι δὲ καὶ πρὸς τὴν ἀντίστροφον σύμφωνον. ὁ μέντοι
> Ἀρίσταρχος γράφει τριτάτῳ.

'With the first step': if 'with the first' were to be written, as it now has been, Apollo will have come from Pytho to Thessaly in one stride. But if, as in some <texts?>, 'with the third step' <were to be written>, it would be a paraphrase of [Homer's] 'three times he strode'. It is more august and fitting for the god to save his child with the first stride, and it is also in accordance [sc. metrically] with the antistrophe. But Aristarchus writes 'with the third'.

Notable here are the use of Homer as part of a dispute over the form and meaning of Pindar's text, and the very different judgements reached by the two scholia as to how Pindar has manipulated the Homeric material. Whereas the Homer scholium condemns Pindar's employment of an unrealistic idea, the scholium on *P*.3 contrasts the simple 'paraphrase' (παραφράζων) that would be at work with the reading τριτάτῳ, entailing a simple reuse of an Homeric motif, with the more apt and powerful (cf. cεμνότερον καὶ πρέπον) effect produced by reading πρώτῳ.

As we saw in the previous section, engagement with Homer and Hesiod is frequently noted in the Pindar scholia, but mentions of this engagement in the scholia to Homer are understandably rarer.[74] The citations of the two passages in the respective commentaries testify to a scholarly consciousness of the primary texts' interrelation, and the contrasting views of the Pindaric text may reflect a conscious attempt to rebut the interpretations put forward by the other scholar(s). These scholia may therefore represent responses to one primary text influencing the process by which another is understood, although we cannot tell which (if either) commentary initially motivated the debate. In view of the connections between the two scholia, however, mutual influence seems likely. Moreover, the gloss in the Homer scholia encourages the reader to see Pindar's description of Apollo as enacting its intertextual antagonism, with Apollo's 'first step' literally outpacing and outdoing (ὑπερβαλέcθαι) his Homeric counterpart.[75] Given the importance of intertextual engagement to the Longinian approach to literature, we might also wonder whether the Homeric scholium reflects the influence of the kind of thinking

[74] This parallels modern commentaries, which tend to be more interested in how a text makes use of its predecessors than in how later texts respond to it.

[75] This is the only occasion in the Homeric scholia where the verb is used in this specifically literary sense, and its use may have been influenced by the subject matter of the two passages. Cf. Σ *N*.5.34b (iii 93–4 Dr) for ὑπερβαλέcθαι used in a similar sense.

mentioned above in connection with the representation of Homer in
N.7.[76] A more elaborated critical notion of literary competitiveness
may well lie behind this analysis, and at the very least the scholium
could have suggested this to readers familiar with the kind of critical
concepts found in Longinus and, presumably, his predecessors.[77]

Most importantly, however, the scholia prompt the reader to reflect
on how intertextual relationships participate in the formation of meaning. By dwelling on Pindar's intertextual daring at a moment when he is
narrating Apollo's self-assertion, the Homeric scholium allows the
reader to correlate the two. At this point, however, an ambiguity should
be noted in the phrasing of ὑπερβαλέcθαι δὲ τοῦτο θελήcαc, in which
τοῦτο could refer either to the words of the Homeric text or to Homer's
narration of them, or to a combination of the two. How a reader
negotiates this ambiguity is interpretatively crucial. If one sees the
engagement as restricted to the form of the words, one would attribute
to Pindar simply a wish to make his Apollo more powerful and impres-
sive (sc. ὑπερβαλέcθαι) than the Homeric Poseidon. But if one were to
suggest that such an intertextual move necessarily implicates narratorial
identity, a situation would emerge in which the actions of narrator and
character were closely connected, with the former's intertextual pose
enacting the latter's action, or perhaps deriving validation from it.
A reader possessed of both relevant commentaries would additionally
have been able to reflect on their different literary judgements (εἰc
ὑπόνοιαν ἦκεν ψεύδουc, cεμνότερον καὶ πρέπον), and to exercise his
own interpretative agency in response.

The opening lines of *O.*1 were probably the most well-known passage
of Pindar in antiquity, and it is not surprising to find that they are
quoted as part of literary analyses.[78] One gloss of especial interest cites
*O.*1 in relation to the simile at *Il.* 18.207–14 which describes Achilles'
appearance when he has been readied for battle by Athena:

> ὡc δ᾽ ὅτε καπνὸc ἰὼν ἐξ ἄcτεοc αἰθέρ᾽ ἵκηται
> τηλόθεν ἐκ νήcου, τὴν δήϊοι ἀμφιμάχωνται,
> οἵ τε πανημέριοι cτυγερῷ κρίνονται Ἄρηϊ

---

[76] Cf. pp. 185–7.

[77] Although uses of ὑπερβάλλομαι in the context of literary engagements do not
feature in the extant portions of *On the Sublime*, the notion of 'competition' between
authors is crucial: cf. p. 187. For his use of the verb in the context of aesthetic
affectivity cf. [Long.] 16.2 τὴν δὲ τῆc ἀποδείξεωc φύcιν μεθεcτακὼc εἰc ὑπερβάλλον
ὕψοc καὶ πάθοc.

[78] Cf. Ch. 3, p. 122.

ἄcτεοc ἐκ cφετέρου· ἅμα δ' ἠελίῳ καταδύντι   210
πυρcοί τε φλεγέθουcιν ἐπήτριμοι, ὑψόcε δ' αὐγὴ
γίγνεται ἀΐccουcα περικτιόνεccιν ἰδέcθαι,
αἴ κέν πωc cὺν νηυcὶν ἀρῆc ἀλκτῆρεc ἴκωνται·
ὣc ἀπ' Ἀχιλλῆοc κεφαλῆc cέλαc αἰθέρ' ἵκανε·

As when smoke going up from a town reaches the sky, from an island
far off, over which fierce men are fighting, who daily are judged in Ares'
hateful contests on behalf of their city: when the sun sets the close-
packed beacons blaze out, and on high a light leaps up for those nearby
to see, that they might come in their ships to ward off harm.[79] So did the
light from Achilles' head reach the heavens.

The gloss on πυρcοί τε φλεγέθουcιν reads simply καὶ Πίνδαροc
"αἰθόμενον πῦρ / ἅτε διαπρέπει νυκτί" (Σ T 18.211a, O.1.1–2). Pindar's
lines are cited in part because of their fame, as being perhaps the best-
known instance of the imagery of fire burning against the night.[80] But
while Homer's πυρcοί have a definite communicative function, Pindar's
αἰθόμενον πῦρ is a free-standing, uncontextualized element, a feature
that enables it to focus the reader's attention on the imagistic quality of
the glossed text. The mode of the citation, which contributes further to
this decontextualization by separating the Pindaric phrase from its
context in the priamel, emphasizes this function. The citation also
juxtaposes two comparisons, and creates a situation in which Achilles'
illumination by Athena, as the subject of the simile, is implicitly
correlated with the Olympian games, the focal point of Pindar's priamel. This correlation connects the status and pre-eminence accorded
the two subjects, and contributes to the Homeric simile in casting
Achilles as an extraordinary figure whose achievements are pitched at
a level above others'.

One of the most complex citations of Pindar in the Homer scholia
occurs in a gloss on the description of the chariot race in *Iliad* 23. At
Σ bT *Il.* 23.362–72, we find a claim about the vividness and pictorial
quality with which the scene is composed:

πᾶcαν φανταcίαν ἐναργῶc προβέβληται ὡc μηδὲν ἧττον τῶν θεατῶν
ἐcχηκέναι τοὺc ἀκροατάc.

---

[79] I give here the text printed by West: for the textual problem see his apparatus
and Janko (1994) 220–1.

[80] They may also have been used to clarify the debate over the relation between the
smoke and the fire, for which cf. Σ bT *Il.* 18.207b.

He [sc. Homer] has projected the whole imaginary scene so clearly that the readers are captured no less than the spectators.

This scholium draws on a concern with vividness (ἐναργεία) and the connection between readers and spectators, both of which are important topoi in ancient scholarship.[81] The equation of readers and spectators reoccurs at *Σ* T 382a, which glosses the line καὶ νύ κεν ἢ παρέλαςς᾽ ἢ ἀμφήριςτον ἔθηκεν ('and now he would have either driven past or put the issue in doubt...') with the statement ςυναγωνιᾶν αὐτοῖς ποιεῖ τοὺς θεατὰς κατὰ Πίνδαρον· "πολλοὶ δὲ {καὶ} μέμνανται, καλὸν εἴ τι ποναθῇ" ('He makes the spectators share in their [sc. the competitors'] anxiety according to Pindar<'s statement> 'Many remember if a good deed is done with toil', *O*.6.11).[82] The phrasing of the scholium is abrupt; κατὰ Πίνδαρον is a compressed version of something like 'according to the logic of Pindar's statement'. Nor is the relation of the cited text to the analysis straightforward. The scholium focuses on how vividly the events appear to the intradiegetic spectators, and the Pindaric citation underlines that the emotional experience of seeing an event fixes it in the memory. But the earlier equation of readers and spectators (*Σ* bT *Il.*23.362–72) also suggests the possibility of seeing that equation (implicitly) at work in *Σ* T 382a. On this reading, the scholium connects the vividness of the Homeric text's presentation of both events and spectators with its memorableness, and uses the Pindaric text to implicitly equate the experience of reading Homer with actually being present at an athletic festival to watch a victory.

While some of this compression is perhaps due to a heavy-handed redaction, it is clear that the citation requires careful thought from a reader in order to draw out the implications created by the juxtaposition of the two texts. The scholium also sheds light on citational practices. Pindar is quoted partly because of the connection between his celebration of athletic achievement and the subject-matter of the glossed text. This shows that the wider context of the cited text,

---

[81] On the reader as spectator in the scholia cf. Nünlist (2009) 153–4, 194–5.

[82] The verb ςυναγωνιᾶν occurs at Polyb. 3.43.8 (τῶν δὲ ςτρατοπέδων ἀμφοτέρων ἐξ ἑκατέρου τοῦ μέρους παρὰ τὰ χείλη τοῦ ποταμοῦ παρεςτώτων, καὶ τῶν μὲν ἰδίων ςυναγωνιώντων καὶ παρακολουθούντων μετὰ κραυγῆς), a passage that draws on the description of the final sea-battle at Syracuse at Thuc. 7.70–1: like their Thucydidean counterparts, Polybius' spectators also share in the suspense of the combatants. Cf. also Diod. Sic. 20.16.6. This topos may well have influenced the conception of readers as spectators.

and not only the local meaning of the quoted phrase, could affect commentators' decisions, as well as being potentially significant for readers. The Pindaric intertext is deployed to equate Homeric ἐναργεία with an historical experience, but the statement also hints at the way epinician poetry aims to immortalize its subjects, the καλόν τι translated into the mnemonically productive medium of textuality. By reusing the statement in this way, the citation reinforces the point of the cited text, and is as such a pointed example of the phenomenon I have noted elsewhere in which Pindar's texts take on new meanings and significances as a result of their contextual transplantations. In this citation, the contextual specificities of Hagesias' victory and its treatment in O.6 have been pared away, leaving only the generalizing remark. Yet the application of the statement to Homer also fulfils an encomiastic function by connecting Pindar's poem, and by extension its *laudandus*, with a programmatic athletic event. The anti-chronological nature of this application underlines the recontextualization to which Pindar's maxim is subject.[83]

Pindar's status as a canonical author is also reflected in how he is quoted in commentaries on the Hellenistic poets. Very often he is cited for information, as a privileged narrator of a myth, or as the source of out-of-the-way details, and I shall return to this mode of citation below. Before that, however, I want to dwell on some of the ways in which Pindaric influence on later authors is reflected in the scholia. We are frequently told that an author has 'taken' a detail from Pindar or based a narrative on his account; such notices are particularly common in the scholia to Apollonius.[84] But a more complex documentation of literary influence is found at Σ Theoc. 1 arg. b (p. 23 Wendel):[85]

αὕτη ἡ ὑπόθεσις εἰς Δάφνιν γέγραπται, ὃς διὰ τούτου μὲν τοῦ εἰδυλλίου τέθνηκε, διὰ δὲ τῶν ἑξῆς ὡς ζῶντος αὐτοῦ μνημονεύει. ὅμως τοῦτο προτέτακται διὰ τὸ χαριέστερον καὶ τεχνικώτερον τῶν ἄλλων μᾶλλον συντετάχθαι· καὶ Πίνδαρος γάρ· 'ἀρχομένου δ' ἔργου', φησί, 'πρόσωπον χρὴ θέμεν τηλαυγές'. ἔστι δὲ ἀμοιβαῖον καὶ δραματικώτερον μὴ ὑποδεικνυμένου τοῦ ποιητικοῦ προσώπου.

This poem has been written for Daphnis, who died during the course of the epyllion, but [the author] recalls him in what follows as if he were

[83] On the transhistorical force of Pindar's gnomai cf. Introduction, p. 41; Ch. 3, pp. 152–4.
[84] Cf. e.g. Σ Ap. Rh. 4.1750–7 (= p. 327 Wendel).
[85] For a similar analysis cf. *Anec. Est.* 5 (= p. 11 Wendel).

alive. Nevertheless, it [sc. the poem] was placed first because it has been constructed more gracefully and skilfully than the others. For Pindar says (*O.*6.3) 'when beginning a work one must set forth a far-shining frontage'. And it is written in dialogue form and more like a drama because the identity of the poet is not revealed.

The editorial practice of placing a poem first in a book might be compared with the comment about Aristophanes' placement of *O.*1,[86] although unfortunately it is not made clear whether the commentator means τοῦτο προτέτακται to be referred to Theocritus or an editor.[87] This imprecision is frustrating not only in view of the light that might have been shed on scholarly conceptions of how authors arranged books, but also because of the interpretative consequences for how the Pindaric gloss is to be interpreted.

Pindar's statement quoted here clearly applies to his own poem as well as having a generalizing force, and as a consequence the citation might suggest that προτέτακται should be imputed to Theocritus by implying that he controls the ordering of his book as Pindar controls the ordering of his poem. The polyptoton of προτέτακται . . . ϲυντε-τάχθαι might also be read as suggesting authorial arrangement of the book, correlating as it does the 'ordering' applied to the individual poem and the book as a whole.[88] Whatever the commentator's views on editorial practice, however, the citation is a fascinating case of poetry being reapplied to new literary contexts; the poet's poetological wisdom is refashioned as a guide to editing poetry books.[89] As in some of the examples examined above, decontextualization is an important feature of the citation.For the purposes of the gloss, the Pindaric text is a generically neutral, disembedded 'work' (ἔργον) that serves to exemplify a general principle. By expropriating the cited text from its context in the poem, the commentator elides the distinction between Pindar's πρόϲωπον . . . τηλαυγέϲ referring in its original

[86] Cf. Ch. 3, pp. 122–3.
[87] On the evidence for Theocritean poetry books cf. Gutzwiller (1996), Sens (1997) 55–6.
[88] This verbal similarity may also serve to underline the reasoning behind *Id.* 1 being placed first, as the most gracefully elaborated of the poems.
[89] Which commentator was responsible for the comment is impossible to say: Gutzwiller (1996) 126, noting that the gloss indicates 'a scholarly commentary of considerable sophistication', observes that Munatius (active in the second century AD) and Theon, who worked in the mid-first century BC and was one of the first scholars known to have worked on Theocritus, are both possibilities.

context to the opening section of the poem, and the role of the citation here as describing a whole poem. Yet the scholium also seems to mobilize the differences between Pindar's text and Theocritus' by playing on different meanings of πρόcωπον as 'front' of a building and the 'identity' of the poet (τοῦ ποιητικοῦ προcώπου).[90] By using πρόcωπον in these senses, the scholium highlights the distinction between the splendid image that the poem presents through its 'graceful and technical' aspect, and the poetic 'identity' that the dramatic form conceals. Unlike Pindar's πρόcωπον ... τηλ-αυγέc, which projects the fame of victor and poet, the Theocritean text creates at least some of its effects by means of disguise and concealment of authorial identity (μὴ ὑποδεικνυμένου ...).

As has frequently been noted, Pindar's use of buildings and other physical structures as part of his self-referential apparatus has a competitive edge, implying poetry's superiority to other art forms, as well as serving to highlight the sophisticated craft that goes into composing and performing a poem.[91] Such imagery also serves as a metaphor for poetry's temporal durability, a feature this citation instantiates. As in the case of O.6.11 above, the rhetoric of the poem is recontexualized in a way that re-routes and adds to its poetological significance. Central to this recontexutalization is the dialogue in the citation between two types of physical structures, Pindar's building and Theocritus' poetry book. The use of the πρόcωπον ... τηλαυγέc as an analogy for *Id*.1 and its place in the book implicitly draws attention to the book's role in instantiating and enabling poetry's dissemination.[92] The metaphor is not only drawn from a poem composed within a performance culture, but is also inscribed by that culture: πρόcωπον ... τηλαυγέc probably references, at least in part, the faces of the dancers, and the image as a whole (χρυcέαc ὑποcτάcαντεc εὐτειχεῖ προθύρῳ θαλάμου / κίονac ὡc ὅτε θαητὸν μέγαρον / πάξομεν) also acts as a metaphor for the physical beauty of the chorus, as well as the verbal sophistication of the poetry.[93] The reapplication of this

---

[90] Cf. LSJ *s.v.* πρόcωπον 3.2.

[91] Cf. Introduction p. 3 n. 9, and Ford (2002) 124.

[92] For the imagery of light (τηλαυγέc) used of books, cf. Posidippus on Sappho's 'bright pages' (Ch. 2, pp. 86–7).

[93] Uhlig (2011) 25 notes that the paradox of 'beginning' with the frontage rather than the foundations expresses how the poem will be 'viewed' in performance, and sees the language of 'fixing' (πάξομεν) and 'setting' (θέμεν) as references to the material form of the book.

metaphor to the poetry book testifies to the appropriations by and through which his poetry exerts its cultural force. But the citation also bespeaks the complex interrelations of Hellenistic 'modernity' and the classical past, in that the very use of the metaphor indicates the strength of the imaginative parameters bequeathed by the culture of the classical period, and their influence in shaping contemporary modes of thought and aesthetic response.

So far my readings have focused on citations in which different kinds of literary effect have been at issue. But it is important to remember that one of the chief functions of canonical texts in the literary culture of the Hellenistic period was their didactic role as sources of information, mined as they were for details about everything from mythology and local traditions to details of dialect and correct grammatical and rhetorical usage. One example of the complexities that such citations could generate is a scholium that glosses Apollonius' account of the foundation of Cyrene (2.498–527), and which assembles and synopsizes various previous accounts. After remarks on the Etesian winds, the scholium's account of Cyrene begins as follows (*Σ* Ap. Rh. 2.498–527a (= pp. 168–9 Wendel)):

περὶ δὲ τῆς Κυρήνης Πίνδαρος ἱστορεῖ ἐν Πυθιονίκαις, ὡς παρθένος οὖσα μέχρι πολλοῦ συνεκυνήγει τῷ Ἀπόλλωνι. διαπαλαίουσα δέ ποτε λέοντι ἠγαπήθη ὑπὸ Ἀπόλλωνος· ὃς καὶ ἁρπάσας αὐτὴν διεκόμισεν εἰς τὴν νῦν ἀπ' αὐτῆς καλουμένην Κυρήνην τῆς Λιβύης, καὶ μιγεὶς Ἀρισταῖον ἐποίησεν.

Concerning Cyrene Pindar gives the following account in his *Pythian Odes* (*P*.9), that when she was a maiden she accompanied Apollo in the hunt for a long time. Apollo had fallen in love with her while she wrestled with a lion. Having snatched her away he conveyed her to the land in Libya that is now called Cyrene, and lay with her and fathered Aristaeus.

This narrative is followed by citations from other authors. Pherecydes (*FGrH* 3 F 58) and Ariaethus (*FGrH* 316 F 3) are cited for the detail that, at Apollo's wish, Cyrene was borne on swans to Cyrene (ἐπὶ κύκνων αὐτὴν ὀχηθεῖσαν κατὰ Ἀπόλλωνος προαίρεσιν εἰς τὴν Κυρήνην ἀφικέσθαι), while Agroetas' *Libyaca* (*FGrH* 762 F 1) is cited for a slightly different version of the story. After noting the account of Mnaseas of Patara, according to which Cyrene went willingly to Africa rather than being abducted (*FHG* III 39), the scholium goes on to record a rationalization of the myth by Acesandrus, narrated in his *On Cyrene* (*FGrH* 469 F 4). According to this version, Cyrene was conveyed by Apollo to Libya during the reign of Eurypylus when a lion was causing damage to the land. He promised the kingdom to whomever slew the beast, and she did so, and afterwards gave birth to Autouchus and Aristaeus. This version in turn is followed by a brief citation from Phylarchus (*FGrH* 81 F 16) that states that Cyrene was accompanied to Libya by attendants.

One notable feature of the citation is how Pindar's account is assimilated to the others. The verb ἱϲτορεῖ used of his account is of course often used of historiographical writing, and there is nothing in the citation apart from the simple reference to the account's provenance (ἐν Πυθιονίκαιϲ) to emphasize that Pindar's account is of a different order from the others mentioned.[94] On the other hand, Pindar's narrative is cited first, while the rationalizing accounts of Acesandrus and Phylarchus fall at the end of the scholium, which suggests a movement from a purely mythological account to more 'historical' ones.[95] A schema of valuation may therefore be implicit. Pindar's priority emphasizes his status as a canonical author and his narrative as privileged source, but the movement from mythopoeia to rationalization also encourages the reader to reflect on the nature of the different accounts, and to consider of what kind of ἱϲτορία Pindar's narrative consists. Another feature of the scholium is that it allows the reader to contrast Pindar's version of the myth, and those of the other authors, with Apollonius', in which Cyrene is shepherdess (Κυρήνη πέφαται τιϲ ἕλοϲ πάρα Πηνειοῖο / μῆλα νέμειν προτέροιϲι παρ᾽ ἀνδράϲιν, ... τήνγ᾽ ἀνερειψάμενοϲ ποταμῷ ἔπι ποιμαίνουϲαν, 'a certain Cyrene is said to have been pasturing her sheep by the Peneian marsh ... [Apollo] snatched her away when she was tending her sheep by the river', 2.500–1, 504). Apollonius' substitution of Pindar's daringly heroic Cyrene for a simple shepherdess also feeds into the contrast between Pindar's text and those of Acesandrus and Phylarchus.[96]

As well as its significance for a reading of Apollonius, however, the scholium may also have affected how readers engaged with *P.9*,

---

[94] The scholium's attribution to Pindar's account of the detail that Cyrene accompanied Apollo in the hunt παρθένοϲ οὖϲα μέχρι πολλοῦ is an error that may have arisen from confusion with the other accounts.

[95] For this opposition cf. Phillips (forthcoming). Cf. also Σ Lyc. *Alex.* 175, 886, 890 for Pindar being cited alongside historians.

[96] See Hunter (1993) 152–3 for further connections between Apollonius' representation of Cyrene and Pindar's presentation of the city in, especially, *P.4* and *P.5*.

potentially disposing them to see the text in more historical than encomiastic terms. It is possible to imagine, for instance, a scenario in which a reader read the scholium, and then referred back to Pindar's account primarily in order to read his narrative of Cyrene, with the poem's generic aims and total structure being of secondary importance. In view of my remarks about (re)singularization above,[97] it is also worth considering the violence of the paraphrase to which *P.*9 is here subjected. The scholium's instrumental account pares away all but the basic story elements from Pindar's account, subordinating *P.*9 to the gloss's exegetical function. As such the gloss deracinates the authorial voice, making Pindar into a transparent recorder of information (Πίνδαρος ἱστορεῖ). This strategy is dictated by the pragmatic aims of the gloss, but it also creates a powerful contrast between the narrative simplicity of the synopsis and the verbal richness of the text itself. This in turn highlights the distance between the poem and the modalities of its contemporary reception, a sense that is reinforced by the positioning of Pindar's text in relation to rationalizing accounts of the Cyrene story.

CONCLUSIONS

The above readings are very far from exhausting the significance of this type of literary interaction. Despite the limitations of the evidence, it is clear that Hellenistic scholars and readers were capable of considerable critical sophistication in construing the relationships between texts. The process of citation, in the Pindaric commentaries and elsewhere, has emerged as multifaceted, mobilized for different purposes, and generating a variety of interpretative situations. As well as serving as a conduit for scholarly judgements about the textual relationships, citations also open up new possibilities for understanding texts, and for reflecting on their cultural significance. In this sense, and despite their specific exegetical function, citations have much in common with some of the other receptive processes I have examined. In a fashion not dissimilar to the recontextualizing effects created by Theocritus in *Id.* 16, citations reposition the utterances they quote, and transform authorial agency by putting it to new uses in new

[97] Cf. Intoduction, pp. 32–4.

contexts. We have seen that, especially in the case of Pindar being used to gloss later poets, citation can suggest ways of associating texts that exceed authorial control, pluralizing not only the meanings of the texts concerned but also the modes of authority employed in regulating meaning: the (often anonymous) commentator becomes, alongside the author, a crucial point in the dialogue through which meaning is generated and sustained. This authority is further complicated by the openness of the ends at which interpretation is directed.

Seen against a more general background, the interpretative situations I have sketched out can be understood as instantiating issues of wider importance to how Hellenistic readers and scholars related to the literature of the past. In particular, there is a connection between the operation of commentaries as compendia of textual material and the libraries in which they were often stored. Recent studies have stressed the political status of Hellenistic libraries: epigraphic evidence shows that aristocratic euergetism was often responsible for the foundation and endowment of public book collections,[98] while for later authors such as Aulus Gellius, Athenaeus, and Vitruvius, libraries functioned in part as symbols of cultural authority,[99] exemplified by the library of Alexandria.[100] The relationship between how libraries are represented and their concrete social functions is not a straightforward one, however, and not only because the textual strategies at work in accounts of early Hellenistic libraries reflect the conceptions and preoccupations of later authors as much as, and perhaps more than, the historical realities they purport to recount.[101] The notion of the library's cultural authority

---

[98] See Johnstone (2014) 352–7: he argues for a 'biblio-political revolution' in the second century BC, in which for the first time 'rich and powerful men began to sponsor the public display of large collections of books'; as a result, books began to be treated in terms of their value as objects as well as being valued for their content.

[99] Jacob (1996); Barnes (2000); Too (2010); Harder (2013) 106–8. Too discusses texts such as Aul. Gell. 7.17 and Athen. 1.3a, in which the movement of book collections tracks shifts in political power, as evidence for this conception of the library.

[100] The origins of the library of Alexandria are obscure, however: see Bagnall (2002) for a critical reading of the evidence.

[101] Johnstone (2014) 357–70 criticizes the common conception of the library of Alexandria as a political foundation, arguing that there is no strong evidence for the early Ptolemies sponsoring the extensive collection of books, as opposed to gathering scholars, and that accounts of the library in the *Letter of Aristeas*, and by Galen and others, retroject later conceptions of libraries as political institutions onto the early Hellenistic period. He does, however, admit that the library was of considerable size by the second century BC (p. 362).

also entails the potential fragmentation of the symbolic power it per-forms. Because it contains a body of texts that often conflict with each other in giving different accounts of the same phenomena, and which give rise to sometimes radically different modes of thinking, and because it constitutes a space in which all manner of different readings and reconfigurations of these texts are possible, the library cannot function as a consistent, self-identical totality.[102] To the library as a unified symbol of political authority can be opposed the notion of it as a space of discontinuity and fragmentation, a potentially infinite labyrinth of texts and textual experiences irreducible to a univocal thematization. Symbolism and actualities intersect in a complex relationship:[103] the Ptolemies exercised concrete political power and reaped cultural bene-fits from the Alexandrian library, while also enabling the creation of a textual multiplicity that exceeded control by any individual. Even in smaller libraries a similar tension would have been at work, especially with regard to the multiplicity of potential textual relationships such collections created.[104]

As spaces in which meanings are debated and multiplied, textual relationships posited and discussed, and classical texts turned to new uses, commentaries give rise to similar dynamics, and instantiate the tensions between cultural politics and textual multiplicity in a par-ticular way. While it is certainly possible to see all scholarly activity at, for example, Alexandria or Pergamum as in a general sense furthering the cultural programmes of the cities' rulers, the marked apoliticality of Pindaric commentaries cautions against oversimplifying this relationship. Nowhere, for example, is there any explicit attempt to see a connection between Pindar's patrons and the Ptolemies, or to legitimize the Ptolemies by way of Pindaric exempla. This does not mean to say that such connections would not have occurred to readers and scholars, but the evidence we have suggests that such modes of interpretation would have been secondary to other

---

[102] The numbers of book-rolls in the library of Alexandria recorded in ancient texts are likely to be considerably exaggerated, but it is clear that the library was of considerable size: see Bagnall (2002) 351–6.

[103] Hence narratives such as Athen. 1.3a can be read as an attempt to exercise a metaphorical control over the contingencies and multiplicities of the library's oper-ation, scripting the history of the library as an ordered progression which is the antithesis of the actuality of the processes of textual transmission, and bestowing on it a mode of authority which counterposes the multiple heteronomies that the library (seeks to) contain(s).

[104] On private libraries see e.g. Dix (2013).

interpretative considerations.[105] Another striking feature of the citations I have examined is that no strong notion emerges from them of what a 'correct', educated reading of Pindar in relation to other poets would consist of. While there are certainly marked traits, such as the agonistic relationship with Homer and the rivalries with contemporaries such as Bacchylides,[106] the commentaries' intertextual juxtapositions generate interpretative possibilities that are not circumscribed by the limited generalizing frames of reference these relationships imply. Becoming a 'learned' reader of Pindar seems to have been more a matter of negotiating interpretative possibilities than of taking on a particular model of intertextual orientation.[107] Taken together, these two features suggest a form of readerly agency in which a sense of the wider cultural implications of reading practices would have developed from the variousness of the dialogues those practices entailed. These considerations will also be of importance for my final two chapters, where I shall turn next to examining a group of poems against wider intertextual and cultural backgrounds. Although the textual interactions I shall examine in relation to those poems will be of a different scale and order from those I have focused on in this chapter, the issues that emerge in the course of those readings will be seen to have numerous connections with the dynamics of recontextualization that I have just analysed.

---

[105] Although cf. Phillips (2013c) 169–75.   [106] See Ch. 1, pp. 78–9.

[107] This reflects the situation that readers would often have been in when asked to adjudicate on scholarly debates between, for instance, Didymus and Aristarchus.

5

Closing the Book: *Olympian* 14

My reading of Theocritus *Id.* 16, and particularly of the role played by the Graces in the poem's finale, provides a useful starting point for thinking about *O*.14 as a material text. As I argued above,[1] Theocritus' appropriation foregrounds the oppositions between text and choral performance, between the Graces as personifications and documents, and the poem's focus on materiality encourages attention to the book as a distinctive space of meaning. The following analysis will explore some of these phenomena in relation to *O*.14. Composed for Asopichus of Orchomenos' victory in (probably) 488 BC,[2] a short poem for a relatively unimportant victor in a minor event, *O*.14 exemplifies the practice of placing the less socially weighty poems towards the end of the book.[3] I shall argue here, however, that it is also a highly effective poem with which to close the Olympian edition, with Echo's journey to the underworld assuming a powerful closural function. I argue below that in the performance economy of the fifth century Echo would have acted as a metaphor for reperformance, and that in the context of written dissemination in later years this role doubles as a metaphor for dissemination more generally, providing a memorable vignette with which to end the book, while also instantiating

---

[1] See Ch. 3, pp. 158–62.

[2] For the date see Del Grande (1956) 115, *Olimpiche* p. 335 n. 2.

[3] *O*.14 is a particularly good example of the pathos potentially attendant on the diachronic process, as the reader confronts the juxtaposition of the splendour of Pindar's commemoration and the town's subsequent bleak history. It was sacked by the Thebans in 364 BC (Diod. Sic. 15.79) and again after the Sacred War (Dem. 19.112). It was later rebuilt (cf. Paus. 9.37.8, Arr. *An.* 1.9.10), but was not again to thrive as an independent political force. Although we cannot be certain that *O*.14 always came last in post-Aristophanic editions, it is likely that this order was the norm: Theon's commentary on *P*.12, for instance, shows that *P*.12 was the last poem in the edition he used.

the transhistorical claims of poetic discourse. Echo's function is balanced by the role of the Graces, discussion of which has dominated criticism of the poem, with scholars attempting to balance the poem's hymnic form with its function as an epinician.[4] In the context of the poetry book the invocation of the Graces and the account of their importance makes for an appropriate closural gesture, capping previous references to poetic inspiration and forming a coda which implicitly restates the book's claims of importance and authority.

A HYMN TO THE GRACES

Καφιcίων ὑδάτων
λαχοῖcαι αἵτε ναίετε καλλίπωλον ἕδραν,
ὦ λιπαρᾶc ἀοίδιμοι βαcίλειαι
Χάριτεc Ἐρχομενοῦ, παλαιγόνων Μινυᾶν ἐπίcκοποι,
κλῦτ᾽, ἐπεὶ εὔχομαι· cὺν γὰρ ὑμῖν τά τε τερπνὰ καί   5
τὰ γλυκέ᾽ ἄνεται πάντα βροτοῖc,
εἰ cοφόc, εἰ καλόc, εἴ τιc ἀγλαὸc ἀνήρ.
οὐδὲ γὰρ θεοὶ cεμνᾶν Χαρίτων ἄτερ
κοιρανέοντι χοροὺc
    οὔτε δαῖταc· ἀλλὰ πάντων ταμίαι
ἔργων ἐν οὐρανῷ, χρυcότοξον θέμεναι πάρα   10
Πύθιον Ἀπόλλωνα θρόνουc,
αἰέναον cέβοντι πατρὸc Ὀλυμπίοιο τιμάν.

<ὦ> πότνι᾽ Ἀγλαΐα
φιληcίμολπέ τ᾽ Εὐφροcύνα, θεῶν κρατίcτου
παῖδεc, ἐπακοοῖτε νῦν, Θαλία τε   15

---

[4] The most recent discussions are Ford (2011) 97–104 and Athanassaki (2003) 4, who sees the poem as a fusion of hymn and epinician, an 'artistic experiment' which leads to 'the creation of a setting where the Graces and Echo make up a most exclusive audience for poet and victor alike'. See also Lomiento (2010–11) 294–301. On the predominance of the hymnic element cf. Wilamowitz (1922) 151: '[h]ier ist alles nur ein Gebet an die Chariten, und das ist nicht nur durch den Ort geboten, sondern kommt ihm von Herzen'; cf. also Kakridis (1979) 145: '[d]er Kult der orchomenischen Chariten muss dem böotischen Dichter schon früher vertraut gewesen sein. Diese Vertrautheit gab ihm die Eingebung, das Siegeslied so zu gestalten, dass ihm die Form eines Gebets an die Chariten annahm'. This less orthodox form fits well with the practice of ending a book with less orthodox examples of the genre, for which cf. e.g. Haslam (1993) 115 on Callim. *Iambi*.

ἐρασίμολπε, ἰδοῖca τόνδε κῶμον ἐπ' εὐμενεῖ τύχᾳ
κοῦφα βιβῶντα· Λυδῷ γὰρ Ἀcώπιχον ἐν τρόπῳ
ἐν μελέταις τ' ἀείδων ἔμολον,
οὕνεκ' Ὀλυμπιόνικοc ἁ Μινύεια
ceῦ ἕκατι. μελαντειχέα νῦν δόμον   20
Φερcεφόναc ἔλθ', Ἀ-
    χοῖ, πατρὶ κλυτὰν φέροιc' ἀγγελίαν,
Κλεόδαμον ὄφρ' ἰδοῖc', υἱὸν εἴπῃc ὅτι οἱ νέαν
κόλποιc παρ' εὐδόξοιc Πίcαc
ἐcτεφάνωcε κυδίμων ἀέθλων πτεροῖcι χαίταν.

You who dwell in a land of fair horses and have as your allotted share
the waters of Cephisus, queens worthy of song, Graces of shining
Orchomenos who watch over the ancient Minyae, listen, since I am
praying to you. For it is by your help that all pleasant and sweet things
come about for mortals, whether a man be wise, or fair, or famous.
Indeed, not even the gods arrange choruses or feasts without the august
Graces, but as stewards of all works in heaven they have their thrones
beside Pythian Apollo of the golden bow and venerate the ever-flowing
majesty of the Olympian father. O noble Aglaea, and Euphrosyne who
loves song, children of the mightiest of the gods, hear me now, and you
Thalia, lover of song, looking upon this revel that steps lightly in
celebration of kindly fortune. For I have come singing of Asopichus in
Lydian mode and with much exertion, since the Minyan land is victorious at Olympia because of you. To Persephone's black-walled house
go now, Echo, carrying a glorious message to his father, so that when
you see Cleodamus you may tell him that his son crowned his hair with
the wings of the famous games, in the renowned folds of Pisa.

The poem begins with the Graces, and it is to them that I turn first.[5]
The extent of the Graces' authority on Olympus (πάντων ταμίαι /
ἔργων ἐν οὐρανῷ, 'stewards of all works in heaven', 9–10) and their
participation in all the positive facets of human culture (5–7) connotes
in the performance scenario the poem's Panhellenic aspirations.[6]
In the situation of reading, however, the Graces function somewhat

---

[5] For a general reading of the Graces' role in the poem see MacLachlan (1993)
42–53.

[6] *Cults* p. 403 argues that the Graces of Orchomenos were the 'original' Graces
from which those in the rest of Greece developed. If this is correct, it would be possible
to see a parallel between O.1's return to the origins of the games, recapitulated in O.10,
and O.14's return to the original site of the Graces. Pausanias' account of the
Orchomenian Graces is a testament to their Panhellenic status. See also MacLachlan
(1993) 43–4.

differently, although the Panhellenic claims are still in play. The poem
directs itself towards two audiences, the divine, composed of the
Graces, and the human.[7] This is recapitulated by the situation of
reading, where the reader partially assumes the situation of the projected audience. The relationship between the human and divine
choruses is of crucial importance here. Critics have often argued for
seeing a close continuity between these choral groups,[8] but the former
is not merely a reflection of the latter. While the Graces' role in overseeing the celebrations on Olympus (8–9) provides a clear parallel with
the performing chorus, Echo's role interposes an important distinction
between the two. While it is possible to see Echo as paralleling the
Graces, and the poem as moving both upwards to Olympus and down-
wards to Hades,[9] the Echo's role as an adjunct to the human chorus also
differentiates it, as the Graces have no need of such recourse. Echo points
up the fact that the human chorus needs to deal with mortality, in a way
which the divine does not. Similarly, Cleodamus' role as an addressee is
distinguished from Thalia's by his mortality.

The performance of the human chorus arises partly out of a need to
deal with and (attempt to) transcend mortality, whereas the Graces'
celebrations on Olympus are bound by no such restraints. This
differentiation is expanded by the diachronic context, in which the
reader assimilates Thalia's role as an internal reader/spectator: ἐπακοοῖτε νῦν, Θαλία τε / ἐρασίμολπε, ἰδοῖσα τόνδε κῶμον ('listen now
Thalia, lover of song, looking on this revel . . . ', 15–16). The phrasing
of the invocation refers to the Graces' role in overseeing the performance (ἰδοῖσα τόνδε κῶμον), enjoining upon readers an awareness of the
secondariness of their activity, and a comparison between their role
and the Graces' power to validate the text. This is offset, however, by
the productive aspect of reading, as the performance rhetoric gives
rise to an awareness of the fleetingness of the moment of performance, and its dependence on the material document for its recreation.
These interactions restage the relations at work between the human
and divine choruses in a performance context, and I shall argue below
that a similar dynamic is at work in the figure of Echo.[10]

[7] Cf. Segal (1985); Athanassaki (2003) 4. For further comment on the prayer see
Wells (2010) 96–7.
[8] Cf. Athanassaki (2003) 6.   [9] Segal (1985) 205.
[10] As with other texts I have examined, the process of commentary is an important
aspect of the text's material transformation. The information given about the Minyae
and Orchomenos in Σ O.14 inscr.c (i 390 Dr), and the bee etymology in Σ O.14.26a

Before exploring Echo's role in more detail, however, I want to focus briefly on an aspect of potential interaction between the text and its performance context. I think processional performance likely,[11] and that in this scenario the description of the underworld as Persephone's 'black-walled house' (μελαντειχέα δόμον) serves as an inverse of the famous temple of the Graces at Orchomenos, the probable destination of the performing chorus. The 'black-walled house' gains additional resonance by substituting for the house of the victor's father, towards which a celebratory revel would normally have been directed.[12] This interpretation is necessarily speculative, but it seems reasonable in view of the importance of the Graces' temple at Orchomenos, and of the structural feature of directing a celebratory revel to the father's house.[13] In the context of processional performance, a parallel would obtain between two moving entities, rather than a static entity and a moving one as would be the case if we were to hypothesize performance outside the temple.

The structural parallel between the μελαντειχέα δόμον and the temple of the Graces would create a tension between different semantic levels, with the earth and the underworld being both separated and drawn together. The μελαντειχέα δόμον is operative as a verbal signifier, the Graces' temple is not. The latter would be gestured to by the

(i 393 Dr) both exemplify the process by which commentary shifts the functionality of the primary text, making it into a setting for scholarly exploration of matters unrelated, or only tangentially related, to the poem itself.

[11] Cf. Athanassaki (2003) 4. Verdenius (1987) ad *O*.14.16 argues against the processional performance thesis, on the grounds that in such circumstances '[the poem] could hardly have been understood and appreciated by the public', but this objection has no weight. For the κῶμος as a procession cf. Bundy (1962) 23; Goldhill (1991) 135–6; Heath (1988) 183; for criticisms of this position cf. Eckerman (2010) 308–9.

[12] For the temple cf. Paus. 9.38.1. The project of connecting Pindaric epinicia to architecture has gathered pace lately: cf. Shapiro (1988) for reading of *P*.6 in relation to the Siphnian treasury at Delphi, and Pavlou (2010) for possible connections between *O*.3 and the temple of Zeus Olympius at Acragas. Cf. also Athanassaki (2011b) on the architectural intertexts in *P*.7. Cf. Pavlou (2010) 316 n. 19 for further references. The relation suggested here is more general than those outlined by these scholars. For the victor's father's house as the destination of the revel cf. *I*.8.1–4:
Κλεάνδρῳ τις ἁλικίᾳ τε λύτρον εὔδοξον, ὦ νέοι, καμάτων / πατρὸς ἀγλαὸν Τελεσάρχου
παρὰ πρόθυρον / ἰὼν ἀνεγειρέτω / κῶμον ('Go, one of you young men, for the sake of Cleandrus and his youth, to the gleaming doorway of Telesarchus his father, and awake the revel, glorious recompense for his labours').

[13] Cf. Segal (1985) 205 for the structural patterns in which the chorus's performance is opposed to that of Echo, and Echo and Persephone are associated as figures who travel between earth and the underworld.

performance itself, and recontextualized by the movement of the
chorus towards it, while being held outside the realm of the text.[14]
This recontextualization juxtaposes the temple of the Graces with the
underworld, drawing on the contrast between the two realms and also
referencing the performance as a means of mediating between them,
and balances the association between the performance and the
Graces' singing on Olympus (8–12). The encompassing of μελαντειχέα δόμον by the text contrasts with the chorus's physical inability
to journey to Hades, and acts as a formal reversal of Echo's journey.

The Graces are given multiple and generalized spatial associations
by their connection with the waters of the Cephisus (Καφιcίων
ὑδάτων / λαχοῖcαι, 'owners of Cephisus' waters', 1–2) and because
their 'seat' (ἕδραν) is Orchomenos as a whole; similarly, they have a
dual role as overseers of the festivities on Olympus (9–12) and the
revel on earth (13–20). This correlates with their temporal extension,
as their status as παλαιγόνων Μινυᾶν ἐπίcκοποι ('guardians of the
Minyans born in ancient times', 4) looks back to the heroic age.
The (non-)presence of the temple of the Graces in O.14 would be,
on my reading, a particular example of the strategy by means of which
Pindar omits to tie a poem too strongly to the specific features of a
particular place in order to allow a poem to appeal to as many
listeners as possible.[15] In this case, the audience of a performance in
Orchomenos would obviously have been well aware of the temple and
would have been able to fill in the details, but the generality with
which the Graces are localized also allows for their transposability in
reperformance and eases the shift from the Graces as specifically
Orchomenian deities in 1–4 to their Panhellenic Olympian status in
6–12. In substituting for the house of the victor's father, the 'black-
walled house' adds a note of pathos by reminding the audience of the
κῶμος that might have been. However, the substitution of Echo's

---

[14] We note the difference from e.g. Sappho fr. 2, where Aphrodite's grove is
described in detail, as well as e.g. P.7 which alludes specifically to the temple of the
Alcmaeonids; see e.g. τεόν / δόμον Πυθῶνι δίᾳ θαητὸν ἔτευξαν, ('they made your
dwelling in divine Pytho a marvel to see', 10–11).

[15] Cf. Carey (2007) 199 on the absence from Pindar's poetry of overly specific
descriptions of particular places, a strategy which 'facilitates the process of projecting
the song and its honorands beyond their polis into the larger performative context of
Greece in fulfilment of the boast/promise of the panegyrists that their song provides a
fame which transcends the boundaries of space and time'. This style of writing does
not completely preclude the possibility of allusions to particular local features: see e.g.
Pavlou (2010).

journey for this never-performed κῶμος is also a celebratory move, replacing a human performance with an event which transcends the mortal sphere, and which, as we shall see below, gestures towards the poem's immortalizing power. The poem can thus be read as a formal and conceptual aggregation; both Echo's journey to the underworld and the κῶμος of the performance directed towards the Graces replace the κῶμος that would have taken place had Cleodamus still been alive.[16]

A (RE)PERFORMANCE TEXT

Before thinking in detail about *Olympian* 14 as part of an edition, I want to examine an aspect of the poem's performance function which is of importance for these considerations. I suggest that Echo, as a figure of reduplication, of the poem/performance going beyond itself, operates as a metaphor for reperformance.[17] The brevity of *O.*14 makes it a particularly good candidate for solo reperformance, as does its unusual structure, which effectively combines a hymn to the Graces with an epinician for Asopichus of Orchomenos. This structure would have fitted easily into a sympotic context, in which a celebration of the Graces' powers in overseeing the Olympian 'choruses and banquets' (9) could easily have doubled as a metaphorical reflection on the participants' current activities, and a desire to accommodate the poem to such scenarios may have been part of what motivated Pindar to design it as he did.[18]

My main focus here, however, is on Echo's role, by means of which Cleodamus' death and the need to include him in the performance is coupled with an implicit meditation on poetry's immortalizing

---

[16] On the κῶμος as a reinterpretation of the performing chorus in epinician more generally see Budelmann (2012).

[17] Probably the clearest reference to reperformance is N.4.13–16 (εἰ δ' ἔτι ζαμενεῖ / Τιμόκριτος ἁλίῳ / cὸς πατὴρ ἐθάλπετο, ποικίλον κι θαρίζων / θαμά κε, τῷδε μέλει / κλιθείς / ὕμνον κελάδηcε καλλίνικον, 'and if your father Timocritus had still been warmed by the mighty sun, often playing subtly the cithara he would have celebrated his victorious son, inclining to this melody'), for which cf. Morrison (2011) 232. The connection between Echo and reperformance is noted briefly by Ford (2011) 104.

[18] On the poem's structure see e.g. Athanassaki (2003).

power. In order to understand the implications of the poem's conclusion, we need to consider how Echo's role is conceived, and
how the content of her utterance is likely to have been understood
by fifth-century audiences. The relevant lines are 21–4:

> πατρὶ κλυτὰν φέροις᾽ ἀγγελίαν,
> Κλεόδαμον ὄφρ᾽ ἰδοῖς᾽, υἱὸν εἴπῃς ὅτι οἱ νέαν
> κόλποις παρ᾽ εὐδόξοις Πίcας
> ἐcτεφάνωcε κυδίμων ἀέθλων πτεροῖcι χαίταν.

... carrying a glorious message to his father so that when you see
Cleodamus you may tell him that his son crowned his hair with the
wings of the famous games, in the renowned folds of Pisa.

Echo's figuration of reperformance is indirect. Her journey to the
underworld differentiates her contextually from reperformers, a distinction that would have been especially strongly felt in the case of
sympotic reperformance. Moreover, Echo's speech act is a deferred
action, existing in a hypothetical future, given by the indefinite
subjunctive εἴπῃc, which is always in advance of the text. Her journey
to the underworld is both a part of the text and that which the text
cannot circumscribe.

There have been various attempts to formulate the content of
Echo's utterance, ranging from seeing her loosely as a personification
of fame, to thinking that she conveyed a precise message to Cleodamus, or that she repeated the whole poem verbatim.[19] These readings
are based on later depictions of Echo, such as that of Aristophanes'
Thesmophoriazusae, where she repeats the last words of Inlaw's and
the Guard's speeches to comic effect (1056–96), and Ovid's famous

---

[19] Cf. Wilamowitz (1922) 151–2 '[ü]berraschend wendet sich die Anrede an Echo,
die hier für [*fama*] eintritt, weil von den Klängen der Oberwelt höchstens ein Wider-
hall in den Hades dringt; durch diesen soll der Vater erfahren, dass Thaleia seinem
Erben den Kranz aufs Haupt gedrückt hat'; it should be noted, however, that his
notion of an echo of the noise of the celebrations reaching Hades is speculative, and
not implied by the text; this may be a metaphorical resonance, but the main focus falls
on Echo as a messenger. Cf. Gianotti (1975) 74 n. 121 who characterizes Echo as 'in
sostanza la voce di *Fama*, chediffonde la notizia della vittoria'. Carne-Ross (1975) 192
thinks 'Pindar bids Echo take the news, the actual sound of the celebration to him'.
Segal (1985) gives a more detailed analysis of the thematics of communication with
the underworld, but does not analyse the contents of Echo's prospective utterance.
Alden Smith (1999) 259 argues for verbatim repetition, but this is unlikely, since it
would entail Echo repeating the poet's command to her, as well as the invocation of
the Graces, which would make little sense in the context of the underworld. For
remarks on personification in Pindar generally, cf. Dornseiff (1921) 53–4.

treatment of the Echo and Narcissus myth (*Met.* 3.334–510). In the absence of any solid contemporary evidence which might indicate how Echo was conceived by Pindar's contemporary audiences, however, we should be wary of retrojecting these later realizations of Echo onto the performance scenario of *O*.14, and of attributing too specific a function to Echo, or an expectation of such a function to her audience.[20] In Homer ἠχή means 'noise',[21] and it is unclear when the more specific meaning of 'echo' developed. A possible contemporary comparandum is *Hom.h.Pan.* 21, where Echo is mentioned as one of the nymphs who accompany Pan in his revels. Here, Echo 'moans around' the mountain top (κορυφὴν δὲ περιcτένει οὔρεοc Ἠχώ), but it is unclear whether this involves the kind of specific repetition that Aristophanes' character engages in.[22] If this kind of repetition was associated with Echo in the early fifth century, Pindar has presented her in a way which draws generally on the idea of echo-as-repetition but also given her a specific function as a conveyor of meaning.

Echo's utterance is deliberately opaque, although it clearly involves a version of the indirect statement of 22–4, telling Cleodamus of his son's victory. Her act of 'taking a message' corresponds in part to the announcement of the victor's name at Olympia during the games,[23] but she is also imagined as dependent on the poem and as a conveying something of its effect. The rhetoric is comparable to the episode at

---

[20] Equally, there is no evidence that the myth of Narcissus and Echo, at least in the form told by Ovid, even existed by this point in the fifth century. Even if the story existed, it is just as likely that Echo would have played the role of a generic mourner, perhaps repeating Narcissus' name, as that she would have engaged in the kind of specific repetition found in Ovid.

[21] Cf. e.g. *Il.* 2.209; 13.389.

[22] For the capitalization cf. Germany (2005) 188; Thomas (2011) 157 n. 19. The dating of the poem is uncertain, although it may well be contemporary with or slightly later than Pindar: cf. Thomas (2011) 169–71. Germany (2005) reads Echo as a figure of intra- and intertextual repetition; *Hom.h.Pan.* 16–18 recalls *Od.* 19.518–21, 'producing a literal mimesis of Echo' (p. 201), who herself metaphorizes the poem's allusive strategies and internal structure.

[23] Thus Nash (1990) 101–3, who thinks that she repeats the last lines of the poem. The poem itself rewrites the announcement at the games, which would have consisted of the victor's name, father, and city: see Nash (1990) 102. This rewriting also has consequences for the poem's status as a meditation on reperformance and poetic power: even the 'original' performance is marked as secondary, situated in relation to a precursor that informs its significance. This in turn anticipates how later performances will be marked by the performance traditions of which they form part.

O.8.81–4, where the personified Angelia, daughter of Hermes, is depicted in a similar role:[24]

> Ἑρμᾶ δὲ θυγατρὸς ἀκούcaic Ἰφίων
> Ἀγγελίαc, ἐνέπο ικεν Καλλιμάχῳ λιπαρόν
> κόcμον Ὀλυμπίᾳ, ὅν cφι Ζεὺc γένει
> ὤπαcεν.

Iphion, hearing from Angelia, daughter of Hermes, could tell Callima-chus of the shining adornment at Olympia, which Zeus granted to their family.

Again, there is in this passage a combination of clear communication (ἀκούcaic . . . ἐνέποι . . . λιπαρόν / κόcμον) without the precise articula-tion of the form or content of that communication; we are not told, for instance whether Iphion duplicated Angelia's message exactly, or whether all of the Blepsiads' victories were mentioned as part of the λιπαρόν / κόcμον, or only the latest one. In a sense, these details do not matter; the fact of the communication is what is important, rather than its mode or content. But from another perspective, the fact that these communications are not explicitly articulated is a means of foregrounding both poetry's immortalizing power but also its limita-tions in the face of mortality.[25] Not attempting to make an empirical claim for a mode of communication that is beyond evidential sub-stantiation is a way of signalling the limits of men's accomplishments and their claims on the world.[26] Similarly here, Echo operates opaquely, and her utterance can only be imagined, a deferral which balances the structural position of the temple of the Graces in the above reading as the destination towards which the poem moves, but which is never realized in the text. The paradox of her role as a messenger, a figure defined by her capacity to vocalize an utterance, who does not have a speaking role within the poem, underscores the alterity of her mode of communication.

---

[24] Comparable also is the opening of Bacch. 2: ἄ[ιξον, ὦ] cεμνοδότειρα Φήμα, / ἐc Κ[έον ἱ]ερáν, χαριτώ- / νυμ[ον] φέρουc' ἀγγελίαν, for which cf. Maehler (1982) 28; Calame (2011) 124–5.

[25] Cf. also Rutherford (1997) 46 on the closural use of references to song in Pindar's epinicians.

[26] Miller (1977) 234 n. 35 compares O.8.77–84 as functionally identical to Echo's role and argues that in each case the poet 'seeks to encompass the dead within the spirit of the occasion'; this formulation overlooks the way in which Cleodamus both is and is not part of the performance.

This scenario has consequences for how we might read Echo as a metaphor for reperformance and the poem's wider dissemination. In each reperformance the singer places himself in the position of Echo *qua* figural representation of song by 'echoing' previous performances, but in doing so, he also addresses Echo, and reruns the deferral of Echo's task. This scenario maps on to the intratextual situation; a monodicreperformance of an original choral performance would replicate the structure of Echo as a solo messenger carrying a message for the chorus.[27] Echo is not, however, an exact metaphor for reperformances,[28] which, although they convey the message (φέροις' ἀγγελίαν) of the victor's achievements, replicate the whole poem in a way Echo does not. The text has already figured its own future as a part of itself, but it is a future that is simultaneously inside and outside, constituted by differing from the performance utterance. In her function as a metaphor, subordinated to but differing from the text, Echo figures the contextual variations of reperformance.

Echo's doubleness as both messenger and metaphor encourages an attention to the wider dynamics of differentiation entailed by the processes of reperformance. Thus Λυδῷ γὰρ Ἀσώπιχον ἐν τρόπῳ / ἐν μελέταις τ' ἀείδων ἔμολον ('I came singing of Asopichus in a Lydian mode and with care') would have a different resonance in a reperformance scenario, particularly one different in form from the original. A monodic performance at a symposium would constitute a metaphorical transposition of the context signified by τόνδε κῶμον, a transposition that picks up on the polyvalent signification of κῶμος.[29] Such a performance scenario would have involved the recontextualization of the poem in a new context, together with the poem's rhetoric imprinting itself on and shaping that context. An audience at, for example, a sympotic performance would be able to respond to the intersection of their present circumstances and the virtual context projected by the text. These transformations also apply to the reperformer, who in taking on the role of the speaker is both assimilated to

---

[27] For monodic reperformance cf. Morrison (2011) 232.

[28] Metaphors necessarily involve a dialogue between similarity and difference, but in this particular case the differentiations that operate within the analogical system are, I argue, productive of meaning, as opposed to being trivial by-products of correspondence.

[29] On references to the κῶμος and their role in performance see e.g. Eckermann (2010); Agócs (2012); Budelmann (2012). For anticipation of sympotic reperformance cf. Theognis 237–40; Bacch. 20b.5; Pind. *O*.1.14–18, with Clay (1999).

and distinguished from the implied author of the poem. The aorist
ἔμολον, for instance, might be read as inscribing the temporal priority
of the original performance, referencing the role of the original
speaker by indicating his singular action by means of the aspect of
the verb, as well as referring to the present performer.[30] The Graces
are also linked to the poem's reperformance; their role in bestowing
benefits on mortals (5–6) and their supervision of the festivities on
Olympus (8–10) both resonate with the poem's wider dissemination
across the Greek world. More particularly, the word order of χορούς
οὔτε δαῖτας marks a performance trajectory for the poem, mapping
the shift from choral premiere to sympoticreperformances. The
'pleasures' given by the Graces (τά <τε> τερπνὰ καί / τὰ γλυκέ ...
πάντα) implicitly include the repute bestowed by the poem's dissemination, and the comprehensive inclusivity of πάντων ταμίαι / ἔργων
ἐν οὐρανῷ is instantiated as a metaphor for the poem's Panhellenic
reach, each reperformance replicating the Graces' role in listening to,
and implicitly favouring, the poem.

   The complexities of the disseminatory process are anticipated by
the temporal structure of 22–4, which point to a moment in the past
(ἐcτεφάνωcε), but also anticipate the utterance of these words (or a
version of them) in a future context by Echo.[31] Equally, the time
signified by the participles ἰδοῖc' and φέροιc' also pertains to this
deferred future, and hence differs from the present of the utterance.
This articulation of the temporal structure of the performance results
in a temporality that is constituted by elements of present, past, and
future without being reducible to any of them. There is also a
distinction between the signified moment of Echo's meeting with
Cleodamus, conceived as a particular moment of time, and the
endless deferral practised by the (non-performative) signification of
that moment within the text.[32] The text's capacity to project itself into
a/the future is linked to its figuration of a particular textual temporality. In this sense Echo's journey spans the distinction between
the future projected by the text (its being reperformed, read, and
participating in the circulation of the *laudandus*' fame) and an

---

[30] On the role of deictics in projecting contexts of performance see e.g. D'Alessio
(2004a) and above, Introduction, pp. 5, 14, 19; Ch. 3, pp. 121–2.

[31] The poem's reworking of the announcement made at the games is also significant in this respect: see above, n. 23.

[32] I use 'performative' here in its Austinian sense, rather than as an adjective from
'performance'.

unforeseeable future, in the form of the particularities of contexts and readings through which it will operate and which participate in its meaning. In the light of the wider performance economy, then, the Echo episode can be understood as both a transcendence of the immediate circumstances of performance, and a pointer towards how these circumstances are exceeded by the text's capacity to structure a distinctive temporality and to project a context of reading for itself. As a figure of reperformance, Echo stands for the ways in which the poem participates in the constitution of its context, and in doing so moves beyond it and destabilizes its borders, and also for the mutually contextualizing interplay of the text and the circumstances in which it is performed. Cleodamus' death is resituated as the site for a meditation on the immortalizing power of poetry, in which the speaker anticipates the text's future as an index of its power, but also the arbitrariness of the future that lies beyond the control of the text's significational economy.

ECHO AND THE POETICS OF THE BOOK

In the context of the book, Echo's journey to the underworld works more generally as a figure for epinician's immortalizing power, its capacity to operate beyond the confines of a particular context. Echo's journey balances closure and aperture: Hades' operation as a limit beyond which mortal life cannot pass invokes a sense of closure that is reinforced by the material ending of the collection, but Echo's role as messenger is also apertural gesture, pointing to reperformance and the *Nachleben* of the poem.[33] In this section I shall explore in detail how this closure operates in the context of the book, and how this recontextualization adds to Echo's significance.[34]

The difference just articulated between the text's projected control and lack of control over its future is sharpened by the situation of the

[33] On the dynamic of closure and aperture cf. e.g. Fowler (2000) 237–307.

[34] The motif of departure is often used in closural sections in later literature: see e.g. Fowler (1997) 114–15. The prevalence of the motif would, I suggest, have helped to sensitize readers to the force of Echo's departure in this poem. Horace gestures to the end of O.14 at C.3.30.16 (see Nisbet and Rudd (2004) ad loc.), and an artful allusion to the poem's closural role may also be at work at Nonn. *Dion.* 25.21, a line that closes a long metapoetic passage, where the position of ἠχώ at the end of the line (Πινδαρέης φόρμιγγος ἐπέκτυπε Δώριος ἠχώ) replicates O.14's position in the Olympian book.

material document, where the reader is confronted by the illusion of Echo moving over the border of the book. Echo's mediatory role also has a temporal aspect. Read diachronically, she is both a symbolic figure partaking of the world of the performance, and a metaphor for, and grounded in, the diachronicity of the text. This dynamic recapitulates the division internal to performance scenarios between the performance as an event and Echo's utterance in the underworld. Echo's supplementary character is also significant for her closural role: as a replication of an originary utterance, she is radically secondary, and yet dramatized as necessary for the text to function.[35] The collection ends with a highlighting of poetry's diachronic aspect, and also prompts a reconsideration of the supplementary dynamics of reading. Dependent on the narrator or performer for the content of her message, but also able to communicate in a way that the performers cannot, Echo therefore symbolizes the power and the limitations of the epinician project. In the context of the book, she also comes to stand for the interdependence of reader and text, and the interactions between the text and the context(s) that affect its dissemination.

Another passage where such resistance is at issue is *P*.5.96–103, where Arcesilas' ancestors are imagined as participating in epinician performance:

> ἄτερθε δὲ πρὸ δωμάτων ἕτεροι λαχόντες Ἀΐδαν
> βασιλέες ἱεροί
> ἐντί· μεγαλᾶν δ' ἀρετᾶν
> δρόςῳ μαλθακᾷ
> ῥανθειςᾶν κώμων ὑπὸ χεύμαςιν,
> ἀκούοντί ποι χθονίᾳ φρενί,
> ςφὸν ὄλβον υἱῷ τε κοινὰν χάριν
> ἔνδικόν τ' Ἀρκεςίλᾳ·

Apart from him before the palace there are other sacred kings, who have Hades for their lot. And they hear in some way, with their minds beneath the earth, of great virtues soaked by soft dew under outpourings of revels, their own prosperity and a blessing justly held in common with Arcesilas, their son.

As in *O*.14, the precise nature of the contact between the underworld and the world of the living is left obscure: the ancestors are described

---

[35] Her secondariness participates in that of the performance utterance itself as an 'echo' of the announcement of the victor's name at the games: see above, n. 23.

as 'hearing in some way' (ἀκούοντί ποι).[36] The text thus construes within itself the possibility of an experience of reading irreducible to its own textuality, and which consequently cannot be archived. The connection between the dead in the underworld and the performance (δρόcῳ μαλθακᾷ / ῥανθεισᾶν κώμων) contrasts with the connection enabled by the archive between the poem as a physical document and generations of readers. Equally, as in the case of Echo, the kings in the underworld prefigure the role of readers in participating in the text, as well as paralleling the activities of the performing chorus. Both passages engage in an imbrication of repeatability and the ineffable, as the unknowable scene of the underworld comes by a metonymical slippage to stand for later rereadings. Seen specifically against the background of the preservation and ordering of texts in the Hellenistic period, in which the written document records a past text and acts as a written trace of performance culture, Echo marks simultaneously the preservative functions of textual dissemination and the elements in it which exceed the archivable. Echo's utterance as a virtual projection of the text can only be a virtual property of the archive.[37]

Further multiplication of her role is also at work: in the context of written dissemination, Echo can also be read as a metaphor both for the book and the reader. Like the latter, she 'reads' the poem and partakes in its dissemination, carrying the text's message beyond its original context; by being addressed as Echo the reader is figuratively transformed into an echo of the text. Likewise, the book enables the poem('s message) to travel, and reduplicates an utterance which precedes it. A contrast emerges between Echo's status as a figure of mobility and the material fixity of the document, offset by the book also being a mobile object whose disseminatory power relies on its capacity to be transported. This symbolic multiplicity itself suggests the interrelatedness of these different aspects of the disseminatory process. Each individual reading of the text is a kind of fulfilment of Echo's journey, in that it enacts the poem's transcendence of its original context, but it also reruns the text's deferral of Echo's message. The text therefore fulfils itself by means of a (series of) transfiguration(s), as no individual reading is ever identical to Echo's

---

[36] Cf. Slater *s.v.* for other uses of ποι.

[37] On the 'archival' aspect of texts in the Hellenistic period see above, Ch. 1, pp. 67–9; Ch. 4, pp. 205–7. For the significance of the relation between event and archive cf. Derrida (1996); Orrells (2010).

function, but acts as a mediated realization of it. Significant for this mediation is the interaction between Echo and voiced readings of the text: Echo's unenunciated message acts as that which cannot be voiced by a reader, asserting the limits of individual appropriations of the text. We have seen that the conceptualization of authorial voice is an important part of Pindaric reception; the epigrams frequently point up the force of Pindar's voice, and the critic Arcesilaus described Pindar as 'terrific at filling [the reader] with voice' (δεινὸν εἶναι φωνῆς ἐμπλῆσαι).[38] This maxim refers to the sonic force of Pindar's poetry, analysed in detail by Dionysius of Halicarnassus, and its impact on the reader's vocalization. Yet in her resistance to vocal reduplication, Echo thematizes what cannot be included within voiced readings.

Receptive mediation also takes the form of concrete interpretations, an instance of which can be seen at Σ *O.*14.28a (i 394 Dr), which equates Φήμη and Echo: παραγενοῦ πρὸς τὸν σκοτεινὸν οἶκον, ὦ Φήμη καὶ Ἠχώ, διηγησομένη καὶ ἀγγελοῦσα τὴν καλλίστην ἀγγελίαν τῷ πατρὶ Ἀσωπίχου Κλεοδάμῳ ('go to the dark house, O Rumour and Echo, and set out and announce the fairest message to Cleodamus, Asopichus' father').[39] This doubling actually shifts the operation of the text, assimilating Echo's role to another personification not mentioned by the poem. As outlined above, there are potential problems with expanding Echo into a more generalized 'rumour' or 'repute', and the scholia's equation glosses over these, leading to a figuration of Echo potentially quite different from that implied by the figure of Echo alone. While there is a distinction to be drawn between the transfiguration of Echo brought about by this concretized exegetical reading, and the transfiguration that occurs as a structural aspect of the interaction between any reader and Echo, the scholium nonetheless illustrates the role of metatexts in displacing the texts they comment on into a new interpretative space.

The unenunciated nature of Echo's message also has significance for the recontextualization of her role in the book. Echo stages the

---

[38] Cf. Introduction, pp. 20–3 above.

[39] See Daude (2009), *Scholies* pp. 352, 412 on paraphrase in the scholia. The use of Φήμη here may have been influenced by her appearance in commemorative epigrams: see e.g. the epigram for Attalus of Pergamum, who won the chariot race at Olympia: Φήμη δ' εἰς Φιλέταιρον ἀοίδιμος ἦλθε καὶ οἴκους / Περγάμου Ἀλείῳ τεισαμένα στεφάνῳ = Ebert (1972) no. 59: see van Bremen (2007) 346. For earlier use of Φήμη in a way that approximates Echo cf. n. 24.

limits of readerly control, in that the content as well as the means of her utterance remains opaque. Hitherto, I have argued that Echo conveys the message of the poem's final lines; this reading entails seeing the text as doubled, narrated both by the speaker or chorus and as representing in advance what Echo will say in the underworld. On this reading, the text would contain Echo's version within itself, but her version of the message would necessarily be contextually different, even if comprising the same words. Thus the 'containment' just mentioned is only provisional. This situation creates an uncertainty over the text's status which resonates with the wider uncertainties of the processes of reception, and impels the reader to question whether reading simply reduplicates the text (which has always been reduplicated in advance, withholding the possibility of a pure reduplication), or whether it is a more active process engaged in a transformation of the text at which it is directed.

I shall argue below that these questions are affected by the depictions of Echo in later texts, but it is also important to note that the narrator's address bears on a reading of Echo as a diachronic figure:

$$\mu\epsilon\lambda\alpha\nu\tau\epsilon\iota\chi\epsilon\alpha \ \nu\hat{\upsilon}\nu \ \delta\acute{o}\mu o\nu \hspace{3cm} 20$$
$$\Phi\epsilon\rho\sigma\epsilon\phi\acute{o}\nu\alpha\varsigma \ \check{\epsilon}\lambda\theta', \ \text{A}$$
$$\chi o\hat{\iota}, \ \pi\alpha\tau\rho\grave{\iota} \ \kappa\lambda\upsilon\tau\grave{\alpha}\nu \ \phi\acute{\epsilon}\rho o\iota\varsigma' \ \grave{\alpha}\gamma\gamma\epsilon\lambda\acute{\iota}\alpha\nu$$

Go now, Echo, to Persephone's black-walled house carrying a glorious message to his father

The simplicity of the command ἔλθ', Ἀχοῖ elides the text's disseminatory complexities by constructing Echo as the simple reflex of a mode of address and conveyance: this can be read as interacting with the erasure of other (later) literary realizations of Echo demanded of the reader by Pindar's distinctive construction, which I shall discuss in more detail below. But the command ἔλθ', Ἀχοῖ is also an inauguration of dialogue, as Echo's reduplicative role comes to stand for the reader's relation to the text. Although Echo's message forecloses the role that the book and the reader can play by figuring it in advance, the ineffability of her language metaphorically exposes that role to a definitional instability, as the exact nature of the dialogue subject to metaphorization is unclear. Reading is metaphorized here in terms of both openness and delimitation, and the concept of metaphoricity upon which this process is based is also implicated in the text's operation. Echo is a symbol of the poetic afterlife, but also stands for transformation. Likewise, Echo as metaphor both stands and does not stand for the reader, in that, as argued above, the exact grounds of the relation are not made explicit, and because Echo's role refigures what reading the text will have meant, thus intervening into that which she ostensibly only stands for. The closural position of the poem also gives this reading of the effects of metaphor a resonance for the collection as a whole: like Echo, the collection transforms what it addresses, and is given over to further transformations in its journey across the centuries.[40]

OTHER ECHOES INHABIT THE GARDEN: THE LIMITS OF INTERTEXTUALITY

One of the central moves of intertextualist theorizing has been to foreground the intertextual determinations that underpin all acts of reading, which are redescribed as bringing into play a potentially endless range of texts in addition to any one particular text on which a reader might focus; this wider intertextual background, comprising not only literary texts but the whole resources of the language user, is essential for the reader to be able to make sense of the text at all. A correlative of this has been an increased awareness of modes of reference not dependent on authorial intentions. As well as consciously formulated allusions, texts also allow for the operation of intertextual resonances that may not have been intended by an author, and for interactions with later texts that an author could not have foreseen.[41] In this section, I shall examine part of the intertextual background that emerges in the Hellenistic period for *O.14* by focusing on post-Pindaric literary representations of Echo, and attempt to understand the kind of effects this may have had for a Hellenistic reader.

*O.*14 is the first extant occurrence of Echo as a personified figure;[42] the next extant occurrence is Soph. *Phil.* 188–90:[43]

---

[40] On the transformational effects of Pindar's language cf. Silk (2007).

[41] Cf. e.g. Hinds (1997) for a detailed discussion of the distinction between allusion and intertextuality.

[42] Cf. (possibly) Aesch. *Per.* 391.

[43] Like Echo's appearance in *O.*14, these lines fall at the end of a strophic pair, which raises the possibility that Sophocles modelled his structure on Pindar's poem: in both cases, a musical echoing of one set of the strophe's lines by their corresponding lines in the antistrophe may have reinforced Echo's thematic role in the text.

ἁ δ' ἀθυρόστομος
Ἀχὼ τηλεφανὴς πικραῖς
οἰμωγαῖς ὑπακούει

Echo, she of the unbarred mouth, appearing far off responds to his bitter cries of grief.

The primary reference here is to the frequency of Philoctetes' lamentations.[44] The use of ὑπακούει leads to a coincidence of significational doubleness and referential function, the verb's two meanings of 'listen to'[45] and 'respond'[46] exactly map onto Echo's dual role. But the word's doubleness also marks her futility, and the futility of Philoctetes's situation; her 'listening' adds nothing to her 'response', which simply reduplicates Philoctetes' laments, connoting the frustrated circularity of his utterances.[47] The visuality of -φανής seems at odds with Echo's auditory and vocal role, but the word accents her distance from Philoctetes, implying the distance travelled by his cries before she echoes them: the adjective's connection with vision enhances the sense of Philoctetes' isolation.

Echo plays a slightly more active role at Eur. *Hec.* 1109–13, where Agamemnon describes returning to the Greek camp after hearing a disturbance among the soldiers:

κραυγῆς ἀκούςας ἦλθον· οὐ γὰρ ἥςυχος
πέτρας ὀρείας παῖς λέλακ' ἀνὰ ϲτρατὸν
Ἠχὼ διδοῦϲα θόρυβον· εἰ δὲ μὴ Φρυγῶν
πύργους πεϲόντας ἦιϲμεν Ἑλλήνων δορί,
φόβον παρέςχ' ἂν οὐ μέϲως ὅδε κτύπος.

I came upon hearing the uproar. For Echo, the unquiet child of the mountain rocks, cries out among the army, raising a din. Did I not know that the towers of the Phrygians were fallen to the Greek spear, this noise would bring no little fear.

Her two actions (λέλακ' . . . διδοῦϲα θόρυβον) are not explicitly marked as derivative, although we are presumably meant to think of Agamemnon understanding her actions as reduplicating and further inciting the noise already being made by the men. Agamemnon is

---

[44] For the meaning of ἀθυρόστομος as ἀθυρόγλωττος cf. LSJ *s.v.* ὑπακούει is a conjecture by Auratus for the ὑπόκειται of the manuscripts. For discussion cf. Lloyd-Jones and Wilson (1990) 183.

[45] *Il.* 8.4; *Od.* 14.485.   [46] Cf. *Od.* 4.283.

[47] Cf. Alexiou (1974) for the repetitiveness of lamentations.

slightly uneasy in 1112–13; Troy has fallen, therefore the noise, whose cause he does not yet know, cannot have anything to do with military matters, and therefore does not cause him any fear, and yet it was enough to cause him to come and find out the nature of the events. His use of Echo might be read as describing the noise as an attempt to downplay a potentially threatening situation by subordinating it to a diminutive metaphorical realization, using Echo to cast the crowd as an unruly child (πέτρας ὀρείας παῖς) shrieking stupidly; her association with the wilderness of the mountains underscoring her (and their) lack of sociality. Notable also in this respect are the multiple synonyms (κραυγῆς, θόρυβον, κτύπος).

As in the *Philoctetes*, Echo's conceptual aspect has an impact on the semantics of the passage. Her nature as a coterminous listener and speaker mobilizes the two different senses of the verb λάσκω, which can refer to things 'ringing' when struck, where the subject of the verb makes a sound as a result of being the object of an action,[48] but also to creatures making noise independently.[49] Both of these senses are appropriate to Echo, who can be read here as acting independently and registering sound made by others. The combination of these senses, together with the context of the disorder of the crowd, connotes Echo's status as a figure who obstructs normal modes of communication. Both passages involve indeterminate and unregulated sound, and in both Echo's appearance marks a threat to comprehensibility. In the *Philoctetes* passage, the interminability of Philoctetes' lamentation, bolstered by the closed circuit of Echo's repetitions, defies readability and mirrors the character's isolation. In the *Hecuba*, the κτύπος unnerves Agamemnon by preceding from an unknown cause. The *Philoctetes* passage is paralleled by Euripides' use of Echo in the *Andromeda*; at fr. 118 Andromeda tells Echo to depart in order that she may lament together with the chorus. As in the *Philoctetes*, Echo symbolizes Andromeda's loneliness, and the mourning that she participates in is distinguished from communal lamentation.

Euripides' use of Echo in the *Andromeda* is parodied by Aristophanes in the *Thesmophoriazusae* in a scene where 'Euripides' dresses up as Echo in order to attempt to befuddle the Guard and free Inlaw. Here Echo's capacity for reduplicating discourse is given a comic

---

[48] e.g. *Il.* 14.25 of bronze, *Il.* 20.277 of a shield.   [49] e.g. *Hom.h.Her.* 145.

spin, again acting as a bar to clear communication. 'Euripides' characterizes (himself as) Echo as λόγων ἀντῳδὸc ἐπικοκκάcτρια (1059). The meaning of ἐπικοκκάcτρια is obscure. It is glossed by the scholia as εἰωθυῖα γελᾶν, γελάcτρια. ἐπεὶ εἰcήγαγε κακοcτένακτον τὴν Ἠχὼ ὁ Εὐριπίδηc ἐν τῇ Ἀνδρομέδᾳ, εἰc τοῦτο παίζει ('given to laughter, a mocker. Since Euripides in his *Andromeda* used Echo as a mourner, he [sc. Aristophanes] makes a joke of this'). However, this looks like a speculation, and on the basis that her 'main characteristic [in this scene] is her relentless, annoying loquacity',[50] and that 'Echo' is not referred to as laughing, ἐπικοκκάcτρια is more likely to mean something like 'babbling', 'chattering'. In what follows, Aristophanes traduces Euripides' use of Echo; instead of assisting his 'Andromeda' in her mourning, her repetitiousness quickly frustrates Inlaw (1070–80).

Later, once Inlaw has grown tired of the dialogue, Echo's repetitions also bewilder the Scythian Archer. Paradoxically, it is the very precision of Echo's replies that precludes both the possibility of a meaningful dialogue and of Inlaw getting on with his lamentations by himself (ὦγάθ᾽, ἔαcόν με μονῳδῆcαι...). Also of interest for the concept of Echo as a metapoetic figure is the decontextualizing nature of her utterances. Her repetitions separate individual words from their original enunciative context, and either make them almost meaningless, as with λίαν (1076), where the adverb is detached from its verb, or humorously alter their meaning. We see this in παῦcαι / παῦcαι, where the very fact of Echo's speaking contradicts Inlaw's command, and the main burden of the word is in its effect, transgressing Inlaw's wishes, rather than its semantic value. Part of this effect has to do with the absence of motivation or intent from Echo's utterances; because she can only repeat what she hears, her utterances cannot be analysed normatively as proceeding from a subject who is attempting to give voice to internal thoughts. Her language is pure exteriority, and cannot be correlated with any kind of projected psychological ground. Thus when 'Echo' repeats Inlaw's ληρεῖc, there is a shift of meaning; whereas his accusation is a result of his frustration, her utterance is simply an empty reflection of his, as well as a confirmation of his comment. Ironically, however, Inlaw himself is babbling at this point. The scene has resonances for the relations between comedy and tragedy,[51] but taken in more general terms, it

---

[50] Austin and Olson (2004) ad loc.
[51] Cf. e.g. Rau (1967) 79–85; Silk (1993).

also reads as a comment on the complications of repetition, which language requires in order to function, but which can also threaten language's capacity to make sense.

Echo also occurs as a mourner in the context of pastoral poetry, a trope doubtless influenced by her role in texts such as the *Philoctetes* and the *Andromeda*.[52] Particularly relevant to an assessment of *O*.14 in the Hellenistic period is the use made of Echo by Bion and [Moschus]. The former uses Echo as part of the *Epitaphius Adonis* 37–8:

'αἰαῖ τὰν Κυθέρειαν· ἀπώλετο καλὸς Ἄδωνισ'·
Ἀχὼ δ' ἀντεβόασεν, 'ἀπώλετο καλὸς Ἄδωνισ'

'Alas Cytherea! Fair Adonis is dead,' and Echo cried out response, 'Fair Adonis is dead.'

This use is picked up by [Mosch.] *Epit. Bion.* 30–1, which neatly inverts Echo's usual loquaciousness, making her mourn the fact that she must remain silent without Bion's songs to repeat:

Ἀχὼ δ' ἐν πέτραισιν ὀδύρεται ὅττι σιωπῇ
κοὐκέτι μιμεῖται τὰ σὰ χείλεα ...

Echo grieved among the rocks, so that she, in silence, no longer imitated your lips ...

Echo's association with the mountainous wilderness (ἐν πέτραισιν) is again, as in the *Philoctetes*, mobilized to enhance her sense of isolation. These pastoral depictions of Echo may be redirecting, in ways now obscure, associations built up around Echo as a figure in comedies such as Eubulus'; if that play, and perhaps others like it, involved some tragicomic or pathetic depiction of Echo based around the restricted repetitiousness of her speech, the pastoral topos of Echo as mourner may have taken over some of the pathos of the comic treatments.

In the late Hellenistic period, Echo is also depicted by Archias 33 GP (= *AP* 16.154), whose representation plays on the conventions of ecphrastic and dedicatory epigram:[53]

Ἠχὼ πετρήεσσαν ὁρᾷς, φίλε, Πανὸς ἑταίρην,
ἀντίτυπον φθογγὴν ἔμπαλιν ἀδομένην,

---

[52] And presumably by the repetitiveness and amoebaean form of many laments. She also occurs in an eponymous play by Eubulus (fr. 35, for which cf. Hunter (1983) ad loc.), and her relationship with Pan is exploited in Moschus fr. 2.

[53] Cf. Call. *Ep.* 28.5–6 Pf. = 2 GP with Gutzwiller (1998) 218–19.

παντοίων cτομάτων λάλον εἰκόνα, ποιμέcιν ἡδὺ
παίγνιον. ὅccα λέγειc, ταῦτα κλύων ἄπιθι.

You see rocky Echo, friend, Pan's girlfriend, who sings back a voice
shaped after your own, the babbling image of all types of tongues, the
shepherds' sweet plaything. Leave, hearing just as much as you say.

Here, Echo's repetitiousness is used to ironize formal conventions.
Such epigrams are normally based on the fiction of the speaking
monument, whereas here Echo can only speak as a result of being
spoken to, an irony pressed home by the double meaning of λάλον
εἰκόνα as speaking statue or image.[54] The erasure of Echo's capacity
for independent vocalization is here presented as playful (ποιμέcιν
ἡδὺ / παίγνιον), and the shepherds speaking to Echo are subjected to
the same erasure. This is complicated by the ambivalence of the
speaker, which could be conceived as either an epigram written on
the statue or as one shepherd speaking to another, or as a shepherd
reading the inscribed epigram. The second alternative would presumably involve Echo (the statue) simultaneously echoing the utterance,
meaning that the text would contain an unenunciated double of itself.
Internal vocalization is signified by ὅccα λέγειc, ταῦτα κλύων ἄπιθι;
thus whether we conceive the epigram as read aloud in its fictional
context, or if we read the epigram aloud ourselves, then we are
effectively playing Echo's role in echoing an utterance. Consequently,
the poem dramatizes the secondariness of the reader's role; like Echo,
the reader is doomed to be an ἀντίτυπον φθογγήν, replicating another's discourse.[55]

Despite their significant generic and contextual differences, all of
these treatments have in common a problematization, whether ironic
or pathetic, of communication through its exposure to the differently
realized types of repetition to which Echo can give rise. Pindar's
treatment of Echo is notably different in that she enables communication, albeit of a complex kind. Consequently, the intertextual
field against which an educated Hellenistic reader is likely to have

[54] On the poem in general see Gutzwiller (2002) 106–7; Meyer (2007) 195–6.
[55] The most famous Echo narrative is Ov. Met. 3.356–99, in which Ovid yokes
together Echo and Narcissus. He also adduces an aetiology for Echo being reduced to
a voice without a body; this state is a punishment from Juno for assisting Jupiter in his
adulteries: *fecerat hoc Iunoquia cum deprendere posset / sub Iou esape suo nymphas
in monte iacentes, / illa deam longo prudens sermone tenebat / dum fugerent nymphae*
(3.362–5).

experienced *O*.14 complicates fidelity to *O*.14's particular realization
of Echo by bringing into play a number of other different models by
means of which Pindar's Echo's might be understood.[56] The intertextual field just outlined opens up the possibility of consciously
allowing one's engagement with *O*.14 to be coloured by later texts; a
reader might, for instance, see the capacity of Pindar's Echo to travel
to Hades as prefiguring her connection with death and mourning in
the pastoral texts. Equally, a reader might privilege the original
context of *O*.14 to the extent of holding the later texts of no account
in a reading. This position, however, would neglect the determinative
impact that later texts will inevitably have on a reading of *O*.14, even
if this impact is only subconscious; moreover, such a position fails to
recognize the extent to which the move of privileging an 'originary'
reading of the poem is not a neutral or necessary move, but itself a
construction of various critical discourses and presuppositions.
A more productive position, I suggest, is to recognize the extent to
which fidelity to the particular demands of *O*.14 requires a kind of
negative intertextuality, a resistance to the possible connections that
could be made between *O*.14's Echo and those of later texts, and an
erasure of the intertextual networks within which the text could be
understood.

This move is not purely negative, however, as it alerts the reader to
the particular features of Pindar's treatment, and allows Pindar's text
to be viewed in a different light. Both *O*.14's emphasis on the communication that Echo allows, and its untextualizable nature, are
clarified by the intertextual nexus in which *O*.14 is situated in the
Hellenistic period, allowing for a changed understanding of Pindar's
Echo in terms of its differences from other treatments. As in the case
of the poems examined above, the diachronic situation has a resin-
gularizing dimension: *O*.14 not only confronts the conceptual categories of its own time with its singularizing force, but also differs
from the prevailing representations of Echo in later periods. Broader
questions are also at stake: the combination of Echo's metapoetic
resonances and the marked differences between Pindar's treatment of
Echo and others mean that *O*.14 becomes the site of a potential
questioning of what is involved in the construction of a context of

---

[56] Symptomatic of this is the tendency of some modern scholars to see hints of the
Narcissus and Echo connection in *O*.14 (e.g. Alden Smith (1999) 259–60); there is no
evidence that this myth was even in existence during the fifth century, and there is no
reference to it in the poem.

reading. Given Pindar's privileged status within the canon, the possibility arises of reading the later texts' Echoes as indirect or distortive
echoes of Pindar's Echo, thus both validating Pindar's Echo as a
symbol of a privileged mode of communication, and buttressing
their own figurations of echoing as distortion, displacement, and
transfiguration. From another angle, the differences between the
later Echoes and Pindar's Echo can also be read as prefigured by the
differentiated repetition which Pindar's Echo represents. But this
privileging of O.14 is problematic: as suggested above, representations
of Echo as a pastoral mourner seem to be drawing on the tragic
poets' uses of Echo, and perhaps that of the *Homeric Hymn to Pan*,
rather than Pindar's. In negotiating possible literary filiations and the
importance of generic considerations in shaping particular representations of a figure, the reader finds himself confronted with various
means of constructing the context in which Pindar's Echo can be
(re)read, and impelled to dwell on what fidelity to Pindar's text
might mean, whether such fidelity is even possible given that it itself
is subject to diachronic variations, and the implications of this for a
reading of the rest of the collection.

6

Pythians 11 and 12: Materiality, Intertextuality, Closure

Pythian 12, for Midas of Acragas, combines the stories of Perseus killing Medusa and Athena inventing the music of the *aulos*. One of my aims in this chapter is to examine how the poem operates in the context of the book, and how its aetiological narrative functions in relation to the exegetical comments in the scholia and the poem's intertextual background. As in the cases of other poems I have looked at, this approach necessitates consideration of its status as a performance piece; as well as requiring interpretation against the background of early fifth-century performance culture, the poem's representation of music and the distinctive way the text records and reconfigures mythical events also intersect challengingly with the text's status as an archival document during the Hellenistic period.[1] Consideration of *P*.12's closural force also entails reading it in relation to the poem that precedes it, a relation complicated by the interpretative challenges posed by *P*.11. My reading rehearses the problems *P*.11 has created for scholars, and aims to reorientate interpretation of the poem in various respects. I shall argue that the poem problematizes laudatory strategies in order to create a distinctive interpretative situation, and that its complex intertextual connections make it a particularly interesting instance of the impact changing cultural contexts can have on the protocols of reading. Addressing the two poems in order, the chapter as a whole explores how they combine to articulate the reader's experience of the end of the Pythian book.

---

[1] For the 'archival' context see Ch.4, pp. 205–7.

CLOSURAL PAIRS

Hellenistic and Roman poets frequently positioned poems to create
literary effects.[2] Although Hellenistic editors may well have been
guided primarily by non-aesthetic considerations in their intratextual
ordering of Pindar's epinicians,[3] it is worth considering both the
effects that these orders may have had in shaping readerly expectations, and that readers' approaches to Pindaric editions may have
been conditioned in part by the practices of modern poets. In order to
foreground the patterns created by the ordering of poems, I shall
begin by comparing the final poems of the Olympian and Pythian
books, before considering *P*.11 and *P*.12 as a pair. Both the former are
short and monostrophic, and both were composed for victors geo-
graphically and personally much less important than the tyrants and
other major political figures, and *P*.12 is the only extant epinician
written for a victor in the musical contests.[4]

Both poems thus exemplify the categorizational principle of putting poems for lesser victors and events towards the end of the book,
but contain closural elements which suit them for and are emphasized
by their position. Another formal similarity between the poems is that
neither dwell much on the achievements of the victors or their
families, unlike the odes for the tyrants, or indeed other odes for
better known figures. This could be read in the context of the book as
producing a certain focus on the narrative and metapoetic elements at
the expense of the laudatory programme, or rather as subsuming the
laudatory programme by means of these features, as the *laudandus*
recedes somewhat and other elements come into the foreground. The
diminution of direct praise combines with the poems' emphasis on
mortality, and is thrown into sharp relief by the contrast with the
poems earlier in the book. This contrast is particularly strong in the
case of *P*.12, where Midas is only mentioned in 5–6, and is presented

---

[2] The bibliography is extensive. See e.g. Hutchinson (2008) 251–66 for an overview, on Horace see e.g. Lowrie (1995) Lune (2005); on Propertius see Phillips (2011)
127–8 with further references. Particularly important for Hellenistic book are the
essays in Gutzwiller (2005).

[3] Above Introduction, pp. 57–9.

[4] The reference to Cephisus in *P*.12.27 might put the reader in mind of *O*.14's
depiction of Orchomenos as a privileged poetic site; Orchomenos is a source of poetic
and musical inspiration in both poems.

as conveyor/practitioner of his craft rather than an individual notable in and of himself.[5]

Yet there are also important differences between the poems. *O.*14's hymn to the Graces is generalizing and, despite the Graces' strong connections with Orchomenos, has a Panhellenic resonance which lends itself to being read as capping the poetic concerns of the book; *P.*12's aetiological narrative is more explicitly local, dealing with one particular mode of performance rather than with poetry generally. Similarly, Echo as a metapoetic figure functions rather differently from the closing gnome in *P.*12; although I shall argue that the latter also has a metapoetic dimension, and both passages dwell on the fragility of mortal life, they emphasize different aspects of how mortality can be confronted. The intertextual backgrounds of the two poems are also notably at odds. Consequently, significant differences between the closural and archival functions of the two poems will become clear in the course of my reading.

The structure of the book encourages intertextual connections between poems, a reading strategy particularly prompted by the various links between *P.*11 and *P.*12. The narratives of both poems involve ephebic triumphs, where young men kill oppressive older figures. In both, the heroes are recipients of divine aid which enables their actions: *P.*11.36–7 describes Ares' assistance to Orestes (ἀλλὰ χρονίῳ σὺν Ἄρει / πέφνεν τε ματέρα θῆκέ τ' Αἴγισθον ἐν φοναῖς, 'but with Ares' timely help, he slew his mother and encompassed Aegisthus with murder'), while Athena aids Perseus at *P.*12.18–19. Deviant sexual relationships and the consequent disorder within the family unit are at issue in both poems. *P.*11.22–7 stress the importance of adultery as part of Clytemnestra's motivation in addition to the killing of Iphigenia:

> πότερόν νιν ἄρ' Ἰφιγένει' ἐπ' Εὐρίπῳ
> cφαχθεῖcα τῆλε πάτρας
>   ἔκνιcεν βαρυπάλαμον ὄρcαι χόλον;
>   ἢ ἑτέρῳ λέχεϊ δαμαζομέναν

---

[5] Compositionally, this may have to do with reasons of social etiquette; if Midas was a foreigner as some scholars have suggested (e.g. Gentili and Luisi (1995)), extended focus on him may have been seen as improper, a problem potentially compounded by his humble social status as a musician. Nevertheless, this strategy has a marked effect as a divergence from the generic norm established by the poems earlier in the book.

ἔννυχοι πάραγον κοῖται; τὸ δὲ νέαις ἀλόχοις
ἔχθιςτον ἀμπλάκιον καλύψαι τ᾽ ἀμάχανον
ἀλλοτρίαιςι γλώςςαις.

Did Iphigenia's slaughter by the Euripus, far from her homeland, goad her to stir up her heavy-handed rage? Or did nightly couplings lead her astray, overcome in another's bed? This lapse is most hated in young wives and impossible to hide because of others' tongues.

The juxtaposition of the two poems opens the possibility of reading Danaë and Clytemnestra against each other. Whereas Danaë is forced into a relationship she does not want (ἔμπεδον / δουλοςύναν τό τ᾽ ἀναγκαῖον λέχος, 'fixed slavery and a forced bed', 14–15) it is suggested that Clytemnestra is impelled into adultery by her desires (ἢ ἑτέρῳ λέχεϊ δαμαζομέναν / ἔννυχοι πάραγον κοῖται;). The contrast between the more abstract, political δουλοςύναν and the animalistic δαμαζομέναν retrospectively points up Clytemnestra's baseness, and implies Danaë's virtue.[6] Similarly, the greater detail of ἔννυχοι πάραγον κοῖται puts Clytemnestra's illicitness in the spotlight, contrasting again with the more neutral, desexualized ἀναγκαῖον λέχος, the emphasis of which is squarely on the compulsion Danaë suffers. Another contrast between the poems is the difference between Perseus rescuing his mother and Orestes killing his mother in order to avenge his father. Comparison strengthens the conflictedness of Orestes, and likewise highlights Perseus as a relatively more straightforward figure.[7]

However incidental the grounds for comparison between *P*.12 and *P*.11 and/or *O*.14, resting as such comparisons do on structural parallels created by the decisions of Hellenistic editors, the formal connections between the poems, both at the level of lexis and narrative and in the case of *O*.14 and *P*.12 at the level of structural function within their respective books, invite readerly consideration and contribute to the poems' resonance in a documentary context. A full exploration of the relation between the two Pythian odes, however, requires an analysis of *P*.11, the argumentative and intertextual aspects of which are also of interest for a reading of the Hellenistic

---

[6] Cf. Illig (1932) 95 on the ethical force of Perseus' act; he compares Heracles' destruction of Augeas in *O*.10.

[7] For the parallel cf. Crotty (1982) 111, 119, and cf. more generally Köhnken (1971) 134–5.

edition of the *Pythians*. Before examining *P*.11 in this context, I shall explore the challenges it posed to its audiences when it was first performed.

PROBLEMATIC PRAISE

Pythian 11 poses numerous interpretative problems. The date of its composition is disputed, a majority of scholars having argued for 474, opposed by a substantial minority favouring 454.[8] The precise location of the performance in Thebes has also occasioned debate.[9] Interpretative controversy has centred on the issue of how the poem may relate to Aeschylus' *Oresteia*, and the connection between the poem's narrative and its encomiastic function. In relation to the former, inextricable from the question of dating, scholars have generally been inclined to see Pindar as composing after and under the influence of Aeschylus' play.[10] This position has been recently asserted in greater detail than in any previous argument as part of an attempt to position the poem in a landscape of choral competition in the mid-450s.[11] Interpretations of the mythical narrative have fallen into two camps, some seeing it as a negative *exemplum* in which the house of Atreus represents a web of immorality and disorder, while others have seen Orestes as a praiseworthy figure whose actions redound to the credit of Thrasydaeus.[12] This reading

[8] Cf. Finglass (2007a) 5–11 for an assessment of the scholia which date the poem, with the remarks of D'Alessio (2010) 283–4: both favour dating to 474. For an argument in favour of 454 based on the political circumstances of that period see Kurke (2013) 150–67.

[9] Sevieri (1997) attempts to reconstruct aspects of the poem's first performance, with questionable success: cf. Finglass (2007a) 74. For objections to Finglass's scepticism see D'Alessio (2010) 284–6, who rightly points out that detailed evocation of a locality should not be used as a ground for thinking that the poem was not performed in that place.

[10] For some treatments of this question cf. e.g. Herington (1984); Robbins (1986); Finglass (2007a) 11–17.

[11] Kurke (2013), building on Hubbard (2010).

[12] For a more balanced analysis cf. Most (1985b) 25–6: 'Orest spielt in diesem Gedicht zwei verschiedene Rollen. Bei seiner Reise, beim delphischen Empfang und bei der Rückkehr gleicht er Thrasydaios und ist ein positives Beispiel; aber in seiner Verstrickung ins Unheil seiner Familie, in seinem Muttermord, gehört er durchaus zu den übrigen Atreiden und funktioniert zusammen mit ihnen als ein negatives Gegenbeispiel.' For objections to Most's parallels between Orestes and Thrasydaeus, cf. Finglass (2007a) 45–7.

will focus mainly on the questions of the relationship between the myth and the frame, and *P.*11's relations with the *Odyssey*.

In part, this approach is motivated by my caution about the poem's date and connection with Aeschylus' *Oresteia*, both of which are susceptible of opposed and compelling interpretations. A more important motivation, however, is that the structurally crucial function of the mythical narrative has been misunderstood in crucial respects. Strategies of seeing the myth as either positive or negative in force, and the theoretical assumptions that underlie these readings, have not taken adequate account of the way the poem problematizes its own generic status.[13] I shall argue that the poem emphasizes the non-identity of Thrasydaeus and Orestes, and thereby creates a distinctive hermeneutic situation that produces a particularly calibrated mode of praise, but also prompts listeners to reflect on their own interpretative mechanisms. Further on in my reading, I shall also suggest that these problematics are enhanced by the poem's diachronic situation. My interpretation of the poem does not exclude the possibility of interaction with the *Oresteia*, but emphasizes the poem's engagement with the *Odyssey* on the grounds of its intertextual importance and that, on the scenario of a dating to 454, it is likely to have been better known to a Theban audience than Aeschylus' work. Likewise, I do not exclude the possibility of the poem having a specific political resonance as a result of performance at a particular time; my argument will instead focus on the generalizing force of the poem's political statements.[14]

Proponents of the positive exemplum thesis have asserted that seeing Orestes as a problematic, tragic figure gives too much weight to the image of him we have inherited from tragedy, and point out that in the *Odyssey* Orestes serves as a positive exemplum for Telemachus. This view, however, neglects an important facet of the interaction of the two texts, namely that *P.*11 puts the matricide to the fore by explicitly mentioning it, and focuses more than does the *Odyssey* on Clytemnestra's immorality.[15] In the *Odyssey*'s accounts of Agamemnon's death, Clytemnestra's role is closely connected to who

[13] See also D'Alessio (2010) 286–7.

[14] For recent politically inflected readings see Hubbard (2010) 189–90, 198–200, Kurke (2013) 129–32, 140–3.

[15] The argument about the differing presentations of the matricide in *P.*11 and the *Odyssey* is made in greater detail by Kurke (2013) 110–12. I recapitulate here the main points of her case.

is telling the story. In Zeus' programmatic account (*Od.* 1.32–43) Clytemnestra's role is minimal, and Aegisthus is the active partner in their attack. It is he who marries Clytemnestra and kills Agamemnon, to whom Hermes speaks (38–9), and to whom Orestes' vengeance is principally directed (ἐκ γὰρ Ὀρέcταο τίcιc ἔccεται Ἀτρεΐδαο, 'from Orestes will vengeance come for the son of Atreus', 40). Similarly at *Od.* 1.298–302 Clytemnestra is nowhere to be seen, and the emphasis falls on the killing of Aegisthus, who also takes centre-stage in Nestor's speech at *Od.* 3.301–10. Although Clytemnestra is mentioned at 310 (μητρός τε cτυγερῆc, 'hateful mother'), the actual act of matricide is not narrated. Nestor's presentation is influenced by pragmatic considerations: eliding Clytemnestra's role equates to a tactful avoidance of the sensitive issue of Penelope's conduct, thus avoiding the possibility of giving offence to Telemachus. But the audience is made aware of the matricide nonetheless; the structuring of the narratives in the *Odyssey* allows us to interrogate the process by which arguments and exempla are constructed, and hence participates in the poem's wider meditation on the deceptiveness, positive and negative, of speech and storytelling.[16]

The narrative dynamics of *P.*11 are very different. Here the main emphasis of the narrative at 17–37 falls on Clytemnestra's actions, and Aegisthus is not mentioned until the end (37).[17] This is a problem for critics who want to see Orestes as an unproblematic figure who avenges his father and brings order to his household. Such readings have to minimize the inherently disturbing nature of the action, and indeed Roberta Sevieri even goes so far as to say that Orestes is not presented as a matricide.[18] This neglects the phrasing of *P.*11.37 πέφνεν τε ματέρα θῆκέ τ' Αἴγιcθον ἐν φοναῖc. Had the poet wanted to gloss over the matricide, he could easily have phrased this line differently; by contrast, the phrasing emphasizes it,[19] and the

---

[16] Kurke (2013) 110 notes that the six mentions of the killing in the Telemachy 'are about Orestes taking vengeance, with Orestes serving as [a] . . . role model for Telemachus' while in the five passages in which Clytemnestra's role is featured, Orestes' vengeance is not mentioned (*Od.* 4.90–2, 11.387–461, 24.20–9, 24.93–7, 24.192–202).

[17] Cf. Robbins (1986) 3; Sevieri (1999) 101–2; Finglass (2007a) 107–8.

[18] Sevieri (1999) 85: 'Pindaro abbia inteso qui presentare non Oreste il matricida, ma Oreste il restauratore della casa paterna.'

[19] Finglass (2007a) 108 compares 'the brevity of the reference to the matricide' to *Od.* 3.309–10, but Pindar's πέφνεν τε ματέρα is a more direct reference than the Homeric lines, where the genitive μητρός τε cτυγερῆc is dependent on τάφον, and the focus on killing (πέφνεν) is more explicit than the Homeric δαίνυ τάφον.

separation of Clytemnestra and Aegisthus encourages us to view them
as individuals as well as a unity. This does not mean, however, that
Orestes functions simply as a negative exemplum, as the matricide
does not negate the positive aspects of Orestes' presentation.[20] Rather,
the matricide appears as an interpretative conundrum, a horrifying act
that is nonetheless necessitated by Orestes' situation, irreducible to
conception as purely positive or negative. The conflictedness of this
action contrasts with the situation of the *laudandus* but is also part of
how the poem problematizes the terms of its own discourse.

Another difficulty for the relation between myth and frame comes
with 55 <ἀλλ'> εἴ τις ἄκρον ἑλὼν ἡςυχᾷ τε νεμόμενος αἰνὰν ὕβριν /
ἀπέφυγεν ('but if a man gains the peak and there dwelling peacefully
has avoided dread *hybris*'). The injunction to avoid 'dread *hybris*' sits
uneasily with the mythical narrative. Although the poem does not
encourage the listener to see Orestes as a hubristic figure, it is not
made clear whether he lived 'peacefully' after his revenge on Clytemnestra.[21] Indeed, details of Stesichorus' *Oresteia* suggest that Pindar's
injunction here may develop a contrast between the idealized subject
and how Orestes was represented in that poem. Of particular relevance is the papyrus commentary that supplies the information that
Euripides follows Stesichorus in referencing the bow given to Orestes
by Apollo to ward off the Eumenides (Eur. *Or.* 268–70). The commentary cites a fragment spoken by Apollo in Stesichorus' poem
(*POxy* 2506 fr. 26 col. ii 21–4 = *PMG* 217):

> τό[ξα . . .] τάδε δώcω παλά-
> μα]ιcιν ἐμαῖcι κεκαcμένα
> . .] . . [ἐ]πικρατέωc βάλλειν

'I shall give you this bow, excellent my hands . . . to shoot mightily . . . '

This fragment shows that Orestes was pursued by the Eumenides in
Stesichorus' poem,[22] which is likely to have included scenes on which,

---

[20] Cf. e.g. Robbins (1986) 4; Instone (1986) 87; Sevieri (1999) 83–5; Finglass
(2007a) 44–5.

[21] The use of the present participle with gnomic aorist denotes an action continuous with the main verb, with the aorist participle describing an action anterior to both.
For νέμομαι as 'live', 'dwell' cf. Slater *s.v.*, who compares *I.*9.4. Cf. Dickie (1984) 86–7,
who argues that leaving a fair reputation to one's descendants depends on avoidance
of *hubris* and 'enjoying . . . success with ἡςυχία, that is, with restraint'. Finglass (2007a)
121 compares *N.*1.70 for the peace that results from toil (ἡςυχίαν καμάτων μεγάλων
ποινὰν λαχόντ' ἐξαίρετον).

[22] Cf. Davies and Finglass (2014) 509–10.

for instance, the opening of Aeschylus' *Eumenides* was modelled.[23] If this was the case, Pindar's ἡϲυχᾷ νεμόμενοϲ would form a pointed contrast with the aftermath of the killing in Stesichorus, further differentiating Orestes and the ideal to which the *laudandus* is made to aspire.

These passages are part of a wider self-consciousness about the relation between *persona loquens* and audience, and between the narrator and his material. By foregrounding points of contrast between itself and previous versions of the story, *P.*11 impels its audience towards consideration of their own role in constructing the intertextual networks through which the poem operates.[24] Yet this self-consciousness also emerges in relation to intratextual discourses, and in what follows I shall analyse two more moments at which these effects are played out. The first is another celebrated crux, containing the *persona loquens*' criticism of tyranny (*P.*11.50–4):

> θεόθεν ἐραίμαν καλῶν,
> δυνατὰ μαιόμενος ἐν ἁλικίᾳ.
>   τῶν γὰρ ἀνὰ πόλιν εὑρίϲκων τὰ μέϲα μακροτέρῳ
> ὄλβῳ τεθαλότα, μέμφομ' αἶϲαν τυραννίδων·
> ξυναῖϲι δ' ἀμφ' ἀρεταῖϲ τέταμαι· φθονεροὶ δ' ἀμύνονται.

May I desire fair things from the gods, striving after what is possible for my age. I reprove the condition of tyrannies, finding as I do in the city the middle way flourishing with the longer-lasting prosperity. I strive for shared achievements: the grudging are warded off.

Champions of the negative exemplum thesis have tended to read this passage as condemning the monarchical structures of the heroic age, the horrors and instabilities of which are illustrated by the myth, in favour of the more stable oligarchy of present day Thebes.[25] Those

---

[23] On the relation between *P.*11 and Stesichorus' *Oresteia* see Finglass (2007a) 16; Davies and Finglass (2014) 489–91, 508–9. The aftermath of the matricide is subject to various retellings by the tragedians, and considerable variation elsewhere. Eur. *Andr.* tells the story of his marriage to Hermione (cf. particularly 881–1008) and his killing of Neoptolemus at Delphi (1067–1165, and cf. Pind. *N.*7.34). Cf. also Eur. *Or.* 1658–90 for his marriage to Erigone. Paus. 2.18.6 says that he had a son Tisamenus by Hermione, who succeeded him as king of Sparta. Σ Eur. *Or.* 1645 and Apollod. *Ep.* 6.28 record that he was killed by the bite of a snake at Oresteum in Arcadia. For further references cf. Frazer's notes on Apollod. *Ep.* 6.28.

[24] For remarks about intertextuality as a feature of Pindar's poetics see Pavlou (2008) 533–41.

[25] Cf. Young (1968); Hubbard (2010) 196.

who see Orestes as a positive figure tend to dissociate him from the criticism levelled at tyrants.[26] But the *sententia* also has a general paraenetic force with ethical relevance for listeners and readers beyond the *laudandus*. When read in conjunction with the exhortation to moderation discussed above (ἡϲυχᾷ ... νεμόμενοϲ), the reference to tyranny has both an encomiastic resonance, pointing up the difference between tyrants and the victor, and a generalized paraenetic function, warning against the kind of excessive behaviour connected with the tyrant's life which implicitly balances the moderation referenced in the previous line.[27] This double function also emphasizes the distinction between the exemplum and the frame. Orestes is the son of a monarchical ruler, with aspirations towards continuing the dynasty, and the problems and challenges of his life are an extreme example of the negative aspects of the αἶϲα τυραννίδων that Thrasydaeus will not have to face.

Phrases such as εὑρίϲκων τὰ μέϲα ... τεθαλότα and ξυναῖϲι δ' ἀμφ' ἀρεταῖϲ τέταμαι could have carried differing charges in various performance scenarios: indeed, a distinctive feature of the modern interpretation of these lines is how they have been made to signify different things according to scholars' understanding of the poem's context.[28] Yet the political position they articulate is perhaps less important than the way they enact the formation of a speaker and subject position. Notwithstanding the social situation of the performance utterance, the generalizing statements dramatize their own disembeddedness, their capacity to speak meaningfully to a variety of contexts. Viewed contextually, the passage gives a picture of a political perspective emerging from the messy specifics of contemporary events, gestured at by αἶϲαν τυραννίδων and φθονεροί. Put in a temporal perspective, the diachronic force of the utterance is already at

[26] See e.g. Sevieri (1999) 104 for a reading of Orestes as an anti-tyrannical killer who restores legitimate governance. Finglass (2007a) 118 subordinates the warnings against tyranny to the poem's laudatory function.

[27] Cf. Pavese (1975) 249. Nagy (1990) 187 and Kurke (1991) 215 see such references as warning against the formation of actual tyrannies, or as diffusing the threat of them. For another type of historicizing reading cf. Gentili (1979). I see such passages as figurative ethical constructions. The emphasis on moderation (τὰ μέϲα μακροτέρῳ / ὄλβῳ τεθαλότα) is connected with the diminishing stress on victor in the final poems and anticipates the minimal role of Midas in *P*.12. For the myth's accent on moderation cf. Bernardini (1993) 416.

[28] For an inventory of political readings cf. Finglass (2007a) 17–18, 37–42, and for some readings of these lines contrast *Pitiche* pp. 663–4 with Hubbard (2010) 196, who sees the lines as advocating friendly relations between Thebes and Sparta.

work in the construction of its speaker.[29] The utterance both scripts
the listener's response to the poem, and enacts the didactic imposition
of the voice of the *persona loquens* on the performing chorus, hinting
at a process of consideration and judgement necessary to make sense
of both the narrative and the vagaries of contemporary politics.

The passage also forms a connection between political positioning
and 'literary' interpretation, the advocation of τὰ μέϲα forming a
sociopolitical correlative to how the *persona loquens* reflects on and
shapes the narrative. In condemning Clytemnestra's excesses through
marked phrasing (e.g. χειρῶν ὕπο κρατερᾶν 18, νηλὴς γυνά 21, ἔκνιϲεν
βαρυπάλαμον ὄρϲαι χόλον 23, ἔχθιϲτον ἀμπλάκιον 26), the *persona
loquens* gives the narrative a strong moral colouring. Yet as I shall
explore further below, the break-off at 38–40 suggests the narrator's
limitations by inviting the judgement of his φίλοι to supplement
his own interpretation of the narrative. By means of this double
manoeuvre of judgement and self-limitation, the *persona loquens*
acts out a poetic version of the sociopolitical ideal described in
50–3, in which co-operation, self-awareness, and restraint are to the
fore. This in turn underscores and complicates how the poem scripts
audience response: the poet asserts his authority, but also puts on
show the dialogic openness through which this authority is validated.

This process reaches its climax at 38–40, responses to which have
ranged from taking the apology at face value to seeing it as a purely
rhetorical gesture:[30]

> ἦρ᾽, ὦ φίλοι, κατ᾽ ἀμευϲίπορον τρίοδον ἐδινάθην,
> ὀρθὰν κέλευθον ἰὼν
> τὸ πρίν; ἢ μέ τιϲ ἄνεμος ἔξω πλόου
> ἔβαλεν, ὡϲ ὅτ᾽ ἄκατον ἐνναλίαν;

Was I indeed, O my friends, whirled away where the path divided,
having previously travelled a straight road, or did some wind cast me
from my course, like a small boat at sea?

On Finglass's reading, 'Pindar presents himself as so keen to get back
to explicit praise of the victor and his family that he presents his
preceding material as the result of a wrong turning. His aim is not to

---

[29] Audience perception is also at issue: listeners are made aware by the generalizing
statement of the poet's capacity to speak to different contexts, and of the disembedded
nature of the utterance: see further Payne (2006).

[30] On the pragmatic effects of such self-corrections, giving a sense of spontaneity
and improvisation, cf. Carey (1981) 5; Mackie (2003) 10–11; Currie (2005) 79.

denigrate the myth, but to exalt the section which follows it. But he also implicitly challenges the audience to see if it can improve on the ill-judged (or perhaps over-modest) condemnation of the myth given by the poem's narrator.'[31] Finglass is right to reject the interpretation which sees the change of tack as an outright rejection of the myth, but his rendering of ἐδινάθην as 'confused' elides the verb's reference to, and interaction with, the bodily actualities of performance.[32] The image contrasts with the physical stylization and the control exerted by the poet during the performance in his role as ἐξάρχων, a contrast reinforced by the verb's connection with dancing.[33] This contrast opens the possibility of seeing the narrator's assertion either as contradicted by the disciplined iconography of choral dance, or of seeing it as a literal description of the chorus's movements. In the latter case, the physicalities of performance would be represented as the outcome of the narrator's mental confusion.

The verb also invokes the image of the eddy or whirlpool, and hence of a static, circling movement in contrast with the complex momentum of the verbal narrative. Both strands of meaning invite analysis of the poem's function in relation to the physicalities of performance, and both involve a testing of the limits of the metaphor and the image's application to physical realities. The polyvalence of the image and its various interpretative implications lend an additional weight to the question of which it forms part. On this point, it is important to note that readings that see the passage as a rejection of the myth diminish the force of the question and its wider interpretative significance.[34] What is voiced is not a declarative statement, but

[31] Finglass (2007a) 109.

[32] His translation of the cited lines reads 'my friends, did I become confused at the place where three roads meet, despite travelling on a straight path beforehand?'

[33] The point would still stand if, as in the case of O.6, Pindar employed a friend in this role, but given the poem's location in Thebes this seems prima facie unlikely. The verb is used of dancing at e.g. Il. 18.494 (κοῦροι δ' ὀρχηστῆρες ἐδίνεον) and 606: cf. LfgrE s.v. δινέω** B2.

[34] Kurke (2013) 115–20 reads κατ' ἀμευσίπορον τρίοδον as an allusion to tragic versions of the Oedipus story in which the crossroads played a crucial role (cf. Aesch. fr. 387a Radt: ἐπῆμεν τῆc ὁδοῦ τροχήλατον / cχιcτῆc κελεύθου τρίοδον, ἔνθα ξυμβολὰc / τριῶν κελεύθων Ποτνιάδαc ἠμείβομεν), and suggests that the crossroads may have already taken on 'a particular association with tragic drama' by this period (p. 117). She then sees Pindar as contrasting the 'straight path' of encomiastic praise with tragedy's 'unstable and shifting landscape of the path-shifting crossroads' (p. 120). This reading, although suggestive, marginalizes the interpretative force of the question in seeing the myth as a negative exemplum, and neglects the extent to which Pindar has rewritten the story in encomiastic terms.

a presentation of alternatives which are held in suspense, compelling the listener to supplement the narrator's indecision. In the context of the problematic relation between myth and frame, the force of this suspense prompts a questioning of how the exemplum relates to the *laudandus* and to the listener, constituting a starting point for the listeners' reflection on their own ethical position.

The scholia on the passage take the questions at face value. The interpretation given at *Σ P.*11.58a (ii 259–60 Dr) sees the digression as functionally inopportune, and the narrator as upbraiding himself for 'using an inopportune digression' (αὐτὸς ἀκαίρῳ παρεκβάcει κεχρημένοc), although its following comment on the nature of the narrator's 'wandering' (ἆρα, ὦ φίλοι, ἐπλανήθην τῆc ὁδοῦ τὸ πρότερον ὀρθὴν πορευόμενοc [ὁδόν], 'indeed, O friends, I wandered from the road having previously travelled straight') does not imply confusion on his part.[35] However, the interpretation recorded in *Σ* 58a goes on to connect the self-address with an encomiastic commitment: εἰ cυνέθου καὶ μιcθὸν ἔλαβεc, ἵν' ἐγκωμιάcῃc τὸν νικηφόρον, δέον ἐcτὶ τὸν ὕμνον ἄλλοτε ἄλλῃ μετάγειν, ἢ περὶ τοῦ Θραcυδαίου τι λέγονταc ἢ περὶ τοῦ πατρὸc αὐτοῦ τοῦ Πυθιονίκου ('if you agreed to compose an encomium for the victor and took money for it, you must take the hymn either in one direction or another, either saying something about Thrasydaeus or about his father the Pythian victor').[36]

The scholia illustrate the difficulty and elusiveness of the phrase κατ' ἀμευcίπορον τρίοδον ἐδινάθην, and it is hard to resist the conclusion that this obscurity is meant to be to some degree performative,

---

[35] Cf. also *Σ P.*11.23b (ii 257 Dr) and also the censorious comments about digressions at *Σ P.*10.46b (ii 245 Dr) and *Σ N.*6.94a (iii 113 Dr) with Instone (1986) 90.

[36] We might wonder whether *Σ P.*11.58a (ii 259 Dr), and specifically the phrase ἀκαίρῳ παρεκβάcει κεχρημένοc can be read as a trace of a negative exemplum-style reading on the part of ancient critics. The phrase does not necessarily justify such a reading, because ἀκαίρῳ does not imply the perception of an ethical disparity between exemplum and frame, and the criterion of relevance might be conceived as without an ethical dimension. However, the criticism does open up the possibility of such a debate. Eustathius *Pro.* 19 offers a more sophisticated general view of Pindar's mythical 'digressions'. In particular, his point that the 'juncture' between myth and frame is not always clear (χρώμενοc ταῖc μὲν τῶν παρεκβάcεων οὐ κατά τινα ἐκφανεcτάτην cυνάρτηcιν) is suggestive for the case of *P.*11, but we are not in a position to say whether this view was derived in part from ancient critical models, or how (or if) he applied it in his commentary to individual poems. Moreover, this comment should be seen against the background of his theory that Pindar deliberately aims at obscurity: for further comments on digressions cf. *Pro.* 4–7, and on obscurity 10–11, 20.

the confusion of the narrator providing a model for interpretative response. The reader's hermeneutic problem, however, is somewhat more wide-ranging; the narrator appears only to be concerned with the efficacy of his story, whereas the reader also questions the reasons for the narrator's decision. The questioning also leads, I suggest, to a self-consciousness about the constructedness of the myth, as a result of which the reader is asked to participate in the process of construct-ing Orestes *qua* exemplum.[37] Like the critics mentioned above, the scholia neglect the force of the question and its interpretative conse-quences. This is clear in the scholia's reduplication of the poem's rhetoric; referring to the myth as a παρέκβαϲιϲ presupposes a certain tangentiality in the exemplum without commenting on what the consequences of this distance between exemplum and frame might be.

The scholia's treatment of *P.*11.38–40 is part of a wider pattern of commentators either ignoring or seeking to minimize the lack of fit between the exemplum and the situation. There are certainly ways in which Orestes can be construed as a positive foil for Thrasydaeus, but critics who have emphasized these factors have neglected the simple but important fact of Orestes as matricidal avenger being very differ-ent from Thrasydaeus the Pythian victor, and, more broadly, the way in which his actions exceed the ethical norms of Pindar's time, a facet emphasized by his difference from the Orestes of the *Odyssey*. Acknowledgement of this difference points towards another, more fruitful way of looking at the poem, one in which the interpretative challenge of reconciling the exemplum to the situation, or of finding points of reconciliation and balancing them with the differences, is itself important ethically and intellectually, both for the listener and for Thrasydaeus himself as an internal reader of the poem. In other words, the whole process of exemplarity is at issue in this poem; it is not simply a matter of reading the exemplum and drawing the 'right' or best thought-out conclusion, but rather of questioning the nature of exemplarity itself, and the degree to which Orestes, or any other figure can function in such a role.[38]

The poem's ethical demands are articulated both by the declarative moralizing statement at 55–8, and by its staging of an encounter with

[37] Cf. D'Alessio (2010) 287.

[38] For acknowledgement of the limitations of the frame/exemplum relation cf. Instone (1986); Sevieri (1999) 107, and Finglass (2007a) 46: '[r]ather than seek a one-to-one correspondence, Pindar instead points to a likeness between the two which does not depend on similarity in every detail'.

a figure who as we have seen exceeds the behavioural norms of
Pindar's own time, and whose ethical significance is not explicitly
construed by the narrator. Both dynamics are crucial to how the
poem positions itself as an instance of and reflection on the social
role played by didactic chorality. We have seen that the poem dramatizes the construction of subjectivity, both of chorus and audience,
through the imposition of the poet's voice, but the poet's authority is
also articulated in part by a delimitation of the interpretative power
he exerts over his mythical material. The poem constitutes itself as a
space of dialogue between these two dynamics. Crucial to this operation is that the questions the text poses and the interpretative
problematics it sets up remain, on its own terms, unforeclosed: as
such, the poem dramatizes itself as a particular kind of event, one that
advocates concrete responses and behaviours, but also articulates its
demands through its resistance to such recuperation. The poem's
rhetoric has the effect of making any interpretation an incursion
that reaffirms the openness of its questions. The poem's final lines
reassert this dynamic through their mention of the afterlife given to
Castor and Pollux: τὸ μὲν παρ' ἆμαρ ἕδραιςι Θεράπνας, / τὸ δ' οἰ-
κέοντας ἔνδον Ὀλύμπου ('[who] dwell one day in their seat at Ther-
apnae, and the next on Olympus', 63–4). The *Nachleben* bestowed by
the poem on Thrasydaeus differs from that of the Dioscuri, but
involves elements that approximate their duality. The poem bestows
a form of immortality, and the reference to the Dioscuri's cult hints at
the parallel cultic setting of the poem itself.[39] Thus the Dioscuri's
alternating immortality articulates differentially the poem's praise of
Thrasydaeus, and acts as a closural gloss on the poem's wider procedures. The projection of the victor in the poem's final lines as an
implied relational term, constituted by his difference from and
approximation to the Dioscuri, correlates with the force of the
poem itself as an event poised between self-assertion and interpretative realization by individual listeners.

These interpretative tensions are sharpened by the poem's diachronic recontextualization. The arguments I have made have
aimed at understanding the text in performance, but they also apply
to the reading situation. Although there are no signs that ancient
scholars formulated a reading of the poem along the lines I have

---

[39] On the parallelism achieved with the opening of the poem cf. Finglass (2007a)
123–4; Hubbard (2010) 198–200. Kurke (2013) 129–32, 143.

outlined, the scholia on the break-off section quoted above suggest an interpretative aporia about the narrative's function that testifies to the success of the poem's self-problematization. But while the basic mechanics of the relation between narrative and frame operates similarly in reading and performance scenarios,thinking about how the poem may have appeared to later readers also entails a reconceptualization of the poem's intertextual filiations. In a Hellenistic context, the issue of how Aeschylus' *Oresteia* and *P.*11 were related can be reformulated in terms of the relations of the texts to each other as part of an intertextual continuum which also includes Euripides' and Sophocles' tragedies about Orestes.[40] As with Echo in *Olympian* 14, an awareness of these accounts serves to highlight the distinctiveness of Pindar's treatment of the story; his Orestes is clearly a long way from the Orestes of Euripides' eponymous play, and indeed from Sophocles' character. Such a contextual situation also affects smaller-scale issues, such as the interpretation of the questions about Clytemnestra's motives at 22–5:

> πότερόν νιν ἄρ' Ἰφιγένει' ἐπ' Εὐρίπῳ
> ϲφαχθεῖϲα τῆλε πάτραϲ
>   ἔκνιϲεν βαρυπάλαμον ὄρϲαι χόλον;
> ἢ ἑτέρῳ λέχεϊ δαμαζομέναν
> ἔννυχοι πάραγον κοῖται;   25

Did Iphigenia's slaughter by the Euripus, far from her homeland, goad her to stir up her heavy-handed rage? Or did nightly couplings lead her astray, overcome in another's bed?

Some scholars have attempted to see these lines as a response to Aeschylus' interrogation of Clytemnestra's motivations in the *Oresteia*, or even as the inspiration for Aeschylus' treatment.[41]

---

[40] Readers in the Hellenistic period may have had access to an accurate dating of the poem, but the controversy in the scholia over dating may suggest that this had always been a matter for debate: see D'Alessio (2010) 283–4. On the other hand, if Finglass (2007a) 5–11 is correct to argue that the poem was originally dated to 474 by Hellenistic scholars and that the confusion in the manuscripts is due to corruption, this may explain why no connection between *P.*11 and Aeschylus' *Oresteia* is mentioned by the scholia (cf. *Σ P.*11.25b (ii 257 Dr) where Pherecydes and Herodorus are cited for alternative stories involving Orestes' nurse). This absence would then simply reflect a *communis opinio* that put *P.*11 before the *Oresteia*. However, absence of references to the *Oresteia* does not mean that this and other treatments of the Orestes myth would not have influenced Hellenistic readers' reception of *P.*11.

[41] e.g. Herington (1984); Kurke (2013) 122–5.

The diachronic context allows for a reorientation of these questions. Finglass explains the lines as follows: 'Pindar presents the narrator as so overcome by the crime that he must search for motives to account for it. Instead of authoritatively stating a single cause, he clutches at possibilities that might go some way towards an explanation. His questioning thus underlines the gravity of the killings.'[42] But the questions also specifically dramatize Clytemnestra's unknowability, a facet underlined by the formal contrast between *P*.11, where no 'Clytemnestra' is present to be the subject of an interrogation, and the plays, where the staged character can explain her actions, albeit in problematic fashion. This formal aspect is also strengthened by the complexity of the question of Clytemnestra's motivation in the tragedians, awareness of which heightens the reader's sense of the difficulty of answering Pindar's questions.[43]

Additionally, the problematizing treatments of the tragedians emphasize the difficulties of the exemplum–frame relation. Hellenistic readers' experiences of *P*.11 would have been shaped to some degree, as are those of contemporary readers, by their knowledge of the tragedies, and such experiences are likely to have given rise at least initially to a sense of confusion over appropriateness of the narrative to an epinician context.[44] How different readers may have responded to this situation is beyond our capacity to say; my argument here is simply that the intertextual situation of the poem sharpens the problematization of reading that is already at work within the text. Readers are free to marginalize such intertexts and attempt to focus on the poem in and of itself as a free-standing entity, but such a process will necessarily be provisional.

---

[42] Finglass (2007a) 13–14.

[43] Herington (1984) sees *P*.11.23–5 as a response to the *Oresteia*'s use of the killing of Iphigenia and the adultery as motives for Clytemnestra's killing of Agamemnon. But Finglass (2007a) 13 rightly points out that Herington's argument that there is a progression in the *Oresteia* from Iphigenia's sacrifice to the adultery as the chief reason for Clytemnestra's behaviour is faulty; the sacrifice is mentioned at e.g. *Ag.* 1521–9, and Agamemnon's adultery with Chryseis at *Ag.* 1437–47. Finglass is therefore rightly sceptical about the necessity of seeing *P*.11.23–5 as influenced by the *Oresteia*. The sacrifice is also mentioned at Soph *El.* 530–3 and Eur. *El.* 1018–29. See further Finglass (2007b) 251–3 for a concise assessment of the analysis of motivations in Aesch. *Ag.*, Soph. *El.*, and Eur. *El.*, and ibid. 257 for Clytemnestra's motivation in the *Choephori*.

[44] Cf. Finglass (2007a) 15–16 for the intertextual influence of the *Oresteia* on modern arguments over dating.

Hellenistic readers are also confronted by the contrast between the reputation of the idealized figure of 56–8 and the literary history of Orestes. In this passage, the narrator comments on the good reputation bestowed by such a man on his descendants (56–8):

μέλανος{δ'} ἂν ἐϲχατιὰν
καλλίονα θανάτου <ϲτείχοι> γλυκυτάτᾳ γενεᾷ
εὐώνυμον κτεάνων κρατίϲταν χάριν πορῶν·

...he would go to a fairer border of black death, bestowing on his sweetest offspring the grace of good repute, strongest of possessions.

The narrator does not comment on whether Orestes bequeaths a εὐώνυμον... χάριν to his descendants. This silence might be read positively, but the absence of explicit comment draws attention to the difference between the event of athletic success and Orestes' actions; even if Orestes is seen as a largely positive figure, we are made aware of the less controversial nature of the athlete's achievement. Moreover, the passage foregrounds a tension between different modes of bequeathing and inheritance, the ideal of εὐώνυμον... χάριν πορῶν contrasting with the conflictedness of Orestes' function as an exemplum. This contrast is reinforced by Orestes' representation by the tragedians as a figure of conflict. In a Hellenistic context a difference opens up between Thrasydaeus' posterity and Orestes' literary history: while the poem's praise of Thrasydaeus effectively accomplishes the ambitions articulated in 56–8, Orestes' figuration in the tragedians provides a literary counterweight to the athlete's poetic *Nachleben*.

In foregrounding these interpretative difficulties, the situation of *P*.11 in the book also influences how readers relate to *P*.12; as argued above, Clytemnestra contrasts with Danaë, and the *sententia* on tyranny contextualizes the actions of Polydectes. Most importantly, however, the conflictedness of Orestes as an ethical exemplum points up the absence of such issues surrounding Perseus. The context of the book also gives rise to a potential conflict between this passage and earlier poems in praise of tyrants. The criticism of the tyrant's life recalls the end of *P*.1, recalling the stress there on the tyrant's conduct and retrospectively highlighting the difficulties of the idealization broached in that passage, and might also prompt a recollection of *P*.3 and its depiction of Hiero's illness. In conjunction with the inverse parallel described above between Clytemnestra and Danaë,

we can also read this passage as anticipating the depiction of Polydectes as a negative ruler in *P.*12. Reading the poetry book thus
involves a confrontation with differing representations of tyranny,
and the attempt to balance their competing claims involves an interrogation of the ethical concepts on which such claims are based.

PERFORMANCE AND TEXT

Before focusing further on *Pythian* 12 as part of the book, I want to
analyse some aspects of how its musical and textual aspects may have
worked together in order to better grasp how the poem may have
operated in performance, and to foreground both the differences and
the continuities between performance and the text as a material
document. I argue elsewhere on the grounds of metre and contextual
probability that Pindar used the 'many-headed *nomos*' as the melodic
basis of the music, vocal and instrumental, that accompanied the
performance of the poem. On my reading, the *nomos* would have
served as a melodic frame which Pindar and his performers would
have applied to the words of the poem and their rhythmical structure
according to the melodizational practices current during the classical
period.[45] Whether or not this was the case, however, it is clear from
the scholia that the scholars of the Hellenistic period had no knowledge of the poem's musical accompaniment, and so this scenario is
not relevant to how readers of the Hellenistic period may have related
to the poem. I shall make reference to this scenario in the following
treatment in order to press the case for a particular reading of the
poem's performance dynamics, but my reading of the text in the
context of its Hellenistic readership should not be taken to rely on
readerly knowledge of a particular mode of musical performance.

The *aetion* narrated in *P.*12 is not the only one related to the
invention of the *aulos* and *aulos*-playing. Perhaps the better-known
story is that of Athena and Marsyas, in which Athena, having
invented the instrument, rejects it on account of the distortion of
her facial features caused by playing it, whereupon it is taken up by

---

[45] Phillips (2013b) 38–41. This section is a lightly revised version of part of that
article, and I would like to thank Cambridge University Press for permission to
reproduce it.

Marsyas.[46] P.12 is our first source for the 'Athena and the Gorgons'
aetion, but we cannot know how original his mythopoeia was.[47]
Crucially, Pindar describes the origin of aulos-playing not only as
the invention of an instrument and of an art in general, as is the
case in the other aetion, but as the origin of a particular piece, the
'many-headed nomos'. One motivation for the mythological grounding of this piece could be that it was the very piece with which
Midas was victorious in his performance at the Delphic contests.[48]
Whether or not this was the case, the paradigmatic association of a
single piece with the origins of aulos-playing as a whole has the
effect of marking the whole art with the characteristics of a particular moment of divine invention. By means of this totalizing redescription, Pindar validates his composition (and Midas' victory, if
it was indeed the 'many-headed nomos' with which he won) by
associating it with the paradigmatic moment of αὐλητική par excellence. This also has the effect of juxtaposing the musical and
circumstantial individuality of Pindar's use of the nomos with its
general cultural importance.

While recent readings of the poem have analysed the text's sociological implications with regard to the disputed place of the aulos in
Greek musical culture of the time, and in relation to contemporary
debates about musico-poetic style,[49] I want to focus here on the role
of the poem's interrelations of text and music, and its reflections on
mimesis. The complexity of these interrelations emerges from the
fact that the accompanying instrument is the subject of the discourse. This involves an audience in a mimetically double structure,
wherein the aulos, both as a concept and as a concrete part of the

[46] Cf. PMG 758 and 805 for fifth-century versions of the Athena/Marsyas narrative. Paus. 1.24.1 describes the famous statue group depicting the myth by Myron on
the Athenian Acropolis. For analysis, see Leclerq-Neveu (1989); Wilson (1999).
Papadopoulou and Pirenne-Delforge (2001) 44–5 explore possible echoes of the
Marsyas story in P.12.

[47] See e.g. Landels (1999) 154–59; Papadopoulou and Pirenne-Delforge (2001) 38.

[48] This is assumed by West (1992) 214 and followed by Porter (2007) 17, but we
are not told that this was the case. Cf. Köhnken (1971) 121 n. 19.

[49] e.g. Frontisi-Ducroux (1994); Papadopoulou and Pirenne-Delforge (2001);
Martin (2003). For disputes about the aulos see generally Wilson (1999) with
Martin (2003). Steiner (2013) 184–94 reads the poem as endorsing the musical
complexity enabled by contemporary developments in the aulos but testimony
about Pindar's melodic conservatism compels caution about the extent to which
mimeticism and heterophony would have been reflected in the poem's music: see
Phillips (2013b).

performance,[50] is redescribed by the verbal narrative, while simultaneously providing a frame in the light of which the words of the text are understood. This doubleness is particularly notable given the explicit redescription of the musicality of the *aulos* at 6–11 and 19–21. These descriptions mark both the originary moment of creation, in implicit opposition to the Athena and Marsyas narrative, and the musicality of the present performance. The music to which the audience listens during the performance is subjected to a transformation which reaches back into the mythical past and simultaneously acts on the present.

The poem's multiple mimeticity (Pindar imitating Athena imitating the Gorgons, to which we may also add the musical and rhythmical mimesis and reconfiguration by *P*.12 of the 'many-headed *nomos*') has often been noted by scholars,[51] but what has been less appreciated is the dual status of the poem's mimetics staged as both production and imitation. Given that the mythical episode narrated in *P*.12 must pre-date Pindar in some form, as does the *nomos* upon which the poem's music draws, we recognize that *P*.12 does not dramatize itself as a purely originary production of what it imitates, but as a reconfigurative intervention into the tradition.[52] This dynamic is reflected in the blurring of figure and ground enacted by the text's mimetic structure.[53] Thus at the lexical level the Gorgons' οὔλιος θρῆνος is both the ground which makes Athena's foundational mimesis possible, and a figuration of the present performance. As a musical texture it functions as an echo heard through the redescribed *aulos* music of the performance, and as its mythical antecedent. The Gorgons' lament is figured as unapproachable (ἀπλάτοις ὀφίων κεφαλαῖς, 'from [their] unapproachable snaky heads', 9), as something which requires Athena's technological intervention to become assimilable to human experience. This is furthered by the semantics of οὔλιος, which in addition to 'baneful' or 'destructive' can also mean

---

[50] See Phillips (2013b) 38–41 for an argument in favour of *aulos* accompaniment.

[51] e.g. Schlesinger (1968); Segal (1998) 99.

[52] My analysis of mimesis as a production of the subjects of imitation differs from the conception of mimesis as ritual enactment, for which see e.g. Nagy (1990) 42–5. On my reading, mimesis is not grounded primarily in its correspondence to a mythical subject, but by its own projection of that subject.

[53] One might compare the performative 'reinvention' of the 'original' dithyrambic circular chorus at *Dith.* 2.1–5: cf. Steiner (2013) 186–7.

'frequently repeated'.[54] The oscillation of these meanings contributes to a sense of the Gorgons' *Unheimlichkeit*, semantic polyvalence enacting uncanniness.[55]

This process is reinforced musically by the *aulos*, the sound of which is a mediated, partial representation of its mythical antecedent; there is obviously a difference, as well as a similarity, between the *aulos* the audience listens to and the Gorgons' lament. If we accept the argument that Athena's 'weaving' (8) of the Gorgons' *threnos* also combines it with the cry of victory uttered by Perseus at 11,[56] then Athena's mimesis is dramatized as a mode of combination and reconfiguration, wherein each of the elements, the lament and the victory cry, contribute to a whole that is different from either of them individually. Understood in these terms, the narrative also formulates the *nomos*' music as a particular type of phenomenon, a substrate which bears the imprint of the two expressions which were woven together to create it. The sonic warp and weft of the *nomos* is made by implication to reflect the emotional states of Perseus and the Gorgons in their respective vaunt and lament. As such, the narrative makes the *nomos* into a phenomenal correlative of the emotional effects that music was felt to have and Athena's act of creation as a proleptic allegory of the text's reception(s).[57] At the same time, however, the simultaneity of text and music dramatizes their different effects; hearing the *aulos*' music alongside the description of Athena 'weaving' the Gorgons' lament (οὔλιον θρῆνον διαπλέξαισ᾽ Ἀθάνα, 8) in order to create the *nomos* cues an awareness of the difference between the signifier διαπλέξαισ᾽ and the sound of the *nomos*. This in turn

---

[54] The former sense is usually favoured by commentators (e.g. Köhnken 1971: 136: 'in seiner Wirkung auf Perseus gleicht der Threnos der Gorgonen einem furchteinflössenden und verderbenbringenden Kriegsgeschrei'). Gerber (1986) 248 follows Greppin (1976) in seeing *P.*12.8 as echoing e.g. *Il.* 17.756 οὔλον κεκλήγοντες and drawing on the repetitiveness of ritual lament: the standard meaning of οὖλος is 'woolly', or 'thick', and is taken to mean 'close-packed' or 'frequent' at *Il.* 17.756 by extension: see LSJ *s.v.* 3.

[55] For a classic analysis of the Gorgons as other see Vernant (1985) 12, and further Segal (1994) 86–8.

[56] Clay (1992) 523, who argues that διαπλέξαισ᾽ must refer to the 'weaving' of more than one 'object', followed by Martin (2003) 163. For Clay (1992) 522, Perseus bringing Medusa's head to Seriphus, rather than the decapitation, forms the focal point of the mythical narrative.

[57] Theory which described the emotional and ethical effects of music is common in the fourth century BC and thereafter; cf. e.g. Pl. *Rep.* 397–401b with further passages in Barker (1984) *s.v.* 'ethos'. *P.*12 can be seen as prefiguring these theorizations.

highlights the provisionality of the poem's description of the foundational event, a description which can only be accomplished via the
metaphorical διαπλέξαιc'. At the point where the text comes nearest
to denoting 'what happened', it has recourse to indirection, a blurring
of significational realms which represents Athena's action by means
of an imperfect analogy with human activities. At the same time,
however, the use of 'weaving' to describe Athena's action also constructs it as a mythical forerunner, and legitimization, of Pindar's
use of weaving vocabulary to describe his own poetry elsewhere.[58]
Something that was an actual event in the mythical fabula serves as
the basis for a metaphorical system.

The poem therefore enacts mimesis as simultaneously a presencing
and a displacement, as a practice which makes a cultural event
available and also dramatizes its otherness,[59] but there is a strong
stress on continuity as well as on difference and distance. At 22, for
instance, the narrator emphasizes precisely the continuity between
Athena's foundational act and the current conditions of auletic
performance: εὗρεν θεός· ἀλλά νιν εὑροῖc' ἀνδράcι θνατοῖc ἔχειν ('the
goddess invented it, but she invented it for mortals to have'). The
auletic art is envisioned here as an embodying continuity of Athena's
practice, in which the physical contingencies of performance assume
a symbolic value by means of their connection with their mythical
precursor.[60] This physical detailing is continued by the description at
25 λεπτοῦ διανιcόμενον χαλκοῦ θαμά καὶ δονάκων, ('often blown
through the reeds and slender bronze') which some scholars have
read as referring to contemporary developments in the design and

---

[58] Pindar uses πλέκω metaphorically of composing songs at *O*.6.86, *N*.4.94. διαπλέκω is used of Hermes making sandals at *Hom.h.Herm.* 79–80 (cάνδαλα δ' αὐτίκα
ῥιψὶν ἐπὶ ψαμάθοιc ἁλίηcιν / ἄφραcτ' ἠδ' ἀνόητα διέπλεκε, θαυματὰ ἔργα). Whereas
Hermes' action is precisely delineated and διέπλεκε used literally, as made clear by the
next line (cυμμίcγων μυρίκαc καὶ μυρcινοειδέαc ὄζουc, 81), albeit to make things
'unthought of, unimagined' (ἄφραcτ' ἠδ' ἀνόητα), Pindar uses the verb metaphorically
to denote a process the constituent aspects of which remain undefined. The shared
features of the two passages, the use of διαπλέκω, the creation by a god of something
extraordinary, suggest an intertextual connection: the greater complexity of Athena's
'weaving' is used to trump the *Hermes* passage, while also suggesting the limitations of
his metaphor for conveying Athena's action. For the dating of the *Hom.h.Herm.* cf.
Thomas (2010) 20–9.

[59] Cf. Segal (1994) 90–3, who stresses the transformation of the Gorgons' cry from
a shriek of primordial pain into a culturally contained and sanctioned practice,
elaborated by Steiner (2013) 179.

[60] On embodiment see Habinek (2005) 4–6 with references.

construction of *auloi*.[61] The personification of the reeds at as πιcτοì
χορευτᾶν μάρτυρεc ('dancers' faithful witnesses', 27) reinforces the
rhetoric of embodiment; the reeds' 'witnessing' gives them an
anthropomorphic character. The use of θαμά also marks *P*.12 as
part of a continuity of performances.

Yet the dynamic by which performance functions as an embodiment of the foundational act is not one of a simple ascription to the
present contingencies of performance of the energies and value
attendant on their precursor. As suggested above, mimesis is presented musically, through the use of the Athena *nomos*, as an appropriation by means of which the *nomos* is reinscribed into a discourse
that reconfigures its significance, and textually as a double practice of
presencing and distancing, reflected in the description of how the
nomos is perpetuated. At 23 the narrator dramatizes the act of
naming (ὠνύμαcεν κεφαλᾶν πολλᾶν νόμον, 'she gave it the name of
"the tune with many heads"'), and the act of linguistic mediation is
made vital to the perpetuation of the specified musical practice. This
deployment of naming, as well as invoking the bestowal of a name as
an act of empowerment, proleptically metaphorizes the appropriation
in which *P*.12 engages by utilizing the melodic frame of the Athena
nomos in a new rhythmical (and linguistic) structure. Athena's act of
naming is figured as the precursor of the (re)naming in which the
poet engages; again, this gesture is both mimetic and productive. The
same mimetic doubleness, in which the poem's language both
imprints itself on a prior event and is itself informed by that event,
is at work in the physical detailing of the *aulos* at 25 (λεπτοῦ διανιcó-
μενον χαλκοῦ θαμὰ καὶ δονάκων, 'often blown through the reeds and

---

[61] Gentili and Luisi (1995); Papadopoulou and Pirenne-Delforge (2001) 47–51. Cf.
also Chuvin (1995). This use of λεπτóc could well have influenced Callimachus'
famous formulation of the Μοῦcαν . . . λεπταλέην (*Aetia* fr. 1.24 Harder) and other
self-referential uses of the adjective in Hellenistic poetry (cf. further Harder (2012) ad
loc). Given the focus of the Pindaric passage, the intertext with *Aetia* fr. 1.24 Harder is
a particularly marked site for the interaction of performance rhetoric and material
texts. In *P*.12, the λεπτοῦ . . . χαλκοῦ has a specific role in the instrument, and the
bronze's 'slenderness' is a practical property which allows sound to be produced in a
particular way, whereas Callimachus' λεπταλέην connotes a more generalized poetic
(and purely verbal) quality. Seen together with *P*.12.25, the specifically conceptual
stress of Callimachus' adjective highlights his appropriative modernity. The Callimachean intertext also stresses Pindar's status as an aesthetic model for the Hellenistic
poets, and raises (or strengthens) the possibility of seeing *P*.12's λεπτóc as a marker of
the sophistication of Pindar's own poetics.

slender bronze'). The description draws attention to the elements shared across the tradition (the reeds, the bronze mouthpiece, the act of emitting the sound), but also creates an implicit tension between the regularity of linguistic signification and the variations in performance style at work in individual performances.[62] Unlike the words that record them, each performance is constituted in part as a transient, unrepeatable event. In relation to such events, the description in 25 acts as an archival moment, translating the individual performance into transcontextual signification, but also implicitly registering that the contingencies of a given performance are not susceptible to a complete translation.[63] As such, the line captures in miniature the tension the poem as a whole articulates between recording and transforming its referents.

It might seem paradoxical that *P.*12 should dramatize the discovery of αὐλητική by means of a mimetic action (Athena's) which imitates an event (the Gorgons' lament) which is only partially appropriable by human activity, of which a performance can only be an indirect echo. But such a strategy serves to glorify the *aulos* by stressing its strangeness, and in turn emphasizes the power of the art, and of the individuals capable of utilizing it. The narrative's foregrounding of alterity, and of the singularity both of Athena's foundational act, and, by implication, of the performance itself, provide an indirect correlative to the power of fate and the divine, invoked at 29–32, as a force incapable of being comprehended or anticipated by mortals (30), and capable of unforeseen and transformational interventions into men's lives (ἀελπτίᾳ βαλών / ἔμπαλιν γνώμας, 'striking with surprise unexpectedly', 31–2). The performance maintains and enacts the dual status of the mythical founding, and the mythical fabula in general, as both other and culturally assimilated. This thematic connection is reinforced by the musical accompaniment, which enacts the embodiment of the Gorgons' lament, while also stressing, by means of its place within the reconfigured structure of the *nomos*, its constructedness,

---

[62] This dynamic would probably have been reinforced by individual performances of the *nomos* involving a certain amount of idiomatic melodic variation: see Phillips (2013b) 38–42 with further references.

[63] Steiner (2013) 200 argues that 'θαμά . . . points to the regularized, recurrent nature of these celebrations [sc. the poetic events in which the *aulos* was involved]', but in referring to multiple performances the adverb also hints at the variations at work in the performance economy.

and the human arts—technical, compositional, and performance-related—needed to realize it.[64]

The conjunction of the extensive description of the *aulos* with a written document gives rise to a general tension between these two modes. In particular, the description of the physicality of the instrument at 20–6 brings about a contrast with the medium of writing; the mention of the reeds used to make the *auloi* as πιϲτοὶ χορευτᾶν μάρτυρεϲ (27), for instance, highlights the fact that it is now the written words that perform this memorializing function, and points up the differences between the two media. The *aulos* is a 'witness' in part because it records the sound created by Athena's mimetic invention, and primarily because it oversees the dancers' performance.[65] The book, however, can only signify these effects indirectly, and the materiality of the document enforces the contrast between music and the verbal signifiers that have to stand in for it. These differences are strengthened by the poet's accenting the melodic range of the *aulos* (παρθένοϲ αὐλῶν τεῦχε πάμφωνον μέλοϲ, 'the maiden created a melody of every sound for the *auloi*', 19) and the specifically mimetic character of Athena's creation (ὄφρα τὸν Εὐρυάλαϲ ἐκ καρπαλιμᾶν γενύων / χριμφθέντα ϲὺν ἔντεϲι μιμήϲαιτ' ἐρικλάγκταν γόον, 'so that she might imitate with instruments the loud-sounding wail that was pushed from Euryale's swiftly moving cheeks', 20–1), neither of which are susceptible to reduplication by the book.[66] Similarly, the *aulos'* role as εὐκλεᾶ λαοϲϲόων μναϲτῆρ' ἀγώνων ('famous reminder of people-stirring contests', 24) points to the secondariness of the book text and the situation of reading in which it operates, removed from the performance context the poem describes.[67] The *nomos* is a form of

---

[64] Cf. Clay (1992) 524–5 on the thematic connections between the concluding passage and the doubleness of the *nomos* as recording suffering and celebration.

[65] Cf. *Pitiche* p. 682.

[66] There are several possibilities for how Athena's imitation relates to the sounds she heard. If one follows Gentili and Luisi (1995) in thinking that the *aulos* being referred to is made of double pipes, which is the most natural way of taking the plural of ϲὺν ἔντεϲι, then the two pipes could be imitating the two Gorgons. Alternatively, the drone pipe might be imitating the Gorgons' wailing, while the pipe on which the melody was played Perseus' victory cry.

[67] The use of λαοϲϲόων is an intertextual pointer to the dynamic of violence and civilization; in Homer, the epithet is frequently applied to deities such as Ares and Athena, and used to refer to their role of 'stirring up' warriors in battle (cf. *LfgrE s.v.* and Sotiriou (1998) 45). Its application here to non-military 'contests' enacts intertextually the movement from violence to its civilized containment. The fact that this is

archive, recording as it does (a version of) the mythical event, albeit one the book cannot reduplicate. Athena's act of invention, on the other hand, functions here as the unarchivable, that which escapes totalizing signification.

As in the case of *O*.14, these interpretative issues bear on the constitution of a voiced reading of the poem. In *O*.14 Echo's unenunciated narrative marked the limits of the text's archival force by not being repeatable, whereas in *P*.12 what the speaking voice cannot recapture (alone) is the relationship between music and text that marked the poem in performance. Yet we should not read the poem's diachronic movement as a juxtaposition of an idealized performance mimesis with the secondary, parasitic mimeticity of the book. As we have seen above, the performance is itself an indirect echo of the foundational mimesis, and combines textuality and music in ways which implicate the concept of mimesis itself. Furthermore, the situation of the material document recapitulates the poem's construction of the interaction between singularity and cultural continuity. Whereas in the performance context, the playing of the *aulos* recorded Athena's invention, now it is the book which plays the role of recording and preserving: the uniqueness of individual texts and readings substitutes for the unique performance events. It is notable that the book archives (and fails to archive) both the signified events of the poem, and the performance itself as an event. Reading *P*.12 as an archive therefore involves an acknowledgement of both the limitations of its archival function, specifically its inability to record the music referenced by the text, and its capacity to shift the text's connotations, to expand its meanings, and broaden the significance of its mediation on artistic creativity.

ENDINGS AND INTERTEXTS

I turn now to an examination of the factors that would have influenced later readers' reception of *P*.12. As in my examination of *O*.14 above,[68] I shall focus on the recontextualizing effects of scholarly

---

achieved via an epic intertext hints at the place of *P*.12 and αὐλητική within a wider cultural continuum. For a differently focused interpretation, cf. Clay (1992) 523–4.

[68] See Ch. 5, pp. 223–35.

reception, and on the poem's interaction with other versions of its myths. The situation of *P.*12 differs somewhat, however, in that Hellenistic readers would have had access to a complete text of Pindar's *Dithyrambs*, an edition that contained at least two poems in which Perseus played an important role. Reading these poems alongside *P.*12 would have allowed readers to compare their different realizations of the narrative.

The dithyrambs (*Dith.* 1 = fr. 70a S–M and *Dith.* 4 = fr. 70d S–M) survive in highly fragmentary form, and nothing is known for certain about their dates of composition, although it seems fairly likely that *Dith.* 1 was composed for performance at Argos.[69] This poem contained a narrative of Perseus' encounter with the Gorgons; at fr. 70a.15, following an invocation of the Muses, Pindar says that 'mortals tell that . . . he, having fled the sea's black enclosure . . . of the daughters (?) of Phorcus, relative of the fathers . . .' (λέγοντι δὲ βροτοί/]α φυγόντα νιν καὶ μέλαν ἔρκος ἅλμας / κορᾶν] Φόρκοιο, σύγγονον πατέρων . . .).[70] How the narrative developed from this point is unknown. More detail can be gleaned from the fragments of *Dith.* 4, however. The first extensive fragment records Zeus setting Perseus' revenge in motion:

```
[   ]φύτευε{ν} ματρί
[   ].αν λέχεά τ' ἀνα[γ]καῖα δολ[          15
[]αν·
[Κρ]ονίων νεῦσεν ἀνάγκᾳ [
[   ] δολιχὰ δ' ὁδ[ὸ]ς ἀθανάτω[ν
```

was planting (?)[71] for the mother . . . and the forced bed . . . the son of Cronus nodded by (?) necessity . . . long is the road of the immortals . . .

The phrasing of λέχεά τ' ἀνα[γ]καῖα is similar to ἔμπεδον / δουλοσύναν τό τ' ἀναγκαῖον λέχος at *P.*12.14–15, but it is unclear to which

[69] A suggestion based on the mention of the city at fr. 70a.7. On the possible performance dynamics of *Dith.* 1 see Lavecchia (2000) 93–5, D'Alessio (2004b) 121–5, who cites the suggestion of Zimmermann (1992) 42 that the poem had to do with the confrontation between Dionysius and Perseus (Paus. 2.20.3), and went on to record the foundation of Dionysiac cult at Argos. On the cultic background see Arrigoni (1999).

[70] It seems likely that the attribution to 'mortals' signals that the story, or at least elements thereof, was a false one to which Pindar was intending to supply corrections: see D'Alessio (2004b) 123.

[71] Or 'planning' (Race): the sense is unclear.

story element the phrase refers: it could be to the imprisonment by Polydectes, as in *P*.12, or the rape by Proetus.[72]

After obscure fragments of sixteen lines, a better-preserved passage records a fragment of the mythic narrative:

> ... μ]έμηλεν πατρὸς νόῳ,   35
> ....]ccέ νιν ὑπάτοιcιᾳ βουλεύμαcι<ν>·
> Ὀλυμ]πόθεν δέ οἱ χρυcόρραπιν ὦρcεν Ἑρμᾶν .[
> καὶ π]ολίοχον Γλαυ-
>   κώπιδ]ᾳ· τὸ μὲν ἔλευcεν· ἴδον τ' ἄποπτα
> ....].· ἦ γὰρ [α]ὑτῶν μετάcταcιν ἄκραν [40
> ..θη]κε· πέτραι δ' [ἔφ]ᾳ[ν]θεν ἀντ[ὶ] φωτῶν
> ....]ν τ' ἔρωτοc ἀνταμοιβὰν ἐδάccατο [
> cτρα]τάρχῳ·

it concerned the father's mind... him with highest counsels... from Olympus he sent to him Hermes of the golden wand and the grey-eyed goddess, protector of cities. He brought it,[73] and they saw things not to be seen... Truly he (?) made their transformation extreme (?) and they became stones instead of men and he gave to the general requital for his lovemaking.

This account differs in various important respects from *P*.12.9–21.[74] Neither Zeus nor Hermes are mentioned in *P*.12, where the focus is restricted to Athena's assistance.[75] Whereas *P*.12 focuses on the creation of the *nomos* and deals briefly with the story of Danaë and Polydectes (14–15), the dithyramb appears to have situated the story against a more elaborate cosmic backdrop (35–40). The passage has a markedly epic feel:[76] the phrasing of ὑπάτοιcιᾳ βουλεύμαcιν recalls and expands on the Διὸc βουλή of the *Iliad*, the despatch of Hermes and Athena parallels an epic type-scene, and this is also the only extant instance of χρυcόρραπιc outside hexameter texts in the archaic and classical periods. Athena's military aspect is specified by πολίοχον

---

[72] See van der Weiden (1991) ad loc. The closeness of the phrasing raises the intriguing possibility that Pindar was alluding to one passage in the other, but our uncertainties about the dithyramb's date render this speculative. A performance scenario connecting *Dith*. 4 to the Argolid would also seem to tell against, or at least complicate, a connection with *P*.12.

[73] Medusa's head.   [74] Cf. Calame (2013) 335–6.

[75] Although they are common in artistic depictions of the myth: see Lavecchia (2000) 237 for references.

[76] For an instance of extended dithyrambic engagement with epic material see Fearn (2007) 269–87.

in a way that contrasts with the emphasis on her technical inventiveness in *P*.12. The climactic event of turning Polydectes and his associates to stone is narrated more directly in the dithyramb (41) than in the allusive phrase λυγρόν τ' ἔρανον Πολυδέκτᾳ θῆκε at *P*.12.14. Finally, the wording of ἔρωτος ἀνταμοιβὰν ἐδάccατο evinces a more explicit concern with justice and requital than is apparent in the epinician's narrative.[77]

These differences are doubtless due in part to generic considerations: the focus of *P*.12 on the invention of the *nomos* disallows a more capacious narration of Perseus' killing of Medusa, whereas the dithyramb's narrative included a greater number of events and may have in part been motivated by a more complex set of political and cultic factors. Although the nature of the fragments limits what can be said about their relations with *P*.12, what is clear is that a Hellenistic reader with access to these texts could have constructed a composite picture of Pindar's engagement with the Perseus myth. How coherent a picture these poems would have presented is impossible to say, but the dithyrambs would certainly have allowed readers to set *P*.12's condensed account in relation to a more extended treatment that expands on the poet's moral and cosmic understanding of the story.

Happily we have more evidence for the scholarly responses to *P*.12, although this evidence also poses interpretative problems. The following readings are not meant to be explications of an ideal grouping of text and scholarly exegesis, but a series of provisional explorations of potential relations that could have emerged between these in different contexts. Following the above discussion of the etymology of the πολυκέφαλος νόμος it is interesting to note how the scholia explain the mimeticity of Athena's creation and the function of the etymology, and how their exegesis affects further readings. The first explanation is given at Σ *P*.12.15b (ii 265 Dr):

---

[77] Cf. van der Weiden (1991) 163, Lavecchia (2000) 242 for discussion of this phrase. Comparable also is the brief narration of the killing of Medusa at *P*.10.46–8: ἔπεφνέν / τε Γοργόνα, καὶ ποικίλον κάρα / δρακόντων φόβαιcιν ἤλυθε νacιώταιc / λίθινον θάνατον φέρων. The difference between the absoluteness of λίθινον θάνατον and the process of change marked by the dithyramb's πέτραι δ' ἔφανθεν ἀντὶ φωτῶν is marked. The latter may have been shaped in part by cultic setting, perhaps designed as a negative inverse of the processes of transformation (cf. μετάcταcιν ἄκραν) undergone by Dionysiac initiates: on the ephebic dimensions of the Perseus myth and its possible relations to Dionysiac cult in the Argolid see Arrigoni (1999) 44–70. In view of the evidential limitations however, such a suggestion remains speculative.

τὸν παρθενίοις: μυθεύεταί τι τοιοῦτον, ὅτι ὅτε ὁ Περσεὺς ἐκαρατόμησε τὴν
Μέδουσαν, αἱ δύο ἀδελφαὶ ἐθρήνουν τὴν ἀδελφήν, καὶ ἐκ τῆς κεφαλῆς
αὐτῶν καὶ τῶν ὄφεων τῶν περὶ τὴν κεφαλὴν συριγμός τις ἀνεδίδοτο.
τούτου τοῦ συριγμοῦ κατακούσασα ἡ Ἀθηνᾶ τοῦ ἐκ τῶν ὄφεων πρὸς
μίμησιν τοῦ θρήνου καὶ τοῦ γινομένου συριγμοῦ ἐκ τῶν ὄφεων ἐπενόησε
τὴν αὐλητικήν, ἣν καὶ ὠνόμασε πολυκέφαλον νόμον διὰ τοῦτο· ἐπεὶ γὰρ ἐκ
τῶν πολλῶν κεφαλῶν τῶν ὄφεων εἷς τις ἀνεδίδοτο συριγμός, πολλὰς δὲ
κεφαλὰς εἰκότως εἶχον οἱ ὄφεις, διὰ τοῦτο πολυκέφαλον νόμον τὴν κατὰ
μίμησιν αὐλητικὴν συνθεῖσα ὠνόμασεν.

'Which from the maidenly . . .': there is a story that when Perseus cut off
Medusa's head, the two sisters sang a lament for their sister, and a
hissing arose from their heads and from the snakes around the head.
Athena, on hearing this hissing from the snakes, devised the art of *aulos*
playing as an imitation of the lament and of the hissing that came from
the snakes, and she also named it for that reason 'the many-headed
nomos'. For since a single hissing arose from the snakes' many heads,
and because the snakes evidently had many heads, she named the
imitative art of *aulos*-playing that she had contrived 'the many-headed
nomos'.

A variety of explanations are then put forward at *Σ P.*12.39a–c
(ii 268 Dr):

a. ἀλλά νιν εὑροῖσα: ἀλλ' εὑροῦσα τὸ τοῦ αὐλοῦ μέλος μετέδωκε τοῖς
ἀνθρώποις ἔχειν, καὶ ὠνόμασε τὸ μέλος πολυκέφαλον νόμον· ἐπεὶ καὶ αἱ
τῶν δρακόντων πλείους ἦσαν κεφαλαὶ αἱ συρίξασαι· ὧν κατὰ μίμησιν
συνέθηκε. **b.** τινὲς δὲ πολυκέφαλον, φασίν, εἶπεν, ἐπειδὴ πεντήκοντα ἦσαν
ἄνδρες, ἐξ ὧν ὁ χορὸς συνεστὼς προκαταρχομένου τοῦ αὐλητοῦ τὸ μέλος
προεφέρετο. **c.** οἱ δὲ κεφαλὰς ἀκούουσι τὰ προοίμια. ᾠδὴ οὖν διὰ πολλῶν
προοιμίων συνεστῶσα, ἣν λέγουσι τὸν Ὄλυμπον πρῶτον εὑρηκέναι.

a. 'but having invented it': but having invented the *aulos* melody she
gave it to men for them to possess, and she named the melody 'the
many-headed *nomos*', since the snakes' heads that made the hissing
were numerous, and she constructed the melody as an imitation of
them. **b.** Some say that she called it 'many-headed' because the chorus,
which presented the melody under the leadership of the aulete, was
composed of fifty men. **c.** Others understand the preludes to be heads,
i.e. an ode comprising many preludes, which they say Olympus was the
first to invent.

The alternatives listed in *Σ* 39b–c are not to be preferred, and the
explanation proposed by 39b cannot be right because the piece itself

was for solo performance by the *aulos*,[78] and the last seems equally fanciful. The fact that the exegesis which links the πολυκέφαλος νόμος to the snakes' heads is mentioned twice probably indicates that it was the more common thesis; regardless of whether or not this reading is historically correct, it preserves a connection between the phrase πολυκέφαλος νόμος and the mythological event itself, rather than in the other cases where it is connected to modes of performance.

This reading recapitulates the connection between language and mythological event described above, albeit in an untheorized form; consequently, a tension arises between the apparently direct connection between the phrase and its origin, and the process of scholarly debate out of which this meaning emerges for the reader. This interplay in turn replays and extends the process described above in which meaning emerges both from the relation of word and object, and from the circulation of signifiers, a process which the varying explanations extend. A similar phenomenon is detectable in the debate over the cry at 11 (*Σ P*.12.19a–b, ii 266 Dr):

a. Περσεὺς ὁπότε τρίτον ἄϋςε κασιγνητᾶν: τουτέςτι τὴν μίαν· τρεῖς γὰρ ἦςαν. τὸ δὲ ἄϋςεν ἤτοι ἐπὶ τῆς μιᾶς τῶν Γοργόνων ἀκουςτέον, ὡς ἄϋςε καρατομουμένη διὰ τὴν ἀλγηδόνα, καὶ τότε ἄϊεν ἡ Ἀθηνᾶ τὸν θρῆνον τῶν ἀδελφῶν αὐτῆς· ἢ ἄϋςεν ὁ θρῆνος καρατομήςαντος τοῦ Περςέως. οἱ δὲ ἀπὸ τῆς ἀϋτῆς ἐςχηματίςθαι θέλουςι, τῆς μάχης· οἷον κατεπολέμηςε τὸ τρίτον μέρος αὐτῶν. **b.** ἄϋςε διχῶς· ἄνυςεν, ἀνυςθῆναι ἐποίηςεν· ἢ ἄϋςεν, ἀντὶ τοῦ ἐκραύγαςεν.

a. 'When Perseus cried aloud... the third [part] of the sisters' [or, according to the reading of a '... Perseus, when the third [part] of the sisters cried out']: that is, one of them, for there were three. 'Cried out' should be understood in relation to one of the Gorgons, since she cried out in pain when her head was being cut off, and then Athena heard her sisters' lament. Alternatively, the lament 'cried out' after Perseus cut off her head. Some wish to it to be taken figuratively from 'cry of battle', i.e. 'battle', meaning he defeated[79] a 'third part' of them. **b.** ἄϋςε [can be taken] in two ways; [reading] ἄνυςεν, 'cause to be achieved'; or 'cried out' instead of screamed.[80]

---

[78] However, it may be that the author of this comment is assuming that the πολυκέφαλος νόμος was used as the melody in the performance of *P*.12, as I argue in Phillips (2013b).

[79] Cf. the use of this verb at *Σ* Ap. Rh. 3.233–4b (p. 226 Wendel).

[80] This scholium gives ἄνυςεν as a variant rather than an alternative interpretation. διχῶς can be used to introduce an alternative meaning (cf. e.g. *Σ P*.4.76a = ii 107 Dr,

The attribution of the cry to all or one of the Gorgons seems improbable.[81] What is of more interest from an interpretative point of view, however, is the ironic contrast between the event described and the process of debate surrounding it, between Perseus' single cry as a marker of his triumph, a univocal signification, and the contortions of the hermeneutic debate. The juxtaposition of text and metatext shapes readerly understanding by suggesting new interpretations and varying exegesis that individual readers may not have considered. But it also draws attention to the singular nature of the text; the text is necessarily open to paraphrase, and yet always resists exact assimilation to such rewritings, which never precisely reduplicate the precise nature, lexical, rhythmical, and contextual, of the text's utterance. Moreover, reading the scholia is not simply a matter of adjudicating on the correctness of various exegeses, because it also implicates readers' conceptual stances, and necessitates a certain self-reflexiveness about reading practices. Thus relating to the comment οἱ δὲ ἀπὸ τῆς αὐτῆς ἐςχηματίcθαι θέλουςι, τῆς μάχης involves thinking about why one might read ἄυce figuratively as a 'battle cry' instead of as a cry of triumph, or whether the battle cry reading would equate to seeing the cry as triumphal. The boundaries between text and exegesis are also at issue here; this comment could be taken as opening up a potentiality of meaning hitherto unforeseen, given that at least some readers will not have thought to read ἄυce figuratively before reading this scholium.

Intertextual considerations are raised by Σ P.11.24b (ii 266–7 Dr) glossing εὐπάραον: διὸ καὶ περὶ κάλλους τῇ Ἀθηνᾷ ἐφιλονείκηcεν, '"fair–cheeked": wherefore she competed with Athena in beauty').[82] This scholium alludes to the separate myth in which Medusa challenged Athena to a beauty contest, and the reference to beauty might also recall the alternative version of the invention of the *aulos*, where Athena rejected her new creation because it distorted her facial features.[83] It is notable that the scholium explains why Medusa

---

διχῶc τὸ cπέρμα δύναται νοεῖcθαι) or a textual variant (cf. e.g. Σ T Il. 5.408b): the latter is clearly more appropriate in this case, despite the absence of a specifying term such as γράφεται.

[81] Cf. *Pitiche* 674–5 for the textual argument, and Clay (1992) 522–3. I follow Race in reading ἄυcεν and taking τρίτον . . . καcιγνητᾶν μέρος as the object of ἄγων.

[82] I use 'intertextual' here in a sense that encompasses mythical plots in addition to realizations of these in specific literary texts.

[83] Cf. Papadopolou and Pirenne-Delforge (2001) for other possible echoes of the Marsyas myth in *P.*12.

competed with Athena (διὸ καί—'wherefore', and note the aorist denoting a completed past action), rather than the reason why the author used the word here, and they do not give any reason for why this connection should be read as obtaining. Nevertheless, the validity of the claim is less important for this analysis than the mode of textuality it presupposes, and which is realized in the interaction of scholia and text. This is not to say that such a reading is only possible in this context; such a connection may well have suggested itself to a spectator at a performance, or indeed in a reading without metatextual accompaniment. As with the intertexts discussed above,[84] the distinctiveness of the interaction between text and scholia resides in its particular configuration of intertextual relations. A mode of reference is implied here without being explicitly theorized, one which sees the text as a weave of the signified and the non-signified, which in turn gives rise to the possibility of the reader rethinking his/her views not only of this passage but of the processes of (inter)textuality more generally. The intertext also pointedly substantiates the polyvalence of εὐπάραον, lending it ironic or perhaps pathetic tone, and might be taken as imputing a possible subsidiary motivation to Athena.[85]

Intertextuality is also at issue in Σ P.12.31 (ii 267 Dr), which glosses ἐρρύcατο and expands on τούτων . . . πόνων by referencing the story of the Gorgons' pursuit of Perseus: ἐπεδίωξαν γὰρ τὸν Περcέα μέχρι Βοιωτίαc ('for they pursued Perseus as far as Boeotia'). Here, Perseus' 'troubles' (τούτων . . . πόνων) are made to include unnarrated as well as narrated events.[86] Again, the ontology of the text is subject to alteration by the critical intervention, as the gloss opens up the unenunciated as a subject of scholarly discourse and readerly attention, hence potentially involving the reader in a rethinking of the workings of narrative and the concepts that orient it. There is, however, a contrast between the semantic modes of εὐπάραον and the expansion required here; the former is a semantic polyvalence arising from a specific intertextual connection, the latter a gap simultaneously opened up and supplemented

---

[84] Ch. 4.

[85] *Pitiche* ad loc. argues, on the basis that Medusa is not represented as beautiful in archaic and early classical art, that εὐπάραον here refers to 'la forza e il gonfiore delle guanche di Medusa . . . che conferiscono al viso l'aspetto rigido di una maschera', and compares *P.*9.17 where he thinks that εὐώλενον refers to Cyrene's strong arms. For the later tradition of Medusa's beauty cf. e.g. Cic. *Ver.* 4.56.124; Ov. *Met.* 4.794.

[86] Pindar's *Dithyrambs* (above, pp. 264–6) are a possible source for such a narrative, but there are no mentions of the pursuit in the extant fragments.

by the scholium. We might simply dismiss the scholium as flawed by saying that one cannot interpret a text on the basis of things which it does not mention, but such an objection relies on an overly simple division on what can be considered 'inside' and 'outside' a text.

This is particularly problematic in the case of the Perseus narrative, which Hellenistic readers are likely to have known from treatments in fifth-century tragedy and Pherecydes. Versions of the pursuit story occur at [Apollod.] *Bibl.* 2.4.3, where his invisibility cap saves Perseus (αἱ δὲ Γοργόνες ἐκ τῆς κοίτης ἀναπτᾶσαι τὸν Περcέα ἐδίωκον, καὶ cυνιδεῖν αὐτὸν οὐκ ἠδύναντο διὰ τὴν κυνῆν· ἀπεκρύπτετο γὰρ ὑπ' αὐτῆς, 'the Gorgons, flying up from their lair, pursued Perseus, but were not able to see him because of his cap, by which he was concealed'), and at Σ Ap. Rh. 1515a (319.9 Wendel = Pherecydes fr. 11 Fowler): αἱ δὲ αἰcθόμεναι διώκουcι καὶ αὐτὸν οὐχ ὁρῶcι ('having perceived him they go in pursuit, but do not see him'). It is likely that the comment at Σ *P*.12.31 is based on Pherecydes' account.[87] The remains of plays involving Perseus are too exiguous to provide much specific evidence for how they may have affected a reader's approach to *P*.12,[88] but in conjunction with the mythographical evidence it is

---

[87] For the Gorgons as capable of flight cf. e.g. *LIMC* 4.2.293, 301, 331, 338. Cf. also the versions at Σ Lyc. 838; Σ Hom. T *Il.* 14.319.

[88] Perseus occurs in several plays of Aeschylus, such as *Dictyulci*, a satyr play describing the aftermath of Perseus and Danaë being washed ashore at Seriphus. This may or may not have been part of a tetralogy which included *Phorcides* and *Polydectes*. Of the latter we know nothing (cf. Sommerstein (2008) 194–5). For the former, cf. Eratosthenes *Catasterisms* 22 (= *TGrF* 3 F 262 Radt = Sommerstein (2008) 260–3). This gives a version of the story apparently told by Aeschylus, in which the Graeae served as 'sentinels' (προφύλακας) for the Gorgons; by tricking them into giving him their eye, which he then throws into Lake Triton, Perseus is able to evade them and attack the Gorgons. Sophocles wrote a *Danaë* and an *Acrisius*, but it has been suggested that they are the same play. For the *Danaë* cf. *TGrF* 4 F 165–70. Little can be guessed about the subject matter of this play. For the *Acrisius* cf. *TGrF* 4 F 60–76. Note also the *Men of LarissaTGrF* 4 F 378–83, which Jacoby argued to be identical with the Acrisius (followed by Lloyd-Jones (1996) 29). It is unclear whether any of these plays dealt with Perseus' killing of Medusa. Euripides also wrote a *Danaë*, which relates the episode of Perseus' birth (*TGrF* 5.1 F 316–30a). More relevant to an assessment of *P*.12 is the *Dictys* (*TGrF* 5.1 F 330b–48), produced with *Medea* in 431, which tells the story of Danaë and Perseus after they have come to Seriphus. Dictys is a fisherman, half-brother of Polydectes, who takes care of Danaë and Perseus. As in the other stories, Polydectes forms a design on Danaë, and sends Perseus to bring back the Gorgon's head. Polydectes is turned to stone, and Dictys becomes king. Danaë may perhaps have become his queen. How the Medusa episode was handled is unclear. On Sophocles' Perseus plays see in general Lucas (1993), and on Perseus in Greek culture more generally Ogden (2008).

safe to say that most readers would have been aware of the compression of Pindar's account. The scholia's supplementation is also interpretatively significant in that the very fact of its addition highlights the gaps in *P.12*'s narrative. It also draws attention to the spatial indeterminacy of the Gorgons which, in the absence of a link to a defined space, registers their alterity, and contrasts with the spatial definition given to Perseus' killing of Polydectes and his supporters, specifically located in Seriphus (12).[89] The unenunciated pursuit correlates with this non-location, recapitulating the text's spatiality, constituted by both places (Seriphus, the Cephisus) and the non-place of the Gorgons' abode, in terms of the interaction of the enunciated and unenunciated events of the fabula.

The scholia's strategy of explaining the final gnomic comment by recourse to the story about Midas' *aulos* breaking during the performance is interestingly parasitic on the aetiological strategy of the poem as a whole:[90]

(inscr.) γέγραπται ἡ ᾠδὴ Μίδᾳ Ἀκραγαντίνῳ. οὗτος ἐνίκησε τὴν κδ′ Πυθιάδα καὶ κε′· φασὶ δὲ αὐτὸν καὶ Παναθήναια νενικηκέναι. ἱστοροῦσι δέ τι ἴδιον σύμπτωμα συμβεβηκέναι περὶ τὸν αὐλητὴν τοῦτον· ἀγωνιζομένου γὰρ αὐτοῦ ἀνακλασθείσης τῆς γλωσσίδος ἀκουσίως καὶ προσκολληθείσης τῷ οὐρανίσκῳ, μόνοις τοῖς καλάμοις τρόπῳ σύριγγος αὐλῆσαι, τοὺς δὲ θεατὰς ξενισθέντας τῷ ἤχῳ τερφθῆναι, καὶ οὕτω νικῆσαι αὐτόν.

The ode was written for Midas of Acragas. This man won at the Pythian games in the 24th and 25th festivals. They say that he had also won at the Panathenaea. It is recorded that a particular misfortune befell this aulete; while he was competing, his mouthpiece broke by accident and became stuck to the roof of his mouth, and he was only able to play his *aulos* with the reeds, in the manner of a *syrinx*, but the spectators were surprised and took pleasure in the sound, and he was thus victorious (ii 263–4 Dr).

This mode of explanation is picked up by Σ *P.12.52* (ii 269 Dr, and cf. 54b):

ἤ τοι σήμερον δαίμων ἢ ὕστερον· τουτέστιν, ἐὰν μὴ παραχρῆμά τις εὐτυχήσῃ, μὴ ἀδημονείτω· ὁ γὰρ θεὸς τὸ εἱμαρμένον ἢ σήμερον τελέσει ἢ

---

[89] Hes. *Th.* 274–5 describes the Gorgons' location at the edges of the earth: Γοργούς θ′, αἳ ναίουσι πέρην κλυτοῦ ᾽ωκεανοῖο / ἐσχατιῇ πρὸς νυκτός. They are located on the island of Sarpedon by *Cypria* fr. 32 B. Pherecydes fr. 11 gives an unspecified location 'near the Ocean' somewhere in the region of Seriphus. Cf. further *Pitiche* p. 685.

[90] Cf. the story of Heracles and Cycnus at Σ *O.10.21a* (i 316–17 Dr).

αὔριον. τοῦτο δέ φησιν, ἐπεὶ ἀπροςδοκήτως ἐνίκηςε κλαςθέντος τοῦ καλάμου.

'Indeed fate either tomorrow or today...': that is, if a man does not meet with immediate success, he should not be downcast, for the god will bring his allotted portion to fruition either today or tomorrow. He says this because he [the victor] won unexpectedly when his reed was broken.

Whereas the poem documents a singular moment of creativity that gave birth to a multiple tradition, the scholia explain a general truth in terms of a particular event, translating concepts into physical realia. It is also notable that the scholia's explanation, for which the poem itself gives no evidence,[91] deproblematizes the unexpectedness of fate by limiting it to a particular event, replacing Pindar's wide canvas with a specific situation. As interpreted by the scholia, the final gnome refers exclusively to Midas and his victory, and is consequently retrospective, diminishing the instability of the future. The gnome, however, literally refers to events yet to come, with a concomitant emphasis on unpredictability that the retrospective reading softens. The lines also have a metapoetic aspect; the unexpected treatment of the myth exemplifies the unpredictability of divine interventions in mortal affairs,[92] and the scholia's stress on definite endings is ironic in the light not only of this structural feature, but also of the unforeseeable processes of textual diachronicity, such as the poem's closural role in the book. The scholia's participation in these processes itself undermines their delimitative strategy by supplementing the text in a way not explicitly licensed by any narratorial statement.

---

[91] Cf. Gentili and Luisi (1995).

[92] The intertextual aspect of the final lines reinforces this effect. Pindar's τὸ μὲν δώςει, τὸ δ' οὔπω reworks Eumaeus' statement about the power of the god(s) at *Od.* 14.443–5 (ἔςθιε, δαιμόνιε ξείνων, καὶ τέρπεο τοῖςδε, / οἶα πάρεςτι· θεὸς δὲ τὸ μὲν δώςει, τὸ δ' ἐάςει, / ὅττι κεν ᾧ θυμῷ ἐθέλῃ· δύναται γὰρ ἅπαντα). There are, however, marked differences of context and social position between Homer's Eumaeus and Pindar's *persona loquens*. The intertext with Eumaeus may be a nod to the humble social standing of the victor (if this was indeed the case), and a subtle means of asserting the potential of such men to participate in meaningful social discourses: just as Eumaeus reflects powerfully if normatively on the gods, so the implication would go, so too does Midas' victorious performance. Making Eumaeus' statement speak through that of the epinician *persona loquens* is also thematically significant: by appropriating the voice of the humble Eumaeus and conflating two markedly dissimilar enunciative moments, the *persona loquens* creates an intertextual version of the 'unexpectedness' the passage comments on.

The processes of dissemination, collection in an edition, and scholarly comment rerun the poem's aetiological strategies in different forms. But the poem also has a metapoetic dimension, arising partly from the correlation mentioned above between the unexpectedness of the myth, which I shall discuss further below, and the unpredictability of fate, and from the poem's musical subject matter. We might expect these factors to be accentuated by its place in the edition, although it is clearly different from the more explicit meditations on poetic craft found elsewhere in Pindar, such as the famous reflections at O.2.86–90 or the comparison of encomiastic song with the bee at P.10.54.[93] Moreover, it also contrasts with the explicitly metapoetic statements of contemporary Hellenistic poetry. Nevertheless, the potentially metapoetic context, as well as the contemporary development of such tropes, encourage the reader at least to reflect on the possibility of seeing P.12 in these terms, and this approach finds support from a comment in a second-century AD papyrus fragment of a hypomnema on the *Pythians* by the late Hellenistic scholar Theon.[94] At POxy 2536 col ii 35 we find the comment τοῦ[τ]ο δὲ ὡϲπ(ερ) ἐπιϲφραγίζων [π]ο̣εῖ ('he creates this as if setting a seal').[95] This comment is not paralleled in the scholia given by the manuscripts, and is likely to originate with Theon himself.[96]

The lemma referred to is not extant in the papyrus, but the fact that the next lemma cited is τὸ δὲ μόρϲιμον οὐ παρφυκτόν shows that the comment on the sphragis must be an interpretation of the gnome in 28–30 (εἰ δέ τιϲ ὄλβοϲ ἐν ἀνθρώποιϲιν, ἄνευ καμάτου / οὐ φαίνεται· ἐκ δὲ τελευτάϲει νιν ἤτοι ϲάμερον / δαίμων, 'if there is some prosperity

---

[93] On metapoetic endings in Pindar see Rutherford (1997) 46–8.

[94] For Theon's role in Pindaric scholarship cf. Deas (1931); McNamee (2007) 33–5. Detailed analyses of the papyrus have been carried out by McNamee (2007) 95–9 and Ucciardello (2012) 119–26. It is written in two hands; from this McNamee concludes that multiple versions of Theon's commentary must have been circulating in order to be the basis for two separate copyings (p. 95), whereas Ucciardello suggests that the papyrus was 'a scholarly product of a reading circle', the members of which had different interests and levels of reading competence, leading to the different kinds of glosses found in the two hands (p. 125).

[95] For the use of ἐπιϲφραγίζειν cf. Σ Aesch. *Sept.* 166–72a αὕτη γὰρ ἐπιϲφραγίζει τὰ κατὰ ϲχέϲιν ᾀδό[μενα ᾄϲμα]τα, where the coronis 'ratifies' or 'sets a seal on' the preceding song.

[96] ϲφραγίϲ vocabulary is found in the Pindar scholia only at Σ O.6.154h (i 190–1 Dr) where it is used of the Spartan message-sending system, and Σ I.1.90b (iii 211 Dr); the latter uses ἐπιϲφραγίζειν 'als Bestätigung für die Wahrheit einiger einzelnen Aussage' (Treu (1974) 82).

among men, it does not appear without toil; and indeed fate will bring it about either today...'). Eric Turner comments that ἐπισφραγίζων [π]ρεῖ could either refer to the poet 'affixing his sphragis' or to χρόνος or the δαίμων 'bringing things to their end', but while this latter reading is possible, the importance of the ϲφραγίϲ as a literary topos makes the former much more likely.[97] The ὥϲπ(ερ) should probably be read as signalling the implicitness of the trope, referencing the fact that the author does not use ϲφραγίϲ or its cognates. This prompts the question of what sort of ϲφραγίϲ these lines constituted according to Theon's reading, and whether it should be read as applying to this poem alone, or to the whole Pythian collection.

The former question centres on whether the ϲφραγίϲ function of the lines should be interpreted as pertaining to authorial identity, as the kind of comment felt to typify the Pindaric narrator, or whether it should be seen as more broadly thematic, as a paradigm of the ethical tone of Pindaric epinician. Given the generalizing force of the lines and the absence of any narratorial self-reference, the latter reading might seem more plausible, and with regard to the applicability of the ϲφραγίϲ its position at the end of the book may imply that the remark was intended to apply to the whole collection. Even if it were not, it could have suggested such an interpretation to an individual reader given the poem's climactic position. It could be objected that the ϲφραγίϲ function of the lines is entirely arbitrary, but as I suggested above the subject matter of the poem and its closural position allow for a certain metapoetic resonance. Theon could have been attempting to read the lines as metapoetic, connoting something like the hard work that Pindar put into his writing and his expectation of both divine and human reward, in order to see them as a generic

---

[97] Cf. Σ P.12.51 (ii 269 Dr): ἐκτελευτήϲει δὲ, φηϲὶ, τὸν ὄλβον ὁ δαίμων, τουτέϲτιν ἐπὶ τέλοϲ ἄξει, ἤτοι ϲήμερον ἢ ὕϲτερον ('he says that the *daimon* will bring about prosperity, that is, will bring it to fruition, either today or the next'), and cf. also Σ 54a (ii 269–70 Dr). Treu (1974) 82–3 reads Theon's comment as elucidating the activity of the δαίμων, partly on the basis of the scholia, but the scholia's readings may be based on a misunderstanding of Theon's exegesis. He is sceptical about Theon's reading: '[s]o hübsch aber nun auch durch den Vergleich mit einem aufgedrückten Siegel Pindars Gnome gekennzeichnet ist; dass Theons Paraphrase ihrem...Inhalt gerecht wird, finde ich nicht. Bei Pindar ist hier eine zweimalige Scheidung durchgeführt: einmal scheidet er die heutige Erfüllung von der künftigen Zeit, zum anderen in der künftigen Zeit eine teilweise Erfüllung der Erwartung von einem "Noch nicht"'. This interpretative infelicity, however, can be explained by the literary interpretation of Theon's phrase.

cφραγίc. Indeed, the specifically narratorial cφραγίc function and the more general ethical one can be read as mutually reinforcing.

We might also wonder whether the cφραγίc was linked to the materiality of the book, with ὥcπ(ερ) pointing to the fact that in performance the lines would not have had a cφραγίc function, which was only necessitated by the book's capacity to go beyond the author's control. This question raises the problem of how the literary cφραγίc was conceived as functioning, and of the precise dynamics of its symbolism. The first and most influential occurrence of the topos is Theognis 18–22:[98]

> Κύρνε, cοφιζομένωι μὲν ἐμοὶ cφρηγὶc ἐπικείcθω
> τοῖcδ' ἔπεcιν, λήcει δ' οὔποτε κλεπτόμενα,
> οὐδέ τιc ἀλλάξει κάκιον τοὐcθλοῦ παρεόντοc·
> ὧδε δὲ πᾶc τιc ἐρεῖ· "Θεύγνιδόc ἐcτιν ἔπη
> τοῦ Μεγαρέωc· πάνταc δὲ κατ' ἀνθρώπουc ὀνομαcτόc."

Cyrnus, for me, a skilled man, let a seal be set on these words, and their theft will not escape notice, nor will anyone ever take something inferior in exchange when the good is at hand. And so everyone will say, 'These are the verses of Theognis of Megara, and he is known among all men.'

These lines have given rise to much scholarly debate, which has revolved around questions about the exact nature of the cφραγίc, and how exactly it is supposed to function.[99] As numerous critics have pointed out, the mere inclusion of the name of the author within a corpus of poems does not guard against the interpolation of

[98] The 'seal' is also employed by Critias (fr. 5 W) in a passage that clearly recalls Theognis: see e.g. Hubbard (2007) 202. There is also the fascinating possibility that Theognis may be engaging in a sophisticated and specifically book-based poetics: his self-naming occurs in the twenty-second line of the collection, mirroring Hesiod's naming of himself at *Th.* 22. As Hubbard (2007) 206 points out, this feature, if not coincidental, suggests that 'the artful arrangement of poems within a book . . . had its origins . . . in archaic Greek elegy'.

[99] Griffith (1983) 42–4 argues that the seal refers to the relationship between poet and audience/addresser and addressee rather than to the 'genuineness' of the discourse. Ford (1985) 89 sees the poem as part of an oral performance culture, and thinks that the name Theognis 'guarantees . . . [the poems'] homogeneous political character': for objections see Hubbard (2007) 194–5. Scholarship has shifted towards accepting that the *sphragis* refers to written texts rather than to a fluid group of orally disseminated poems: see e.g. Scodel (1992) 75–6; Friis Johansen (1993) 26–9; Hubbard (2007). See also Cerri (1991), who thinks that the lines refer to the depositing of an authenticated copy of the text in a temple. One important issue here is whether the poem as a whole or just the name 'Theognis' has the value of a sphragis: see Hubbard (2007) 208–9 for a reading of the elegy as a whole as marking a shift from spoken to written discourse.

substandard verses (20).[100] Louise Pratt has argued that the passage references the fixing in writing of the Theognidean corpus; the author, by setting his name on the written text, asserts his ownership of and authority over the poems collected therein.[101] A distinction should be made, however, between the ϲφραγίϲ as a signifier within a textual system and as a functional element within a (series of) concrete material document(s). The fixing of a written text is only provisional and can still be subject to interpolations, losses, and damage; the function of the ϲφραγίϲ is therefore necessarily partial in respect of the circumstances of dissemination over which the author attempts to exert control. Furthermore, the interaction between signifier and material reality has consequences for the specific kind of authorial or narratorial identity constructed by the ϲφραγίϲ. For Theognis, the ϲφραγίϲ has to be both repeatable in order to make the author known (πάνταϲ δὲ κατ᾽ ἀνθρώπουϲ ὀνομαϲτόϲ) and a marker of the author's distinctive skill (ϲοφιζομένωι μὲν ἐμοί).

As such, we may compare it to the signature, which in Derrida's analysis is both the unique mark of the presence of the individual whose name it bears, the signifier of a unique event, and a repeatable trace. In Geoffery Bennington's neat formulation: '[a] signature marking the uniqueness of an event must be repeatable as the signature that it is in order validly to mark the singularity of an event that it marks'. We can see from this analysis that the ϲφραγίϲ and the signature are not identical; the latter has to be both repeatable and a unique mark; the former is a conjunction of verbal signifiers, and as such is repeatable, but its uniqueness arises from its disposition of non-unique lexical units. The signature marks the indisputable presence of an individual; the ϲφραγίϲ marks rather the performativity of literary discourse, its capacity to construct itself as such, although it is notable that this self-construction takes place by means of a reference to a non-literary mode of activity.[102] Whereas the signature marks the physical presence of the only person capable of making exactly that mark in exactly that way, the ϲφραγίϲ marks the figuration of the individual *qua* author or narrator, a figuration which divides the

---

[100] Pratt (1995) 171–2.

[101] Pratt (1995), an argument made in more detail by Hubbard (2007). Edmunds (1997) argues that the name Theognis refers not to an individual author but is a mark of a particular mode of writing; for objections see Hubbard (2007) 198–206.

[102] For the sphragis as a seal cf. e.g. Cerri (1991); Hubbard (2007) 205–6.

individual by exposing him to the mechanics of textuality, where identity is mediated by a variety of generic and intertextual factors. Therefore Theognis' cφραγίc does not do what it says it will, but rather attempts to bestow a certain authoritative force on its own language, and on the name it uses of itself. But like the signature, this manoeuvre also presupposes the repeatability of the text, and consequently entails an exposure of the author's name and the associated narratorial identity to a multiplicity of rereadings and recontextualizations. The cφραγίc is constituted by its exposure to such repetition.

The concept of the cφραγίc also gives rise to a particular interaction with the written dissemination of the text. Each copying of the text is a unique event based on a repeatable practice, writing, and therefore structurally replays the conjunction of individuality and repeatability that takes place in the cφραγίc, but simultaneously each copying shapes the text into a new physical form; in this sense, individual material copies of the poem are more like signatures, each written in a uniquely distinctive hand although without the signature's claim to express the presence of an individual. The uniqueness of these individual copyings fracture the attempt of the cφραγίc to master its text by instantiating the text's differential repeatability. Theon's reading of P.12.29–30 captures some of the problematics of how the cφραγίc operates. By, on a sceptical reading, imposing the cφραγίc on the text, or, on a more sympathetic reading, identifying a cφραγίc function not explicitly flagged as such by the author, Theon highlights the force of the mark's constitutive repetition and the transferability of the concept, which is such as to shape readings of poems even in the absence of an obvious deployment of the topos. It also focuses attention on the interaction between the text and its documentary situation; Theon's cφραγίc exemplifies the conjunction of generic topos and material context in framing critical readings.

As my earlier readings of the scholia demonstrated, however, the material context is only one aspect of the text's resituation. In order to elaborate this further, I conclude with a discussion of the relationship between metapoetics and intertextuality, a relation which will emerge as central to P.12's closural function. As has already been noted, the poem's aetiology of the *aulos* contrasts with the more common version in which Marsyas discovered the *aulos* after Athena cast it aside.[103]

---

[103] Steiner (2013) 195–9 reads Pindar as 'Hellenizing' the invention of the *aulos* and freeing the instrument of its eastern associations.

The form of the book and its participation in an archival culture encourages us to see this version of the narrative not only in terms of a particular performance context but in terms of a wider debate about the nature of the *aulos*. Moreover, the poem's closural position and metapoetic elements point us towards taking the myth as a wider comment on Pindar's mythopoeia, exemplifying his determination to select or invent myths with a cogent moral structure, or which make a particular ethical point.[104] These two points then combine; as noted above when discussing the scholia, the archival and intertextual form of the poem encourages a certain relativizing, seeing Pindar's telling of the story as only one of several, and the story itself as contested and contestable.

The poem's place within an intertextual continuum informed by later versions of the myth gives these considerations particular point. We know that the Athena and Marsyas narrative was important to the so-called New Musicians of the later fifth century, as well as being of wider cultural significance,[105] from two fragments of the period. The first comes from a version by Melanippides, according to which Athena cast the *aulos* away (*PMG* 758):

> ἁ μὲν Ἀθάνα
> τὤργαν' ἔρριψέν θ' ἱερᾶς ἀπὸ χειρὸς
> εἶπέ τ'· ἔρρετ' αἴσχεα, σώματι λύμα·
> ὔμμε δ' ἐγὼ κακότατι δίδωμι.

Athena cast the instruments from her holy hand and said, 'Perish, disgraceful things, outrage to the body. I give you over to ruination.'

This account is contradicted by a fragment of another New Musical poet, Telestes, who argues instead that the *aulos* was a clever invention which Athena would not have discarded (*PMG* 805):

> †ὅν† σοφὸν σοφὰν λαβοῦσαν οὐκ ἐπέλπομαι νόωι
> δρυμοῖς ὀρείοις ὄργανον
> δίαν Ἀθάναν δυσόφθαλμον αἶσχος ἐκφοβη-
> θεῖσαν αὖθις χερῶν ἐκβαλεῖν
> νυμφαγενεῖ χειροκτύπωι φηρὶ Μαρσύαι κλέος·

---

[104] Cf. above, p. 273.

[105] The frequency with which the Athena and Marsyas myth is represented shows that it was much the commoner version. Cf. Paus. 1.24.1 on the statues on the Athenian Acropolis representing Athena casting the *aulos* away. Cf. also e.g. Ov. *Fasti* 6.697–710; Hyg. *Fab.*165; Athen. 14.616e–f.

τί γὰρ νιν εὐηράτοιο κάλλεος ὀξὺς ἔρως ἔτειρεν,
ἇι παρθενίαν ἄγαμον καὶ ἄπαιδ᾽ ἀπένειμε Κλωθώ;

I do not believe in my mind that the clever, divine Athena, took the clever instrument in the mountain thickets and immediately, terrified by ugliness offensive to the eyes, cast it from her hands to be the fame of that nymph-born, hand-clapping beast Marsyas. For why should a sharp desire for lovely beauty distress her to whom Clotho has assigned maidenhood without marriage and children?

This fragment is notable for its rationalistic rebuttal of the canonical narrative, in arguing (with a possibly ironic functionalism) that concern for her own beauty would have been no motivation to the virgin Athena. We do not know how Telestes continued the story, but presumably his version had Athena exercising some form of patronage over the *aulos*.[106]

My interest here, however, lies not in the place of these poems in the musico-poetic debates of the fifth century,[107] but in their potential importance for a reading of *P*.12 in the Hellenistic period. It is clear from these and other sources that by this time the Athena and Marsyas narrative was more common than Pindar's form of the story, although we must be cautious about making such a claim about the poem in its original performance scenario due to our lack of evidence for the early history of the myth. It seems likely, however, that Hellenistic readers would have been more familiar with the versions involving Athena and Marsyas.[108] There is consequently a case for claiming that a Hellenistic reader would have been encompassed by a hermeneutic version of the kind of instability described in the final lines, and, as claimed above, we might see the final lines as a comment on Pindar's own handling of the myth, surprising his readers with an unexpected version, with the δαίμων as that which gives or not unexpectedly (ὃ καί τιν᾽ ἀελπτίᾳ βαλών / ἔμπαλιν γνώμας τὸ μὲν δώςει, *P*.12.31–2) becoming a correlative for Pindar's storytelling. We can therefore observe a collusion of contextual cultural factors with the text's rhetorical strategies, as the intertextual background reinforces the

---

[106] On Telestes' response to Pindar's depiction of Athena's invention see LeVen (2014) 108–9.

[107] For which cf. Wilson (1999), Martin (2003). See LeVen (2014) 167–8 on the poetic effects of Telestes' description.

[108] Again, the state of the evidence precludes an awareness of the kind of variations between different versions which may have further influenced readers.

unexpectedness of Pindar's version of the story, which in turn exemplifies the closing gnome about the unexpectedness of divine action. This collusion in turn impacts on the poem's closural force, juxtaposing the generalizing force of the statement with an implicit openness to the reconfigurative effects of diachronicity.

The end of the poem, then, provides an opportunity to reflect not only on its singular disposition of cultural materials, but also on the transfigurative effect of archival processes and textual dissemination. There is a certain paradox about the intertextual scenario described above, which reinforces the text's unexpectedness by means of just the kind of unpredictability that the final gnome predicts, and hence tries to control. Recontextualization both reinforces and undermines the text's claims by underscoring its arguments and pointing up the extent of its porousness and its exposure to the very uncertainties it documents. A contrast can also be observed between the collusive intertextual background of *P*.12 and the intertextual situation that obtained in my analysis of *O*.14, where intertextuality threatened to occlude a reading of Echo, as later depictions blurred the distinctiveness of Pindar's depiction. Taken together, these two poems exemplify the variety of recontextualizing and receptive effects to which poems are subject in their diachronic situations.

Conclusion

Looking at receptions of Pindar in Athenaeus' *Deipnosophistae* takes us somewhat beyond the temporal frames of reference within which I have been working so far, but also sheds helpful light on the methodological considerations that have underpinned my readings. The text's omnivorous coverage of literary genres encourages reflection on its processes of ordering and containment,[1] both containing and creatively fragmenting the literary traditions it feeds off.[2] As a text in which a group of self-consciously learned men wittily joust for intellectual and discursive status, and compete with each other in establishing different and often competing identities, it provides a convenient vantage point for looking back over issues central to this study, of literary receptive one-upmanship and creative engagement, and the dynamic relations between 'past' and 'present' texts.[3]

The *Deipnosophistae* establishes numerous points of contact with the Pindaric corpus. At 1.3b, *O*.1.14–17 is cited as part of a eulogy of Larensis, the symposium's host, praising his cultural sophistication. This quotation comes at the end of a catalogue of men who had possessed large book collections, beginning with the archaic tyrants Polycrates of Samos and Pisistratus, and moves on through Ptolemy Philadelphus and others to Larensis, who is made a modern equivalent of these earlier models, and indeed is made to outdo them in the number of books he owns (1.3a). The passage describes the transfer of culture authority across the ages, and is programmatic of the *Deipnosophistae*'s own archival

---

[1] See e.g. Jacob (2013) 33–40 on the issue of structure.

[2] Cf. Too (2010) 111–13 on *Deipnosophistae* as an archival text.

[3] For identity politics in *Deipnosophistae* cf. McClure (2003) 260–1, and for the significance of the sympotic form cf. Lukinovich (1990). See Milanezi (2000) 401; McClure (2003) 261 on metasymposiastic discourse.

qualities. The quotation's application to Hiero is de-emphasized by the process of citation and the lines made to illustrate a transhistorical ideal. The emphasis on music (ἀγλαΐζεται δὲ καὶ / μουсικᾶς ἐν ἀώτῳ, 'he is glorified by the flower of music') serves as a reminder, in its application to Larensis, of the continuing importance of performance culture, while also marking a difference between performance-based and reading-based cultures. Yet the citation also redescribes the situation in which it is placed: the reader is encouraged to see a connection between the unmentioned Hiero and the idealized rulers mentioned in the previous passage, and between Pindar's symposiastic image and *Deipnosophistae*'s own virtualized symposium. This interplay between a citational decontextualization which enables the cited text to be reimagined within the strategies of the main text, and the situational force of the cited text which spills over into the situation in which it is cited, reproduces in miniature the dynamics of the wider literary economy.

At 11.503f–4a, a Pindaric quotation is integrated into the characterization of an individual symposiast:[4]

τοсαῦτα εἰπὼν ὁ Πλούταρχος καὶ ὑπὸ πάντων κροταλιсθεὶς ᾔτηсε φιάλην,
ἀφ' ἧς сπείсας ταῖς Μούсαιс καὶ τῇ τούτων Μνημοсύνῃ μητρὶ προὔπιε
πᾶсι φιλοτηсίαν. ἐπειπὼν <δέ> (O.7.1–3)·

> φιάλαν ὡς εἴ τις ἀφνεᾶς ἀπὸ χειρὸς ἑλὼν
> ἔνδον ἀμπέλου καχλάζοιсαν <δρόсῳ>
> δωρήсεται,

οὐ μόνον 'νεανίᾳ γαμβρῷ προπίνων', ἀλλὰ καὶ πᾶсι τοῖς φιλτάτοις ἔδωκε
τῷ παιδὶ περιсοβεῖν [ἐν κύκλῳ] κελεύσας . . .

Having said these things and been applauded by everyone, Plutarch asked for a drinking cup, from which he poured a libation to the Muses and to Mnemosyne their mother. He then toasted everyone with a friendship-cup, saying 'Just as if someone, taking from his rich hand a drinking cup plashing within with the dew of the vine, and gives it' (O.7.1–3), not only 'drinking to his young son-in-law', but also all his closest friends, he gave the cup to the slave bidding him to 'chase it around' . . .

Plutarch then explains the meaning of περιсοβεῖν as 'to drink in a circle' with a quotation from Menander. As well as being a pointer to how Pindaric quotations may have been used in real symposia, the passage shows Plutarch integrating a Pindaric quotation into his

---

[4] On the symposium in Athenaeus see Jacob (2013) 27–30; on the practice of 'drinking in a circle' see Wecowski (2014) 88–9.

discourse and his physical comportment. Recontextualization is central, as Plutarch turns Pindar's sympotic imagery into an 'actual' sympotic utterance, a transformation given further point by the narrator's differentiation of the different enunciatory positions of Plutarch and the Pindaric *persona loquens* (οὐ μόνον 'νεανίᾳ γαμβρῷ προπίνων', ἀλλὰ καὶ πᾶσι τοῖς φιλτάτοις). Again, the specific context of the cited passage is de-emphasized, and the quotation's transfiguration of Plutarch's gesture arises from the speaker's particularizing appropriation, his skill in using the quotation in a certain way, as well as from the cultural cachet of the poetry itself.[5]

Many of the leitmotifs of this study, then, can be seen at work in these two passages. They testify to the importance of books and of libraries as cultural institutions, to the reconstitutive force of literary and cultural receptions, and to the capacity for 'classic' texts to impose their own economies of meaning on the contexts in which they operate. They also point up the complexities of citational practices, exemplifying the reconfigurative as well as the explicatory force that such manoeuvres can have.[6] Both passages evince the complexity of the opposition between performance and writing. Reading Pindar on the page is not a matter of reading 'only' a material text or a trace of performance, but a negotiation between the two that is further complicated by the virtualities of 'performance' generated by the poems themselves, and by readerly awareness of performance as a cultural institution subject to diachronic change. In both passages, the celebratory and idealizing force of the cited poems is appropriated and put to new ends, grounding the citational strategy while also being (partially) displaced by it. In addition to their role within the *Deipnosophistae*, these textually self-conscious citations invite readings sensitive to the modes of recontextualization that might be at work in readers' own encounters with Pindaric (and other) texts.

This study has likewise sought to foster an attention to the various contexts in which readers encounter Pindaric epinicians, paying particular attention to the changing intellectual horizons within which these encounters took place. In thinking about these poems as diachronic

---

[5] Athenaeus' separation of νεανίᾳ γαμβρῷ προπίνων from the quotation may also operate as an allusion to textual critical debate: Σ O.7.5b (i 200 Dr) records that some scholars read προπέμπων, arguing that προπίνων was an error of transmission (cf. above, Introduction, p. 10).

[6] The *Deipnosophistae* can from this sense be seen as a 'metacitational' text, reflecting not only on the processes of citation in literary texts, but also on the effects generated by scholarly citation.

texts, mediated by material instantiation as well as by changing literary, cultural, and socio-political frames, I have tried to explicate some of the influences that would have affected how ancient readers approached this corpus, and to understand how the meanings and significances of the texts themselves can be variously interpreted in relation to their contexts. Consideration of the poems in performance, however, has also been crucial. In part this is because of the intrinsic importance of this textual mode, and I have argued for new ways of approaching some of Pindar's poems as performance pieces. In this respect, the multiple functions of mythological narratives and poetological discourses have emerged as central to the poems' operation. Moreover, no study of Pindaric textuality in later antiquity can neglect the modalities of performance projected by the texts, and readers' imaginative projections of such modalities. One result of dwelling on Pindar's poems specifically as material texts is that it allows for a heightened sense of the *virtuality* of the images of performance projected by the texts, and consequently the complexity of the interactions that would have arisen in concrete performance scenarios between these textual projections and the historical circumstances of the performance itself.

A leitmotif of this study not so obviously present in these citations from Athenaeus is the importance of epinician's ethical demands, and the complex interconnections Pindar achieves between *didaxis* and praise. In order to dwell again on this issue, I turn back to Leonidas of Tarentum's epigram on Pindar (99 GP 2556–7 = *AP* 7.35): ἄρμενος ἦν ξείνοισιν ἀνὴρ ὅδε καὶ φίλος ἀστοῖς, / Πίνδαρος, εὐφώνων Πιερίδων πρόπολος ('gracious to strangers was this man and dear to his townsmen, Pindar, a servant of the fair-voiced Muses').[7] Like the epigrams examined previously,[8] the lines mobilize the reuse of Pindaric vocabulary as a metaliterary device. The characterization of the author as ἄρμενος, a relatively rare term in this sense, recalls uses of the word by Pindar himself.[9] Pindar, however, uses it of 'fitting things' rather than persons. By shifting the term's application, the speaker of the epigram presents 'Pindar' as an image constructed from his own reinflected idioms. As well as foregrounding Leonidas' deftness, the epigram operates as both a reflection of and guide to

---

[7] Cf. Barbantani (1993) 15–18. [8] Ch. 2, pp. 92–6.

[9] Cf. *O*.8.73, *N*.3.58. Nor is this the only significant intertext that the epigram mobilizes: the description of Pindar also recalls e.g. *N*.5.8, where Aegina is described as φίλαν ξένων ἄρουραν.

reading practices. In focusing on Pindar's ethical status, the poem implies his continuing significance as a model, and anticipates a reading of his poetry in these terms, but its rewriting of Pindaric idiom also foregrounds the dialogic nature of the relationship into which modern authors, and by extension readers, enter with the poets of the past. Leonidas has generated an image of Pindar based on a creative (mis)reading of his work, a manoeuvre that requires alertness from the reader, both to respond to the intertext and to recognize its figuration of receptional dynamics.

This intertextual representation of reading is not simply a piece of philological sophistication, however. In the context of the epigram's subject matter, the mechanisms of rewriting/reading implied by the use of ἄρμενος take on a wider resonance. The implication of the emphasis on writerly/readerly agency is that we need to understand what makes Pindar ἄρμενος ξείνοιcιν . . . καὶ φίλος ἀcτοῖc *on our own terms*. Simply by treating Pindar in this way, Leonidas emphasizes the importance of ethical considerations to an engagement with the Pindaric corpus. But the intertextual dimension of ἄρμενος also implies that the terms in which Pindar's ethics are couched are open to redefinition by authors and readers: mirroring that of the epigrammatic speaker, the reader's capacity for creative reconfiguration is implied to be a necessary feature of engagement with Pindar's ethical discourses. This element of reception extends processes that are already at work in Pindar's epinicians themselves. As my readings have elaborated, poems such as *Olympian* 14 and *Pythian* 11 produce forms of interpretative response that act as models for socio-political comportment, but also underline how the move from interpretation to response is itself a productive activity. These texts figure interpretation, and indeed recreation in performance and reading, as transformative manoeuvres, and in doing so insist on the particularity of the 'textual' space, however this is realized.

This ethical dimension, in turn, is reflected in and exercises effects on other modes of approach to the Pindaric corpus.[10] This study has examined numerous aspects of literary culture, such as the physical characteristics of books, scholarly literature, literary receptions, biography, and cultic practice, that scholars have not traditionally sought to connect with the practice of reading the author with whom

---

[10] Pindar's status as a cultic figure is especially important in this respect: see Ch. 2, pp. 99–100.

these cultural data are concerned. It might be objected that much of the material I have assessed in this respect bears either not at all or only minimally and contingently on concrete acts of Pindaric interpretation, but one of the concepts that this study has attempted to complicate is that of what counts as a 'literary' experience. At stake in considering the textual and cultural relations which I have examined is the status of the 'literary' itself (or at least the 'literariness' or particular textuality of an author), how it is experienced, regulated, and contested, and how it is influenced and potentially reconfigued by the various influences that bear on it.

As my readings have argued, attention to such processes cannot be divorced from considerations of why Pindar matters, for whom, and in what ways. Defining what is coincidental or irrelevant to the operation of a particular text at a given historical moment, and how that operation might itself be conceived, is an important, and necessarily non-saturable, critical move, and one to which epinician, with its multivalent relations to history and contexts, incessantly impels its readers. Moreover, the decisions involved in such constructions of context entail reflection on wider issues of cultural value, the status of individual texts and authors, and the presuppositions that orientate the reading process. I have argued that various types of receptions are part of the ongoing (re)construction of the epinician corpus, and that the varied resonances of Pindar's epinicians during their unpredictable voyages are necessarily implicated in a series of wider cultural discourses and influenced by the strategies, literary and exegetical, of a variety of other texts. But what has also emerged is the continuing force and wonder of these poems, their capacity for being regrafted and for imposing their distinctive textuality on later readers.

Bibliography

Acosta-Hughes, B. (2010) *Arion's Lyre: Archaic Lyric into Hellenistic Poetry*, Princeton.

Acosta-Hughes, B., and Barbantani, S. (2007) 'Inscribing Lyric', in P. Bing and J. S. Bruss (eds.), 429–57.

Acosta-Hughes, B., and Stephens, S. (2002) 'Rereading Callimachus' *Aetia* Fragment 1', *CP* 97.3, 238–55.

Agócs, P. (2012) 'Performance and Genre: Reading Pindar's κῶμοι', in P. Agócs, C. Carey, and R. Rawles (eds.) (2012a), 191–223.

Agócs, P., Carey, C., and Rawles, R. (eds.) (2012a) *Reading the Victory Ode*, Cambridge.

Agócs, P., Carey, C., and Rawles, R. (eds.) (2012b) *Receiving the Komos*, London.

Alcock, S., Cherry, J., and Elsner, J. (2001) *Pausanias: Travel and Memory in Roman Greece*, Oxford.

Alden Smith, R. (1999) 'Pindar's Ol. 14: A Literal and Literary Homecoming', *Hermes* 127, 257–62.

Alexiou, M. (1974) *The Ritual Lament in Greek Tradition*, Cambridge.

Armstrong, D. (1995) Translation of Philodemus *On Poems* 5, in D. Obbink (ed.), 255–69.

Arrigoni, G. (1999) 'Perseo contro Dionisio a Lerna', in F. Conca (ed.) *Ricordando Raffaele Cantarella: Miscellanea di studi*, Milan, 9–70.

Asmis, E. (1992) 'Crates on Poetic Criticism', *Phoenix* 46, 138–69.

Asmis, E. (1995) 'Philodemus on Censorship, Moral Utility, and Formalism in Poetry', in D. Obbink (ed.), 148–77.

Asmis, E. (2004) 'Philodemus on the Sound and Sense in Poetry', *Cron. Erc.* 34, 5–28.

Athanassaki, L. (2003) 'A Divine Audience for the Celebration of Asopichus' Victory in Pindar's Fourteenth Olympian Ode', in G. Bakewell and J. Sickinger (eds.), 3–15.

Athanassaki, L. (2004) 'Deixis, Performance, and Poetics in Pindar's *First Olympian Ode*', *Arethusa* 37.3, 317–41.

Athanassaki, L. (2009) 'Narratology, Deixis, and the Performance of Choral Lyric: On Pindar's *First Pythian Ode*', in J. Grethlein and A. Rengakos (eds.), 241–73.

Athanassaki, L. (2011a) 'Giving Wings to the Aeginetan Sculptures: The Panhellenic Aspirations of Pindar's *Eighth Olympian*', in D. Fearn (ed.), 257–93.

290 *Bibliography*

Athanassaki, L. (2011b) 'Song, Politics, and Cultural Memory: Pindar's *Pythian* 7 and the Alcmaeonid Temple of Apollo', in L. Athanassaki and E. Bowie (eds.), 235–67.

Athanassaki, L., and Bowie, E. (eds.) (2011) *Archaic and Classical Choral Song: Performance, Politics and Dissemination*, Berlin.

Attridge, D. (2004) *The Singularity of Literature*, London/New York.

Austin, C., and Olson, D. (2004) *Aristophanes Thesmophoriazusae*, Oxford.

Austin, R. G. (1971) *P. Vergili Maronis Aeneidos Liber Primus*, Oxford.

Bagnall, R. S. (2002) 'Alexandria: Library of Dreams', *PAPS* 146.4, 348–62.

Bakewell, G., and Sickinger, J. (eds.) (2003) *Gestures: Essays in Ancient History, Literature, and Philosophy Presented to Alan L. Boegehold*, Oxford.

Bakker, E. (1997) *Poetry in Speech: Orality and Homeric Discourse*, Ithaca.

Bakker, E. (2005) *Pointing to the Past: From Formula to Performance in Homeric Poetics*, Washington DC/Cambridge, Mass.

Balanza, A., and Cássola Guida, P. (eds.) (1975) *Studi Triestini di Antichità in onore di Luigia Achillea Stella*, Trieste.

Balogh, J. (1927) '"Voces Paginarum": Beiträge zur Geschichte des Lauten Lesens und Schreibens', *Philologus* 82, 84–109, 202–40.

Barbantani, S. (1993) 'I poeti lirici del canone alessandrino nell'epigrammistica', *AevAnt* 6, 5–97.

Barbantani, S. (2012) 'Hellenistic Epinician', in P. Agócs, C. Carey, and R. Rawles (eds.) (2012b), 37–55.

Barchiesi, A. (2000) 'Rituals in Ink: Horace on the Greek Lyric Tradition', in M. Depew and D. Obbink (eds.), 167–82.

Barker, A. (1984) *Greek Musical Writings I: The Musician and his Art*, Cambridge.

Barnes, R. (2000) 'Cloistered Bookworms in the Chicken Coop of the Muses: The Ancient Library of Alexandria', in R. MacLeod (ed.), 61–77.

Baron, C. A. (2013) *Timaeus of Tauromenium and Hellenistic Historiography*, Cambridge.

Barthes, R. (1973) *Mythologies*, London.

Battezzato, L. (2009) 'Techniques of Reading and Textual Layout in Ancient Greek Texts'. *CCJ* 55, 1–23.

Bell, S., and Davies, G. (eds.) (2004) *Games and Festivals in Classical Antiquity: Proceedings of the Conference Held in Edinburgh 10–12 July 2000*, Oxford.

Bennett, A. (ed.) (1995) *Readers and Reading*, London.

Bergemann, J. (1991) 'Pindar: das Bildnis eines konservativen Dichters', *MDAI(A)* 106, 157–89.

Bernardini, P. (1993) 'Il mito di Oreste nella *Pitica* 11 di Pindaro', in R. Pretagostini (ed.), 413–26.

Bing, P. (1988) *The Well-Read Muse: Present and Past in Callimachus and the Hellenistic Poets*, Göttingen.

Bing, P. (2009) *The Scroll and the Marble*, Ann Arbor.

Bing, P., and Bruss, J. S. (eds.) (2007) *Brill's Companion to Hellenistic Epigram*, Leiden.

Bitto, G. (2012) *Lyrik als Philologie: zur Rezeption hellenistischer Pindarkommentierung in den Oden des Horaz. Mit einer rhetorisch-literarkritischen Analyse der Pindarscholien*, Rahden.

Blanchot, M. (1955) *L'espace littéraire*, Paris.

Blum, R. (1991) *Kallimachos: The Alexandrian Library and the Origins of Bibliography* (translated by H. Wellisch), Wisconsin.

Boeke, H. (2007) *The Value of Victory in Pindar's Odes: Gnomai, Cosmology, and the Role of the Poet*, Leiden.

Bona, G. (1995) 'Pindaro tra poeti e filologi alessandrini', *AevAnt* 8, 87–103.

Bonner, S. F. (1939) *The Literary Treatises of Dionysius of Halicarnassus: A Study in the Development of Critical Method*, Cambridge.

Bosher, K. (2012) *Theatre Outside Athens: Drama in Greek Sicily and Southern Italy*, Cambridge.

Bourdieu, P. (1993) *The Field of Cultural Production: Essays on Art and Literature*, New York.

Bowra, C. M. (1953) 'Pindar, *Pythian* II', in C. M. Bowra, *Problems in Greek Poetry*, Oxford, 66–92.

Bowra, C. M. (1964) *Pindar*, Oxford.

Bradshaw, D. (ed.) (2003) *A Concise Companion to Modernism*, London.

Braswell, B. K. (1992) *A Commentary on Pindar Nemean One*, Fribourg.

Braswell, B. K. (2012) 'Reading Pindar in Antiquity', *MusHel* 69.1, 11–27.

Braswell, B. K. (2013) *Didymos of Alexandria: Commentary on Pindar*, Basel.

Braund, D., and Wilkins, J. (eds.) (2000) *Athenaeus and his World*, Exeter.

Bremer, J. (2008) 'Traces of the Hymn in the *Epinikion*', *Mnemosyne* 61, 1–17.

Broggiato, M. (2011) 'Artemon of Pergamum (*FGrH* 569): A Historian in Context', *CQ* 61.2, 545–52.

Brulé, P., and Vendries, C. (eds.) (2001) *Chanter les dieux: musique et religion dans l'antiquité grecque et romaine*, Rennes.

Budelmann, F. (2012) 'Epinician and the symposion: a comparison with the epinicia', in P. Agócs, C. Carey, and R. Rawles (eds.) (2012a), 173–90.

Bulloch, A. (1985) *Callimachus: The Fifth Hymn*, Cambridge.

Bulman, P. (1992) *Phthonos in Pindar*, Berkeley.

Bundy, E. (1962) *Studia Pindarica* (2nd edition 1986), California.

Burnett, A.-P. (2005) *Pindar's Songs for Young Athletes of Aigina*, Oxford.

Burnyeat, M. F. (1997) 'A Postscript on Silent Reading', *CQ* 47, 74–6.

Cairns, F. (1977) 'ἔρωc in Pindar's First Olympian Ode', *Hermes* 105, 129–32.

Calame, C. (2001) *Choruses of Young Women In Ancient Greece*, Lanham/Oxford.

Calame, C. (2011) 'Enunciative Fiction and Poetic Performance: Choral Voices in Bacchylides' *Epinicians*', in L. Athanassaki and E. Bowie (eds.), 115–38.

Calame, C. (2013) 'The Dithyramb, a Dionysiac Poetic Form: Genre Rules and Cultic Contexts', in B. Kowalzig and P. Wilson (eds.), 332–52.

Calder, W., and Stern, J. (eds.) (1970) *Pindaros und Bakchylides*, Darmstadt.

Cameron, A. (1995) *Callimachus and his Critics*, Princeton.

Canfora, L. (1989). *The Vanished Library: A Wonder of the Ancient World*, Berkeley/Los Angeles.

Cannatà Fera, M. (1990) *Pindari Threnorum Fragmenta*, Rome.

Cannatà Fera, M., and D'Alessio, G. B. (eds.) (2001) *I lirici greci: forme della comunicazione e storia del testo*, Messina.

Cannatà Fera, M., and Grandolini, S. (eds.) (2000) *Poesia e religione in Grecia: Studi in onore di G. Aurelio Privitera*, Perugia.

Carey, C. (1981) *A Commentary on Five Odes of Pindar*, Salem.

Carey, C. (1989) 'The Performance of the Victory Ode', *AJP* 110, 545–65.

Carey, C. (2001) 'Poesia pubblica in performance', in M. Cannatà Fera and G. B. D'Alessio (eds.), 11–26.

Carey, C. (2007) 'Pindar, Place, and Performance' in S. Hornblower and C. Morgan (eds.), 199–210.

Carey, C. (2011) 'Alcman: From Laconia to Alexandria', in L. Athanassaki and E. Bowie (eds.), 437–60.

Carne-Ross, D. (1975) 'Three Preludes for Pindar', *Arion* 2, 160–93.

Carson, A. (1999) *Economy of the Unlost: Reading Simonides of Keos with Paul Celan*, Princeton.

Casson, L. (2001) *Libraries in the Ancient World*, New Haven.

Cavallo, G. (1999) 'Between *Volumen* and Codex: Reading in the Roman World', in G. Cavallo and R. Chartier (eds.) *A History of Reading in the West: Studies in Print culture and the History of the Book*, Boston, 64–89.

Cavarzere, A., Aloni, A., and Barchiesi, A. (eds.) (2001) *Iambic Ideas: essays on a poetic tradition from archaic Greece to the late Roman empire*, Lanham.

Cerri, G. (1991) 'Il significato di sphregis in Teognide e la salvaguardia dell' autenticità testuale nel mondo antico', *QS* 17.33, 21–40.

Chantraine, P. (1950) 'Les verbes grecs signifiant "lire": ἀναγιγνώϲκω, ἐπιλέγομαι, ἐντυγχάνω, ἀναλέγομαι', *Annuaire de l'Institut de Philologie et d'Histoire Orientales et Slaves* 10, 115–26.

Chartier, R. (1995) 'Labourers and Voyagers: From the Text to the Reader', in A. Bennett (ed.), 132–49.

Christesen, P. (2007) *Olympic Victor Lists and Greek History*, Cambridge.

Chuvin, P. (1995) 'Un éloge paradoxal de l'*aulos* dans la douzième *Pythique*', in C. Meillier and L. Dubois (eds.), 119–27.

Clapp, E. B. (1913) 'Two Pindaric Poems by Theocritus', *CP* 8, 310–16.

Clark, T. (2005) *The Poetics of Singularity: The Counter-Culturalist Turn in Heidegger, Derrida, Blanchot and the Later Gadamer*, Edinburgh.

Clarke, K. (2008) *Making Time for the Past: Local History and the Polis*, Oxford.

Clay, D. (2004) *Archilochos Heros: The Cult of Poets in the Greek Polis*, Washington.

Clay, J. S. (1992) 'Pindar's Twelfth Pythian: Reed and Bronze', *AJP* 113, 519–25.

Clay, J. S. (1999) 'Pindar's Sympotic Epinicia', *Qucc* 62, 25–34.

Clay, J. S. (2011) '*Olympians* 1–3: A Song Cycle?', in L. Athanassaki and E. Bowie (eds.), 337–45.

Cooper, C. (ed.) (2007) *The Politics of Orality*, Leiden.

Cribbiore, R. (2001) *Gymnastics of the Mind: Greek Education in Hellenistic and Roman Egypt*, Princeton/Oxford.

Cropp, M., Fantham, E., and Scully, S. (eds.) (1986) *Greek Tragedy and its Legacy: Essays Presented to D.J. Conacher*, Calgary.

Crotty, K. (1982) *Song and Action: The Victory Odes of Pindar*, Baltimore.

Currie, B. (2004) 'Reperformance Scenarios for Pindar's Odes', in C. Mackie (ed.) *Oral Performance and its Context*, Leiden/Boston, 51–69.

Currie, B. (2005) *Pindar and the Cult of Heroes*, Oxford.

Currie, B. (2011) 'Epinician *Choregia*: Funding a Pindaric Chorus', in L. Athanassaki and E. Bowie (eds.), 269–310.

Curtis Wright, H. (ed.) (1977) *The Oral Antecedents of Greek Librarianship*, Utah.

Dale, A. (2009) *Callimachus Lyricus: The Lyric Fragments of Callimachus and the Greek Lyric Tradition*, Oxford DPhil Thesis.

D'Alessio, G. B. (1994) 'First Person Problems in Pindar', *BICS* 39, 117–39.

D'Alessio, G. B. (1997) 'Pindar's *Prosodia* and the Classification of Pindaric Papyrus Fragments', *ZPE* 118, 23–60.

D'Alessio, G. B. (2000) '"Tra gli dèi ad Apollo, e tra gli uomini ad Echecrate": *P. Louvre* E 7734 + 7733 (Pind. fr. dub. 333 S.-M.)', in M. Cannatà Fera and S. Grandolini (eds.), 233–62.

D'Alessio, G. B. (2004a) 'Past Future and Present Past: Temporal Deixis in Archaic Greek Lyric', *Arethusa* 37, 267–94.

D'Alessio, G. B. (2004b) 'Argo e l'Argolide nei canti cultuali di Pindaro', in *La città di Argo. Mito, storia, tradizioni poetiche. Atti del Convegno internazionale*, Rome, 107–25.

D'Alessio, G. B. (2005) 'Il primo *Inno* di Pindaro', in S. Grandolini (ed.), 113–49.

D'Alessio, G. B. (2007) 'Per una ricostruzione del "Primo Inno" di Pindaro: la "Teogonia" tebana e la nascita di Apollo', *Sem. Rom.* 10, 101–17.

D'Alessio, G. B. (2010) 'Recensione di P. J. Finglass, *Pindar. Pythian Eleven*, Cambridge University Press, 2007', *ExClass* 14, 283–91.

D'Alessio, G. B. and Ferrari, F. (1988) 'Pindaro, Peana 6,175–183: una ricostruzione', *SCO* 38, 159–180.

Damon, C. (1991) 'Aesthetic response and technical analysis in the rhetorical writings of Dionysius of Halicarnassus', *MH* 48, 33–58.

D'Angour, A. (2006) 'The 'new music': so what's new?' in S. Goldhill and R. Osborne (eds.), 264–83.

D'Angour, A. (2007) 'The Sound of μουϲική: Reflections on Aural Change in Ancient Greece', in R. Osborne (ed.), 288–300.

D'Angour, A. (2011) *The Greeks and the New*, Cambridge.

Daude, C. (2009) 'Problèmes de traduction liés à la reformulation du texte pindarique par les scholiastes', in S. David, C. Daude E. Geny, and C. Muckensturm-Poulle (eds.), 19–57.

David, S., Daude, C., Geny, E., and Muckensturm-Poulle, C. (eds.) (2009) *Traduire les scholies de Pindare . . . I: De la traduction au commentaire: problèmes de méthode*, Besançon.

Davies, M. (1988) 'Monody, Choral Lyric, and the Tyranny of the Hand Book', *CQ* 38, 52–64.

Davies, M. (2014) *Theban Epics*, Cambridge, Mass.

Davies, M., and Finglass, P. J. (2014) *Stesichorus: The Poems*, Cambridge.

Davis, G. (ed.) (2012) *A Companion to Horace*, Oxford.

Deas, H. T. (1931) 'The Scholia Vetera To Pindar', *HSCP* 42, 1–78.

Debray, R. (1996) 'The Book as Symbolic Object', in G. Nunberg (ed.), 139–51.

de Jong, I. (2007) 'Metalepsis in Ancient Greek Literature', in J. Grethlein and A. Rengakos (eds.), 87–115.

de Jong, I. and Sullivan, J. P. (eds.) (1994) *Modern Critical Theory and Classical Literature*, Leiden.

Del Grande, C. (1956) 'Lettura Della Quattordicesima Olimpica', *Filologia Minore*, Milan, 115–20.

Depew, M., and Obbink, D. (eds.) (2000) *Matrices of Genre: Authors, Canons, and Society*, Cambridge, Mass.

Derrida, J. (1976) *Of Grammatology*, Baltimore.

Derrida, J. (1978) *Writing and Difference*, London.

Derrida, J. (1981) *Positions*, Chicago.

Derrida, J. (1982) *Margins of Philosophy*, Brighton.

Derrida, J. (1985) *The Ear of the Other*, Nebraska.

Derrida, J. (1990) 'Some Statements and Truisms about Neo-logisms, Newisms, Postisms, Parasitisms, and other Small Seismisms', in D. Carroll (ed.) *The States of 'Theory'*, Oxford/New York, 63–94.

Derrida, J. (1992) *Acts of Literature* (ed. D. Attridge), London/New York.

Derrida, J. (1996) *Archive Fever: A Freudian Impression*, Chicago.

Derrida, J. (2006) *Geneses, Genealogies, Genres and Genius: The Secrets of the Archive*, Edinburgh.

de Vleeschauwer, H. J. (1973) 'Origins of the Mouseion of Alexandria', in C. Rawski (ed.) *Toward a Theory of Librarianship: Papers in Honour of Jesse Hauk Shera*, New Jersey: reprinted in H. Curtis Wright (ed.) (1977), 175–201.

Dickie, M. (1984) '*Hêsychia* and *hybris* in Pindar', in Gerber (ed.), 83–109.

Dissen, L. (1830) *Pindari Carmina II*, Gotha and Erfurt.

Dix, T. K. (2013) '"Beware of Promising Your Library to Anyone": Assembling a Private Library At Rome', in J. König, K. Oikonomopoulou, G. Woolf (eds.), 209–34.

Dornseiff, F. (1921) *Pindars Still*, Berlin.

Dougherty, C., and Kurke, L. (eds.) (2003) *The Cultures within Ancient Greek Culture: Contact, Conflict, Collaborations*, Cambridge.

Duguid, P. (1996) 'Material Matters' in G. Nunberg (ed.), 63–101.

Duncan, A. (2012) 'A Theseus Outside Athens: Dionysius I of Syracuse and Tragic Self-Presentation', in K. Bosher (ed.), 137–55.

Dunn, L., and Jones, N. (eds.) (1994) *Embodied Voices: Representing Female Vocality In Western Culture*, Cambridge/New York.

Dupont, F. (2009) 'The Corrupted Boy and the Crowned Poet: or, The Material Reality and the Symbolic Status of the Literary Book at Rome', in W. Johnson and H. Parker (eds.), 143–63.

Eagleton, T. (1976) *Criticism and Ideology: A Study in Marxist Literary Theory*, London.

Ebert, J. (1972) *Griechische Epigramme auf Sieger an gymnischen und hippischen Agonen*, Berlin.

Eckermann, C. (2008) 'Pindar's κοινὸς λόγος and Panhellenism in Olympian 10', *RhM* 151, 37–48.

Eckermann, C. (2010) 'The κῶμος of Pindar and Bacchylides and the Semantics of Celebration', *CQ* 60, 302–12.

Edmunds, L. (1997) 'The Seal of Theognis', in L. Edmunds and R. Wallace (eds.) *Poet, Public, and Performance in Ancient Greece*, Baltimore, 29–48.

Edmunds, L. (2001) 'Callimachus *Iamb.* 4: From Performance to Writing', in A. Cavarzere, A. Aloni, and A. Barchiesi (eds.), 77–98.

Eidinow, J. S. C. (2009) 'Horace: Critics, Canons, and Canonicity', in J. Houghton and M. Wyke (eds.), 80–95.

Elsner, J. (1992) 'Pausanias: A Greek Pilgrim in the Roman World', *P&P* 135, 2–29.

Elsner, J. (1994) 'From the Pyramids to Pausanias and Piglet: Monuments, Writing and Travel', in S. Goldhill and R. Osborne (eds.), 224–54.

Elsner, J. (2001) 'Structuring "Greece": Pausanias' *Periegesis* as a Literary Construct', in S. Alcock, J. Cherry, and J. Elsner (ed.) 3–20.

Elsner, J. (2007) *Roman Eyes: Visuality and Subjectivity in Art and Text*, Princeton.

Erbse, H. (1970) 'Bermerkungen zu Pindars 10 Olympischer Ode', in *Silvae: Festschrift für Ernst Zinn*, Tübingen, 21–34 (reprinted in H. Erbse, *Ausgewählte Schriften zur Klassischen Philologie*, Berlin (1979) 92–103).

Erskine, A. (ed.) (2003) *The Blackwell Companion to the Hellenistic World*, Oxford.

Fairweather, J. (1974) 'Fiction in the Biographies of Ancient Writers', *AncSoc* 5, 231–75.

Fantuzzi, M. (2000) 'Theocritus and the "Demythologizing" of Poetry', in M. Depew and D. Obbink (eds.), 135–51.

Fantuzzi, M. (2014) 'Tragic Smiles: When Tragedy Gets Too Comic for Aristotle and Later Hellenistic Readers', in R. Hunter, A. Rengakos, and E. Sistakou (eds.), 215–33.

Fantuzzi, M., and Hunter, R. (2004) *Tradition and Innovation in Hellenistic Poetry*, Cambridge.

Farrell, J. (2009) 'The Impermanent Text in Catullus and Other Roman Poets', in W. Johnson and H. Parker (eds.), 164–85.

Faulkner, A. (ed.) (2011) *The Homeric Hymns: Interpretative Essays*, Oxford.

Fearn, D. (2007) *Bacchylides: Politics, Performance, Poetic Tradition*, Oxford.

Fearn, D. (ed.) (2011) *Aegina: Contexts for Choral Lyric Poetry*, Oxford.

Fearn, D. (2011) 'Introduction: Aegina in Contexts' in D. Fearn (ed.), 1–37.

Fearn, D. (2013) '*Kleos* v Stone? Lyric Poetry and Contexts for Memorialization', in P. Liddel and P. Low (eds.) *Inscriptions and their Uses in Greek and Latin Literature*, Oxford, 231–53.

Feeney, D. (2007) *Caesar's Calendar: Ancient Time and the Beginnings of History*, Berkeley.

Felson, N. (1999) 'Vicarious Transport: Fictive Deixis in Pindar's *Pythian Four*', *HSCP* 99, 1–31.

Felson, N. (2004) 'The Poetic Effects of Deixis in Pindar's *Ninth Pythian Ode*', *Arethusa* 37.3, 365–89.

Ferrari, F. (1992) 'La sigla ζ^η/ζ nei papiri pindarici', *SCO* 42, 273–6.

Figueira, T. J., and Nagy, G. (1985) *Theognis of Megara: Poetry and the Polis*, Baltimore.

Finglass, P. J. (2007a) *Pindar Pythian 11*, Cambridge.

Finglass, P. J. (2007b) *Sophocles Electra*, Cambridge.

Finkelberg, M., and Stroumsa, G. (eds.) (2003) *Homer, the Bible, and Beyond: Literacry and Religious Canons in the Ancient World*, Leiden.

Finley, M. I. (1979) *Ancient Sicily*, London.

Fish, S. (1980) *Is There A Text In This Class?*, Cambridge, Mass.

Fisker, D. (1990) *Pindars Erste Olympische Ode*, Odense.

Ford, A. (1985) 'The Seal of Theognis: The Politics of Authorship in Archaic Greece', in T. Figueira and G. Nagy (eds.), 82–95.

Ford, A. (2002) *The Origins of Criticism* (Princeton).

Ford, A. (2003) 'From Letters to Literature: Reading the "Song Culture" of Classical Greece', in H. Yunis (ed.), 15–37.

Ford, A. (2011) *Aristotle as Poet: The Song for Hermias and its Contexts*, New York/Oxford.

Foshay, R. (2009) 'Derrida on Kafka's "Before the Law"', *Rocky Mountain Review* 63.2, 194–206.

Foucault, M. (1977) 'Fantasia of the Library', in M. Foucault, *Language, Counter-Memory, Practice: Selected Essays and Interviews*, Ithaca, 87–109.

Fowler, D. (1996) 'Moderne Literaturtheorie und lateinische Dichtung', *Anregung* 42, 311–18.

Fowler, D. (1997) 'On the Shoulders of Giants: Intertextuality and Classical Studies', in D. Fowler and S. Hinds (eds.) *Memoria, arte, allusiva, intertestualità / Memory, Allusion, Intertextuality*, 13–34 Pisa: reprinted in D. Fowler (2000), 284–308.

Fowler, D. (2000) *Roman Constructions*, Oxford.

Fowler, D. (forthcoming) *Unrolling the Text*.

Fowler, P. (1997) 'Lucretian Conclusions', in D. H. Roberts, F. M. Dunn, and D. Fowler (eds.), 112–38

Fraser, P. (1972) *Ptolemaic Alexandria*, Oxford.

Friis Johansen, K. (1993) 'A Poem By Theognis, Part II', *C&M* 44, 5–29.

Frontisi-Ducroux, F. (1994) 'Athéna et l'invention de la flûte', *Musica e storia* 2, 239–57.

Fuhrmann, F. (1988) *Plutarque, Œuvres morales, III: Apophtegmes de Rois et de généraux and Apophtegmes Laconiens*, Paris.

Furley, P., and Bremer, J. (2001) *Greek Hymns: Selected Cult Songs from the Archaic to the Hellenistic Period, I–II*, Tübingen.

Gadamer, H.-G. (2005) *Truth and Method*, London/New York [first English edition 1975, London].

Gavrilov, A. K. (1997) 'Techiques of Reading in Classical Antiquity', *CQ* 47, 56–73.

Genette, G. (1997) *Paratexts: Thresholds of Interpretation*, Cambridge.

Gentili, B. (1979) 'Polemica antitirannica (Pind. *Pyth.* 11; Aesch. *Prom.*; Herodt. 3.80–1; Thuc. 2.65.9', *QUCC* 32.2, 153–6.

Gentili, B. (1988) *Poetry and Public in Ancient Greece*, Baltimore.

Gentili, B. (2002) '*Addendum*. La memoria operativa e la colometria del testo poetico', *QUCC* 71.2, 21–3.

Gentili, B., and Luisi, F. (1995) 'La *Pitica* 12 di Pindaro e l'aulo di Mida', *QUCC* 49, 7–31.

Gerber, D. (1982) *Pindar's Olympian One: A Commentary*, Toronto.

Gerber, D. (ed.) (1984) *Greek Poetry and Philosophy: Studies in Honour of Leonard Woodbury*, Chico.

Gerber, D. (1986) 'The Gorgons' Lament in Pindar Pythian 12', *MH* 43, 247–9.

Germany, R. (2005) 'The role of Echo in the "Homeric Hymn to Pan", *AJP* 126, 187–208.

Gianotti, G. F. (1975) *Per Una Poetica Pindarica*, Paravia.

Gigante, P. (1978) 'Meleagro, *A.P.* XII 257,2', *PP* 33, 58–9.

Gildersleeve, B. (1890) *Pindar: The Olympian and Pythian Odes*, New York.

Gleason, M. (1995) *Making Men: Sophists and Self-Presentation in Ancient Rome*, Princeton.

Gloy, K., and Rudolph, E. (eds.) (1985) *Einheit als Grundfrage der Philosophie*, Darmstadt.

Goldhill, S. (1991) *The Poet's Voice*, Cambridge.

Goldhill, S. (1994) 'The Failure of Exemplarity', in de Jong and Sullivan (eds.), 51–73.

Goldhill, S. (1996) 'Collectivity and Otherness—The Authority of the Tragic Chorus: Response to Gould', in Silk (ed.), 244–56.

Goldhill, S. (1999) 'Literary History Without Literature: Reading Practices in the Ancient World', *Substance* 88, 57–89.

Goldhill, S. (2010) 'What is Local Identity? The Politics of Cultural Mapping', in T. Whitmarsh (ed.). 46–68.

Goldhill, S., and Osborne, R. (eds.) (1994) *Art and Text in Ancient Greek Culture*, Cambridge.

Goldhill, S., and Osborne, R. (eds.) (1999) *Performance Culture and Athenian Democracy*, Cambridge.

Goldhill, S., and Osborne, R. (eds.) (2006) *Rethinking Revolutions through Ancient Greece*, Cambridge.

González, J. (2010) 'Theokritos' *Idyll* 16: The Χάριτες and Civic Poetry', *HSCP* 105, 65–116.

Gould, J. (1996) 'Tragedy and Collective Experience', in M. Silk (ed.), 217–43.

Gow, A. S. (1950) *Theocritus, Vols. I and II*, Cambridge.

Gow, A. S. F., and Page, D. (1968) *The Greek Anthology: The Garland of Philip, and Some Contemporary Epigrams*, Cambridge.

Grandolini, S. (ed.) (2005) *Lirica e teatro in Grecia. Il testo e la sua recezione. II Incontro di Studi (Perugia, 23–24 gennaio 2003)*, Naples.

Grant, J. (ed.) (1989) *Editing Greek and Latin Texts*, New York.

Gray, V. J. (2007) *Xenophon On Government*, Cambridge.

Graziosi, B. (2002) *Inventing Homer*, Cambridge.

Graziosi, B., and Haubold, J. (2010) *Homer Iliad VI*, Cambridge.

Greppin, J. (1976), '*Oulos*, "Baneful"', *TAPA* 106, 177–86.

Grethlein, J. and Rengakos, A. (eds.) (2009) *Narratology and Interpretation*, Berlin/New York.

Griffith, M. (1983) 'Personality in Hesiod', *CA* 2, 37–65.

Griffith, R. D. (1989) 'Pelops and Sicily: The Myth of Pindar Ol. I', *JHS* 109, 171–3

Griffith, R. D. (1991) 'Person and Presence in Pindar (*Olympian* 1.24–53)', *Arethusa* 24, 31–42.

Griffith, R. D. (1999) 'Leaves in Pindar', *Eranos* 97, 54–8.

Griffith, R. D. (2000) 'Pelops and the speal-bone (Pindar Olympian 1.27)', *Hermathena* 168, 21–4.

Gutzwiller, K. (1996) 'The Evidence For Theocritean Poetry Books', in M. Harder, R. Regtuit, and G. C. Wakker (eds.), 119–48.

Gutzwiller, K. (1998) *Poetic Garlands: Hellenistic Epigrams in Context*, Berkeley.

Gutzwiller, K. (2002) 'Art's Echo', in A. Harder, R. Regtuit, and G. Wakker (eds.) *Hellenistic Epigrams*, Groningen, 85–112.

Gutzwiller, K. (ed.) (2005) *The New Posidippus: A Hellenistic Poetry Book*, Oxford.

Habinek, T. (2005) *The World of Roman Song*, Oxford.

Hadjimichael, T. (2010–11) 'Epinician Competitions: Persona and Voice in Bacchylides' *Poesia, musica, e agoni nella Grecia antica: Atti di convegno internazionale di Moisa*, 332–56.

Hall, E., and Easterling, P. A. (eds.) (2002) *Actors and Acting in Antiquity*, Cambridge.

Halliwell, S. (2011) *Between Ecstasy and Truth: Interpretations of Greek Poetics from Homer to Longinus*, Oxford.

Hamilton, T. (2003) *Soliciting Darkness: Pindar, Obscurity, and the Classical Tradition*, Cambridge, Mass./London.

Harder, M. A. (2002) 'Intertextuality in Callimachus' *Aetia*', in F. Montanari and L. Lehnus (eds.), 189–223.

Harder, M. A. (2012) *Callimachus* Aetia *Vol. II*, Oxford.

Harder, M. A. (2013) 'From Text to Text: The Impact of the Alexandrian Library on the Work of Hellenistic Poets', in J. König, K. Oikonomopoulou, G. Woolf (eds.), 96–108.

Harder, M. A., Regtuit, R. F., and Wakker, G. C. (eds.) (1993) *Callimachus*, Groningen.

Harder, M. A., Regtuit, R. F., and Wakker, G. C. (eds.) (1996) *Theocritus*, Groningen.

Harris, W. (1989) *Ancient Literacy*, Cambridge, Mass.

Harrison, S. (1995) 'Horace, Pindar, Iullus Antonius, and Augustus: Odes 4. 2', in S. Harrison (ed.) *Homage to Horace*, Oxford, 108–27.

Harvey, A. (1955) 'The Classification of Lyric Poetry', *CQ* 5, 159–75.

Haslam, M. (1978) 'The Versification of the New Stesichorus (*P.Lille* 76abc)', *GRBS* 19, 29–57.

Haslam, M. (1993) 'Callimachus' Hymns', in M. A. Harder, R. F. Regtuit, and G. C. Wakker (eds.), 111–25.

Heath, M. (1988) 'Receiving the κῶμος: The Context and Performance of Epinician', *AJP* 109, 180–95.

Heath, M. (1989) *Unity In Greek Poetics*, Oxford.

Heath, M. (2002) *Interpreting Classical Texts*, London.

Heller, J. L., and Newman, J. K. (eds.) (1974) *Serta Turyniana: Studies in Greek Literature and Palaeography in Honour of Alexander Turyn*, Urbana.

Henderson, C. (ed.) (1964) *Classical, Mediaeval and Renaissance Studies in Honour of B. L. Ullman, Vol. I*, Rome.

Hendrickson, G. (1929) 'Ancient Reading', *CJ* 25.3, 182–96.

Herington, C. J. (1984) 'Pindar's Eleventh Pythian Ode and Aeschylus' *Agamemnon*', in D. Gerber (ed.), 137–46.

Herington, C. J. (1985) *Poetry into Drama*, Los Angeles/London.

Hillis Miller, J. (1995) 'Reading Unreadability: de Man', in A. Bennett (ed.), 205–21.

Hinds, S. (1997) *Allusion and Intertext*, Cambridge.

Hirsch, E. D. (1967) *Validity in Interpretation*, New Haven/London.

Hitch, S. S., and Rutherford, I. (eds.) (forthcoming), *Animal Sacrifice in the Ancient Greek World*, Cambridge.

Hopkinson, N. (1984) *Callimachus Hymn to Demeter*, Cambridge.

Hornblower, S. (2004) *Thucydides and Pindar: Historical Narrative and the World of Epinikian Poetry*, Oxford.

Hornblower, S. (2012) 'What Happened Later to the Families of Pindaric Patrons — and to Epinician Poetry?', in P. Agócs, C. Carey, and R. Rawles (eds.) (2012a), 93–107.

Hornblower, S., and Morgan, C. (eds.) (2007) *Pindar's Poetry, Patrons and Festivals*, Oxford.

Houghton, J., and Wyke, M. (eds.) (2009) *Perceptions of Horace*, Cambridge.

Houston, G. (2009) 'Papyrological Evidence for Book Collections and Libraries in the Roman Empire', in W. Johnson and H. Parker (eds.), 233–67.

Howie, J. G. (1984) 'The Revision of Myth in Pindar *Olympian* I: The Death and Revival of Pelops (25–27; 36–66)', *Liverpool Lat. Semin. IV*, 277–313.

Howie, J. G. (1991) 'Pindar's Account of Pelops's Contest With Oenomaus', *Nikephoros* 4, 55–120.

Hubbard, T. K. (1985) *The Pindaric Mind: A Study of Logical Structure in Early Greek Poetry*, Leiden.

Hubbard, T. K. (1986) 'Pegasus' Bridle and the Poetics of Pindar's *Thirteenth Olympian*', *HSCP* 90, 27–48.

Hubbard, T. K. (2001) 'Pindar and Athens After the Persian Wars', in D. Papenfuss and V. Strocka (eds.), 387–97.

Hubbard, T. K. (2004) 'The Dissemination of Epinician Lyric: Pan-Hellenism, Reperformance, Written Texts', in C. Mackie (ed.), 71–93.

Hubbard, T. K. (2007) 'Theognis' *Sphrêgis*: Aristocratic Speech and the Paradoxes of Writing', in C. Cooper (ed.), 193–215.

Hubbard, T. K. (2010) 'Pylades and Orestes in Pindar's *Eleventh Pythian*: The Uses of Friendship', in P. Mitsis and C. Tsagalis (eds.), 187–200.

Hubbard, T. K. (2011) 'The Dissemination of Pindar's Non-Epinician Lyric', in L. Athanassaki and E. Bowie (eds.), 347–63.

Hummel, P. (1992) 'Poluphatos/poluphantos: morphologie étymologique et morphologie formulaire', *RPh* 66.2, 289–299.

Hummel, P. (2001) 'Polysyntaxe et polysémie dans la poésie de Pindare', *QUCC* 68, 41–48.

Hunter, R. (1983) *Eubulus: The Fragments*, Cambridge.

Hunter, R. (1993) *The Argonautica of Apollonius: Literary Studies*, Cambridge.

Hunter, R. (1996) *Theocritus and the Archaeology of Greek Poetry*, Cambridge.

Hunter, R. (2003) *Theocritus Encomium of Ptolemy Philadelphus*, Berkeley/London.

Hunter, R. (2009) *Critical Moments in Classical Literature: Studies in the Ancient View of Literature and its Uses*, Cambridge.

Hunter, R. (2012) *Plato and the Traditions of Ancient Literature: The Silent Stream*, Cambridge.

Hunter, R. (2014) 'Theocritus and the Style of Hellenistic Poetry', in R. Hunter, A. Rengakos, and E. Sistakou (eds.), 55–74.

Hunter, R., and Fuhrer, T. (2002) 'Imaginary gods? Poetic theology in the *Hymns* of Callimachus', in F. Montanari and L. Lehnus (eds.), 143–75.

Hunter, R., Rengakos, A., and Sistakou, E. (eds.) (2014) *Hellenistic Studies at a Crossroads: Exploring Texts, Contexts, and Metatexts*, Berlin/Boston.

Hunter, R., and Russell, D. (2011) *Plutarch: How To Study Poetry*, Cambridge.

Hunter, R., and Rutherford, I. (2009) *Wandering Poets in Ancient Greek Culture: Travel, Locality, and Pan-hellenism*, Cambridge.

Hutchinson, G. (1988) *Hellenistic Poetry*, Oxford.

Hutchinson, G. (2001) *Greek Lyric Poetry*, Oxford.

Hutchinson, G. (2008) *Talking Books*, Oxford.

Hutton, W. (2005) *Describing Greece: Landscape and Literature in the 'Periegesis' of Pausanias*, Cambridge.

Illig, L. (1932) *Zur Form der pindarischen Erzählung*, Berlin.

Immerwahr, H. R. (1964) 'Book Rolls on Attic vases', in C. Henderson (ed.), 17–48.

Immerwahr, H. R. (1973) 'More Book Rolls on Attic Vases', *AK* 16, 143–7.

Indergaard, H. (2011) 'Thebes, Aegina, and the Temple of Aphaia', in D. Fearn (ed.), 294–322.

Innes, D. (1995) 'Longinus, Sublimity, and Low Emotions', in D. Innes, H. Hine, and C. Pelling (eds.) *Ethics and Rhetoric: Classical Essays for Donald Russell on his Seventy-Fifth Birthday*, Oxford, 323–33.

Instone, S. (1986) 'Pythian 11: Did Pindar Err?', *CQ* 36, 86–94.

Irigoin, J. (1952) *Histoire du texte de Pindare*, Paris.

Iser, W. (1978) *The Act of Reading: A Theory of Aesthetic Response*, Baltimore.

Itsumi, K. (2009) *Pindaric Metre: 'The Other Half'*, Oxford.

Jackson, S. (2000) *Istrus the Callimachean*, Amsterdam.

Jacob, C. (1996) 'Lire pour écrire: navigations alexandrines', in M. Baratin and C. Jacob (eds.) *Le pouvoir des bibliotheques*, Paris, 47–83.

Jacob, C. (2013) *The Web of Athenaeus*, Washington.

Jaeger, W. (1946) *Paideia: The Ideals of Greek Culture, Vol. I*, Oxford.

Janko, R. (1994) *The Iliad: A Commentary. Volume IV: books 13–16*, Cambridge.

Janko, R. (2011) *Philodemus* On Poems *Books Three and Four, With the Fragments of Aristotle* On Poets (Oxford).

Jauss, H. R. (1982) *Toward an Aesthetic of Reception*, Minneapolis.

Jeffery, L. H., and Johnston, A. W. (1990) *The Local Scripts of Archaie Greece*, Oxford.

Jensen, C. (1923) *Philodemus Über die Gedichte, Fünftes Buch*, Berlin.

Johnson, W. A. (2000) 'Towards a Sociology of Reading in Classical Antiquity', *AJP* 121, 593–627.

Johnson, W. A. (2004) *Bookrolls and Scribes in Oxyrhynchus*, Toronto.

Johnson, W. A. (2009) 'Constructing Elite Reading Communities in the High Empire' in W. A. Johnson and H. Parker (eds.), 320–30.

Johnson, W. A. (2010) *Readers and Reading Culture among the Greeks and Romans: A Study of Elite Reading Communities in the High Empire*, Oxford.

Johnson, W. A., and Parker, H. (eds.) (2009) *Ancient Literacies: The Culture of Reading in Greece and Rome*, Oxford.

Johnstone, S. (2014) 'A New History of Libraries and Books in the Hellenistic Period', *CA* 33.2, 347–93.

Kahn, C. (1979) *The Art and Thought of Heraclitus: An Edition of the Fragments with Translation and Commentary*, Cambridge.

Kakridis, J. T. (1930) 'Die Pelopssage bei Pindar', *Philologus* 463–77.

Kakridis, J. T. (1979) 'Die 14. olympische Ode: Ein Beitrag zum Problem der Religiosität Pindars', *Serta Philologica Aeripontana* 3, 144–8.

Kallendorf, C. W. (ed.) (2007) *A Companion to the Classical Tradition*, Oxford/Malden.

Kambylis, A. (1965) *Die Dichterweihe und ihre Symbolik: Untersuchungen zu Hesiodos, Kallimachos, Properz und Ennius*, Heidelberg.

Kenney, E. J. (1982) 'Books and Readers in the Roman World', *CHCL* 2.1, *The Roman Republic*, 3–32.

Kerkhecker, A. (1999) *Callimachus' Book of Iambi*, Oxford.

Kimmel-Clauzet, F. (2013) *Morts, tombeaux, et cultes des poètes grecs*, Bordeaux.

Kirkwood, G. (1981) '*Pythian* 5.72–6, 9.90–2, and the Voice of Pindar', *ICS* 6.1, 12–23.

Kivilo, M. (2010) *Early Greek Poets' Lives: The Shaping of the Tradition*, Leiden.

Knox, B. (1968) 'Silent Reading in Antiquity', *GRBS* 9, 421–35.

Köhnken, A. (1971) *Die Funktion der Mythos bei Pindar*, Berlin.

Köhnken, A. (1974) 'Olympian I: Pindar as Innovator', *CQ* 27, 199–206.

König, J., Oikonomopoulou, K., Woolf, G. (eds.) (2013) *Ancient Libraries*, Cambridge.

Kowalzig, B. (2007) *Singing for the Gods: Performances of Myth and Ritual in Archaic and Classical Greece*, Oxford.

Kowalzig, B. (2011) 'Musical Merchandise "on every vessel": Religion and Trade on Aegina', in D. Fearn (ed.), 129–71.

Kowalzig, B., and Wilson, P. (eds.) (2013) *Dithyramb in Context*, Oxford.

Krischer, T. (1985) 'Pindars erste *Pythische Ode* und ihre Vorlage', *Hermes* 113, 491–4.

Kroll, W. (1924) *Studien zum Verständnis der römischen Literatur*, Stuttgart.

Krummen, E. (1990) *Pyrsos Hymnon: Festliche Gegenwart und mythisch-rituelle Tradition also Voraussetzung einer Pindarinterpretation (Isthmie 4, Pythie 5, Olympie 1 und 3)*, Berlin.

Kurke, L. (1991) *The Traffic In Praise*, Princeton.

Kurke, L. (2013) 'Pindar's Pythian 11 and the *Oresteia*: Contestatory Ritual Poetics in the 5th c. BCE', *CA* 32.1, 101–75.

Landels, J. (1999) *Music in Ancient Greece and Rome*, London.

Lavecchia, S. (2000) *Pindaro I Ditirambi*, Rome.

Leclerq-Neveu, B. (1989) 'Marsyas, le martyr de l'aulos', *Metis* 4, 251–68.

Lee, H. M. (1983) 'Athletic Arete in Pindar', *AncW* 7, 31–7.

Lefkowitz, M. (1975) 'The Influential Fictions in the Scholia to Pindar's Pythian 8', *CP* 70.3, 173–85.

Lefkowitz, M. (1976) *The Victory Ode*, Park Ridge.

Lefkowitz, M. (1980) 'Autobiographical Fiction in Pindar', *HSCP* 84, 29–49.

Lefkowitz, M. (1981) *The Lives of the Greek Poets*, London.

Lefkowitz, M. (1985) 'The Pindar Scholia', *AJP* 106, 269–82.

Lefkowitz, M. (1988) 'Who Sang Pindar's Victory Odes?', *AJP* 109, 1–11.

Lefkowitz, M. (1991) *First Person Fictions: Pindar's Poetic 'I'*, Oxford.

Lefkowitz, M. (1995) 'The First Person Reconsidered — Again', *BICS* 40, 139–50.

Leonard, M. (ed.) (2010) *Derrida and Antiquity*, Oxford.

LeVen, P. (2014) *The Man-Headed Muse*, Cambridge.

Lightfoot, J. (2002) 'Nothing to Do With the Artists of Dionysus?', in E. Hall and P. A. Eastertin (eds.), 211–26.

Lloyd-Jones, H. (1973) 'Modern Interpretation of Pindar: The second Pythian and seventh Nemean Odes', *JHS* 93, 109–37.

Lloyd-Jones, H. (1996) *Sophocles*, Cambridge, Mass.

Lloyd-Jones, H., and Wilson, N. G. (1990) *Sophoclea: Studies on the Text of Sophocles*, Oxford.

Lobel, E. (1925) (απφος μέλη: *The Fragments of the Lyrical Poems of Sappho*, Oxford.

Lockwood, J. (1937) 'The Metaphorical Vocabulary of Dionysius of Halicarnassus *CQ* 31.3, 193–203.

Lomiento, L. (2010–11) 'Inno alle Cariti con epinicio in Pindaro, *Olimpica* 14', *Rudiae* 22–3, 287–305.

Lowe, N. (2007) 'Epinikian Eidography', in S. Hornblower and C. Morgan (eds.), 167–76.

Lowrie, M. (1995) 'A Parade of Lyric Predecessors: Horace *C.* 1.12–1.18', *Phoenix* 49, 33–48.

Lowrie, W. (2009) *Writing, Performance, and Authority in Augustan Rome*, Oxford.

Lucas, J.-M. (1993) 'La mythe de Danaé et Persée', in A. Machin and L. Pernée (eds.), 37–48.

Lukinovich, A. (1990) 'The Play of Reflections between Literary Form and the Sympotic Theme in the Deipnosophistae of Athenaeus', in O. Murray (ed.), 263–71.

Lyne, R. O. A. M. (2005) 'Horace *Odes* Book 1 and the Alexandrian Edition of Alcaeus', *CQ* 55.2, 542–5.

Ma, J. (2003) 'Kings', in A. Erskine (ed.), 177–95.

McClure, L. K. (2003) 'Subversive Laughter: The Sayings of Courtesans in Book 13 of Athenaeus' "Deipnosophistae", *AJP* 124, 259–94.

McDonald, P. (2003) 'Modernist Publishing: "Nomads and Mapmakers"', in D. Bradshaw (ed.), 221–42.

McDonald, P. (2006) 'Ideas of the Book and Histories of Literature: After Theory?', *PMLA* 121, 214–28.

McGann, J. (1991) *The Textual Condition*, Princeton.

Macherry, P. (2006) *A Theory of Literary Production*, London.

Machin, A., and Pernée, L. (eds.) (1993) *Sophocle: Le texte, les personnages*, Provence.

McKenzie, D. M. (1999) *Bibliography and the Sociology of Texts*, Oxford.

McKenzie, D. M. (2002) 'Typography and Meaning' in D. M. McKenzie, P. McDonald, and M. Suarez (eds.) *"Printers of the Mind" and Other Essays*, Amherst, 198–236.

Mackie, C. (ed.) (2004) *Oral Performance and its Context*, Leiden/Boston.

Mackie, H. (2003) *Graceful Errors: Pindar and the Performance of Praise*, Ann Arbor.

MacLachlan, B. (1993) *The Age of Grace: Charis in Early Greek Poetry*, Princeton.

McLaughlin, G. (2004) 'Professional Foul: Persona in Pindar', in S. Bell and G. Davies (eds.), 25–32.

MacLeod, R. (ed.) (2000) *The Library of Alexandria: Centre of Learning in the Ancient World*, London.

McNamee, K. (1982) *Marginalia and Commentaries in Greek Literary Papyri*, Ph.D. Thesis, Duke University.

McNamee, K. (2007) *Annotations in Greek and Latin texts from Egypt*, Oakville, Conn.

Maehler, H. (1982) *Die Lieder des Bakchylides. I Die Siegeslieder*, Leiden.

Martin, R. (2003) 'The Pipes are Brawling: Conceptualizing Musical Performance in Athens', in C. Dougherty and L. Kurke (eds.), 153–80.

Martin, R. (2004) 'Home is the Hero: Deixis and Semantics in Pindar *Pythian* 8', *Arethusa* 37.3, 343–63.

Martindale, C. (1993) *Redeeming the Text: Latin Poetry and the Hermeneutics of Reception*, Cambridge.

Martindale, C. (2005) *Latin Poetry and the Judgement of Taste*, Oxford.

Martindale, C. (2006) 'Introduction: Thinking through Reception', in C. Martindale and R. Thomas (eds.) *Classics and the Uses of Reception*, Oxford, 1–13.

Martindale, C. (2007) 'Reception', in C. W. Kallendorf (ed.), 297–311.

Massimilla, G. (1996) *Callimaco Aitia, Libro Primo e secondo*, Pisa.

Matthaios, S., Montanari, F., and Rengakos, A. (2011) *Ancient Scholarship and Grammar: Archetypes, Concepts, and Contexts*, Berlin/New York.

Meijering, R. (1987) *Literary and Rhetorical Theories in Greek Scholia*, Groningen.

Meillier, C., and Dubois, L. (eds.) (1995) *Poésie et lyrique antiques*, Villeneuve d'Ascq.

Merkelbach, R. (1952) 'Bettelgedichte', *RhM* 95, 312–27.

Meyer, D. (2007) 'The Act of Reading and the Act of Writing in Hellenistic Epigram', in P. Bing and J. Bruss (eds.) *Brill's Companion to Hellenistic Epigram*, Leiden, 187–210.

Milanezi, S. (2000) 'Laughter as Dessert: On Athenaeus' Book 14, 613–16 in D. Braund and J. Wilkins (eds.), 400–12.

Milkau, F. (ed.) (1952) *Handbuch der Bibliothekswissenschaft III*, Wiesbaden.

Miller, A. (1977) 'Thalia Erasimolpos: Consolation in Pindar's Fourteenth Olympian', *TAPA* 107, 225–34.

Mitsis, P., and Tsagalis, C. (eds.) (2010) *Allusion, Authority, and Truth: Critical Perspectives on Greek Poetic and Rhetorical Praxis*, Berlin/New York.

Montana, F. (2011) 'The Making of Greek Scholiastic *Corpora*', in F. Montanari and L. Pagani (eds.), 105–61.

Montanari, F. (1993) 'L'erudizione, la filologia, la grammatica', in *Lo spazio letterario della Greca antica*, Rome, 235–81.

Montanari, F., and Lehnus, L. (eds.) (2002) *Callimaque: sept exposés suivis de discussions*, Vandœuvres-Genève.

Montanari, F., and Pagani, L. (2011) *From Scholars to Scholia: Chapters in the History of Ancient Greek Scholarship*, Berlin/New York.

Morgan, T. (1998) *Literate Education in the Hellenistic and Roman Worlds*, Cambridge.

Morrison, A. (2007) *Performances and Audiences in Pindar's Sicilian Victory Odes*, London.

Morrison, A. (2011) 'Aeginetan Odes, Reperformance, and Pindaric Intertextuality', in D. Fearn (ed.), 227–53.

Morrison, A. (2012) 'Performance, Re-performance, and Pindar's Audiences', in P. Agócs, C. Carey, and R. Rawles (eds.) (2012a), 111–33.

Most, G. (1985a) *The Measures of Praise: Structure and Function in Pindar's Second Pythian and Seventh Nemean Odes*, Göttingen.

Most, G. (1985b) 'Der verschieden gesinnten Sinnesverbindung: zur poetischen Einheit der Alten', in K. Gloy and E. Rudolph (eds.), 1–29.

Muckensturm-Poulle, C. (2009) 'L'énonciation dans les scholies de la *Sixième Olympique*', in S. David, C. Daude, E. Geny, and C. Muckensturm-Poull (eds.), 77–91.

Mullen, W. (1982) *Choreia: Pindar and Dance*, Princeton.

Murray, O. (ed.) (1990) *Sympotica*, Oxford.

Nadon, G. (2001) *Xenophon's Prince*, Berkeley.

Nagy, G. (1990) *Pindar's Homer*, Baltimore.

Nagy, G. (2000) 'Reading Bacchylides Aloud: Evidence from the Bacchylides Papyri', *QUCC* 64.1, 7–38.

Nash, L. (1990) *The Aggelia in Pindar*, New York.

Nassen, P. J. (1975) 'A literary Study of Pindar's Olympian 10', *TAPA* 105, 219–40.

Nauck, A. (1848) *Aristophanis Byzantii Grammatici Alexandrini Fragmenta*, Hildesheim.

Negri, M. (2004) *Pindaro ad Alessandria: le edizioni e gli editori*, Brescia.

Neumann-Hartmann, A. (2009) *Epinikien und ihr Aufführungsrahmen*, Hildesheim.

Nisbet, R., and Rudd, N. (eds.) (2004) *A Commentary on Horace, odes, Book III* Oxford.

Nisetich, F. (1975) 'Olympian 1.8–11. An Epinician Metaphor', *HSCP* 79, 55–68.

Nunberg, G. (ed.) (1996) *The Future of the Book*, Berkeley.

Nünlist, R. (2009) *The Ancient Critic at Work*, Cambridge.

Obbink, D. (ed.) (1995) *Philodemus and Poetry: Poetic Theory & Practice in Lucretius, Philodemus, & Horace*, Oxford.

Obbink, D., and Rutherford, R. (eds.) (2011) *Culture in Pieces: Essays on Ancient Texts in Honour of Peter Parsons*, Oxford.

Ogden, D. (2008) *Perseus*, London/New York.

Olivieri, O. (2011) *Miti e culti tebani nella poesia di Pindaro* (Pisa/Rome).

Orrells, D. (2010) 'Derrida's Impression of Gradiva: Archive Fever and Antiquity', in M. Leonard (ed.), 161–84.

Osborne, R. (ed.) (2007) *Debating the Athenian Cultural Revolution: Art, Literature, Philosophy, and Politics 430–380 BC*, Cambridge.

Papadopoulou, Z., and Pirenne-Delforge, V. (2001) 'Inventer et réinventer l'*aulos*: autour de la XIIe *Pythique* de Pindare', in P. Brulé and C. Vendries (eds.), 37–58.

Papenfuss, D., and Strocka, V. (eds.) (2001) *Gab es das Griechische Wunder? Griechenland zwischen dem Ende des 6. und der Mitte des 5. Jahrhunderts v. Chr.*, Mainz.

Parke, H. (1933) 'The Bones of Pelops and the Siege of Troy', *Hermathena* 48, 153–62.

Parker, H. N. (2009) 'Books and Reading in Latin Poetry', in W. Johnson and H. N. Parker (eds.), 186–229.

Pavese, C. O. (1975) 'La decima e undecima Pitica di Pindaro', in A. Balanza and P. Càssola Guida (eds.) 235–53.

Pavlou, M. (2008) 'Metapoetics, Poetic Tradition, and Praise in Pindar *Olympian* 9', *Mnemosyne* 61, 533–67.

Pavlou, M. (2010) 'Pindar *Olympian* 3: Mapping Acragas on the Periphery of the Earth', *CQ* 60, 313–26.

Payne, M. (2006) 'On Being Vatic: Pindar, Pragmatism, and Historicism', *AJP* 127, 159–84.

Pelliccia, H. (2003) 'Two Points About Rhapsodes', in M. Finkelberg and G. Stroumsa (eds.), 97–116.

Pernot, L. (1993) *La rhétorique de l'éloge dans le monde Gréco-romain: Tome II: Les valeurs*, Paris.

Perrotta, G. (1925) 'Teocrito imitatore di Pindaro', *SIFC* 4, 5–29.

Pfeiffer, R. (1968) *History of Classical Scholarship Volume I*, Oxford.

Pfeijffer, I. (1999a) *Three Aeginetan Odes of Pindar*, Leiden.

Pfeijffer, I. (1999b) *First Person Futures in Pindar*, Stuttgart.

Phillips, T. (2011) 'Propertius and the Poetics of the Book: 1.18 and 3.15–17', *CCJ* 57, 105–35.

Phillips, T. (2013a) 'Callimachus On Books: *Aetia* fr. 7.13–14', *ZPE* 187, 119–21.

Phillips, T. (2013b) 'Epinician Variations: Music and Text in Pindar Pythians 2 and 12', *CQ* 63.1, 37–56.

Phillips, T. (2013c) 'Callimachus in the Pindar Scholia', *CCJ* 59, 152–77.

Phillips, T. (forthcoming) 'Historiography and Ancient Pindaric Scholarship', in B. Currie and I. Rutherford (eds.) *The Reception of Greek Lyric Poetry 600BC–400AD: Transmission, Canonization, and Paratext*. Proceedings of the Network for the Study of Archaic and Classical Greek Song, Vol. 3 (Leiden).

Picard, C. (1952) 'Le Pindare de l'exédre des poètes et des sages au serapeion de Memphis', *MMAI* 46, 5–24.

Pöhlmann, E. (1994) *Einführung in Die Überlieferungsgeschichte und in die Textkritik der Antiken Literatur*, Darmstadt.

Pontani, F. (2013) 'Noblest *Charis*: Pindar and the Scholiasts', *Phoenix* 67.1–2, 23–42.

Porro, A. (2009) 'Forms and Genres of Alexandrian Exegesis on Lyric Poets', *Trends in Classics* 1, 183–202.

Porter, J. (2001) 'Ideals and Ruins: Pausanias, Longinus, and the Second Sophistic', in S. Alcock, J. Cherry, and J. Elsner (eds.), 63–92.

Porter, J. (2007) 'Lasus of Hermione, Pindar and the Riddle of S', *CQ* 57, 1–21.

Porter, J. (2010) *The Origins of Aesthetic Thought in Ancient Greece*, Cambridge.

Pratt, L. (1995) 'The Seal of Theognis, Writing, and Oral Poetry', *AJP* 116, 171–84.

Prauscello, L. (2006) *Singing Alexandria: Music Between Practice and Textual Transmission*, Leiden/Boston.

Prauscello, L. (2009) 'Wandering Poetry, "Travelling" Music: Timotheus' Muse and Some Case-Studies of Shifting Cultural Identities', in R. Hunter and I. Rutherford (eds.), 168–94.

Prèaux, C. (1978) *Le monde hellénistique I*, Paris.

Pretagostini, R. (ed.) (1993) *Tradizione e innovazione nella cultura greca da Omero all'età ellenistica*, Rome.

Priestley, J. (2014) *Herodotus and Hellenistic Culture: Literary Studies in the Reception of the* Histories, Oxford.

Prioux, E. (2007) *Regards Alexandrins*, Leuven.

Quinn, K. (1982) 'The Poet and his Audience in the Augustan Age', *ANRW* 30.1, 75–180.

Race, W. (1986) *Pindar*, Boston.

Race, W. (1987) 'P. Oxy. 2438 and the Order of Pindar's Works', *RhM* 130, 407–10.

Race, W. (1990) *Style and Rhetoric in Pindar's Odes*, Atlanta.

Race, W. (2012) 'Horace's Debt to Pindar', in G. Davis (ed.), 147–73.

Rau, P. (1967) *Paratragodia:Untersuchung einer komischen Form des Aristophanes*, Munich.

Renehan, R. (1969) 'Conscious Ambiguities in Pindar and Bacchylides', *GRBS* 10, 217–28.

Richardson, N. (1980) 'Literary Criticism in the Exegetical Scholia to the *Iliad*: A Sketch', *CQ* 30, 265–87.

Robbins, E. (1986) 'Pindar's *Oresteia* and the tragedians', in M. Cropp, E. Fantham, and S. Scully (eds.), 1–11.

Roberts, D. H., Dunn, F. M., and Fowler, D. (eds.) (1997) *Classical Closure: Reading the End in Greek and Latin Literature*, Princeton.

Rohde, G. (1963) 'Über das Lesen im Altertum', in G. Rohde, *Studien und Interpretationen zur antiken Literatur, Religion, und Geschichte*, Berlin, 290–303.

Rosenmeyer, P. (1992) *The Poetics of Imitation: Anacreon and the Anacreontic Tradition*, Cambridge.

Rossi, L. (1971) 'I generi letterari e le loro leggi scritte e non scritte nelle letterature classiche', *BICS* 18, 69–94.

Ruffa, M. (2001) 'La questione dell'autenticità dell' "Olimpica" 5 di Pindaro', in M. Cannatà Fera and G. B. D'Alessio (eds.), 27–45.

Russell, D. (1964) *Longinus On the Sublime*, Oxford.

Russell, D. (1979) 'De imitatione', in D. West and A. Woodman (eds.), 1–16.

Rutherford, I. (1997) 'Closure in Greek Lyrik', in D. H. Roberts, F. M. Dunn, and D. Fowler (eds.), 43–61.

Rutherford, I. (2001) *Pindar's Paeans*, Oxford.

Rutherford, I. (2012) 'On The Impossibility of Centaurs: The Reception of Pindar in the Roman Empire', in P. Agócs, C. Carey, and R. Rawles (eds.) (2012b), 93–104.

Schadewaldt, W. (1928) *Der Aufbau des pindarischen Epinikion* (Halle–Saale) = *Schriften der Königsberger Gelehrten Gesellschaft. Geisteswissenschaftliche Klasse 5. Jahr, heft 3*, 259–343.

Schironi, F. (2010) *To Mega Biblion: Book-Ends, End-Titles, and Coronides in Papyri with Hexametric Poetry*, Durham, NC.

Schlesinger, E. (1968) 'Pindar Pyth. 12', *Hermes* 96, 275–86.

Scodel, R. (1992) 'Inscription, Absence, and Memory: Epic and Early Epitaph', *SIFC* 10, 57–76.

Scodel, R. (2001) 'Poetic Authority and Oral Tradition in Hesiod and Pindar', in J. Watson (ed.), 109–37.

Segal, C. (1959) 'ὕψος and the Problem of Cultural Decline in the De sublimitate', *HSCP* 64, 121–46.

Segal, C. (1985) 'Messages to the Underworld: an Aspect of Poetic Immortalization in Pindar', *AJP* 106, 199–212.

Segal, C. (1987) 'Writer as Hero: The Heroic Ethos in Longinus, *On the Sublime*', in J. Servais, T. Hackens, and B. Servais-Soyez (eds.), 207–17.

Segal, C. (1994) 'The Gorgon and the Nightingale: The Voice of Female Lament and Pindar's Twelfth *Pythian Ode*', in L. Dunn and N. Jones (eds.), 17–34: reprinted in C. Segal (1998) 85–104.

Segal, C. (1998) *Aglaia: The Poetry of Alcman, Sappho, Pindar, Bacchylides, and Corinna*, Langham.

Sens, A. (1997) *Theocritus* Dioscuri (Idyll 22), Göttingen.

Servais, J., Hackens, T., and Servais-Soyez, B. (eds.) (1987) *Stemmata: Mélanges de philologie, d'histoire et d'archéologie grecques offerts à Jules Labarbe*, Liège.

Sevieri, R. (1997) 'Un canto sul far della sera: autoreferenzialità e mimesi cultuale nella *Pitica* XI di Pindaro per Trasideo di Tebe', *Aevum Antiquum* 10, 83–100.

Sevieri, R. (1999) 'Un eroe in cerca di una identità', *MD* 43, 77–110.

Sevieri, R. (2004) 'The Imperfect Hero: Xenophon's *Hiero* as the (Self-) Taming of a Tyrant', in C. Tuplin (ed.), 277–87.

Shapiro, K. D. (1988) 'ὕμνων θηcαυρὸc: Pindar's Sixth Pythian Ode and the Treasury of the Siphnians at Delphi', *MH* 45, 1–5.

Sherwin-White, S. (1978) *Ancient Cos*, Göttingen.

Sicking, C. (1980) 'Pindar's First Olympian: An Interpretation', *Mnemosyne* 36, 60–70.

Silk, M. (1993) 'Aristophanic Paratragedy', in A. Sommerstein (ed.) *Tragedy, Comedy, and the Polis*, Bari, 477–504.

Silk, M. (ed.) (1996) *Tragedy and the Tragic*, Oxford.

Silk, M. (2007) 'Pindar's Poetry as Poetry: A Literary Commentary on *Olympian* 12', in S. Hornblower and C. Morgan (eds.), 177–97.

Slater, W. (1971) 'Pindar's House', *GRBS* 12, 141–50.

Slater, W. (1986) *Aristophanis Byzantii Fragmenta*, Berlin/New York.

Slater, W. (1989) 'Problems in Interpreting Scholia on Greek Texts', in J. Grant (ed.), 37–61.

Snell, B. (1953) *The Discovery of the Mind: The Greek Origins of European Thought*, Oxford.

Sommerstein, A. (2008) *Aeschylus Fragments*, Cambridge, Mass.

Sotiriou, M. (1998) *Pindarus Homericus: Homer-Rezeption in Pindars Epinikien*, Göttingen.

Stehle, E. (1997) *Performance and Gender in Ancient Greece: Nondramatic Poetry in its Setting*, Princeton.

Steiner, D. (1986) *The Crown of Song: Metaphor in Pindar*, London.

Steiner, D. (1994) *The Tyrant's Writ: Myths and Images of Writing in Ancient Greece*, Princeton.

Steiner, D. (1998) 'Moving Images: Fifth-Century Victory Monuments and the Athlete's Allure', *CA* 17, 123–53.

Steiner, D. (2013) 'The Gorgons' Lament: Auletics, Poetics, and Chorality in Pindar's *Pythian* 12', *AJP* 134.2, 173–208.

Stenger, J. (2004) *Poetische Argumentation: die Funktion der Gnomik in den Epinikien des Bakchylide* Berlin.

Stephen, G. (1959) 'The Coronis', *Scriptorium* 13, 1–14.

Strauss, L. (2000) *On Tyranny* (1947 Ithaca), rev. edn. V. Gourevitch and M. S. Roth (eds.), Chicago.

Svenbro, J. (1976) *La parole et le marbre*, Lund.

Swift, L. (2007) *The Hidden Chorus: Echoes of Genre in Tragic Lyric*, Oxford.

Tanzi-Mira, G. (1920) 'Paragraphoi ornate in papiri letterari greco-egizi', *Aegyptus* 1, 224–7.

Tatum, J. (1989) *Xenophon's Imperial Fiction*, Princeton.

Tessier, A. (1995) *Tradizione metrica di Pindaro*, Padua.

Thomas, O. (2010) *A Commentary on the* Homeric Hymn to Hermes *184–396*, Oxford DPhil Thesis.

Thomas, O. (2011) 'The Homeric Hymn to Pan', in A. Faulkner (ed.), 152–73.

Thomas, O. (forthcoming) 'Sacrifice and the Homeric Hymn to Hermes 112–41', in S. S. Hitch and I. Rutherford (eds.).

Thomas, R. (1989) *Oral Tradition and Written Record in Classical Athens*, Cambridge.

Thomas, R. (1992) *Literacy and Orality in Ancient Greece*, Cambridge.

Thomas, R. (2007) 'Fame, Memorial, and Choral Poetry: The Origins of Epinikian Poetry—an Historical Study', in S. Hornblower and C. Morgan (eds.), 141–66.

Thummer, E. (1968) *Die Isthmischen Gedichte I*, Heidelberg.

Too, Y. L. (1998) *The Idea of Ancient Literary Criticism*, Oxford.

Too, Y. L. (2010) *The Idea of the Library in the Ancient World*, Oxford.

Treu, M. (1974) 'Theons Pindarkommentar (Pap. Oxy. 2536)', in J. L. Heller and J. K. Newman (eds.), 62–85.

Tuplin, C. (ed.) (2004) *Xenophon and His World*, Stuttgart.

Turner, E. (1987) *Greek Manuscripts of the Ancient World* (2nd edn. ed. P. Parsons), Oxford.

Ucciardello, G. (2012) 'Ancient Readers of Pindar's *Epinicians* on Egypt: Evidence from Papyri', in P. Agócs, C. Carey, and R. Rawles (eds.) (2012b), 105–40.

Uhlig, A. (2011) *Script and Song in Pindar and Aeschylus*, Princeton PhD Thesis.

Vaahtera, J. (1997) 'Phonetics and Euphony in Dionysius of Halicarnassus', *Mnemosyne* 50, 586–5.

Van Bremen, R. (2007) 'The Entire House is Full of Crowns: Hellenistic *Agones* and the Commemoration of Victory', in C. Morgan and S. Hornblower (eds.), 345–75.

Van der Weiden, M. (1991) *The Dithyrambs of Pindar: Introduction, Text, and Commentary*, Amsterdam.

Van Sickle, J. (1980) 'The Book-Roll and Some Conventions of the Poetic Book', *Arethusa* 13, 5–42.

Vassilaki, E. (2009) 'Aristarque interprète des odes siciliennes de Pindare: explication interne et explication externe', in S. David, C. Daude, E. Geny, and C. Muckensturm-Poulle (eds.), 121–45.

Verdenius, W. (1987) *Commentaries on Pindar, Volume I*, Leiden.

Verdenius, W. (1988) *Commentaries on Pindar, Volume II*, Leiden.

Vernant, J-P. (1985) *La mort dans les yeux*, Paris.

Versnel, H. (1990) *Ter Unus: Inconsistencies in Greek and Roman Religion, I*, Leiden.

Vessey, M. (2010) 'Writing Before Literature: Derrida's Confessions and the Latin Christian World', in M. Leonard (ed.), 290–318.

Vetta, M. (1983) *Poesia e simposia nella Grecia antica*, Rome.

Walsh, G. (1988) 'Sublime Method: Longinus on Language and Imitation', *CA* 7, 252–69.

Watson, J. (ed.) (2001) *Speaking Volumes: Orality and Literacy in the Greek and Roman World*, Leiden.

Wecowski, M. (2014) *The Rise of the Greek Aristocratic Banquet*, Oxford.

Wells, J. B. (2010) *Pindar's Verbal Art: An Ethnographic Study of Epinician Style*, Washington, DC/Cambridge, Mass.

West, D., and Woodman, A. (eds.) (1979) *Creative Imitation in Latin Literature*, Cambridge.

West, M. L. (1989) 'An Unrecognized Injunctive Use in Greek', *Glotta* 67, 135–8.

West, M. L. (1992) *Ancient Greek Music*, Oxford.

West, M. L. (2001) *Studies in the Text and Transmission of the Iliad*, Munich/Leipzig.

West, M. L. (2011) 'Pindar as a Man of Letters', in D. Obbink and R. Rutherford (eds.), 50–68 (reprinted in M. L. West, *Hellenica: Selected Papers in Greek Literature and Thought, Vol. II*, Oxford (2013) 129–50).

White, H. (1999) *Figural Realism: Studies in the Mimesis Effect*, Baltimore.

White, P. (2009) 'Bookshops in the Literary Culture of Ancient Rome', in W. A. Johnson and H. Parker (eds.), 268–87.

Whitmarsh, T. (2001) *Greek Literature and the Roman Empire: The Politics of Imitation*, Oxford.

Whitmarsh, T. (2010) 'Thinking Local', in T. Whitmarsh (ed.), 1–16.

Whitmarsh, T. (ed.) (2010) *Local Knowledge and Microidentities in the Imperial Greek World*, Cambridge.

Wifstrand, A. (1933) *Von Kallimachos zu Nonnos*, Lund.

Wilamowitz, U. (1922) *Pindaros*, Berlin.

Willett, S. (2002) 'Working Memory and its Constraints on Colometry', *QUCC* 71.2, 7–19.

Wilson, N. G. (1967) 'A Chapter in the Histoy of Scholia', *CQ* 17, 244–56.

Wilson, P. (1980) 'Pindar and his Reputation in Antiquity', *PCPS* 26, 97–114.

Wilson, P. (1999) 'The *aulos* in Athens', in S. Goldhill and R. Osborne (eds.), 58–75.

Wilson, P. (2000) *The Athenian Institution of the Khoregia: The Chorus, the City, and the Stage*, Cambridge.

Winiarczyk, M. (2013) *The Sacred History of Euhemerus of Messene*, Berlin/Boston.

Wüst, E. (1967) *Pindar als geschichtschreibender Dichter*, Tübingen.

Young, D. C. (1968) *Three Odes of Pindar*, Leiden.

Young, D. C. (1970) 'Pindaric Criticism', in W. Calder and J. Stern (eds.), 1–95.

Young, D. C. (1971) *Pindar, Isthmian 7, Myth and Exempla*, Leiden.

Yunis, H. (ed.) (2003) *Written Texts and the Rise of Literate Culture in Ancient Greece*, Cambridge/New York.

Zimmermann, B. (1992) *Dithyrambos: Geschichte einer Gattung*, Göttingen.

Index Locorum

MNASEAS OF PATARA
FHG III 39: 205

MOSCHUS
Eur.
49: 151 n. 83
Fragments
2: 232 n. 52

[MOSCHUS]
Epit. Bion.
30–1: 232

NONNUS
Dion.
25.21: 222 n. 34

OVID
Fasti
6.697–710: 279 n. 105
Met.
3.334–510: 219
3.356–99: 233 n. 55
3.362–5: 233 n. 55
4.752: 270 n. 85
PAnt
21: 142 n. 60
P.Lond.Litt
11.136: 109 n. 68
44: 106 n. 64
PLouvre
E 7733: 106 n. 64
E 7734: 106 n. 64
PMG
867: 50 n. 8
POxy
659: 106 n. 64
841: 54, 69 n. 75, 106 n. 64, 114
841 col. 19–22: 106
1015.13: 130 n. 26
1231 fr. 1 col. i 12–13: 106
    n. 61
2440: 106 n. 64
2441: 106 n. 64
2442: 54, 106 n. 64
2438.35: 55, 57, 58, 59, 142
    n. 61
2506 fr. 26 col. ii 21–4: 244
2536: 61 n. 44, 169
2536 col. ii 35: 274–6
2637 fr. 30: 106 n. 62
2735 fr. 45: 106 n. 62
2737 fr. 1 col. i 20–6: 169
2803 fr. 1 col. ii 12–13: 106 n. 62
2878 fr. 10: 106 n. 62

PAUSANIAS
1.8.4: 15 n. 46
1.24.1: 256 n. 46, 279 n. 105
2.18.6: 245 n. 23
2.20.3: 264 n. 69
5.13.4–6: 128 n. 23
9.16.1: 100 n. 40
9.23.2: 98, 99
9.23.3–4: 97 n. 31
9.37.8: 211 n. 3
9.38.1: 160 n. 100, 215 n. 12
10.24.5: 99

PHERECYDES
FGrH 3F 58: 205
fr. 11 Fowler: 271, 272 n. 89

PHILODEMUS
De poem.
1 fr. 117.17: 21 n. 66
1 fr. 184: 21 n. 65
4.120: 53 n. 18
5 col. xxv 2–xxix 18: 21 n. 65
5 col. xxxii 6–10: 21 n. 65

PHYLARCHUS (*FGrH* 81)
F 16: 206

PINDAR
Olympians
1.1–11: 124
1.1: 53 n. 18, 57, 58, 143, 144
1.1–2: 200
1.3–4: 125
1.7: 125
1.8: 126, 126 n. 15
1.10–17: 125
1.10–11: 126, 127
1.11: 134
1.14–18: 221 n. 29
1.14–17: 126 –7, 283–4
1.25–7: 128 n. 23
1.28–32: 133
1.28–9: 128
1.30–2: 128
1.30–5: 44
1.33–4: 133, 153 n. 89
1.47–51: 127, 133
1.47: 127, 140–1, 143
1.55–6: 155
1.87: 196
1.88: 196
1.90–6: 128–9
1.93–5: 129
1.91: 131, 131 n. 29

Index of Subjects

reader:
 agency of 26–7, 33, 34, 35, 42, 170,
  188, 199, 280–1
 as projection of text 31–2, 200–1,
  225–6, 232–3
 interpretative demands on 44–6, 140,
  242, 247, 250–1
 see also audience, reading
reading:
 as communal activity 170–1
 contextualization of 85–6, 103–4,
  111–17, 131–3, 139–42, 211 n. 3,
  233–5, 252–3, 281, 285–6
 in the Hellenistic period 50, 131–3
 influenced by literary criticsm 20–3,
  69–70, 77, 81–2, 170, 188, 199,
  209–10
 influenced by literary
  reception 164–5, 233–5
 relation to performance 5, 13, 19, 95
  n. 25, 121–2, 124–8, 145–8,
  214, 270
 voiced and silent 19–20, 226
 rehearsal 24, 42–3
reperformance:
 anticipation of as poetic strategy 5,
  126–7, 137–8, 148, 151–2,
  211–12, 216, 217–23
 compared with reading 13–15, 37–8,
  66, 121–2
 in fifth century 3–4, 24–5, 122
  n. 2, 126
 in the later classical period 64–5, 126
  n. 17
 sympotic 155 n. 90
Rhodes 3, 183–5

Sappho 87, 94–5, 216 n. 14
scholia:
 as school texts 61, 63 n. 51, 81–2,
  170, 174
 citational practices of 169–70
 evidential problems of 60–1, 167–8
 interpretative strategies of 79–82,
  Ch. 4 *passim*
 intertextuality in 67–9, Ch. 4 *passim*
 origins of 61–3, 69
 references to scholarly predecessors
  in 174 n. 33
 scholars contributing to 61–3, 62 nn.
  48–9
 use by and possible effects on
  readers 26–7, 69–70, 70 n. 77,

81–2, 170, 188, 209–10, 214 n. 10,
 267–9
secondary poetic 27 n. 82
Seriphus 258 n. 56, 271 n. 88, 272
Sevieri, R. 243
Simias 87–8
Simonides:
 classification of poetry 58
 in epigram 94
 in Theocritus 158, 161
 in Xenophon 135–8
singularity:
 and performance 261, 263
 and reception 32–4, 207, 234–5,
  277–8, 281
 definition 29–32
σκυτάλη (message stick) 2, 2 n. 3
Sophocles 73, 87–8, 228–9
σφραγίς 276–8
Stesichorus 244–5
sublime (ὕψος):
 in [Longinus] 75–7
 politics of 76 n. 97
 possible instances in scholia 78–9,
  78 n. 101
symbolic capital 25, 39 n. 125, 163
symposium:
 as setting for performance 217,
  222
 as setting for reading 170
 fictional 126–7, 284–5

Telestes 279–80
text:
 diachronic 27, 252–3, 280–1
 type/token 16–17
Thebes:
 and Pindar's poetry 92–3, 94–6
 and Orchomenos 159–60, 211 n. 3
 as performance location 241,
  248 n. 33
 as possible site for collection of
  Pindar's poems 4 n. 16
 Pindar commemorated at 99
 politics of 245–6
 sack of 99
 site of composition in
  scholia 10 n. 32
Theocritus 157–65, 202–5, 211
Theognis 276–8
Theon:
 as Pindaric commentator 169,
  274–5, 278